Groping for
Ethics in Journalism

FOURTH EDITION

Groping for
Ethics in Journalism

Ron F. Smith

 IOWA STATE UNIVERSITY PRESS • Ames

RON F. SMITH, professor of journalism at the University of Central Florida, Orlando, has worked as a reporter for newspapers in Indiana, Ohio and Florida. His journalistic experience includes stints as police and court reporter, sports copy editor, wire editor and news editor. He co-authored the third edition of *Groping for Ethics in Journalism* with Gene Goodwin. Smith and Loraine O'Connell wrote *Editing Today*, also published by Iowa State University Press.

©1999 Iowa State University Press
All rights reserved

Orders: 1-800-862-6657
Office: 1-515-292-0140
Fax: 1-515-292-3348
Web site: www.isupress.edu

The author and publisher gratefully acknowledge permissions to reprint the following:
Society of Professional Journalists Code of Ethics
Radio-Television News Director Association Code of Ethics

Authorization to photocopy items for internal or personal use, or the internal or personal use of specific clients, is granted by Iowa State University Press, provided that the base fee of $.10 per copy is paid directly to the Copyright Clearance Center, 222 Rosewood Drive, Danvers, MA 01923. For those organizations that have been granted a photocopy license by CCC, a separate system of payment has been arranged. The fee code for users of the Transactional Reporting Service is 0-8138-1319-0 / 99 / $.10.

♾ Printed on acid-free paper in the United States of America

First edition, 1983
Second edition, 1987
Third edition, 1994

Library of Congress Cataloging-in-Publication Data

Smith, Ron F.
  Groping for ethics in journalism / Ron F. Smith. — 4th ed.
    p.   cm.
  Rev. ed. of: Groping for ethics in journalism / Gene Goodwin and
Ron F. Smith. 3rd ed. 1994.
  Incluces bibliographical references and index.
  ISBN 0-8138-1319-0
  1. Journalistic ethics—United States.   I. Goodwin, H. Eugene,
Groping for ethics in journalism.   II. Title.
  PN4888.E8G66   1999
  174'.9097—dc21   99-20431

The last digit is the print number: 9 8 7 6 5 4 3 2

CONTENTS

Chances are, you're planning a career in TV or newspaper journalism. If you're like many of us, you chose your career because you like to write and think you're pretty good at it. Or maybe you want the excitement and prestige of being an anchor on TV. Or perhaps you want the challenge of meeting lots of people, ranging from the powerful and the famous to the powerless and forgotten.

You understand why you are required to take courses in newswriting and editing. Your employers are going to expect you to perform these tasks. And you probably won't balk at taking a mass media law course. You know you don't want to lose a million-dollar libel suit.

However, why must you read books like this one? Why must you study journalism ethics? I'm going to offer two reasons. You and your instructor are welcome to add to this list.

- Journalism is going through a tough time. Nearly every poll shows that people are losing respect for journalists and that they doubt if they can trust the news media. Their dissatisfaction is not with our technical abilities. It is with our ethics and our sense of what our role is in society. Your technical skills as a writer, editor or producer are not going to amount to much if the public doesn't believe you.
- You need to think about what your role is as a journalist. Journalism plays a greater role than just allowing us to satisfy our desire to write, to be on TV or to have the proverbial front-row seats to history. Journalists give communities an opportu-

nity to see themselves. We point out the problems in society and show its successes. We are also playing a role in America's experiment in self-government by informing voters about their government. If we lose sight of the important role the news media play in American society, then the profession of journalism will dwindle into another form of entertainment. Our society will be the worse for it.

As you read this book, challenge yourself. Put yourself in each story that opens a chapter. If you were in that situation, how would you handle the problem? What responsibilities do the journalists have to their sources, their readers and viewers, and their employers? Are there other ways to handle the problem? But also ask yourself how would you react to the reporter's conduct if you were a source. And ask yourself what impact the story would have on you as a reader or viewer.

This book began its life in the perceptive mind of Gene Goodwin, while he was a journalism professor at Penn State University in 1983. Gene wanted to compare the practices of working journalists with the profession's codes of ethics. The first edition won the Frank Luther Mott–Kappa Tau Alpha Research Award as the best book involving journalism research in 1983.

The state of journalism in 1983 did not please Goodwin. Ten years later, he was no more encouraged. He began the preface to the third edition in 1994 with this apology:

> We wish we could report that the ethics of journalists have improved since the first and second editions of this book were published in 1983 and 1987, but we cannot. . . .
> We are not happy with our mostly negative conclusions about the state of ethics in journalism.

As I write this, journalism just endured one of its worst summers: Important writers were caught plagiarizing and making up stories, CNN and the *The Cincinnati Enquirer* had retracted major stories and the Monica Lewinsky story was daily fodder. One hopes that as you are reading this, the profession is no longer suffering through such hard times.

Journalists today are better trained than ever before. Our technical skills are superb. We need to ensure that our understanding of our role in society allows us to use these skills wisely.

Many people helped me as I continued Goodwin's work. Rene Stutzman, a reporter in *The Orlando Sentinel*'s Sanford bureau, critiqued and improved nearly every chapter. About a dozen other newspaper and TV reporters, editors and anchors read parts of the book. Their contributions were vital in ensuring the accuracy and completeness of the material.

My students have also shaped this work. Many have done so directly. Michelle Martinez and Maureen Tisdale made key contributions to the chapter on diversity. Other students have also helped track down references and anecdotes. As anyone who has taught can attest, my students, through class discussion and written work, have broadened my understanding of the issues. They have also been candid in their critiques of early drafts of the manuscript, helping me to avoid dry passages and long-windedness.

Iowa State University Press assigned a great staff to this endeavor. Editor-in-chief Gretchen Van Houten has been very supportive of the project. Acquisitions editor Judi Brown helped provide a fresh look to the book and has helped make it even more accessible to students. Production editor Linda Ross kept the project moving forward gracefully. As a former copy editor myself, I was most impressed with the work of Betsy Hovey. Her detailed editing of the manuscript saved me from some embarrassing mistakes. Designer Kathy Walker has given the work a much needed facelift.

Despite the quality of the people who read portions of the manuscript, the observations of my students and the care taken by ISU Press staff, I am sure you will find an occasional mistake. We'll try to get it right next time. If you have comments or questions about the book, feel free to e-mail me at rsmith@pegasus.cc.ucf.edu.

Ron F. Smith
Professor
University of Central Florida

Principles and Guidelines

Abbreviations

ABC = American Broadcasting Company
AEJMC = Association for Education in Journalism and
Mass Communication
AIM = Accuracy in Media
AJR = American Journalism Review
AP = Associated Press
APME = Associated Press Managing Editors association
APSE = Associated Press Sports Editors association
ASNE = American Society of Newspaper Editors
CBS = Columbia Broadcasting System
CJR = Columbia Journalism Review
CNN = Cable News Network
FCC = Federal Communications Commission
IRE = Investigative Reporters and Editors association
NAA = Newspaper Association of America
NAB = National Association of Broadcasters
NABJ = National Association of Black Journalists
NBC = National Broadcasting Company
NCEW = National Conference of Editorial Writers
NPPA = National Press Photographers Association
ONO = Organization of News Ombudsmen
PBS = Public Broadcasting System
RTNDA = Radio-Television News Directors Association
SND = Society of Newspaper Design
SPJ = Society of Professional Journalists
UPI = United Press International

1

The Search for Principles

Imagine a city as big as New York suddenly grafted onto North Carolina's Coastal Plain. Double it. Now imagine that this city has no sewage treatment plants. All the wastes from 15 million inhabitants are simply flushed into open pits and sprayed onto fields.

Turn those humans into hogs, and you don't have to imagine at all. It's already here.

A vast city of swine has risen practically overnight in the counties east of Interstate 95. It's a megalopolis of 7 million animals that live in metal confinement barns and produce two to four times as much waste, per hog, as the average human.

All that manure—about 9.5 million tons a year—is stored in thousands of earthen pits called lagoons, where it is decomposed and sprayed or spread on crop lands.

That's the beginning of a series of news stories that appeared in the Raleigh *News & Observer*. Having that much manure in your backyard can lead to problems. The paper talked to experts and reported:

- New scientific studies had determined that contaminants from hog lagoons are getting into groundwater. One North Carolina State University report estimated that as many as half of existing lagoons—perhaps hundreds—are leaking badly enough to contaminate groundwater.
- The industry also is running out of places to spread or spray the waste from lagoons. On paper, according to state Agriculture Department records, North Carolina's biggest swine counties

3

Hog factory. From the Raleigh *News & Observer*'s award-winning "King Hog" series. *Photo courtesy of* The News & Observer.

are already producing more phosphorus-rich manure than available land can absorb.

• Scientists are discovering that hog farms emit large amounts of ammonia gas, which returns to earth in rain. The ammonia is believed to be contributing to an explosion of algae growth that's choking many of the state's rivers and estuaries.

The owners of the hogs rarely lived nearby. It was the residents of rural, working-class sections of North Carolina who had to put up with the stench of all that manure, as *The News & Observer* described this way:

> At 11 o'clock sharp on a Sunday morning, the choir marched into the sanctuary of New Brown's Chapel Baptist Church. And the stench of 4,800 hogs rolled right in with them.
>
> The odor hung oppressively in the vestibule, clinging to church robes, winter coats and fancy hats. It sent stragglers scurrying indoors from the parking lot, some holding their noses. Sharekka Leveston, 4, pulled her fleecy white sweater over her face as she ran.
>
> "It stinks!" she cried.
>
> It was another Sunday morning in Browntown, a Greene County hamlet that's home to about 200 people and one large hog farm. Like many of its counterparts throughout Eastern North Carolina, the town hasn't been the same since the hogs moved in a couple of years ago.

Experts said the odor not only collected on clothing but was also absorbed by the fatty tissues in the human body: "That's why some people say they can smell the odor on their breath long after they left the farm." The odor may be more than a nuisance. A Duke University researcher said that it was affecting residents' mental health. She found that people living near large hog farms experienced "more tension, more depression, more anger, less vigor, more fatigue and more confusion."

With all the concerns about the environment and health of the residents, you might imagine that government agencies investigated this situation. Guess again. According to *The News & Observer* series:

> You don't have to look hard to spot the pork industry's connections in North Carolina politics and government. Just start at the top.
>
> U.S. Sen. Lauch Faircloth, a Republican who leads a congressional subcommittee on the environment, is a wealthy hog farmer.
>
> Democratic Gov. Jim Hunt is the top recipient of political contributions from Wendell H. Murphy, whose Duplin County hog company is the biggest in the nation.

The chairman of the environment committee in the state House, Republican John M. Nichols, is building a large hog operation in Craven County and will raise pigs for Murphy.

The chairman of the Senate committee on environment and agriculture, Democrat Charles W. Albertson of Duplin County, is a friend of Murphy's, and—judging from contributions—the pork industry's favorite legislator.

Murphy himself, a former Democratic state senator, is honorary chairman of the Jim Graham Committee, a group working to raise $5 million for scholarships in the name of North Carolina's agriculture commissioner.

And Murphy and the governor are friends from their student days at N.C. State University. Murphy's seats at Wolfpack home games are next to Hunt's.

To people with grievances against big pork, the alliances look like a power bloc.

"We have not found a sympathetic ear anywhere," said Robert Morgan of Lillington, a former U.S. senator who represents plaintiffs in four lawsuits against large-scale hog farms.

The ethics rules of the North Carolina Legislature do not bar representatives with a personal stake in a bill from pushing it in the Legislature. The result:

Wendell H. Murphy, who became the nation's biggest hog producer during the 10 years he served in the General Assembly, helped pass laws worth millions of dollars to his company and his industry.

The Duplin County executive voted for, and sometimes co-sponsored, bills giving hog and poultry producers tax breaks, protection from local zoning and exemptions from tougher environmental regulations.

Those laws kept counties from using zoning laws to control odors. They also allowed the large hog farms to be classed as family farms, thereby exempting them from wage requirements, truck-weight limitations and some environmental laws. One law even kept the state's agriculture agency from sharing information about hog farms with other state agencies, thus making it more difficult for regulators to investigate the farms.

The "King Hog" series was a major project for *The News & Observer.* Special projects editor Melanie Sill and reporters Pat Stith and Joby Warrick spent seven months interviewing hundreds of people and searching through mounds of records. Photographers, graphic artists and editors also worked on the project. The result was a series of stories that provided a detailed portrait of the growth of hog factories and stirred many North Carolinians to reconsider the factories' impact on the state.[1]

The series, which won a Pulitzer Prize for public service in 1996, is an example of thorough reporting, exciting writing and solid presentation. Nearly everyone would agree it is first-rate journalism. We would take that a step further and say that it exemplifies "ethical journalism."

Journalism and Ethics

To many, "ethical journalism" is an oxymoron in the same category as "jumbo shrimp" and "military intelligence." In an Internet discussion group for journalists, a police reporter ridiculed ethical questions as "mental masturbation for people who want to get master's degrees." He's not the only journalist who has a faulty understanding of ethics. Perhaps the most common misconceptions are these:

- Some think of ethics only as a list of rules that spell out what they can and cannot do: Do not accept freebies, do not engage in activities that may create a conflict of interest, do not plagiarize, etc.
- Others fear that if reporters get "too ethical," they will produce wishy-washy journalism: They will be so concerned about hurting someone's feelings or doing the wrong thing that they will not pursue the truth aggressively.
- And some write off the whole area as little more than a public relations ploy to make people like reporters. Reporters aren't supposed to be liked, they say. They're supposed to report the news.

But ethics is broader than these people recognize. To philosophers, ethics is the study of the distinctions between right and wrong, virtuous or vicious, and beneficial or harmful. Professional ethics is more specific. Most professions place ethical demands on their practitioners. Lawyers, for example, are required to give their clients the best possible defense even if they doubt their innocence. Physicians swear they will do no harm to their patients. Priests and psychologists are obliged not to repeat what they are told during confession or counseling.

Just as lawyers, doctors and priests have special responsibilities, journalists too have obligations that define their profession. Although some might quibble with this list, most American journalists would agree that they share these goals:

- **To inform the public about incidents, trends and developments in society and government.** Journalists are obliged to gather information as best they can and to tell the truth as they find it. They must be undaunted in their pursuit of truth and unhampered by conflicting interests.
- **To treat people—both those in the audience and those who are making news—with fairness, respect and even compassion.** It does journalists little good to strive for the truth if a large number of people do not believe news reports because they do not trust or respect the news media.
- **To nurture the democratic process.** For people to govern themselves, they must be informed about the issues and the actions of their government. The news media are the chief providers of that information.

The News & Observer series provides a clear example of ethical journalism because it met these obligations. The series informed citizens about a major development in their state and heightened voters' awareness of an important societal issue. It gave voters a better understanding of their government and provided information about their elected leaders. Through their stories and pictures, the journalists showed compassion for people who lacked the political clout to make their concerns known. And the paper's management displayed courage in criticizing powerful people in business and politics.

The series illustrates another truth about journalism ethics. *The News & Observer* gave the journalists the time and support they needed to prepare the series. Unlike most lawyers and many doctors, most journalists do not work for themselves. They are not completely in control of how well they fulfill the responsibilities of their profession. They work for corporations. Decisions made by corporate executives, who may never have worked a day in a newsroom, affect the ability of individual journalists to live up to their own professional ideals. Their work will suffer if they are not given the time and resources they need. (The business side of journalism is dealt with in Chapter 12.)

Journalism and Democratic Society

The expectation that journalists should explore both social and political issues has long been fundamental in our country. Before the American Revolution, newspapers were leading fights on religious, health and political issues. For example, a newspaper founded by Ben Franklin's older brother, James, clashed with Puritan clergy on the issue of smallpox inoculations. As the Revolution neared, colonists used pamphlets and newspapers to rally support against England. After the British imposed the hated Stamp Act, interest in politics grew and so did the number of American newspapers. These publications were so much a part of American intellectual life that once the new country was established, the First Amendment to the Constitution guaranteed press freedom.

Although historians debate what the Founding Fathers had in mind when they wrote the First Amendment, early American editors believed they understood what their role was to be in this new democracy. Their comments sound very modern. One South Carolina editor argued that as long as newspapers were keeping tabs on Congress, senators could not "betray their trust; convert serious matters into jokes; or transfer mountains into molehills." Another editor interpreted the First Amendment much as the Supreme Court would more than 180 years later in *Times v. Sullivan*. He wrote, "Considerable Latitude must be allowed in the Discussion of Public Affairs, or the Liberty of the Press will be of no Benefit to Society."[2] To these Colonial journalists, freedom of the press was vital if the American experiment in democracy was to work.

Modern editors feel much the same way. "If you look at the history of this country ... the thing that makes this experiment in government unique among democracies has been the continued independence of the daily newspaper serving as a critic and watchdog of government," said James D. Squires, when he was editor of the *Chicago Tribune*. "It goes hand in hand with us being the forum in which the political debate is played out."[3] For the past 20 years, four large-scale research projects have tried to find out what values are important to American journalists. In each study, a large majority of journalists said investigating government claims was among their top priorities.[4]

Journalists have been talking about their "watchdog role" since the early days of our republic. But another popular phrase used to define the role of journalists is relatively new. "The public's right to know" became a chant of American journalists after World War II. They used it as a slogan in their fight to expand their access to information about government, business and other areas of society that have found ways to hide from public scrutiny.

The phrase seems to have started with Kent Cooper, a former top executive of the Associated Press, and then it became cemented into the conventional wisdom of journalism when Harold Cross used it as the title of a book in 1953. The general theme of his book and of the doctrine the slogan represents is that the public has a legal right to know what its government is doing and the press is the representative of the public in finding out. Thus "the public's right to know" became a flag for those many journalists who feel responsible for protecting the people from abuses by government.

Journalists in recent years have used the phrase "the public's right to know" less and less. Some shy away from the phrase because it seems to suggest a constitutional right even though the courts have not supported that view. Other journalists are tired of seeing some of their colleagues turn the doctrine to their own ends, invoking it, for example, as a justification for questionable conduct, such as stealing or lying to get a story.

Yet it remains a basic principle of journalism ethics that the press makes a vital contribution to our democracy when it monitors the activities of politicians and gives citizens information they need to know. Many reporters have sensed that special responsibility when covering some important public meeting with no members of the public present except perhaps an observer for the League of Women Voters and a couple of lawyers representing special interests. Reporters in that all-too-common circumstance usually make a special effort to report actions that might affect those absent citizens—not to sell more papers or increase the station's ratings, but out of a sense of duty. This same sense of representing the public has spurred journalists as they have tried to shed light on the less obvious activities of business and other areas of society.

The Ugly Journalist

Journalists sometimes see themselves in heroic terms. Lurking in the backs of their minds are phrases like "eyes and ears of the public," "representatives of the citizenry" and "the public's watchdog." However, many in the public use less complimentary terms when they describe journalists. A straw poll a few years back found that people felt the ethical standards of reporters were below those of used-car salespeople. Scientific polls are not much more encouraging. Although most reporters enjoy exposing the foibles and chicanery of politicians, polls show that the public is convinced that politicians are more ethical than journalists.[5]

Many people think journalists are foul. Opinion polls suggest the public believes that journalists are arrogant and ruthless. Among the findings:

- Only a third of Americans think reporters care anything at all about the people they report on.

- Fully 73 percent think the media do not respect people's privacy.
- Nearly half the public is unwilling to call journalists moral.[6]
- More than half think reporters abuse their constitutional privileges.[7]
- About half think reporters do not get their facts straight, and more than half think the media cover up their own mistakes.[8]

The problem is deeper than not being able to please all the people all the time. If journalists cannot earn the respect and trust of the public, they will face increasing difficulties in gathering the news and in being believed by the public. A poll by the *Los Angeles Times* found that a third of the public favors limits on news media access to government records and files. An even more discomforting finding was that a third of Americans believe that a government official should have the right to stop the media from reporting a story that the government official believes might be inaccurate. A majority said newspeople should be licensed like doctors or lawyers, and if they behave badly, they should have their licenses revoked.[9]

Perhaps, the most damning indictment of the press was reported in a large-scale survey by journalism Professor Robert O. Wyatt. American journalists take a great deal of pride in the First Amendment and the protection it gives them. Yet, according to Wyatt's survey, Americans would probably not ratify the First Amendment if it were on the ballot today. Two-thirds of them would limit such media practices as endorsing candidates, criticizing the government and military, and reporting on politicians' past mistakes. About a fourth of the people said the media should not be involved in these kinds of activities at all.[10]

Not only would many in the public like to limit journalists' access to news and allow some censorship, they would like the media to suffer financially for their mistakes. Pollsters found that nearly half the people believe that expensive libel suits are a good way to keep the media in line. More than half would allow the courts to fine the media for inaccurate stories.[11] Many believe that jurors have already shown a desire to punish the media. They point to the size of two jury awards against ABC News in 1992. Jurors awarded the Food Lion supermarket chain $5.5 million in one case and banker Alan Levan $10 million in another. Both awards were reduced by appeals court judges.

The public's distrust of the media is getting worse, according to surveys by the Pew Research Center. "What we found 12 years ago was that the public was willing to excuse the press its performance sins, because they took comfort in the watchdog role that the press played, and they liked the news product." For example, in 1985, 55 percent of Americans said national newspapers and the broadcasters reported the facts accurately. By 1997 only 37 percent thought the national news media were accurate. The media took a beating in all social and political groups.

One Pew Center finding was particularly troublesome: The public is not only less supportive of the watchdog role of the press but it thinks journalists are the bad guys. A third of Americans said the national news media get in the way of political leaders and make it harder for them to do their jobs. Unlike 12 years ago, when most people thought reporters were trying to perform an honest public service, today they think news reports are filled with sensationalism, bias and inaccuracy. They believe reporters are chasing stories not for the public good, but for higher ratings and career advancement.[12]

Are Things Really That Bad?

Here's a conundrum. Many would argue that today's news coverage is much better than that of, say, 30 years ago. Both TV and newspaper reporting today provides more thorough stories on a wider variety of topics. Advances in technology allow TV news to provide live reports on most breaking stories. Newspapers are emphasizing thorough reporting and stories with depth. The Internet has created hundreds of new sources of information and commentary. Today's journalists are better trained, better educated, better paid and more professional than ever before. Yet the public has less respect for journalists and the news media.

Many have tried to explain this mystery by pointing out that Americans' respect for all organizations, including churches, schools and government, has declined. To some degree they are right. Yet none of these groups has lost as much respect as the news media.

A more convincing explanation may be that the public is more familiar with how the news is gathered, and that familiarity has bred contempt. Not long ago, if a politician or military leader held a press conference, the public would either read about it in the newspaper or watch highlights on the evening news. The public would never know whether journalists asked stupid questions or behaved brutishly. Today, the news conference is likely to be broadcast live. The public can see journalists in action. Often that isn't pretty. They see reporters yelling over each other to ask questions and photographers elbowing others out of the way. As CNN Washington Bureau Chief Frank Sesno put it, "You look at [Special Prosecutor Ken] Starr coming out of his office, and he's mauled by the cameras and the sound crews and the reporters, and the visual image is 'Yuck, what's going on here.'" Other times, the public sees reporters and photographers chasing after or badgering people who clearly want to be left alone. Or they watch as dozens of reporters and TV remote trucks turn formerly quiet neighborhoods into circuses.

Another factor in the decline in respect for journalists is the tendency of many people to lump all news outlets into one big monolithic entity. They condemn the entire profession for the sins of a few. For example, after the death of Princess Diana, early news accounts suggested that free-lance photographers, the paparazzi, may have contributed to the car crash that killed her. The next day, photographers working for news outlets in small-town America were cursed by passers-by as "the killers of Di." When Gennifer Flowers was asked at a news conference if Bill Clinton used condoms, many people condemned the conduct of insensitive reporters. The question was asked by a "reporter" from Howard Stern's radio program, which prides itself in its tastelessness.

None of this suggests that people confuse their local paper with the *National Enquirer*. Still, they may not create mental footnotes. They will recall hearing some news item but may not remember whether the report was on the *CBS Evening News, Hard Copy* or a shock jock's radio show. If these nuggets of news are obnoxious or prove to be untrue, they often shrug it off as another thing "the news media" did that was wrong.

Movies and TV shows shape some perceptions of journalists. Only police officers are shown more often than journalists during entertainment programs on prime-time television. But these portrayals are rarely flattering. Only 14 percent of the fictional newspaper reporters and 24 percent of their TV brethren are shown favorably, according to one study. Most reporters are depicted as unethical, sloppy, insensitive and foolish.[13] They go about their day lying, stealing, eavesdropping, trespassing and seducing. They diligently avoid letting the facts get in the way of good stories. Then they run back to the newsroom to tell their gleeful editors about their big scoops.

Things are no better in the movies. After viewing more than 1,000 films depicting journalists, one researcher said only a few showed journalists as the least bit competent.[14] Rarely do journalists come across as great humanitarians. In one movie popular a few years ago, a reporter, played by Kirk Douglas, was so desperate to write a series of front-page stories that he bribed rescuers to slow their efforts to free a man trapped in a cave. When the reporter himself found a way to free the man, he didn't tell anyone. Instead, he let the miner die a slow death so he could continue to write front-page stories.[15] In a *New York Times* story headlined "Movies Blast Media, Viewers Cheer," Glenn Garelik pointed out that in the 1930s, reporters often were depicted in screwball comedies as fun-loving, "blue-collar, salt-of-the-earth types." But today, the image has changed. The wise-cracking of earlier reporters has become arrogance, and reporters who had been shown as the working-class enemies of pretension are now seen as pretentious themselves.[16]

"The Enemy Is Us"

CBS newsman George Crile learned the hard way why so many in the public distrust the news media. Crile was in court to answer a libel suit after a CBS documentary contended U.S. Gen. William Westmoreland had deliberately overstated the success of the American military effort in Vietnam. The trial, featuring charges of official misconduct by the military and of questionable reporting techniques by CBS, was big news. When Crile left the courthouse, he was surrounded by packs of reporters shouting questions and TV camera crews jockeying for the best angle. The veteran journalist later remarked, "I'm shocked at the way the media cover these things; they're like a bunch of hungry animals." To which another journalist responded: "George, you have met the enemy and he's in our business."[17]

The media's reputation took one blow after another in the summer of 1998. Major investigative stories were withdrawn. CNN retracted a highly promoted investigation of U.S. soldiers using poison gas in Southeast Asia. The network's own investigation into the story concluded it was not supported by the facts. *The Cincinnati Enquirer* ran an apology across the top of its front page for three days straight after a reporter allegedly stole phone mail messages that he used in an investigation of illegal activities by the Cincinnati-based Chiquita Banana Co. *The Boston Globe* and *The New Republic* magazine fired reporters after it was determined they had made up stories, some of which contained "news" that damaged the reputations of real people.

Perhaps the biggest blow to press credibility was the ongoing stories about President Clinton and White House intern Monica Lewinsky. Rumors flew fast and furious, and news organizations were reporting them, then withdrawing them and then re-reporting them with dizzying speed. Editors at *The Dallas Morning News* decided to retract a story *while* it was being printed.

Journalists point out that these are aberrations, involving only a handful of the nation's 1,500 daily newspapers and hundreds of broadcast news outlets. But the public is less forgiving. In a *Newsweek* poll taken shortly after these revelations, 62 percent said these events made them "less likely to trust the media's reporting," compared with only 30 percent who said these were just isolated incidents. It should have come as no surprise to journalists that nearly seven out of 10 people told pollsters that they believed the news media could not be trusted to get the facts right—or, for that matter, trusted period.

Improving the Profession

The chapter opens with portions of *The News & Observer*'s "King Hog" series, an example of "ethical journalism." To produce this exceptional series, the journalists

- **Practiced the principles of ethical journalism.** As noted earlier, the journalists found a story that shed light on a part of society that probably had been overlooked by many people. They produced a series that told the voters of North Carolina about their state government and their elected officials. And they showed compassion for the residents living near the hog farms and related their stories with care and sincerity.
- **Were talented at their crafts.** To be ethical and credible, journalists must be competent at what they do. If a story is incomplete or has errors, the public is misinformed. And if the story is not told well, the public may not bother to read it or watch it on television. Most of us will not wade through a sea of bad writing, dull video and uninspired design. *The News & Observer* staff was more than competent. Reporters and editors gathered thousands of facts, talked to dozens of sources and scrutinized scores of documents. All that reporting gave their series the ring of truth. They then wrote the story compellingly, and the paper's designers put together a package that reinforced the information and enticed readers to peruse all eight days of coverage.
- **Worked for a strong news organization.** *The News & Observer* gave them support and was brave enough to challenge powerful forces in their state. While first-rate journalism is produced every day in second-rate newsrooms, having enlightened owners and managers of news organizations is a major ingredient in the practice of ethical journalism.

2

Accountability

Assume you are a doctor practicing general medicine in a medium-sized city. You enter the doctor's lounge of the hospital just after checking on your patients and are greeted by a fellow general practitioner who says, "Now we know how you can afford that new house!" Then he shows you an article in the morning paper listing the fees charged by various medical specialists in the area. Your name is listed at the top of a column of general practitioners. You look at the list, and the fee shown is more than twice what you really charge.

Does this mistake upset you? It probably would.

You decide to call the paper to get it to print a correction. You leave your name and phone number with an editor you know. But he doesn't call you back. So you call the reporter whose byline is on the story. He's not in, but the city editor listens to you and tells you he'll get back to you. A week later, you still haven't heard from him. You call back, and he tells you he sees no reason to print a correction because the figures were based on Medicare records. After you exchange a few unpleasant words, he suggests you need to talk to the reporter.

Finally, you get the reporter on the line. You explain how unreliable the sources were that he used for the story. You tell him you wished he had talked to you before the story appeared in the paper and suggest he should recheck his figures. His response floors you. He tells you (1) he didn't have time to check his figures and (2) even if he had checked with you, he wouldn't have changed anything in the article.[1]

If you were the doctor this happened to, what might you do? The first thing you might think of is suing the newspaper. But you are unsure if you could collect enough money to make it worth your while. Lawyers are expensive, and court cases often drag on for years.

You might wonder if there are rules that apply to journalists like those that apply to the medical profession. To become a doctor, you had to pass tests and meet standards set by state law and by the medical societies. You swore an oath promising to abide by ethical codes. If you violate those codes, you can be called before a committee of the medical society, and in severe cases, the committee can even take away your ability to practice medicine. You know that lawyers, dentists, optometrists and other professionals have similar organizations that can sit in judgment of a practitioner's ethics.

Do journalists face those same kinds of standards? Are there codes of ethics for journalists like the codes for other professions? Are there ethics panels that will listen to your grievances against the media? What do you do, short of suing for libel, if you believe you have been wronged by the media? Some people joke that journalism is a game in which the batter gets to call balls and strikes. Are they right?

At many newspapers today, if you were the doctor, you would have no other alternatives. You could either sue the paper or spend the rest of your life complaining about the media. But the doctor in this story had other options. That's because he was dealing with the Louisville *Courier-Journal* and the year was 1980. The Louisville papers were leaders in bringing higher ethical standards to journalism. In 1980, staffers were bound to a code of ethics, and the paper had an ombudsman to listen to reader complaints. Also in 1980, the doctor could appeal his case to an organization called the National News Council.

Codes of Ethics

If the doctor wondered whether journalism is a profession with a uniform code of ethics, he stumbled into a debate that has been raging for years on podiums at journalism conferences, in trade journals and even in courts of law. The belief that journalists should be bound by a uniform code has been around for a long time. In fact, one of the first things the American Society of Newspaper Editors did when it was organized in 1923 was to propose such a code.[2]

But the push for codes of ethics did not pick up momentum until the 1970s. The Society of Professional Journalists, which had endorsed the ASNE canons as its code of ethics in 1926, created its own code in 1973. During the 1970s, codes were either written or revised by the Radio-Television News Directors Association, the Associated Press Managing Editors association, the ASNE, and the national organizations of travel writers, sportswriters, editorial writers and business writers.

News organizations also began to write codes. In the mid-1970s fewer than one in 10 daily newspapers had codes.[3] Today, most do. News organizations initially copied the national codes.[4] But now most of them write their own codes and are constantly revising them as they encounter new problems and as technology creates unanticipated ethical concerns.

Suggestions or Rules?

Within a year of the establishment of its first code of ethics, the ASNE was hit by a question that still troubles national journalism groups: What do you do with journalists who violate your code of ethics?

When the ASNE finished codifying its ethics in 1923, several of the 124 charter members of ASNE wanted their society to have powers similar to those of the legal and medical societies. These societies can punish unethical practitioners and even ban them from their professions. Many ASNE members wanted to flex the muscles of their new code of ethics by expelling F.G. Bonfils, publisher of *The Denver Post,* from their organization. Bonfils had accepted $1 million in bribes not to print stories about government oil reserves in Wyoming that were being sold illegally to private interests. At first, ASNE members voted to expel Bonfils. But then Bonfils threatened to sue the group and each of its directors for slander. He offered to drop the suits if the society would forget about expelling him. The directors agreed, and the debate about punishing him for apparently violating virtually all of its canons of ethics ended.[5] A few years later, the society formally passed a motion spelling out that adherence to its code would be strictly voluntary.[6]

A similar debate consumed SPJ meetings in 1985. Finally, the SPJ board of directors voted not to change its code into binding rules with penalties for offenders. The reason? Board members feared that if they punished someone for breaking the code, the society would be sued and the legal fees might bankrupt it.[7] Today, none of the codes written by professional organizations like ASNE, SPJ and RTNDA are binding. There's no real punishment if a member violates their provisions.

However, that's not true of codes written by news organizations themselves. Most media outlets have some kind of code that their employees must abide by. The original codes could often be printed on one sheet of paper, but now codes fill entire chapters in style books. ABC News' new code is 75 pages long. Many address difficult issues like anonymous sources, privacy and accuracy. These codes often spell out the penalties for breaking the rules, ranging from verbal warnings to dismissal.

Problems with Codes

One objection to codes is that they often deal only with cut-and-dried issues. They may forbid reporters from accepting freebies or moonlighting as publicists for politicians. But they say little about more substantial issues. Jeremy Iggers, a reporter for the Minneapolis *Star Tribune,* argued that because most codes concentrate on banning bad behavior, a journalist can follow the codes to the letter and yet "produce journalism that is utterly irresponsible or destructive."[8]

Other journalists say codes don't help them deal with real reporting problems. For example, many codes of ethics indicate the news media "must guard against invading a person's right to privacy." That admonition offers little guidance to working journalists, said Laurie A. Zenner, a media lawyer.[9] Worse, the codes could be used against journalists in libel and privacy trials. By showing that an accused reporter did not follow a code of ethics, plaintiffs' attorneys try to sway juries into awarding larger settlements against the media.

Mark Zieman, managing editor of the Kansas City *Star,* wonders if it is possible to write a universal code of ethics given the variety of working conditions that journalists face. He explained that "the resources, community and mission of *The Boston Globe* are not the same as those of the *Atchison (Kan.) Daily Globe,* nor should their ethics codes be the same. Their voices are different and so are their values and that's perfectly fine."[10]

Abe Rosenthal, who held most of the top editing positions at *The New York Times,* complained that codes apply only to journalists, not to corporations that own media and media executives whose decisions often shape news coverage. He contended that codes should cover everyone in the news process, including management and owners. Rosenthal argued: "If you're going to have a code, it has to be tough and it has to deal with questions of how much news, how much profit and how much space."[11] (The role media owners play in journalism ethics is discussed in Chapter 12.)

Both journalists and researchers have a more basic question: Do codes really do any good? Andrew Barnes, former editor and president of the *St. Petersburg Times,* was bothered by the tendency in some newsrooms to hang a code of ethics on the wall, declare themselves ethical and then go back to getting the paper out with no real change in their behavior.[12] Journalism research suggests Barnes may be right. Studies have found that frequently reporters are unaware of their organizations' codes.[13] Other studies have raised questions about whether journalists at newspapers with strong codes of ethics behave any differently from those at papers that don't have codes.[14] And many news organizations have bent their codes badly in the heated competition that often surrounds major stories.

News Councils

When the doctor complained to one of the reporters at the Louisville paper, the reporter told him about the National News Council. News councils are voluntary institutions that listen to disputes between the news media and the public. For 11 years, the United States had the National News Council, which was charged with the responsibility of monitoring the news media in this country. Its investigators looked into the complaints, and then the council listened to both sides and decided who was right.

When investigators reviewed the doctor's case, they discovered that he did not deal directly with Medicare. Instead he asked his patients to file for whatever reimbursements they were due. The council suggested that since his "billing system was less than ideal," some patients might have submitted blanket fees instead of itemized ones, which would have skewed his Medicare profile.

The newspaper responded that the paper had made clear efforts to ensure the accuracy of the story. (1) It had hired an outside computer firm to double-check the reporters' study of the Medicare data; (2) the paper had interviewed 60 of the 400 physicians listed (although not the doctor who complained); and (3) when the reporter found that charges for an initial visit can vary because of billing inconsistencies, he inserted that explanation at the top of the list of doctors and charges, directly above the complaining doctor's name. However, the council didn't think that was enough. It concluded:

> The *Courier-Journal* listing was accurate insofar as the Medicare computer records listed Dr. Hogge's charges. What seemed essential was a direct check with Dr. Hogge and all others listed in the top rank of fees recorded, the most sensitive area in the lists. It is clear such a recheck with Dr. Hogge would have brought instant protest and a deeper check. However, the newspaper opted for random checking. Moreover, the newspaper's statement seeking to clarify differentials was

not fully informative. The *Courier-Journal*'s motivation was sound and the paper did publish a patient's letter supporting Dr. Hogge's view. Nevertheless, Dr. Hogge was done an inadvertent injustice and the complaint is found warranted.

The *Courier-Journal* reported the council's finding on its front page, and then its executive editor apologized to the doctor in his column 10 days later. The editor said he accepted the council's decision "without a quibble." The doctor said he "was surprised to get anything near this much redress of injustice. It shows that if you're right—and willing—you *can* fight 'bad press'—and even win."

The doctor might not have fared so well today. The National News Council died of neglect in 1984. Richard Salant, the former head of CBS News who was president of the council when it folded, said he believed news media opposition to the council "was rooted in the traditional reluctance of the press to have any outside body . . . looking over its shoulder, and in the conviction of the press that each individual news organization could best solve its own problems and in its own way."[15]

At about the same time the National News Council was founded, local news councils were set up in California, Hawaii, Oregon, Missouri, Illinois, Minnesota and most Canadian provinces. Today, every Canadian province except Saskatchewan still has a provincial or regional news council.[16] But the only remaining statewide council is in Minnesota.[17]

News councils are not courts of law, and they cannot penalize wrongdoing. In fact, before the Minnesota council will listen to a complaint, all parties must agree that they will not file suits in the case. They then discuss the disputed story and explain their positions. About 95 percent of the complaints are dropped or settled at this stage. If the case goes to a formal hearing, both sides present their cases and are questioned by the 24 members of the council—half from the news media and half from the public. A member of the Minnesota Supreme Court serves as chair. If the media win, that's the end of it. However, if the news outlet loses, it must agree to report the council's decision. The Minnesota council has sided with the media in about half its decisions.[18] The council's $180,000 annual budget is funded by a variety of media and nonmedia organizations with the largest contribution—$ 12,500—coming from the Minneapolis *Star Tribune*.

Many would like to see a resurgence in news councils. Columnist Martin Schram wrote, "A news council seems like a sane middle-ground alternative to the old standard media response to complaints: (1) 'Write a letter to the editor' or (2) 'Sue us.'"[19] CBS's Mike Wallace argued that news councils might cause the public to regain confidence in the news media. "The American public might be reassured by our willingness to open ourselves up to the kind of public scrutiny that we ourselves use in evaluating the work, the accomplishments—and the failings—of others."[20]

Not everyone agrees. Some news organizations in Minnesota refuse to participate in their state's news council. KSTP-TV chief executive officer Stanley Hubbard sees no need for councils: "If somebody feels we've done something wrong, they can talk to us directly, or they have recourse in the courts. I don't want to be in a situation where a panel of people are sitting in judgment on our judgment."[21]

Others are concerned that news councils may chill the pursuit of controversial stories by tying up reporters and editors with complaints that would not be allowed in a court of law. Former WCCO-TV news director John Lansing worries that because news councils are not bound by the same rules that the courts are, they will give powerful institutions "further protection from public scrutiny and a big club to wield against the press." A news council does not limit what participants can say before or after its hearings. When Northwest Airlines brought a complaint against WCCO, Lansing claimed the corporations aroused public opinion against the station by using "advertising channels, labor unions and competing media in a textbook display of a corporate power play. Any media outlet in Minnesota will think twice before taking Northwest on again."[22]

Also of concern is the potential for biased council members. Former *Washington Post* editor Benjamin Bradlee said the old National News Council was "taken over by kooks."[23] Although most concede the Minnesota council has fared well, some worry that other councils may be made up of "do-gooders" who may have axes to grind against the media. Eventually, they foresee the need for an appeals council to hear objections about council rulings.

Ombudsmen

The Louisville doctor missed one avenue of complaint at the *Courier-Journal*: the paper's ombudsman. The *Courier-Journal* and its sister paper, *The Louisville Times*, were the first newspapers in America to have ombudsmen. The ombudsman at the time later said that he believed if the complaint had come to him, the problem "wouldn't have gone as far as it did."

Ombudsmen or reader representatives are in-house consciences.

Part of their job is listening to readers' complaints. Most papers print their phone numbers and e-mail addresses daily. When they receive a complaint, they often discuss it with the journalists involved. Sometimes they use these complaints for columns in which they explain and occasionally criticize the conduct of their own papers. Most also write columns and news stories about the big journalistic issues of the day such as objectivity, anonymous sources or privacy. Occasionally they answer questions that have been bugging readers. For example, Miriam Pepper, reader representative of the Kansas City *Star,* recently explained how the paper chose the "thought for the day" and why play reviews don't appear the morning after performances (early deadlines, she said). Dennis Foley, ombudsman at *The Orange County (Calif.) Register,* answered complaints from middle-school students about a picture showing the winner of a mud race smoking a cigar. They thought it encouraged smoking.

Several newspapers experimented with ombudsmen in the 1960s. Ombudsmen even formed an association, called the Organization of News Ombudsmen, which they call by its initials "Oh, no," said to describe the ombudsman's typical reaction to the paper's latest goof. However, the movement has never really caught on. Today, fewer than 40 of America's 1,500 dailies have ombudsmen, and that number has held steady for years. None of the TV networks had ombudsmen until 1993, when NBC named one. A few months later, ABC appointed its first-ever director of news practices.[24] The concept is more common among Canadian newspapers.[25]

Editors haven't hired ombudsmen for several reasons. Some say ombudsmen are an unwanted barrier between readers and journalists. Editors themselves should "feel the wrath of readers" after they have made controversial news decisions.[26] Norman Isaacs, the editor who appointed the first ombudsman in Louisville, complained that too often ombudsmen "are purely cosmetic; some guy writing a media column in which all he does is explain the virtues of the newspaper."[27]

However, Lynne Enders Glaser, who writes the ombudsman column for *The Fresno Bee,* said she does not see her job as making the paper popular or beloved by explaining away its problems, but as regaining the respect of readers by showing that the newspaper cares about readers' reactions and that it is trying to be fair.[28] Lou Gelfand, reader representative of the *Star Tribune* in Minneapolis, counted his columns once and found that more than half the time he sided with readers in their complaints against his paper. Gelfand contends that by showing such honesty, newspapers may win back respect and even help stop the decline in readership.[29]

Explaining Ourselves

When the Hutchins Commission was looking at the news media in the 1940s, it urged the press to be more honest with its readers. "We recommend that the members of the press engage in vigorous mutual criticism," it said. "Professional standards are not likely to be achieved as long as the mistakes and errors, the frauds and crimes, committed by units of the press are passed over in silence by other members of the profession."

The news media today are a little better at critiquing themselves. David Shaw has been writing well-read stories about media issues for the *Los Angeles Times* since 1974. He is often critical of the *Times* itself in his stories. Other news organizations, including *The Wall Street Journal, The Washington Post, Chicago Tribune, The New York Times, Newsday, Newsweek* and *Time,* also have insightful coverage of the media.

Some believe the news media are becoming more willing to report the shortcomings of other news organizations. They point to the extensive coverage given to *The Cincinnati Enquirer* and CNN when they retracted major investigative stories and to *The New Republic* magazine and *The Boston Globe* when they fired writers for making up stories. Reese Cleghorn, journalism dean at the University of Maryland, contended, "Without a doubt, the press' continuing exposure of the press is the best protection the public has against bad journalism."[30]

Another positive development has occurred at news organizations that are explaining their decisions to readers. When *The Boston Globe* published a story about the drinking habits of a candidate for governor, deputy managing editor Benjamin Bradlee Jr. wrote a sidebar explaining why the paper decided to delve into such a private matter. He told readers that he believed "we should explain our thinking."

Readers appreciate being told the motives of editors. When Richard Davis was convicted in a highly publicized murder trial of killing Polly Klaas, he turned toward the family and extended both middle fingers. Both the *San Jose Mercury News* and the *San Francisco Chronicle* ran photographs of the killer's gesture. The *Mercury News* explained its decision in a front-page letter to readers; the *Chronicle* did not. In the letter to readers, *Mercury News* executive editor Jerry Ceppos wrote:

> The decision to publish the front-page photograph of Richard Allen Davis' obscene gesture wasn't an easy one. Let me tell you why we

San Jose Mercury News

FINAL EDITION · 25 CENTS   *Serving Northern California Since 1851*   WEDNESDAY ... JUNE 19, 1996

S.J. parents to be liable for taggers

The city council voted Tuesday to make San Jose the first city in the state to bill parents for the costs of cleaning up their children's graffiti. The plan, which faces one more vote, would allow the city to place a lien on parents' property to reclaim costs if amounts due go unpaid. Mayor Susan Hammer said: "There has to be a way to get these parents to understand they have to work with us."

See story, Page 1B.

Gun ban approved; test likely

Hundreds of people jammed the city council chambers on Tuesday night to voice their opinions on a proposal to ban the sale of "Saturday night specials" in San Jose city limits. The council approved the ban by a 6-5 vote. A similar measure in West Hollywood was challenged, and San Jose's city attorney believes the local effort is likely to be found in violation of state law.

See story, Page 1B.

Agency ousts regulator in major shift of focus

FAA vows to make safety its sole mission

BY RALPH VARTABEDIAN
Mercury Times

WASHINGTON — The Federal Aviation Administration, acknowledging for the first time that its ability to enforce airline safety standards was in question, announced basic changes Tuesday in the way it oversees the airline industry. Transportation Secretary Federico Peña recommended that Congress amend the FAA's legislative charter by eliminating its role in promoting air commerce and making safety its sole mission. In addition, the agency ousted its longtime safety czar, Anthony Broderick. And it announced that it was instituting six major regulations.

See FAA, Page 7A

Is ValuJet on its deathbed?
PAGE 9E

THE POLLY KLAAS CASE: DAVIS FOUND GUILTY

Now, life or death?

Convicted on all counts, defiant killer awaits sentencing

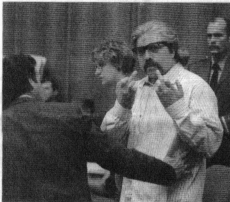

■ Next: Special circumstances make him eligible for capital punishment.

BY SANDRA GONZALES
Mercury News Staff Writer

Seconds after hearing the guilty verdicts, Richard Allen Davis told the world what he thought.

He didn't say a word.

With both middle fingers extended, Davis suddenly turned in the direction of the TV camera and Polly Klaas' family and winked his right eye and kissed the air.

"He was showing us what he is: just a contemptible little punk who's been flipping off society from Day 1," said Marc Klaas, father of the girl Davis had just been convicted of killing. "This is the beginning of the end for Richard Allen Davis."

For the 16 minutes before he made his vulgar salute, Davis had remained mostly impassive while the court clerk read the 21-page verdict forms proclaiming him guilty of the kidnapping and murder of Polly and eligible for the death penalty.

Klaas, who sat in the front row of the San Jose courtroom with his parents, clasped a district attorney's investigator at his side and held onto his mother with his other. Much of the time, Klaas kept

Polly Klaas kidnapped during a 1993 slumber party.

See DAVIS, Back Page

After standing impassively as the guilty verdicts were read at television camera. Then he winked in the direction of the Klaas length, Richard Allen Davis turns suddenly and gestures to the family and kissed the air.

Dear reader,

[letter text box]

Marc Klaas clutches the hand of former Petaluma police Sgt. Mike Meese as verdicts are read.

Arrogance, stupidity, contempt: Killer has it all

A WORD to Richard Allen Davis, killer of Polly Klaas. You're toast, sleaze bag. Of all the stupid stunts that anyone could expect to see from a man whose life is in the hands of a Superior Court jury, Davis topped them all Tuesday afternoon when he turned in the specific direction of the TV camera and in the

JIM TROTTER

general direction of the family of the murdered child and flipped them off with both hands. Gave them a little wink and a gesture of contempt with his mouth, too. A kiss and two birds from a sociopath who is trying to avoid the death penalty. The jury found Davis guilty Tuesday of all 10 counts with which

See TROTTER, Back Page

Driving toward his goal
Recent Santa Clara University graduate Steve Nash's NBA dream is in sight — the point guard is expected to be among the top 25 picks in the draft. *See story,* Page 1D.

WEATHER
■ Sunny with highs about 80.

Yeltsin makes ex-rival his top security aide

With Lebed, he gains stronger hold on first place in campaign

BY MICHAEL R. GORDON
New York Times

MOSCOW — In two bold strokes, Boris Yeltsin on Tuesday consolidated support and tightened his grip on first place in next month's presidential runoff election.

Yeltsin dismissed unpopular Defense Minister Pavel Grachev and named Alexander Lebed, a retired general who finished a strong third in Sunday's first round, as his top national security adviser.

The move gave him a claim to the 15 percent of the electorate who supported the gruff-talking Lebed in the first round of presidential balloting.

And a supremely confident Lebed immediately did his best to turn his image of toughness and personal rectitude to Yeltsin's advantage, announcing he would work with the president to fight the crime and corruption that have alarmed many voters during Yeltsin's first term.

In addition, Lebed claimed that he had foiled an attempt by a small group of military commanders to reverse Yeltsin's dismissal of Grachev.

The plot, Lebed said, involved

See RUSSIA, Page A4

Polly Klaas' murderer. The *San Jose Mercury News* took the unusual precaution of including a front-page letter explaining its decision to publish this photograph of Richard Allen Davis' obscene gesture.

Photo courtesy of the San Jose Mercury News.

decided to do it. Ever since Davis' arrest, I've wanted to know more about the character of a man who could kill Polly Klaas. . . . Even though it's unclear precisely who the target of the gesture is, I believe the photograph tells us something about Allen's contempt for the system that convicted him. . . . For those reasons, I thought the photograph was worth publishing. I'd be interested in your views, too.[31]

The *Mercury News* received about 1,200 responses, two-to-one in favor of publication. The *Chronicle* got 130 calls, nearly all of which were critical. Ceppos told *American Journalism Review* that he credited the positive reaction to the short explanation. Explaining to readers "how we operate and make decisions is probably the only subject in the world of journalism where there shouldn't be any controversy," Ceppos said. "People love to know how and why you make decisions. It's an easy way to get some of our credibility back."[32]

Allan Siegal, an assistant managing editor of *The New York Times,* agrees that the days when editors can tell readers to "just shut up and trust me" have passed. His paper prints a variety of editor's notes and clarifications. During the height of the Clinton-Lewinsky frenzy, the paper printed a story headlined "Trust Me: A Media Guide," which punctured many of the rumors that had been reported in mainstream media, including *The New York Times.* "We have a very intelligent readership, and we've always believed in treating our readers like grown-ups. We tend to level with people," Siegal said.

The shortage of such reporting, however, has left the American people with no firm understanding of the news media. They have no way of knowing why certain events and activities are "newsworthy" and others are not, how the news staff is deployed, and often even who owns the newspaper or TV station. The news media analyze and criticize nearly every aspect of society: government, business, education, sports, entertainment, lifestyles, fashion, health, relationships, literature, religion and on and on. But one institution is conspicuously missing: the news media themselves. As a *Sacramento Bee* ombudsman once said, "The press does an abysmal job of explaining itself."[33]

Two Professional Codes

Society of Professional Journalists

Preamble

Members of the Society of Professional Journalists believe that public enlightenment is the forerunner of justice and the foundation of democracy. The duty of the journalist is to further those ends by seeking truth and providing a fair and comprehensive account of events and issues. Conscientious journalists from all media and specialties strive to serve the public with thoroughness and honesty. Professional integrity is the cornerstone of a journalist's credibility. Members of the Society share a dedication to ethical behavior and adopt this code to declare the Society's principles and standards of practice.

Seek Truth and Report It

Journalists should be honest, fair and courageous in gathering, reporting and interpreting information. Journalists should:

Test the accuracy of information from all sources and exercise care to avoid inadvertent error. Deliberate distortion is never permissible.

Diligently seek out subjects of news stories to give them the opportunity to respond to allegations of wrongdoing.

Identify sources whenever feasible. The public is entitled to as much information as possible on sources' reliability.

Always question sources' motives before promising anonymity. Clarify conditions attached to any promise made in exchange for information.

Keep promises.

Make certain that headlines, news teases and promotional material, photos, video, audio, graphics, sound bites and quotations do not misrepresent. They should not oversimplify or highlight incidents out of context.

Never distort the content of news photos or video. Image enhancement for technical clarity is always permissible. Label montages and photo illustrations.

Avoid misleading re-enactments or staged news events. If re-enactment is necessary to tell a story, label it.

Avoid undercover or other surreptitious methods of gathering information except when traditional open methods will not yield information vital to the public. Use of such methods should be explained as part of the story.

Never plagiarize.

Tell the story of the diversity and magnitude of the human experience boldly, even when it is unpopular to do so.

Examine their own cultural values and avoid imposing those values on others.

Avoid stereotyping by race, gender, age, religion, ethnicity, geography, sexual orientation, disability, physical appearance or social status.

Support the open exchange of views, even views they find repugnant. Give voice to the voiceless; official and unofficial sources of information can be equally valid.

Distinguish between advocacy and news reporting. Analysis

and commentary should be labeled and not misrepresent fact or context.

Distinguish news from advertising and shun hybrids that blur the lines between the two.

Recognize a special obligation to ensure that the public's business is conducted in the open and that government records are open to inspection.

Minimize Harm

Ethical journalists treat sources, subjects and colleagues as human beings deserving of respect. Journalists should:

Show compassion for those who may be affected adversely by news coverage.

Use special sensitivity when dealing with children and inexperienced sources or subjects.

Be sensitive when seeking or using interviews or photographs of those affected by tragedy or grief.

Recognize that gathering and reporting information may cause harm or discomfort.

Pursuit of the news is not a license for arrogance.

Recognize that private people have a greater right to control information about themselves than do public officials and others who seek power, influence or attention. Only an overriding public need can justify intrusion into anyone's privacy.

Show good taste. Avoid pandering to lurid curiosity.

Be cautious about identifying juvenile suspects or victims of sex crimes.

Be judicious about naming criminal suspects before the formal filing of charges.

Balance a criminal suspect's fair trial rights with the public's right to be informed.

Act Independently

Journalists should be free of obligation to any interest other than the public's right to know. Journalists should:

Avoid conflicts of interest, real or perceived.

Remain free of associations and activities that may compromise integrity or damage credibility.

Refuse gifts, favors, fees, free travel and special treatment, and shun secondary employment, political involvement, public office and service in community organizations if they compromise journalistic integrity.

Disclose unavoidable conflicts.

Be vigilant and courageous about holding those with power accountable.

Deny favored treatment to advertisers and special interests and resist their pressure to influence news coverage.

Be wary of sources offering information for favors or money; avoid bidding for news.

Be Accountable

Journalists are accountable to their readers, listeners, viewers and each other. Journalists should:

Clarify and explain news coverage and invite dialogue with the public over journalistic conduct.

Encourage the public to voice grievances against the news media.

Admit mistakes and correct them promptly.

Expose unethical practices of journalists and the news media.

Abide by the same high standards to which they hold others.

(Present version of the Code of Ethics of the SPJ adopted in September 1996)

Radio-Television News Directors Association

The responsibility of radio and television journalists is to gather and report information of importance and interest to the public accurately, honestly and impartially. The members of the Radio-Television News Directors Association accept these standards and will:

1. Strive to present the source or nature of broadcast news material in a way that is balanced, accurate and fair.
   A. They will evaluate information solely on its merits as news, rejecting sensationalism or misleading emphasis in any form.
   B. They will guard against using audio or video material in a way that deceives the audience.
   C. They will not mislead the public by presenting as spontaneous news any material which is staged or rehearsed.
   D. They will identify people by race, creed, nationality or prior status only when it is relevant.
   E. They will clearly label opinion and commentary.
   F. They will promptly acknowledge and correct errors.
2. Strive to conduct themselves in a manner that protects them from conflicts of interest, real or perceived. They will decline gifts or favors which would influence or appear to influence their judgments.
3. Respect the dignity, privacy and well-being of people with whom they deal.
4. Recognize the need to protect confidential sources. They will promise confidentiality only with the intention of keeping that promise.
5. Respect everyone's right to a fair trial.

6. Broadcast the private transmissions of other broadcasters only with permission.
7. Actively encourage observance of this Code by all journalists, whether members of the Radio-Television News Directors Association or not.

(Unanimously adopted by the RTNDA Board of Directors, August 31, 1987)

Telling the Truth

3

Truth and Objectivity

The images on their TV screens grabbed the attention of people in Minneapolis. A Boeing 747 appeared to be headed for a disastrous crash that would surely kill everyone aboard. An announcer told viewers to watch that night's local news to learn about safety problems at Northwest Airlines, the Minnesota-based carrier that handles most flights in and out of Minneapolis.

What Minnesotans saw on WCCO news that week was unsettling. The station reported that Northwest wanted to maintain its on-time standards so badly that it pressured mechanics to let unsafe airplanes fly. The station, which is a CBS affiliate with a reputation for top-notch investigative journalism, reported that

- A Northwest jet flew 291 flights with bolts missing from its engines, a condition that made the plane "unairworthy," according to the Federal Aviation Administration.
- The FAA said Northwest had repeated problems with oxygen masks on 22 Boeing 747s between May 1993 and October 1993, making those planes unairworthy.
- Northwest's faulty maintenance had "endangered the lives of passengers" on a 1993 flight between Boston and Minneapolis.
- Northwest repeatedly failed to properly repair directional and radio equipment on a jet that flew in an unairworthy condition on 33 flights in 18 days. On the 18th day, while flying through bad weather, the pilots warned that they were "down to a basic gyro and mag compass."

- An engine caught fire and nearly fell off a Northwest jetliner as it was landing at Narita Airport in Japan. The cause? Parts that helped hold the engine on the plane had been left off during a maintenance check in Minneapolis 10 days earlier. "And no one noticed they were missing, not even supervisors or inspectors who signed off that the plane was fit to fly," reported WCCO-TV's Don Shelby. "It fell off on landing in Japan: a disaster averted by sheer luck." The plane had flown 14 flights in this condition.
- Northwest paid fines to the FAA amounting to $725,000 for dozens of safety violations.
- Northwest corrected defective wiring in 42 jets only after constant surveillance and prodding by the FAA.

The series was presented with all the gusto of a tabloid TV newscast. As Shelby read the reports, words pulled from FAA documents like "catastrophic failure," "investigation," "careless," "endangered lives" and "unairworthy condition" popped onto the screen. Videotape of the damaged Northwest plane in Japan was shown several times. Northwest mechanics were taped working on jets at night. Because of the type of lighting used in the large hanger, the footage had an eerie greenish glow.

To bolster their case, WCCO reporters interviewed Northwest employees, including one "whistle blower." He was a welder who said Northwest management had ordered him to repair parts that he thought were beyond repair. They also interviewed a group of women employees who said Northwest managers had pressured them after they complained of sexual harassment. Although their complaints were not related to safety issues, WCCO contended that their experiences showed that Northwest managers had a history of pressuring employees who did not toe the company line.

WCCO's reports triggered a torrent of discussion. The labor union that represents the mechanics bought full-page advertisements in newspapers denying that its members would allow unsafe airplanes to fly. Northwest also mounted a publicity program aimed at discrediting the news reports. Viewers debated the stories in letters-to-the-editor columns and on talk-radio shows. Some praised the bravery of the station for taking on an important and controversial issue. They lauded the work of Shelby, the popular and respected WCCO anchor who presented the reports. But other viewers attacked the station for badmouthing one of the area's major employers, a company that paid good wages and had just fought its way back from near-bankruptcy.

WCCO expected the report to draw comment. Nevertheless, even the most seasoned reporters were stung by one criticism: Northwest contended the reports were "untruthful." Shelby, an award-winning reporter, took the criticism personally. "I would like to say that in the 19 years of serving this community I have never told a lie," he said. "If you want to know the truth, I've never tried to deceive or mislead anyone."

The station backed Shelby and defended the story's accuracy. Reporters said that they had spent nearly a year collecting documents and that much of their information had come directly from FAA records. They noted that Northwest had not contested any of the information in those findings and had paid the fines without disputing the charges. Furthermore, news executives explained, the reports did not say Northwest was an unsafe airline, only that Northwest could improve its safety. Each report ended with Shelby saying that Northwest had one of the best safety records among the world's airlines.

These arguments did not placate Northwest. It wanted vindication. However, it did not want to be drawn into a long and costly court battle. Fortunately for the airline, the dispute happened in Minnesota, which has an active news council. News councils, which are discussed more thoroughly in Chapter 2, are community panels that listen to complaints against the news media and decide who is right. They are not courts of law and cannot punish offenders, except by exposing them to negative publicity.

Members of the Minnesota News Council read piles of documents and conducted a daylong public hearing at which both Northwest and WCCO presented their sides of the story. The council then issued a decision that stunned WCCO. Council members voted 17–2 that the reports were untruthful, distorted and lacking in context. After the decision was read, Shelby told the council that the ruling "took the wind out of my sails." He vowed he would never do another investigative report. Pointing out that most of the information in the report was taken directly from government documents, Shelby asked viewers, "What would you have us do?"[1]

Shelby's question is perplexing. American journalists tend to see themselves as objective pursuers of truth. Yet problems begin to arise when you try to decide how "truth" relates to the daily rigors of the newsroom and what "objectivity" means. Over the years, journalists have defined these words in many ways. In this chapter, we will look at some of those definitions.

The Evolution of "Truth"

Early American papers had little "news" as we think of the term, and they employed no reporters. Instead, the editors filled their papers with lots of political essays and announcements about the availability of products and services at local businesses. What news they did report, they injected with strong doses of their own opinions. Many of these early editors considered their opinions right, and therefore reporting those opinions was truthful journalism. They scoffed at the idea of presenting opposing viewpoints. One editor likened presenting the other side of an argument to preaching Christianity in the morning and then advocating paganism in the evening.[2]

The ideals of journalism, of course, have changed since then. Most journalists in the 20th century have believed that it was their job to provide the truth as objectively—or, at least, as fairly—as possible. Throughout much of the first half of the 20th century, journalists defined objectivity very strictly. To them, truthful reporting meant getting the facts right. In practice, this often meant that they would interview one official source and relay that person's comments as accurately as possible. If that source was wrong, it was assumed someone else would tell the reporter about the mistake and the reporter would then write another story. Under this definition of truth-telling, reporting became such a nonjudgmental task that a *Washington Post* editor once said he would prefer to hire reporters who didn't think at all.

While this method of reporting seemed more truthful than the strident political pontificating of earlier papers, the problem was, as former University of Illinois Communications Dean Theodore Peterson pointed out, the press made a fetish of its commitment to objectivity.[3] Michael J. O'Neill, a former editor of the New York *Daily News,* learned about this narrow definition of objectivity when he covered a meat packers' strike in Chicago for United Press International around 1950. The union claimed the company had scabs working inside the plant, but management denied it. O'Neill climbed over the fence and discovered nonunion workers living inside the plant and sleeping on 125 cots. When O'Neill got back to his office, his editor told him he could not use what he had seen unless he could quote some company official.[4] Other journalists of that era told stories of calling their newspapers in the middle of hurricanes and having editors order them to get sources such as fire chiefs or police officers to confirm that the wind was blowing hard.

The Press Learns from McCarthy

The press received a major lesson in the flaws of this kind of objectivity and this notion of truth-telling. Sen. Joseph McCarthy of Wisconsin won election to the Senate when many Americans believed that

Communists were slowly taking over America by secretly infiltrating the leadership of our government, military, political parties and media. Once in the Senate, McCarthy wanted to make a name for himself, and the Washington press corps was unwittingly ready to help. McCarthy learned that if he made a sensational charge, the papers would report what he said almost word for word. Armed with this knowledge, McCarthy began a campaign that made him one of the most feared men in Washington in the 1950s.

McCarthy would announce to reporters that through diligent investigation, he had learned that key people in the State Department were members of the Communist Party. Following the journalistic ideals of their day, the reporters believed they were obligated to report the statements of a U.S. senator. Even if the reporters doubted what he said, their stories the next day would report that a diligent junior senator from Wisconsin said he had discovered known Communists in the State Department. McCarthy was getting the publicity he craved. Before long, McCarthy had claimed to have found Communists in most branches of government, the military and the media, although he would rarely name names.

The shallowness of such reporting angered many reporters. They knew they were being used. Some asked to be taken off the McCarthy beat. Others stayed on the beat and were totally frustrated. In *The Powers That Be,* David Halberstam described the plight of Phil Potter, a reporter for the Baltimore *Sun:*

> During the various McCarthy hearings, [Potter] would astonish admiring colleagues by coming back to the *Sun* bureau and writing a first draft of a story in which all his anger, all his rage at what McCarthy was doing would come forth: "Joseph R. McCarthy, the no good lying son of a bitch from Wisconsin . . ." Then, having vented his spleen and released his anger, he would tear up the story and sit down and go to work. Often when Potter had finished for the day he would go to the National Press Club, where he would find some of his colleagues and tell them that they had to start covering McCarthy, trying to explain what McCarthy was like, what he was doing. It was, he thought, missionary work. Most of his colleagues thought he was simply too involved. A story was a story. If Joe said something, you reported it; that was all it took.[5]

Many of Potter's colleagues were wedded to a notion of objectivity that made very little distinction between fact and truth. It was a fact that McCarthy had said there were Communists in high-ranking positions in the military. And since he was a U.S. senator, his statements were news. Whether his statements were likely to be true was not the responsibility of reporters.

But not all journalists of that era saw their jobs as repeating whatever charges McCarthy made. The biggest challenge to McCarthy's credibility came from a news medium that was then in its infancy—television. CBS's Edward R. Murrow exposed some of McCarthy's tactics on his program *See It Now,* and soon McCarthy's bubble began to burst. After the Senate in 1954 voted 67 to 22 to censure him for his reckless and abusive conduct, many in the press took a hard look at how they had been used by this skillful abuser of truth.

The Impact of Vietnam

Conventional journalistic practices took a further beating during the Vietnam War, in the 1960s and early 1970s. Official sources in Washington tried to paint pictures of South Vietnamese leaders as patriots who were popular with the people and would soon lead their country to victory. At military press conferences in Vietnam, reporters were told that victory was near. Frequently the official government line often clashed dramatically with what reporters were seeing in the field. However, when reporters filed their own stories, their editors often rejected them. The editors were accustomed to the friendly relationship that existed between the press and the military during World War II. They preferred to run the official Washington versions of the war.

Even *New York Times* reporter David Halberstam, who eventually won a Pulitzer Prize for his Vietnam War coverage, claimed he felt pressure. "Some editors disliked what they felt was my lack of balance and wished my reporting were more conventional, with more articles directly quoting high-level officers about how well things were going," he wrote.[6]

The reliance on strict objectivity was so strong during the early part of the war that editors made some strange decisions. Journalism Professor Daniel Hallin recounted one occasion during which the State Department in Washington and the U.S. Embassy in Vietnam each gave "official" versions of an incident in Vietnam. The two versions disagreed on many key points. *Times* editors in New York argued among themselves and then made a decision that would be inconceivable today. The paper ran both stories side by side with a note apologizing to its readers for the contradictions.[7]

Getting the Other Side

During the 1960s and 1970s, many reporters and editors were recognizing that truth-telling meant more than just compiling facts of what officials said. Researcher Leon Sigal documented this when he studied front-page stories in *The New York Times* and *The Washington Post.* In the 1950s, he found that reporters often used only one source, usually some high official. By the 1970s, they were using many more sources, including some who disagreed with the official version or provided another interpretation of the information.[8] Getting the other side became the definition for truth-telling. If a Democratic senator made a statement, reporters would track down a leader of the Republican Party to get the GOP's reaction. The reporter would then write a story quoting both sides, and the public would be left to decide what to believe.

Although these stories have more depth than single-source stories, the practice of "getting the other side" has problems too. For one thing, few issues have two clearly defined sides. Even such "simple" proposals as new roads or new schools can touch off reactions from widely divergent community groups. If reporters settle for stories that quote, for example, a city council member who is for a project and one who is opposed to it, their stories will probably be accurate and seemingly objective. Yet the stories may present an incomplete and simplistic understanding of the issues.

Another problem is that getting the other side may lead to stories that overemphasize conflict. "Journalists keep trying to find people who are at 1 and at 9 on a scale of 1 to 10, rather than people at 3 to 7 where most people really are," Cole Campbell, editor of *The Virginian-Pilot* in Norfolk, has said. "Journalism should say that the people from 3 to 7 are just as newsworthy and quotable as those at either end of the spectrum lobbing bombs toward the middle."[9]

Stephen L. Carter, a Yale law professor who has written extensively on abortion, has seen that happen. "Both sides in the public debate are dominated by hard-liners who can see no compromise and give no quarter," he said.[10] The abortion-rights side of the argument is presented by advocates who "feel that any step in the other direction can lead them down a slippery slope to taking away all their basic rights." The anti-abortion position is often advanced by people who equate every abortion with first-degree murder. Yet, according to polls, most Americans fall into neither of these camps.

Also, the practice of "getting the other side" can introduce subjectivity into stories. Reporters are no longer limited to repeating the comments of officials. Instead, they choose their sources. During Special Prosecutor Kenneth Starr's investigation of reports that President Clinton had sex with a White House intern, reporters from both *The Washington Post* and *The Wall Street Journal* interviewed different sets of former prosecutors. The *Post* headlined its story:

"Ex-Prosecutors Uncomfortable with Starr's Tactics." The same day, a *Wall Street Journal* headline read, "Ex-Prosecutors Defend Starr's Handling of Clinton Probe."[11] This is perhaps an extreme example. But it seems likely that no matter how hard reporters try to be fair, their selections of sources can have an impact on the way some issues are presented.

The problem is further compounded when some groups are well-organized, with public relations programs, while other groups with equally valid viewpoints are not media savvy. Reporters who are drawn to the easier sources may produce stories that are accurate but not complete. The problem of tracking down divergent sources is made even more sticky because journalists want to quote people with some claim to credibility. Therefore, they seek out people with titles (Professor, Mayor, the Reverend, Attorney) or other signs of "authority." TV journalists have an even tougher time because they need to find sources who can speak well on the air and present their views quickly, preferably in 20-second sound bites.

Social Responsibility

Questions about the relationship between news and truth aren't new. In the 1940s, Robert Hutchins, chancellor of the University of Chicago, assembled some of the best minds of the era to study the news media. He sought out philosophers, legal scholars, political scientists and a poet, but no one with a media background. After two years of study, Hutchins' Commission on Freedom of the Press issued a report that the press was in serious trouble. The commissioners objected to the growth of chains, feared the concentration of so much power in the hands of a few wealthy media owners and complained about the poor quality of news coverage.

More importantly, one part of the commission's report called on journalists to rethink their obligations to the truth. It claimed newspapers were too concerned with "scoops and sensations" and suggested ways that the press could better go about informing the American citizenry. The report challenged the press to provide

1. A truthful, comprehensive and intelligent account of the day's events in a context that gives them meaning. . . . It is no longer enough to report the fact truthfully. It is now necessary to report *the truth about the fact.*
2. A forum for the exchange of comment and criticism.
3. The projection of a representative picture of the constituent groups in the society.

4. The presentation and clarification of the goals and values of the society.
5. Full access to the day's intelligence.[12]

The commission's report was lambasted by the press when it was released. Robert McCormick, publisher of the *Chicago Tribune,* railed against the report, claiming it would lead to government control of the press.[13] Journalism groups branded its members "eggheads" and said their ideas would destroy freedom of the press. The work of the commission might have been forgotten if it had not been for Theodore Peterson, a journalism professor and former dean of the College of Communication at the University of Illinois. He wrote a chapter in the book *Four Theories of the Press* in which he articulated the commission's concerns and gave the name "social responsibility theory" to its ideals.[14]

Applying Hutchins' Standard of Truth

For the most part, today's reporters would not be shocked that someone would expect them to get the "truth about the facts." They would not only report the fact that a modern-day McCarthy said he had discovered Communists in the government. They would try to discover the truth about the Communists or expose the lies of the senator.

Today's journalists have broadened their definition of news. At one time crime and politics dominated the news. Now news of business, health and science, and changing lifestyles are important parts of papers and TV newscasts. Reporters have also expanded the kinds of sources they use. They are no longer as dependent on official versions of the news. The best examples of modern journalism include in-depth stories on social issues like poverty, AIDS and homelessness that contain comments not only from politicians, welfare agency officials and sociologists but from lower-level staff in the agencies and from the impoverished, sick and disenfranchised themselves.

However, in many cases, the news media fail to produce journalism that would meet the standards for "truth" set by the Hutchins Commission. One frequently cited example is the way crime dominates TV newscasts in many cities. At some local stations, law-and-order stories fill 60 percent of their newscasts. The national average is about a third. For station managers, showing lots of crime makes financial sense. Crime gets good ratings, and it's cheap and easy to cover. That translates into higher profits. (The relationship between news and media economics is covered in Chapter 12.)

So if both viewers and station owners are happy, what's wrong with emphasizing crime? To many, the answer relates to the distinction between truth and fact. Each individual crime story may be factual, but the abundance of them may not give the public a truthful picture of crime in their communities. "Violent crime is dropping like a rock in the country overall, and in many big metropolitan areas particularly," said Ray Suarez, a network TV reporter before joining the news staff of National Public Radio. "At the same time, the portion of the late local [TV] news hole filled by crime has grown 30 percent. You explain that to me."[15] Network newscasts have also discovered crime. The number of crime stories on the new major network newscasts tripled from 1992 to 1995, according to one study. Although the FBI reported that between 1990 and 1995 the number of murders dropped 13 percent, network news coverage of murder jumped 336 percent, *not* including coverage of the O.J. Simpson case.[16]

One result of this emphasis on crime is that many people do believe violence is rampant. "It makes people fearful," Carole Kneeland, news director from 1988 to 1996 at KVUE in Austin, Texas, said. "And it makes them far more likely to believe they're going to become victims of a crime than they are." As in the rest of the nation, crime has been declining in Los Angeles. Yet a survey by the *Los Angeles Times* found that nearly three out of four people believed crime was the same or worse. In that poll, 80 percent thought media reports increased their fear of crime. Nationally, an ABC News poll in 1997 found that half of Americans were more afraid of crime than they had been five years earlier.[17]

Not only does the coverage of crime lead many to assume that crime is more common than it is, the coverage may give the public a mistaken impression of the nature of crime. Newscasts often concentrate on robberies, muggings and home invasions. These random acts of violence are particularly frightening because they can strike anyone at any place. Yet the majority of violent crimes are committed by family, friends or acquaintances of the victims. These crimes are less likely to make the news. For example, in most cities, if a woman is beaten by a mugger, it's news; if she's beaten by her husband, it isn't. Crimes by teens also tend to be given disproportionate attention.

Patricia Dean, a broadcast journalism professor at Northwestern University, studied local TV news and was surprised at what wasn't being reported. Her study found that education receives about 2 percent of the news time and race relations, perhaps America's most complex social problem, about 1.2 percent. "If you don't have a teachers' strike or a racial incident, there is no coverage at all."[18]

Many worry that by emphasizing crime and not reporting other kinds of news, the media may be unintentionally misguiding public policy. If viewers see many more stories about crime than about problems in the schools, they may conclude that more tax dollars should be spent on building prisons than improving schools and hiring better teachers, according to Franklin Gilliam Jr., a professor of political science and communications at UCLA.

Some station managers and newspaper editors are trying to find better ways to cover crime. KVUE-TV in Austin no longer chases every report of violent crime. For a crime story to be broadcast, it must meet one of these criteria:

1. Is there an immediate threat to public safety?
2. Is there a threat to children?
3. Does someone need to take action?
4. Is there significant impact to the community?
5. Are there crime prevention efforts involved?

These guidelines have changed the way reporters work, according to Michelle Kemkes, a news producer. "When the police scanners scream out 'Homicide responding,' we don't blindly change the rundown," she explained. "I wait until we have enough information to decide how, or if, this story will affect our viewers."[19] Jeffrey Weiss of *The Dallas Morning News,* wrote, "At its essence, the KVUE guidelines translate to mean that editors and reporters are forced to ask 'So what?' before proceeding on any potential crime story."[20]

The answer to the so what question often makes KVUE look different from other Austin stations. For example, a domestic murder in a park was a major story for several days on every Austin station except KVUE. The KVUE staff thought it was an interesting story, but it did not pass the so what test. "This may be stuff eventually for a real good movie of the week, but it's not the kind of thing we put on the air," said KVUE executive producer Cathy McFeaters.

The station also has begun to put crime news into perspective. When a 12-year-old girl killed a small child, every station, including KVUE, broadcast the story. But KVUE also pointed out that crimes by children that young are very rare and looked into the issue of trying young criminals in adult courts. KVUE's ratings have not been affected by its new way of covering crime. Its newscasts have continued to hold the top spot in ratings in Austin.

Other news directors are also asking if the emphasis on crime accurately reflects their communities. "I don't think obsessive crime coverage is reflective of the reality we live in," Jim Sanders, vice president of news at San Diego's KNSD-TV, told *The San Diego Union-Tribune.* "TV news has to be about more than misdemeanor crime. We have to address people's lives and what's important to those lives.

The reality of most people's lives is not crime. Education is a huge issue, jobs are a huge issue. Politics, as it affects people's lives, is important."[21]

However, many TV reporters remain hamstrung by station management. A reporter in a Top 25 market complained that his station concentrates on covering crime to the point that reporters do not have time to develop stories about significant issues in his community. "We've become the police blotter," he said. In his city, the schools were so overcrowded that students attended classes in decaying portable classrooms. He said at his station these problems were not considered "TV stories" because good video was often hard to obtain.

Although newspapers today give less extreme coverage to crime than local TV stations do, many editors are revamping their coverage too. When a teenager opened fire at a school in Springfield, Ore., in 1998 and killed two people and injured 22, the editor of the *Chicago Sun-Times* broke ranks with most news organizations and did not put the story on the front page.

"I took the view that we had to balance our responsibility to report the news against our responsibility to society as a whole," editor Nigel Wade wrote. "If such a tragedy happened in Chicago—in one of our schools, involving our children—our readers would want to read about it on page 1. But I did not think it safe to go on treating every new schoolyard incident the same way." Wade said he feared the stories might lead to copycat killings. And, he stated, "I also did not want to alarm young children packing their bags for another day at school by sending them off with front-page pictures from Oregon burning in their minds."[22]

Truth and the Pressures of Journalism

The Wall Street Journal had a scoop. Its reporters knew they were the only media people who had nailed the story. Paul Steiger, the *Journal*'s managing editor, said he "lived and died, worried that the scoop would leak" to other reporters before the *Journal* got a chance to break the story. The big news? The Barbie doll was getting "a wider waist, slimmer hips and—in a stunning front-end realignment—a reduction of her legendary bust line." Steiger admitted to *Los Angeles Times* media writer David Shaw that he knew that most people would just get a laugh from the story. But, he said, when toy-maker Mattel makes a major change in a product, "we want to be first with it."[23]

While it may be easy to snicker at a major media outlet scrambling to find the measurements of a plastic doll, the desire to be first has always been fundamental to journalists. In earlier days, papers printed extras to avoid being beaten. The two major wire services, the Associated Press and United Press International, would brag when their reporters beat the competition by a few minutes. An adage from an earlier generation of journalists said, "Nothing is older than yesterday's paper." With 24-hour news on television and the Internet, the news ages even faster today. Readers and viewers expect to learn new information every time they open the paper or turn on a newscast.

Also, reporters' egos push them to be first with that news. Shaw noted that "most journalists can recall with great detail—and even greater pride—their biggest scoops, no matter how long ago they happened." CBS anchor Dan Rather told Shaw, "There are few things in journalism better than that feeling that you got the story right, you got it alone and the other guys are chasing your taillights." Rather recalled a story he broke 25 years earlier that President Richard Nixon would name Henry Kissinger as his secretary of state. Shaw described Rather's retelling of the story:

> "We had a world beat . . . what's known in the business as a 'clean kill,'" Rather says, grinning triumphantly at the recollection. "Not only did nobody else have it, they weren't even in the same area code. . . . I still remember it . . . like I remember catching a touchdown pass when I was in high school."

Not only do reporters' egos push them to be first, editors and news directors pressure them. They watch the competition closely, and reporters who get beat on stories may have some explaining to do. "When you're behind and . . . getting hammered by [your] . . . bosses: 'You got beat again, you got beat again, you got beat again,' you're so desperate to break one of these [exclusives] . . . that there's a risk that you'll get driven into jumping too fast" and making mistakes, Tom Bettag, executive producer of ABC's *Nightline,* told Shaw.

Everyone, it seems, has a favorite story about a news outlet that jumped too fast. The *Chicago Tribune* reported that Dewey had defeated Truman in the 1948 election. A banner headline in the Baltimore *Sun* proclaimed that all passengers had been rescued from the sinking Titanic. *The Miami Herald* had a front-page scoop when it reported that an aircraft company was buying massive amounts of swampland in Central Florida for a huge airplane factory. A few days later, plans for Walt Disney World were unveiled.

Everette Dennis, director of the Center for Communications at Fordham University, understands the desire to be first. But he believes the rush to report is best used when stories involve a "really urgent matter that [people] need to know about—an economic catastrophe, a coup . . . a chemical spill, a dangerous criminal at large—something where public health or safety is really a factor. If it's not urgent, then I think it's just journalistic ego . . . just doing it to beat the competition and not necessarily doing a thorough job. Then I think the reader gets cheated."

Deciding when a story is ready to run or should be held for more reporting is not always an easy call. "The best of journalism doesn't sit on its ass; it produces the copy," said Marvin Kalb, a former NBC and CBS newsman who now heads a media research center at Harvard. He told Shaw that when done properly, "the best journalism is hot, fast, first instinct, burst of energy, do it, get it done, let me learn what you've just learned."

However, Kalb is not advocating hasty reporting. He contends that sometimes journalists have to report a story that is 80 percent complete and then add information in the following days until the story is more complete. Kalb makes a distinction between a story that is 80 percent complete and one that is 80 percent accurate. An 80 percent complete story may lack some detail and supplemental information; an 80 percent accurate story lacks essential information and confirmation. To him, that's the distinction between a story that is ready to be printed or broadcast and one that needs to be held.

The Hutchins Commission would probably agree with Kalb. The commission did not define what it meant by truth. But Professor Theodore Peterson, whose writing helped prevent the commission from being forgotten, suggested that the commission did not expect the press to discover absolute truth but did expect the press to discover "a number of lesser truths, tentative truths, working truths."

WCCO's Northwest Story: Facts or Truth?

In the opening section of this chapter, Northwest Airlines charged that WCCO's series about the airline's safety was untruthful. In many ways the case represents the struggle between "reporting the facts truthfully" and "reporting the truth about the facts." The airline acknowledged that most of the facts in the series were accurate. The airline had been fined for safety violations and faced a sexual harassment suit. But, the airline contended, these were presented without context that would allow viewers to make comparisons with the performance of other airlines. The Minnesota News Council agreed.

A few months after the council's decision, Shelby, the anchor and reporter, said he believed the premise of the stories was accurate, but he acknowledged he too had misgivings about the way WCCO produced the series. He told *Columbia Journalism Review* (1) the station should have built a more convincing case against the airline before airing the charges, (2) the series stretched too far when it used the sexual harassment complaints as part of a story about air safety, and (3) the promos, featuring a plane flying at an angle that made it look as if it were about to crash, never should have appeared.

Shelby's major concern, however, was that reporters used techniques that resembled tabloid TV journalism. He said that originally the tabloid TV shows tried to look like traditional newscasts. But when the tabloids became popular, many local TV journalists tried to make their newscasts look like the tabloids. "We legitimate journalists in television have gotten the worst end of that deal," Shelby told *Newsworthy*, "and we've lost customers and trust." He said the flashy graphics in the Northwest story distorted and exaggerated the facts. The station's new manager is opposed to such tabloidism. "She's very clear that we're going to play on the straight and narrow, and there will be no funny business," Shelby said. "That's a relief to a lot of us."

In a larger sense, the news council reminded all journalists of an important truth: As Gary Gilson, the council's executive director, stated, "No one has to tell lies to produce an untrue picture. When you stand in front of a wavy mirror in a funhouse, you are indeed looking at a reflection of yourself, but a distorted, untruthful one."[24]

The Question of Objectivity

The notion of objectivity is so intertwined with America's perception of journalism that most Americans are surprised to learn that objectivity is primarily a North American ideal. European papers often allow their stories to contain a distinct political slant. In London, for example, readers of *The Guardian* expect the paper to give a liberal interpretation to the news while *The Times* of London and the *Sun* provide conservative views. The French, Italian and German newspapers are even more overt in their blending of news and analysis and portray a much wider spectrum of political thought than American newspaper readers are used to. David Shaw of the *Los Angeles Times* noted that in Europe "seven different journalists might put seven different spins on a given story."[25]

Although few American journalists embrace this European notion of journalism, many are backing away from the word "objectivity," preferring to substitute words like "fair" or "balanced." For years, the Code of Ethics of the Society of Professional Journalists had a section titled "accuracy and objectivity." That section—and the word "objectivity"—disappeared entirely when SPJ revised its code of ethics in 1996. The new code suggests reporters should be fair, honest and thorough.

Objectivity means different things to different journalists. Some define objectivity as being profoundly neutral, much like a scientist working with cold, hard facts. It is this notion of objectivity that many believe is unobtainable. They argue that journalists, like everyone else, are shaped by their background, training and social experiences. They can see the world only through their own, subjective, vantage points. When they decide that one thing is newsworthy and another is not, their culture, beliefs and social heritage play a major role.

Robert Scheer, whose reporting and editing career has included stops at the rabble-rousing *Ramparts* and the mainstream *Los Angeles Times,* said, "It's stupid and dishonest for journalists to continue to insist that they are without gut feelings, values, politics, et cetera. . . . To me the more important question is not whether you can be neutral but how you do your job in a fair and honest way."[26]

Professor John Merrill's definition of objectivity is similar to Scheer's. Merrill doesn't believe objective journalists must be completely detached from society or behave like emotionless zombies. He acknowledges that journalists "strain reality through their perceptual filters, and [the news] comes out with some distortion." Yet a journalist "with the proper attitude and who is diligent and persistent can go very far along the objective continuum." To Merrill, objective journalists are those who guard against any kind of intentional bias. Using his definition, objectivity becomes more than a goal journalists strive to obtain. It is a professional obligation that can be practiced.[27]

Others argue that objective reporting is possible. Facts, they insist, are independent of people's backgrounds. If journalists accurately accumulate enough facts, their stories will be objective. Professor Judith Lichtenberg applied this definition of objectivity to the sinking of the oil tanker Exxon Valdez in 1989. She stated that it is a fact that the ship wrecked in Alaska's Prince William Sound. Few people, regardless of their backgrounds, would disagree. It's a fact that more than 10 million gallons of oil poured into the sound.

Objective journalists can report these facts. Reporters will also want to look into questions like what caused the crash and who, if anyone, was to blame. These questions, too, can be answered by gathering more facts, according to Lichtenberg. Reporters can find out, for example, if the captain was drunk, if he was on the bridge or if weather conditions were bad. Eventually, Lichtenberg argued, enough facts may be assembled to allow people to draw conclusions about what really happened that day in Prince William Sound. To Lichtenberg, objective journalists are in pursuit of the truth—or, at least, "truth beyond a reasonable doubt"—and they find truth by the accumulation of facts.[28]

Experts or Fancy Stenographers?

The Hutchins Commission, Lichtenberg and Scheer are describing a different kind of journalism than was commonly practiced in the 1950s. They want reporters to worry about the truthfulness of their accounts, to examine events in terms of their own knowledge of the community and to relate the news so that readers and viewers can understand its social significance.

Geneva Overholser, former editor of *The Des Moines Register,* believes that the shift away from objectivity is long overdue. "All too often, a story free of any taint of personal opinion is a story with all the juice sucked out," Overholser said in a speech at the University of Southern California. "A big piece of why so much news copy today is boring as hell is this objectivity god. Keeping opinion out of the story too often means being a fancy stenographer." Although she said that she understands the concerns of editors who believe moving away from objectivity "will open the floodgates of opinion writing," she argued that a greater danger is posed by the boredom of "wishy-washy, take-it-or-leave-it writing that is wholly objective."[29]

Many newspapers too are asking their reporters to put more context in their reporting, to "write with authority." They are expected to research their stories so thoroughly that they can explain the significance of the developments.

Staffers at the *Portland (Maine) Press Herald* call the technique "expert reporting." Lou Ureneck, who was the paper's executive editor when the paper's policy was formulated, told an ASNE conference, "Too many daily newspapers use only the eyes and the ears of their reporters and don't use their brains." When one of his reporters was investigating the workers' compensation system in Maine, Ureneck said editors told him "to get beyond the whipsaw of competing quotes that are often put into a story for 'balance.' We told him to avoid bogging down in excessive attribution, weasel words and hedging phrases. We told him to support his conclusions with facts and to write forcefully in plain language." Ureneck said reader response was overwhelmingly positive. "These techniques," he told *American Journalism Review,* "can put some meaning back into journalism."[30]

Someday "journalists will be seen as information experts, just as bankers are relied upon for financial expertise and jewelers for appraisals of gems," in the view of Carl Sessions Stepp, former *Charlotte Observer* reporter and editor who became a University of Maryland journalism professor. What sense does it make for "journalists to research subjects with increasing thoroughness and expertise and then hold back their conclusions, depriving readers of what may be the most trustworthy, studied assessments available anywhere?[31]

However, in providing the public with these assessments, journalists are walking a tightrope. They want to use their knowledge and experiences as reporters to make their stories more complete and more truthful. They want to provide analysis based on the insights they have gained by spending weeks or even months covering a story. Yet they run the risk of appearing to be partisan. "They tell us they want analysis, background, interpretation, and when we do that and it's not entirely keeping with their view of the world, they say we're biased," *St. Petersburg Times* political editor Ellen Debenport told *Washington Journalism Review.*[32] (The question of political bias is discussed in Chapter 9.)

Objectivity and Judging Sources

During the 1950s and 1960s, scientists began to find striking evidence that smoking cigarettes was linked to several diseases. Reporters would quote from these scientific studies and then attempt to get the other side by calling the tobacco companies for their responses. Often a representative for an industry group would attempt to debunk the scientific research. Applying the understanding of objectivity that was popular at the time, reporters would give equal weight to both sides.[33] The reader was left with two conflicting claims and given little help in trying to sort out the truth.

Today, many reporters don't believe they should practice such evenhandedness. Perhaps no event in the 1990s illustrated their concerns more than the coverage of the war in Bosnia. In the early years of the war, America and most European governments considered it a civil war and did not want to get involved. But when journalists arrived in Bosnia, many came to the conclusion that they were not covering a civil war. They saw a Serb army that was killing, raping and looting civilians and packing many of them off to death camps. *The Washington Post*'s Mary Battiata said, "This was not a Muslim story or a Serb story. There was only one story—a war of aggression against a largely defenseless, multiethnic population. It was very simple." CNN's Christiane Amanpour saw the war the same way: "There was a clear aggressor and a clear victim."

Journalists disagreed on how "neutral" they should be in these circumstances. Amanpour wrote in *Quill,* "The very notion of objectivity in war becomes immensely important. What does that word mean? I have come to believe that objectivity means giving all sides a fair hearing, but not treating all sides equally. Once you treat all sides the same in a case such as Bosnia, you are drawing a moral equivalence between victim and aggressor." If the press remained neutral, it would be "an accessory to all manners of evil; in Bosnia's case, genocide." In a larger sense, she wrote, treating both sides equally would be going along with the official notion that Bosnia was experiencing a civil war.

Amanpour cited an example. When a shell landed in a market in Sarajevo killing 68 people, mostly Muslims, the Muslims said the Serbs had fired it. But the Serbs said that the Muslims had fired the shell themselves to gain sympathy. Rather than reporting both sides equally, Amanpour wrote she put the bombing in context by citing United Nations figures that the "overwhelming number of mortar shells and sniper fire and fire into the city was from the Serb side." She called the notion that the Muslims had deliberately killed their own people "disgusting." Other journalists came to similar conclusions. "If a guy from the Serbian Information Ministry tells you a bunch of baloney," James O'Shea, deputy managing editor of the *Chicago Tribune,* said, "you have absolutely no obligation to report it unless you're going to characterize it for what it is."

The Washington Post's Peter Maass told the *Christian Science Monitor* that it was difficult for him to maintain the traditional journalistic distance and impossible to present the transgressions on both sides in a way that appeared to put them on equal footing. Maass is not concerned that some have called him "pro-Bosnian": "I assume that no journalist from the Second World War would be dishonored by being called 'pro-Jewish.'"

Many thought the attitudes of these journalists stepped over the line between honest reporting and advocacy. Bill Kovach, a former journalist and current curator of the Nieman Foundation, is worried that if the news appears to be tainted with partisanship, the public may lose even more trust in the news media. David Binder, a foreign correspondent for *The New York Times,* also rejected the argument by Amanpour and others that objectivity creates a "moral equivalence between aggressor and victim." He said, "It's a garbage argument out of garbage minds. Our job is to report from all sides, not to play favorites." He cautioned journalists about "playing God" and asked, "Who gave them the right to decree morality?"

Amanpour understands their argument. She wrote in *Quill,* "This increases the burden upon us journalists in the field to act responsibly, to weigh what we do or say, to understand that in these dangerous situations, words we utter matter and can have consequences." She concluded, "How many times have you heard crusty old TV newsmen say, 'It ain't brain surgery, it's just TV.' But if we go back to the original premise that TV has become the most powerful medium of our time, then it is as important as brain surgery. It's about feeding minds."[34]

4

Errors and
Corrections

Suppose you are a sexual harassment officer at a large university. Your job requires you to win the trust of the college community. Students must feel free to come talk to you about very personal problems. They must believe you will take their problems seriously and do your best to solve them. Faculty and administrators rely on your judgment, sensitivity and diligence in dealing with these delicate issues. Since part of your job is educating people about the problem, you give speeches to campus and community groups and are interviewed by reporters frequently.

One day you are reading your local paper, and you are shocked. You see a story about efforts to reduce sexual harassment on your campus. The story cites a case you know about, an incident involving a note-taking pool in the university's medical school. Two male students took notes at a lecture on the female reproductive process and passed them along to other students in the pool. The notes included many sexist comments, leading one student in the pool to file an official complaint with the university.

Then you see your name in the article and begin to read what you supposedly said. In the article, you sound as if you don't take harassment complaints very seriously. You are quoted as saying you believe the note-taking incident "is a situation for an apology and a night at the bar rather than a formal investigation." The article goes on to quote you as attacking professors in the university's professional schools. It claims you expected many sexual harassment problems in those schools because "the whole construct of their reality is male- and power-oriented." And, although you know that the university has no double standard in the way it treats students and faculty accused of sexual harassment, you are quoted as saying it's a lot trickier to get your university's administrators to deal with complaints against faculty members than those against students.

You know these are not your opinions. And you know you did not say these things to the reporter because the reporter never even interviewed you! What can you do?

This was the circumstance that Donna Ferrara-Kerr, a sexual harassment officer at the University of Calgary, found herself in after the *Calgary Herald* "quoted" her. When the story appeared, she said the reaction was "immediate, fierce and detrimental." The misquotations undermined her ability to win the trust of harassed people on the university's campus and damaged her relationships with many people on campus. She said she received several calls from outraged people, many of whom doubted her when she said those were not her opinions.

After she complained to the newspaper, the reporter sent Ferrara-Kerr a note admitting she had made a mistake: She had mistakenly attributed quotes to Ferrara-Kerr that someone else had said. The paper printed a correction.[1]

Unfortunately, Ferrara-Kerr's experience with the news media is not unique. Journalists make mistakes. Much of the time, reporters who make errors are just proving they are human. ("Doctors bury their mistakes," some editor once said. "We print ours.") Nevertheless, on occasion, as we'll see in this chapter, journalists pass along inaccurate information for less forgivable reasons.

Why So Many Errors?

When pollster George Gallup Jr. asked people who had been interviewed by newspaper and TV reporters about the accuracy of their stories, about a third told him the reporters had gotten the facts wrong.[2] The finding may overestimate the incompetence of American journalists. When people accuse the media of getting the story wrong, often they are judging the story on subjective rather than factual grounds. For example, they may say the story is wrong if the reporter's slant is different from theirs.[3] Also, mistakes aren't always the fault of journalists. Sources sometimes give reporters incorrect information or deliberately bend the truth.

Yet far too many avoidable errors make their way into the news. "If you make mistakes, it taints everything you do," one editor said.

"If you don't get the date of the daughter's wedding right, how can people believe what else you write?" That's one reason editors and news directors want to reduce the number of mistakes.

At some publications, people who make mistakes are held publicly accountable. Corrections may say "due to a reporter's error," which identifies the reporter if the story was bylined. Some papers even name the sinner in the corrections. The *Houston Post* once took this form of discipline a step further and required a reporter who got the date of a conference wrong to stand outside the conference hotel holding a sign and passing out corrections.[4] *The Sioux City (Iowa) Journal* has required staffers who make mistakes to write letters of apology to the people involved.[5]

Other papers handle corrections internally. At *The Cincinnati Enquirer,* people responsible for mistakes must meet with the paper's editor and explain "what happened and here's why it's never going to happen again," according to David Wells, the paper's local news editor. "We jokingly call it going to the woodshed." Staffers at the *Chicago Tribune* are required to fill out a form each time an error is found in their copy. Editors then read through the forms and try to identify problems in the newsroom that led to errors. The *Tribune* pays bonuses to senior managers who reduce the number of errors in their sections.[6]

If journalists are better trained and better paid than ever before, why are there so many mistakes? The answers range from not knowing the community to yielding to competitive pressures.

Not Knowing the Community

Many errors in news stories are caused by reporters' isolation from their communities. Ironically, some of this isolation is the result of tougher ethical guidelines that require journalists to be very careful about the organizations they join and the people with whom they socialize. This may prevent conflicts of interest, but it does little to increase journalists' sensitivity, understanding and knowledge about the people and events they cover. The problem is worsened by the tendency of journalists to make friends primarily with other journalists.

The mobility of newspeople also keeps them from becoming part of their communities. Many journalists at smaller dailies and small-market TV stations expect to live in the community only until their big break comes along and they land a job with a major paper or larger-market station. So they don't bother developing ties and friendships or learning much about their communities. Mayor Gus Morrison of Fremont, Calif., described the reporters who have covered his city as "bright, young people who don't know anything—eager and low paid. By the time they learn anything, they go to a different newspaper. There's no history."[7]

Some barriers between reporters and the public are not the reporters' doing. Because of bomb threats, problems with "crazies," and the amount of expensive equipment lying around modern newsrooms, nearly all news organizations have uniformed guards and security systems. Modern phone mail systems can also separate reporters and the public. Negotiating the phone system often becomes an ordeal that ends with callers talking to bored newsroom clerks who treat them all as if they are cranks.

Carelessness

Carelessness can lead to silly errors that make the paper itself look foolish, as did this paragraph in *The Seattle Times:*

> It isn't as though the use of nitrous oxide by dentists has just appeared on the scene. It was first used as an anesthetic gas Dec. 11, 1844. That's not a typo. Eighteen eighty-four.[8]

Other times, sloppy note taking can result in stories that hurt the reputations of people. Recall what happened when the Calgary paper put someone else's words in the mouth of the sexual harassment officer. Speed can also lead to errors. *Orange County (Calif.) Register* reporter Bill Rams explained, "A story breaks at 2 p.m. I'm supposed to have it in by 5. My editor has to have it a half-hour later with all the wrinkles ironed out and so forth. That makes it difficult to be perfect."[9]

Perhaps the most common errors caused by carelessness are misspelled names and incorrect addresses and dates. Many editors consider these errors unforgivable. The *St. Petersburg Times* fired a veteran photographer for making errors in photo captions. The paper's photo director said its policy was that if in one year "you have three spelling errors [in names], your future on the photo team is in question." The fired photographer had misspelled a name while he was on probation for earlier errors.[10]

Carelessness in reporting can result in more subtle errors. That's what Colorado Gov. Richard D. Lamm thought happened to him after an informal session with lawyers and reporters. *The Denver Post* story began:

> Elderly people who are terminally ill have a "duty to die and get out of the way" instead of trying to prolong their lives through artificial means, Gov. Dick Lamm said Tuesday.

People who die without having their lives artificially prolonged, Lamm said, are similar to "leaves falling off a tree and forming humus for other plants to grow up."

"You got a duty to die and to get out of the way. Let the other society, our kids, build a reasonable life," the governor told a meeting of the Colorado Health Lawyers Association at St. Joseph's Hospital.

Senior citizens groups and others throughout the country were outraged when they read this story, distributed by the Associated Press. So was the governor, who claimed he was quoting a philosopher and that he did not urge terminally ill oldsters to get out of the way but instead urged society to take a harder look at life-extending machines. A tape recording proved that the governor had said:

> The real question gets into, then, high-technology medicine. We have a million and a half heart attacks a year. Every year in the United States we have a million and a half heart attacks. Six hundred thousand of them die. How many Barney Clarks [a heart transplant patient] can we afford? You know we at least ought to be talking about that. . . .
>
> A terrific article that I've read, one of the philosophers of our time, I think, is a guy named Leon Kass. Has anybody seen his stuff? He's just terrific. In *The American Scholar* last year he wrote an article called "The Case for Mortality," where essentially he said we have a duty to die. It's like if leaves fall off a tree, forming the humus for the other plants to grow out. We've got a duty to die and get out of the way with all of our machines and artificial hearts and everything else like that and let the other society, our kids, build a reasonable life.

The *Post* published a correction of its use of "you" instead of the "we" the governor used, but it did not correct the reference to "elderly people" because its reporter said the governor had made several allusions to the aged in his remarks.[11] News stories rarely die. Ten years after Lamm made the comments, he considered running for president on Ross Perot's Reform Party ticket. When reporters wrote background stories about Lamm, many included, without qualification, that Lamm had once said he thought older Americans had a duty to die.

Ignorant Reporters?

Journalists are no longer the uneducated louts that the legendary editor and writer H.L. Mencken saw in the American newsrooms of the 1920s. Mencken wrote, "It is this vast and militant ignorance, this widespread and fathomless prejudice against intelligence, that makes American journalism so pathetically feeble and vulgar, and so generally disreputable."[12] But unfortunately ignorance is still a problem.

Only 10 percent of editors and publishers in America felt their reporters were well prepared to cover complicated governmental issues, one study found. The editors said reporters need better education in economics, political science, business and other subject areas.

Mathematics is also a trouble spot for journalists. Doron Levin, a business writer at the *Detroit Free Press,* joked that he doubted if half the reporters and editors in the nation could calculate a simple percentage. "That amount of numeric incompetence in newsrooms is horrifying," he said.[13] Reporters confuse "percentages" with "percentage points," miscalculate averages and misunderstand basic statistical data. Errors involving math are found in papers ranging from *The New York Times* to small-town weeklies. In 1996, *The Atlanta Journal-Constitution* ran a lead story headed "No. 1 Again: Atlanta Ranked Most Violent." Two days later, also in the lead spot, the paper ran this headline: "Wrong Number: Atlanta's Not No. 1 in Crime." The story acknowledged that reporters had made a mistake in their mathematical calculations and analyses.[14]

Reporters' ignorance also shows in the coverage of the legal system and of business. Several lawyers told David Shaw of the *Los Angeles Times* that they were "astounded by the number of reporters who accepted what they said—or did not say—without either question or challenge, either out of laziness, ignorance, or a fear of being perceived as ignorant." And a survey of business executives found that only 27 percent of them thought business reporting was fair and accurate.[15] One business executive said he had encountered reporters who did not know the difference between stocks and bonds or recognize the significance of a company buying back its own stock, even though these issues were fundamental to the stories they planned to write.[16] Wayne Curry, supervisor of Prince George's County in Maryland, said reporters have no real understanding of county budgets. "Most of the journalists think they have satisfied their role when they come talk to you, get a quote, go back to the office, describe the numbers, and then go to some chronic naysayer and get a counter quote." Curry thought the coverage was so superficial that he began to mail a newsletter to taxpayers explaining the budget.[17]

After the 1996 presidential elections, economists interviewed by *Business Week* paid journalists a backhanded compliment. They said they could find no political bias in news coverage of economic issues. But, the economists said, this lack of bias was not caused by the reporters' objectivity. They said reporters simply did not understand the issues. The result was that the news media allowed both Bill Clinton and George Bush to play fast and loose when they spoke about the economy.[18]

Ignorance can also result in stories that fail to give perspective. "Too many stories are very broad but only a quarter-inch thick" because the reporter does know the background and significance of news events, according to Sandra Mims Rowe, editor of *The Oregonian* in Portland. She believes reporters need expertise so they can report with authority. "You can't just grab a quote or two or stick a microphone in somebody's face. We need to know as much as our readers."

Rowe also faults journalists for not doing basic research before contacting experts. She recalled a conversation she had with Dr. Arthur Caplan, a medical ethicist who is frequently interviewed by the media on issues ranging from doctor-assisted suicide to in vitro fertilization. Caplan told her that "way less than half, probably less than a quarter" of the questions he was asked were reasonable or showed that the reporter had any level of knowledge of the subject.[19]

Journalists need to do their homework before asking questions. Robert Scheer of the *Los Angeles Times* sees library research as the first line of ethical reporting. He said reporters have to make themselves authorities on the subjects they write about. The ethical question, he said, is "whether you're really going to put out, or whether you're going to surrender to . . . cynicism . . . and just shove it into the paper." Scheer said he wants "to be able to pick up the piece two or three years later and say 'God, this holds up!'"[20]

Some are so concerned about journalists' lack of knowledge that they believe journalism education needs to be overhauled. Eugene C. Patterson, editor emeritus of the *St. Petersburg Times,* has called for more specialized courses and graduate degrees. And the American Society of Newspaper Editors continues to push for requirements that journalism majors spend most of their undergraduate days taking classes outside their major in the liberal arts and sciences.[21] Some newspapers turn their newsrooms into classrooms. They invite experts and college professors to teach staffers short courses in economics, computer spreadsheets, policy issues and other topics.

Perhaps it is asking too much of journalists that they have at least above-average knowledge of the many subjects they deal with every working day. But, today, journalists have many quick sources of information, including the Internet and electronic databases. Since reporters can't be expert in all areas, they can at least be quick studies who know how to gather the background they need.

Competitive Pressures

Competitive pressures have become an even bigger concern in recent years. The number of news outlets has increased dramatically. Most cities have four or five broadcast stations providing local news, and many have 24-hour local news channels on cable. Just a few years ago, news on national television consisted of the 30-minute evening newscasts, occasional documentaries and *60 Minutes*. Today, most homes receive three or four 24-hour cable news channels, and almost every night the networks broadcast newsmagazines like *Dateline NBC* and *20/20*. By the mid-1990s, the Internet had also become a major source of news. Most major news organizations are on the Web, and their sites attract millions of hits.

Having all these news outlets lessens the chances that stories the public needs to know about will go unreported. And once a story develops, scores of reporters will begin to chase it. But these advantages can come at a high price.

Thirty years ago, during the Nixon administration, when the Watergate scandal was a developing story, a relatively small number of reporters were digging into it. Much of the early coverage was done by *The Washington Post,* which required reporters Robert Woodward and Carl Bernstein to have two independent sources for their stories. Editors at the *Post* held stories until they were satisfied the information was confirmed. Today, a story like Watergate would be covered by hundreds of reporters from the networks, the cable news channels, the major wire services and the dozens of newspapers with Washington bureaus. This competition increases the likelihood that reporters will use stories before the information is confirmed. Dan Rather, anchor for the *CBS Evening News,* told the *Los Angeles Times* media writer David Shaw that there are now so many more players and so many more news outlets that the pressure to be first is "greater and stronger . . . and that increased pressure has increased not just the probability of inaccuracy but . . . the number of inaccuracies. I don't even think that's arguable. I think it's a matter of record and fact."[22]

That's what happened during the coverage of rumors that President Clinton had sex with Monica Lewinsky, a White House intern. A *Newsweek* reporter wrote a story saying that Clinton was being investigated for perjury in the case. However, just before deadline, his editors withdrew the story. Almost immediately, someone tipped Internet gossip guru Matt Drudge. Without doing any original reporting, Drudge put the item on his Internet newsletter. Soon nearly every news organization was racing to be first with stories about a semen-stained dress and expensive gifts to the intern from the president.

The desire to beat the competition led some news organizations to relax their rules on the use of anonymous sources. One result was that many stories were wrong or premature. For example, *The Dallas*

Morning News reported that a witness had seen Clinton and Lewinsky in a compromising position. The story appeared both on the paper's Internet site and in the early edition. However, 45 minutes after the first edition of the *Morning News* was printed, the paper recognized the story had problems and retracted it in its second edition that day. By then, however, it had become a national story. Producers of ABC's *Nightline* had seen it on the paper's Web site and repeated it in the opening section of their program. The wire services also picked up the story, and several newspapers gave it prominent play. Days later, *The Wall Street Journal* retracted a similar story that had been repeated by scores of newspapers and TV stations.

A few weeks after the Lewinsky-Clinton scandal became public, Richard Smith, editor of *Newsweek,* observed: "There are probably two dozen reporters in Washington right now who have good sources on these [Clinton scandal] stories and are in a position to make judgments about the quality of the sources and the quality of the information they're getting from the sources. And there are a thousand people chasing the story."[23]

Getting Caught up in the Story

In 1998, CNN had an eye-popping story for the debut of *NewsStand,* an investigative news program. The story claimed that the United States had used nerve gas in Southeast Asia during the Vietnam War era. It also reported that American troops had hunted down and killed American deserters. Reporters said a retired admiral who was chairman of the Joint Chiefs of Staff had confirmed the information.

The story was questioned even before it was broadcast. CNN's own Pentagon reporters were troubled that the story used interviews with the retired admiral, who was 86 years old and lived in an assisted-care retirement home. They had stopped using him as a source several years earlier. The program was billed as a joint effort of CNN and *Time* magazine, both owned by Time-Warner. But *Time* reporters, who had not been involved in the original story, questioned the validity of the report and started their own investigation. Once the story aired, the Pentagon and several other groups rejected the allegations.

All of these well-publicized doubts about the report prompted CNN to do its own in-house review of the report. Soon CNN retracted the story. In a detailed analysis, CNN concluded that the reporters and producers had not been deceitful. They believed every word they wrote. "If anything, the serious flaws in the broadcast . . . may stem from the depths of those beliefs," CNN's report concluded.

It said that reporters and producers were so certain the allegations were true that they discounted any information that was contrary to what they believed.

The reporters, however, stood firm. They were angered by CNN's retraction and said the report was valid. They accused CNN of caving in to government pressure.[24]

The "Infallibility Syndrome"

A sports copy editor tells the story of a beginning sportswriter who wrote a basketball story in which he misspelled the name of one of the high schools. When the editor pointed out the error, the reporter became indignant. He said he was there and that's the way the name was spelled. Even after the editor showed the reporter a picture with the name clearly visible on team uniforms, the reporter continued to insist he was right.

Although his may be an extreme case, many reporters and editors suffer from a malady that can only be called "infallibility syndrome." This syndrome may be a by-product of the pressures journalists face. Reporters, producers and editors are expected to achieve a superhuman feat: They must be right all the time. This pressure causes many to resist any suggestions that they may be wrong. This syndrome can strike seasoned pros just as strongly as it does beginners like the sportswriter. A PBS camera crew doing a special report on CBS's *60 Minutes* caught reporter Mike Wallace and producer Don Hewitt in an argument so heated that Wallace finally stormed out of the room. The argument started when Hewitt asked Wallace to use more attribution in the opening to a story he was preparing.

Clashes between reporters and editors are not the only way this syndrome affects the news. Sometimes reporters become so sure they are right that they fail to check and double-check their information, or they assume that they understand what their sources mean. Reporters who have their egos in check recognize that they can make mistakes. To avoid errors, they repeat information back to sources and look things up in reference materials. They also recognize that sources can be wrong. So they call additional sources just to verify the facts.

Checking Facts and Quotes with Sources

An editor of *The Atlanta Journal-Constitution* once said he had been interviewed countless times through the years and had been quoted correctly only once.[25] And ABC religion correspondent Peggy

Wehmeyer said she always asks reporters who interview her if she can see the story before it's printed. "Almost always if they do let me see it, I find mistakes." Unfortunately, their experiences are not uncommon. Researchers compared stories about trials with the official transcripts. Often the quotes in the newspaper did not match the transcripts. Clearly reporters can get quotes wrong.

However, most journalists would not grant Wehmeyer's request to check the story before it was printed. "I don't think it's ever acceptable to show stories or read back quotes," Matthew V. Storin, the editor of *The Boston Globe,* told *American Journalism Review.* "One of the dangers of reading quotes back is that person will say, 'I didn't say this.' You leave yourself open to being pressured to change what they said." Sources may also pressure editors to kill or change stories that are unfavorable to them. Other reporters are afraid readbacks may create legal problems.[26] To some, showing stories to sources is "weak-kneed journalism." Frank Stansberry, a *Business Week* reporter before becoming a corporate public relations executive, said, "As a PR person, I never had the temerity to ask a reporter to see a story, and as a reporter, I would have been offended to have been asked."[27]

However, readbacks are common at magazines like *Time, National Geographic* and *The New Yorker.* Some metropolitan dailies like *The Philadelphia Inquirer* as well as smaller papers like the *Keokuk Daily* in Iowa have similar procedures, especially for lengthy or difficult stories.[28] Many journalists would like to see the practice spread. They think making sure stories are correct is worth the additional hassle. "I just have a really hard time seeing the downside," investigative reporter Rosemary Armao said.

Some reporters routinely let sources read stories. Jay Matthews of *The Washington Post* claimed he has read or faxed copies of stories to sources for the past 10 years. "I've done it this long without any serious mishap. Every year I'm more confident about the process." Matthews stated that he became a believer the first time he read back a story to a source. He had made a serious error but was able to correct it before the story was printed. Since then, Matthews has argued that it is time for journalists to stop "defending a rotting corpse" and consider readbacks. He wrote: "Double-checking selected facts is fine. Competent reporters do that. The process catches the vast majority of potential mistakes. What a readback would catch are the unconscious errors, the verbal misunderstandings, the odd misspellings, the mental lapses that occur in communication between human beings."[29]

Reporter Steve Weinberg contends that in the 10 years he has been permitting readbacks, he is convinced that the practice "had led to more accurate, fair and thorough newspaper pieces, magazine articles and books." Weinberg rejects the argument that readbacks give the sources too much control over the work. He makes it clear to his sources that he will consider any comments they make about the stories, but he reserves the right to decide what he will change. If sources claim he has misquoted them, Weinberg checks the quotes against his tape recordings or his notes. "If the source is incorrect or acting in a self-serving way that obscures rather than illuminates the truth, I change nothing," Weinberg explained.[30]

Even opponents of readbacks agree that sometimes calling back sources to check facts is necessary. Storin said he was surprised to hear one of his reporters at *The Boston Globe* telling a source about a story before it ran in the paper. After talking with her, he decided she was doing the right thing. "When she does medical stories with medical sources, she calls them to go over the gist of what they say. I consider that not only acceptable, but . . . it makes sense."

Other journalists would agree with Storin. They aren't comfortable showing their stories to sources. But when dealing with stories with complicated details or with statistics or numbers, they call back sources to check if their understanding of the information is accurate. Robert Benincasa, who does computer-assisted reporting for *The Burlington (Vt.) Free Press,* said that "sharing computer analyses with sources in the know almost inevitably yields an insight that helps you refine your findings or turn up a quirk in the data." However, he balks at allowing sources to read the story because he considers "the tone and rhetorical nuance" of the story to be his prerogatives.

Jerry Ceppos, executive editor of the *San Jose Mercury News,* used to be strongly opposed to allowing a source review a story. But he decided that a "very, very complex story" about the stock market was an exception. It was shown to officials of the Nasdaq stock exchange. Ceppos told the *San Francisco Examiner* that the feedback was helpful and that changes had been made to the story as a result. He wouldn't say what was changed. The reporter, Chris Schmidt, said letting the sources see the story was his idea. Schmidt said that to show a story to the subject of the piece, "you have to be pretty confident in your material. If your goal is a stronger story, and if you don't give up editorial control, and if you listen, you can get a stronger story."

Many journalists, including some in the *Mercury News* newsroom, disagreed with the decision.[31] Professor Herb Strentz of Drake University also disagreed. "The reporter certainly should verify, corroborate, etc., information in the news story—that goes without saying. All that checking can be done without having the news source review the story."[32]

Even readbacks won't prevent all errors as Kansas City *Star* columnist Hearne Christopher learned the hard way. Christopher wrote a column in which he quoted a woman as saying, "I've been cleaning silver for 10½ months." He was confident the quote was correct. He knew the woman had an expensive home and assumed that she must have a lot of silver. Besides, following his usual practice, he called her and read back to her the quotes he planned to use. The day after his column was printed, he received a thank you note from her with a P.S. that read, "I've been clean and sober for 10½ months, not cleaning silver. I thought that was cute!"[33]

Correcting the Record

In the opening anecdote of this chapter, the *Calgary Herald* made a bad mistake. It reported that a university official had said things she had never said. The paper promptly printed a correction. That's the way most news outlets deal with their errors.

Perhaps the most prominent correction was printed by *The New York Times* in 1987. The headline on the main story on the front page was "Correction: *Times* Was in Error on North's Secret-Fund Testimony." A close second was one by *The Cincinnati Enquirer,* which ran a lengthy apology across the top of its front page for three straight days in 1998 after it retracted a series of stories about the Chiquita Banana Co. *Newsweek* once recalled hundreds of thousands of copies of a special edition that contained an article that mistakenly told parents to feed infants raw carrots. It should have said that infants can eat pureed carrots, but that they would choke on raw ones.[34]

Occasionally, a paper will go back and correct the record years later. The *Northwest Arkansas Times* apologized to a mayoral candidate four years after it reported erroneously that the candidate had a criminal past. Even though the candidate lost a libel suit against the paper, its new publisher and new editor looked over the stories and decided to print a correction titled "An Apology Is Long Overdue."[35]

Some corrections are undoubtedly more painful than others. *San Jose Mercury News* won considerable praise and attention with its "Dark Alliance" series, which left many readers with the impression that the CIA had played a role in supplying crack cocaine to inner city areas of Los Angeles. Several months after the series ran, Jerry Ceppos, the paper's executive editor, said that he had concluded that the reports had oversimplified the relationships among CIA operatives, Nicaraguan Contras and the crack cocaine epidemic in Southern California. In a letter to readers, he wrote that "we presented only one interpretation of complicated, sometimes conflicting pieces of evidence. In one such instance, we did not include information that contradicted a central assertion of the series." Furthermore, he conceded, "Through imprecise language and graphics, we created impressions that were open to misinterpretation."36

Thankfully, few media outlets need to run corrections on that scale. However, nearly all newspapers try to correct most or some of their errors. Commonly, they place their corrections in a set place in the paper every day to make them easier to find. Often that's the second or third page of the front section. But *The Mobile (Ala.) Register* in Alabama prints all of its corrections on the front page. A few newspapers, like *The News-Sentinel* in Fort Wayne, Ind., place corrections on the page where the error occurred, including Page 1.

In addition to corrections, many papers print clarifications if editors believe stories were misleading, ethically unsound or improperly sourced. *The New York Times* is perhaps the most active newspaper in printing clarifications. After it ran a story about a company allegedly selling military supplies to Iraq, a *Times* clarification read: "It was unfair to report an accusation by an unidentified informant who was himself relying on an anonymous source." If the problem is more complex, the paper prints an "Editor's Note" in which problems are discussed in detail.

Exactly which errors will be corrected and which will be overlooked varies from paper to paper. *The Hartford Courant* runs corrections for even minor errors like an incorrect middle initial. The *Courant* averages 100 corrections a month. Other papers show more restraint. "We won't correct the most arcane mistake," said John Bull of *The Philadelphia Inquirer.* "It has to be an error of reasonable substance."37

Some newspapers have been known to drag their feet when it comes to printing corrections. The *New York Post,* rarely considered a leader in media ethics, gave banner-headline treatment to a story about the rape of a 3-year-old. The story stated that motorists on a major highway in Manhattan stopped their cars to watch. "Shame of the City—Shocking Story of New York at Its Worst," the headline charged. The paper never corrected the record with the real story. A rape did take place, but three motorists saw the incident and pursued the rapist. Traffic was stopped not because people were watching the rape but because the rescuers of the little girl had left their cars on the highway in their haste to help the child.38

Broadcast journalism has an equally unimpressive history when it comes to correcting errors. Lawrence Grossman, president of NBC News in the late 1980s, had firsthand experience with television's reticence. He once proposed that the network run a weekly segment in which viewers with legitimate gripes could complain about news reports, much like newspapers carry letters to the editor. However, Grossman stated that the "producers and anchors so resented having to put those spots in their shows that they made a successful end run around management" and the idea was dropped.[39]

Although codes of ethics at all of the TV networks now require prompt corrections, corrections remain rare. "*The Washington Post* and *The New York Times* ran 2,000 corrections between them last year," Michael Gartner, former president of NBC News, said. "The TV networks ran fewer than a half-dozen. Corrections should not be so rare that when they are made they are big news."[40]

Many local stations are also not very forthcoming in admitting their mistakes. Despite findings that as many as one-third of the stories on local TV news have inaccuracies, only a sixth of the stations run corrections as often as once a month, according to one study. Many news directors said they believed that admitting mistakes might cause viewers to lose confidence in their news.[41] But former NBC executive Grossman disagrees: "News organizations can save themselves a good deal of grief and earn a much-needed measure of respect by reporting their own blunders with as much alacrity and gusto as they report the blunders of others. They should overcome their fear of those two credibility-building words, 'We're sorry.'"[42]

It is not journalistic integrity but fear of libel that causes some newspapers and TV stations to run corrections. In some states printing corrections can be a mitigating factor in libel suits. But more importantly, legal studies have found that if news organizations are willing to admit mistakes and print corrections, often they can head off lawsuits. Many libel suits are filed only after the people, who are already angry because of the news report, call the news organization and are snubbed by the journalists who did the story.[43]

Are Corrections Enough?

Not all people who have been mistreated by the media are satisfied that running a correction rights the wrong. Sexual harassment officer Ferrara-Kerr is one. The Calgary paper printed a nine-line correction, but as she told the paper's ombudsman, many more people read the story than saw the correction. Months after the correction appeared, she was still getting phone calls from people angry with her for what she was quoted as saying. "How do you repair the damage?" she asked.

Jim Stott, ombudsman at the *Calgary Herald* at the time, understood her plight. He thought papers ought to do more than print paragraph-long corrections when they make mistakes like the one involving Ferrara-Kerr. He suggested in his column that papers might adopt a "more flexible" policy concerning corrections. Although the regular correction box was adequate for most errors, he thought that in this case, the paper should have run a "prominent article on the same page where the original error occurred."[44]

Other ombudsmen have faced similar questions about repairing the damage of journalists' mistakes. Richard Harwood, when he was the ombudsman at *The Washington Post*, wrote that a much maligned labor secretary asked him, "Who will give me back my good name?" Harwood answered, "Not the press. That isn't our style." Nor do the news media usually do postmortems on their errors, he said. "Our follies and ineptitudes become family secrets, talked about in barrooms and classrooms but rarely in print."[45]

5

Diversity

An African-American reporter looked at the daily assignment list at a Midwestern TV station. He noticed that no one was being assigned to cover the city's Juneteenth activities. When he asked the assignment editor about it, he recognized that not only did the editor not know activities were planned, but he had no idea what Juneteenth was. After he explained that it's the day many people celebrate the freeing of slaves by President Lincoln, the editor assigned him to cover the activities.

A recent college graduate landed her first reporting job at a small newspaper. A few weeks later, she was assigned to cover an incident in the local Mexican-American community, where she would be competing with much more experienced reporters from larger papers in nearby cities. A Mexican-American herself, she understood the nuances and customs of her sources and won their trust. Her stories provided a depth and authenticity that were missing from the other reporters' stories.

Shortly after being elected, President Clinton announced plans to change the military's restrictions on gays. One national broadcast network described the ongoing controversy as "the problem with gays in the military." The network's gay journalists thought the description was poorly worded. After a staff discussion, the network adopted the phrase "the military's problems in dealing with gays." To some, the distinction may be subtle. However, to many, the new phrase was more accurate.

During the 1996 presidential primary, Republican candidates were appearing at a forum. A woman asked the candidates whether they believed she should be allowed to have an abortion if she were brutally raped. Tamala Edwards, writing in *Media Studies Forum,* described their answers—and how the media reported them:

> Dole answered first and, so concerned about alienating the religious right, brusquely said no, without further explanation. Pat Buchanan, ardently pro-life, gave a fuller and more compassionate answer, even though he reached the same conclusion. Dole, realizing how harsh he looked, came back during the next question and awkwardly tried to round out his answer. The men writing the main stories barely touched the issue, let alone Dole's graceless flub; most of them probably didn't realize how jarring that stark "No" had been to female ears. Women reporters like Katharine Q. Seelye of *The New York Times* realized that this was the lead.[1]

A newspaper in the Southwest was gearing up for protests by Operation Rescue, a militant anti-abortion group. As editors were planning the coverage, they noticed that many of the journalists involved in the coverage were pro-choice. So they asked a well-respected staff member who was anti-abortion to explain his position. Editors thought the ongoing discussions led to a more balanced coverage of the protests.

Staffers in a rural newsroom wanted to broaden their paper's perspectives but found themselves stumbling over Jewish customs and religious holidays. When the paper hired a reporter who was Jewish, the staff looked to her for guidance and often asked her to read stories before they appeared in print. She later acknowledged that it was awkward being the "designated Jew" but said she was glad the coverage had improved.

Incidents like these happen every day in America's newsrooms. Our communities are increasingly diverse, and news organizations are trying to broaden their coverage. For the media to provide insightful and truthful news of a diverse society, newsroom managers understand the need for journalists with a variety of backgrounds.

However, the movement toward more diverse newsrooms and news coverage has not been a smooth one. "Journalists, like the country they cover, have a tough time dealing with race," said Keith Woods of the Poynter Institute. "Fear, ignorance and unexamined prejudices render many of those who assign, edit or write stories about race timid at best and cowardly at worst."[2]

Minority Voices

Many early American newspapers fought against the evils of slavery. Although some papers published articles by blacks, all of them were edited by whites, and the coverage of the black community was limited primarily to the debate over slavery.

Some black writers recognized the need for a newspaper that would present news from a black perspective. In 1827 they established *Freedom's Journal,* America's first black-published newspaper. The paper's first edition declared, "We wish to plead our own cause. Too long have others spoken for us." The paper achieved that goal and became an important voice. As journalism Professor Frankie Hutton points out, *Freedom's Journal* and other early black papers were more than anti-slavery tracts. *Freedom's Journal* emphasized news from black communities and told the stories of successful African-Americans. The paper, which directed its message to both white and black readers, emphasized that blacks were Americans too.[3] By the time the Civil War began in 1861, more than 40 black-owned papers had been started. The most famous was Frederick Douglass' *The North Star,* which rallied many in the fight against slavery.

After the Civil War, black-owned businesses sprang up and flourished, and the ranks of the black middle class grew. Since these communities were largely ignored by the mainstream press, more than 1,000 black papers appeared between the end of the Civil War in 1865 and 1900. Some of these papers became vital parts of their communities while others lasted only a few months.

By the 1920s and 1930s, many black newspapers were no longer small publications. The *Pittsburgh Courier* had a circulation of nearly 300,000. Other papers like the *Chicago Defender* and the *Amsterdam News* in New York City had circulations of more than 100,000. Editors championed the fight against color barriers throughout American society and encouraged black migration from the South to northern cities. These papers covered sports, particularly those of the historically black colleges, and heralded the integration of Major

League baseball by Jackie Robinson. Most had lively pages devoted to society and entertainment news. Two black-operated wire services, patterned after the Associated Press, provided them with national and international news.[4]

The *Pittsburgh Courier* and the *Chicago Defender* were circulated nationally. However, local governments in the South often banned them, and the papers had to be smuggled into some cities, often by blacks who worked on passenger trains. The papers were passed from family to family, and some ministers read them aloud to their congregations. Black papers "penetrated just about every black household in the country" at that time, according to Brent Staples of *The New York Times.*

However, in the 1950s and 1960s, changing economic and social conditions weakened many of these papers. They were partly the victims of their own successful fight against segregation. Staples wrote that "with the civil rights movement finally under way—and white papers belatedly interested in Negro news—black readers slipped steadily away."[5] Also, with desegregation many African-Americans moved away from traditional black communities and stopped buying the community newspaper. Also, the movement of African-Americans away from black communities caused businesses in those communities to suffer. At the same time, shopping malls and discount stores were becoming popular. Many small community stores were unable to compete. At most black newspapers, these businesses were the core advertisers. When they cut back on their advertising budgets, the newspapers suffered.

In the late 1990s, black papers continued to struggle to find advertising revenue. Ken Thomas, publisher of *The Los Angeles Sentinel,* a 20,000-circulation weekly, said, "There is a misconception that the majority media can reach our customers better, and advertisers are buying it." High newsprint prices in the 1990s were particularly hard on black publishers and contributed to the death of once strong papers like the *Richmond (Va.) Afro-American Planet,* which was founded in 1883. Today, about 230 black papers are published; nearly all are weeklies.

Other minority newspapers are also playing a role in their communities. Asian-American newspapers, particularly those on the West Coast, have healthy circulations. Some, like *The Korea Central Daily* in San Francisco, provide serious coverage of their communities. Gay-oriented newspapers are doing well in many cities. The *Washington Blade,* perhaps the largest gay-oriented paper in America, has a weekly circulation of 50,000.

The fastest growing minority media in America is Latino. In 1990 the circulation of Hispanic papers was 4.2 million; by 1995 it was 8.1 million. In the late 1990s, there were more than 400 Hispanic news-papers, including about 20 dailies. Spanish-language TV stations are also successful in many areas. In Miami in 1997, WLTV's 6 o'clock newscasts drew the second-highest ratings and trailed the top-rated ABC affiliate by only two share points. In Los Angeles, KMEX's 6 o'-clock news was third-rated, drawing more viewers than the local CBS affiliate; and in Houston, KXLN was the most watched early evening newscast among 18- to 35-year-olds, a major target group for adver-tisers. Two networks, Telemundo and Univision, were supplying pro-gramming to these stations.

Although some research indicates that Hispanics prefer to get the news in Spanish, station managers argue that broadcasting in Spanish accounts for only a small part of their success. Surveys in 1996 indi-cated that only a third of America's Hispanics are dependent on Spanish.[6] "The key is our viewers know we understand them," said KMEX news director Luis Patiño. Patiño cited an example: Cinco de Mayo festivities in the Los Angeles area in 1997 drew more than 80,000 people. All the city's media covered the festival. But, Patiño said, the Anglo stations devoted about 60 seconds to it, usually con-sisting of a live broadcast from Olvera Street, a major tourist area in the Mexican-American community. However, KMEX's reporters went to three areas of the city to show ways in which different Latino communities observed the holiday.

These stations also provide solid hard news coverage of interest to the Latino populations. KMEX's Cinco de Mayo coverage came 15 minutes into the newscast after hard news stories that included an in-depth look at welfare reform. The situation is much the same in Miami. Every news organization covered the trial of Miami Mayor Raul Martinez, a Cuban-American, who was charged with political corruption. "But," WLTV assignment editor Angela D'Costa said, "we would not have covered the trials as extensively . . . every day . . . if we were Anglo."[7]

However, some in the Latino communities are concerned about the narrow scope of coverage in some Hispanic news outlets. Syndicated columnist Myriam Marquez wrote, "My guess, after decades of watching Spanish-language television news programs, is that Spanish-language news media too often center on advocacy and not on straight facts. That can be a hindrance. By focusing so much coverage on anti-Latino bigotry or discrimination in this country, Spanish-language news media can give Hispanics here a skewed sense of reality." Marquez faults mainstream news for covering Hispanics only when they are involved in crimes. Yet she worries that the prominence that the Spanish-language networks give to discrimination stories "can be just as damaging to the Hispanic psyche as the English-language TV news' obsession with crime reporting and little else about Hispanics.[8]

Diversity in the Newsroom

For many years, critics have attacked the mainstream media for its lack of minority coverage. The Hutchins Commission in the 1940s demanded that the media provide "a representative picture of the constituent groups in the society." (The commission is discussed more fully in Chapter 3.) The commission's call was all but ignored. In the 1960s, President Johnson appointed the Kerner Commission to study the race riots that wreaked havoc in many cities. The commission concluded that America was moving toward two societies, one black and one white. By failing to portray blacks "as a matter of routine and in the context of the total society," the commission stated in its report, "the news media have, we believe, contributed to the black-white schism in this country."

Despite these calls for diversity, newspaper newsrooms remained almost exclusively white until 1978. That year a study by the American Society of Newspaper Editors found that only 4 percent of people working at daily newspapers were members of minority groups. The society pledged that by the year 2000, minority representation in the newsroom would equal that of the general population. Although newspapers are now doing a better job of hiring and promoting qualified minority journalists, the society's goal is far from being met. In the late 1990s, minorities were estimated to be approximately 25 percent of the population, yet they comprised about 11.3 percent of newsroom workforce. In 1997, about 5.4 percent of print journalists were African-American; about 3.3 percent were Hispanic; 2.1 percent were Asian-American; and less than half a percent were Native Americans.[9]

Many contend that newspapers have not taken diversity seriously. "Affirmative action is the only goal in American journalism that media managers profess to be important but for which people are judged largely on the basis of effort and not results," said DeWayne Wickham, a *USA Today* columnist and past president of the National Association of Black Journalists. "If you don't get the newspaper to bed on time, somebody's going to lose their job. If you don't meet your affirmative action goals, seldom, if ever, does that happen."[10]

Minority journalists tend to work at large newspapers. About 47 percent work at papers with circulations of more than 100,000. Put another way, about half of minority journalists—compared with a quarter of white journalists—work for papers with circulations of more than 50,000.

While bigger newspapers are making progress in achieving racial equality, smaller papers are having more problems. Three out of four dailies with less than 10,000 circulation have no minority employees. Editors at small and midsize papers say they have trouble recruiting minorities. One reason is the better salaries paid by larger papers. Mark Bowden, managing editor of *The Gazette* in Cedar Rapids, Iowa, said, "If we are successful in recruiting a racial minority here, whether they're right out of school or a longtime professional, it's like, how long are they going to be here before the *Chicago Tribune* calls, and we just can't match those offers." *The Gazette* and other papers in smaller cities have also found that many minority journalists prefer to live in metropolitan areas.

To overcome these problems, Bowden's paper has developed a youth advisory council to identify high school students who might be interested in journalism and offer them scholarships. "If we want more diversity in our newsroom, we have to continually work closely with students who are from this region who want to spend their lives here," he said.

Another problem that smaller newspapers face is the reluctance of many young journalists to be the only minority in the newsroom. One journalism student, Dawn Booker, told *Presstime* that she turned down an internship at the Duluth, Minn., *News-Tribune,* which at the time had an all-white newsroom. "It would have been very scary going into that alone," she said. She said she would have taken the job if there had been one other African-American reporter.[11]

Other minority journalists, however, like the opportunities for advancement that smaller news operations offer. Claudia Ortega left the Reno *Gazette-Journal* for the smaller *News-Press* in Savannah, Ga., a city that is less than 1 percent Hispanic. "I didn't expect to find my culture here," she explained to *Presstime.* "I just knew it would have taken forever to get to the assistant art director's position" at a larger paper.[12]

Minorities Experience Difficulties

Unfortunately, many news staffs have not handled diversity well. Surveys in the late 1990s found that two-thirds of African-American journalists and just over half of Hispanics believed their newsrooms were divided along racial lines. Several studies have found that white and minority journalists disagreed on several issues.[13] Some examples:

- Minorities—especially African-Americans—tended to think they spent more time in entry-level positions and were less likely to be promoted. Whites thought minorities were more likely to be promoted and were promoted faster. "I have been at this newspaper for two decades," a Hispanic journalist said. "It took 10 years to move from entry level up one notch and another six years to go one more step. I don't believe most Hispanic reporters are valued for their skills or talents."
- Minorities—especially African-Americans—tended to think newly hired minority journalists were more qualified than white new hires. White journalists believed many minority beginners were less qualified.
- Whites were much more likely to believe that their accomplishments were appreciated. African-American women were especially negative on this assessment.

As in many workplaces, some whites tended to see new minority employees as "quota-fillers." One white woman at a West Coast metro said that "these people are hired to fill quotas, and quotas don't write stories as well as experienced reporters do." These attitudes were common enough that many minority journalists believed they had to do more to prove themselves than white new hires. More than 80 percent of black journalists and 66 percent of Latino journalists believed that newsroom managers doubted their abilities. One female African-American reporter in the Midwest said, "Managers see minorities and think, 'Remedial.'"

A study by two journalism professors, Ted Pease and J. Frazier Smith, found that many minority journalists believed "they sometimes have been neglected, ignored and passed over for promotion and advancement, left to die on the vine in one corner of the newsroom." One minority reporter said, "I think the top editors at my paper do care about diversity, but they don't understand the reasons why it's important. They hire a lot of young minority journalists, myself included, pat themselves on the back and then virtually ignore us until they require our assistance." Even experienced African-American journalists said they are hesitant to write from a distinctly black viewpoint. A black columnist told *Newsday*'s Les Payne, "I keep one eye on my white audience and another on my bosses."[14]

More troubling, the Associated Press Managing Editors Newsroom Diversity Study found that more than four in 10 minority journalists said they had personally experienced or witnessed incidents of overt racism in their newsrooms. Six in 10 said they sometimes felt racial tension or subtle prejudice. In the mid-1990s, a newly graduated African-American took a job in an all-white newsroom in a small central Florida city. He said most of the staff responded well to him. Nevertheless, one sportswriter would call him only "the Negro" or "the black kid," never by his name. At a New York paper, a columnist was suspended for calling a young Asian-American colleague "a yellow cur."

Diversity in Broadcast News

TV stations began to diversify their newsrooms in 1970. That year, the Federal Communications Commission, which regulates broadcasting, mandated affirmative action at licensed stations. By 1978, minorities held 16 percent of jobs in TV news and 8 percent in radio news.

Vernon Stone, a professor emeritus at the University of Missouri who has studied trends in broadcast newsrooms, found that minority employment has changed little since then. Today, about 18 percent of TV journalists are minority: About 10 percent are African-American, 5 percent Hispanic, 2 percent Asian-American and less than 1 percent Native American. They tend to work in larger markets. About 25 percent of the news staffs in Top 25 markets are minority, dropping to about 11 percent in the 60 smallest markets. The percentage of minority journalists is higher among independent stations than those affiliated with ABC, CBS or NBC, primarily because many large independents are Spanish stations.

Although more minority journalists are being hired, Stone is not optimistic: "At the rate we're going, no news medium will reach the ASNE goal [for representative newsrooms by the year 2000] even by the middle of the 21st century." The Census Bureau estimates that the population will be 47 percent minority by the year 2050. Stone estimated that if newsrooms keep moving at the same average annual rate, the minority shares in 2050 would be 15 percent in radio news, 26 percent in TV news and 35 percent at daily newspapers. "Still nowhere near the goal," he pointed out.[15]

The lack of progress does not surprise Sharon Stevens, an education reporter at KSDK-TV in Kansas City and an officer in the NABJ. "It's clear that we're losing numbers," she said.[16] A report by the Freedom Forum suggested that black journalists have not felt welcome in many TV newsrooms. Its findings include:

• About 37 percent of black TV journalists said their race has hurt their careers. Only 4 percent of Hispanics believed that was true in their cases.

- More than one in four blacks said that racial discrimination may drive them out of the field. About 13 percent of Hispanics felt the same way.
- Blacks are least likely to be managers—3 percent of black broadcast journalists are managers compared with 8 percent of both Hispanics and whites of non-Hispanic origin.
- Blacks are least often supervisors—22 percent compared with 35 percent of Hispanic and 37 percent of white respondents.
- Blacks are least often decision makers on program content—41 percent compared with 57 percent of whites and 60 percent of Hispanics.

"Demographic Assignments?"

Three-fourths of African-Americans and about two-thirds of Hispanic and Asian-Americans believed news coverage of their communities would improve if they were covered by reporters of similar ethnicity.[17] Many journalists agree. Bob Lynch, a gay Native American who has worked at the *Houston Chronicle* and *Los Angeles Times,* believes diverse staffs give newsrooms "a great toolbox of reference." He said, "It would be unwise for any newspaper not to use its people in this way."

However, questions arise when the editors use reporters as what *Time* correspondent Andrea Sachs called "demographic resources," that is, assigning minority reporters to "minority beats" and sending them to cover news involving minorities. Many are concerned that being assigned minority-affairs stories may limit their careers. An African-American reporter understood why he was sent to cover rioting in a predominantly black area. "I had access that white reporters wouldn't have and to people they wouldn't have access to." But, he added, "I would not feel comfortable if my bosses at the paper expected me only to be the paper's eyes and ears in the black community. I wouldn't want them to pigeonhole me in that way." Similarly, David Gonzalez of *The New York Times* said he's volunteered to do stories about Latinos, "but if that was all they asked me to do, yes, I'd be worried."[18]

Others contend that covering minority news may mean fewer Page One stories, thus making advancement harder. Also, editors may not take minority-affairs beats as seriously as the city hall or political beats. One Latino reporter said editors jokingly called minority affairs the "Taco beat."

Sometimes minority journalists face another kind of problem: They have to deal with unrealistic expectations from some people in minority communities who want them to provide only favorable coverage. "I've been accused several times of being an Uncle Tom because of my reporting of a story," said Don Hudson, managing editor at the *Jackson (Tenn.) Sun.* Other journalists say they too have been expected to do cheerleading instead of reporting. This troubles syndicated columnist Juan Williams, an African-American: "It seems some black readers want journalists to lie. My job is to pursue stories . . . not to ignore glaring needs in America's black communities."[19]

Occasionally, journalists have been accused of becoming cheerleaders for parts of the community. When openly gay *New York Times* reporter Jeffrey Schmalz covered a gay march in Washington, he was accused of focusing on the solidarity of the marchers and not on the "topless lesbians, the men in leather harnesses and the cross-dressers," William McGown wrote in *Columbia Journalism Review.* "Of course, the bizarre behavior of a few shouldn't have discredited the cause espoused by the thousands who really were the boys and girls next door. But neither should the *Times'* coverage have deliberately denied the obvious."[20]

Women in the Newsroom

Women have gained ground in the news business. In 1971, nearly 80 percent of newspaper journalists were men. That dropped to 66 percent by 1981 and has continued to drift downward. A survey in 1992 found that about 45 percent of new hires were women and that when adjusted for years of experience, salaries of men and women were about the same.[21] Between 1977 and 1990, the number of women calling the shots at American dailies tripled.[22]

An ASNE study concluded that women are underrepresented in the managerial ranks, but not significantly so. Whereas 23 percent of the men in the workforce are supervisors, 19 percent of the women are in that category. "We're very much the bone and muscle in the newsroom," Caroline Phillips, assistant managing editor of *The Wall Street Journal*, said. "We're not the exception any more."[23] Yet they are still a rarity in the top job at most papers. Only about 15 percent of the 850 members of the ASNE in 1998 were women.

Many believe that women do not get treated equally. The ASNE study found 27 percent of the women and 11 percent of men believe that women are treated unfairly in their newsrooms. Jeannine

Guttman, editor of the *Portland (Maine) Press Herald,* told Mark Jurkowitz of *The Boston Globe* that she knows how it can be when there's only one woman in a roomful of editors. "When you talk, your colleagues stare at the ceiling or look at their watches or interrupt you," she explained. "I think when it comes to readers feeling [disenfranchised], we understand it because we've been there."[24] In 1997, a memo was circulated at the *Los Angeles Times* about the "woman problem." The memo pointed out that only 12 of 42 staffers and one of six editors at the *Times'* prestigious Washington bureau were women.[25]

Women have made gains in broadcast newsrooms. Women made up 33.7 percent of all broadcast journalists in 1990, 34.9 percent in 1993 and 36.2 percent in 1994. The percentage is about the same regardless of the size of the market. Women are also moving into TV newsroom management. In 1996, 24.1 percent of the news directors were women, up from 20.6 percent in 1994 and 15.5 percent in 1993.

"Gone are the days when female news directors were found mostly in understaffed, low-paying shops at independent stations," Vernon Stone, professor emeritus at the University of Missouri, stated. During the 1990s, women moved from heading 12 percent of the network-affiliate newsrooms to 20 percent. At smaller stations, their gains are even more impressive, up from 16.5 percent to 27.6 percent in midsize markets and from 18.4 percent to 30.8 percent in the 60 smallest markets. "These are feeder markets, stepping stones to bigger things," Stone notes.

Perhaps the most infamous battle that women journalists faced was covering sports. Stories in newspaper sports sections often not only describe what happened during the game but emphasize the "whys." Therefore, sportswriters usually interview players immediately after games. In some professional sports like tennis, these interviews take place in the pressrooms. However, for major professional team sports like football and baseball, these interviews usually occur in locker rooms. Initially, this created problems. Some male athletes objected to allowing women into their locker rooms as they undressed and took showers. A few retaliated by flashing the women reporters while others sent "gifts" of dead rats and phallic-shaped cakes. Some teams forced women sportswriters to wait outside the locker room while team officials brought players to them. Because of the delays, women sportswriters had much more trouble meeting deadlines than men did.

In the late 1970s, syndicated columnist Elinor Kaine and *Sports Illustrated's* Melissa Ludtke sued professional football and baseball teams and won equal treatment. But women still experience occasional harassment. In 1990, three New England Patriots were fined by the league after they sexually harassed Lisa Olson of the *Boston Herald* in the locker room after a game. Because of her complaint, Olson was so heavily criticized by Patriot fans that she quit her job.

The old "locker-room" question was raised again in 1997 with the start of the Women's National Basketball Association. Some wondered if the women would allow men in their locker rooms. The WNBA decided to follow the NBA's practice of opening locker rooms after the games. Unlike men in the NBA, however, the women wait to take showers until after the reporters leave.[26]

Problems in Coverage

Many news organizations including ABC's *Nightline*, the New Orleans *Times-Picayune* and Long Island's *Newsday* have done exceptional stories on race relations. The *Akron (Ohio) Beacon Journal's* reporting on race won it a Pulitzer Prize. Others like *The Orlando Sentinel* have done feature sections illustrating the diversity in their communities. However, daily news coverage of racial issues is often criticized. Polls suggest that African-Americans are the least satisfied minority group. Nearly two out of three surveyed said that at least once a week, they saw something in the news media's coverage of black-oriented issues that offended them.[27]

Newspapers took the brunt of African-American respondents' criticism. In one poll, less than half said they were satisfied with coverage of news related to African-Americans, and 47 percent said they thought the coverage worsens race relations. TV news fared a little better: 58 percent were satisfied with it, and 44 percent thought it worsened relations. Most didn't expect coverage to improve. Two-thirds said they doubt if the media pay any attention to criticisms of coverage of black issues.

Hispanics and Asian-Americans surveyed were somewhat less troubled by media coverage of their communities. However, that may not be a sign that all's well, according to Héctor Ericksen-Mendoza, owner of the Hispanic Link News Service. He said there's so little Hispanic news coverage that there's nothing for Latinos to get upset about. "African-Americans are still marginalized, to be sure, but their opinions can be found on the op-ed pages," he explained. He said most newspapers don't carry Latino columnists and that the media rarely seek out Latino sources. "There's no Hispanic perspective on *Nightline* unless they're talking about bilingual education."[28]

When surveyed, minority and white journalists in the newsroom disagreed on how well their news organizations cover minorities. Eighty-five percent of whites and 52 percent of minority journalists thought their papers strived for sensitive and balanced coverage of race-related issues. However, 57 percent of minorities—but only 16 percent of whites—said their newspapers did not cover minorities well.

Minorities and Crime Stories

Crime coverage is especially contentious. A survey asked African-Americans about crime news. About 47 percent said newspaper coverage was unfair, 53 percent said local TV coverage was unfair, and 55 percent thought national TV news coverage was unfair.[29]

This discontent with the media became clear during rioting in St. Petersburg, Fla., after a white police officer killed a black man in 1996. Rioters firebombed one of WTOG-TV's trucks and attacked other journalists. Vickie Oldham, president of the Sarasota-Manatee Association of Black Journalists, told the *Sarasota Herald-Tribune* that rioters were "lashing out" at journalists. "There is a feeling that the media report only on the bad things that happen in the black community. They only show up when there's a crisis. So often on television, the only black faces you see are involved in drugs or committing crimes. The community holds the media responsible for this negative portrayal."[30]

Los Angeles Times' writer David Shaw agreed that the "overwhelming majority of press coverage still emphasizes the pathology of minority behavior—drugs, gangs, crime, violence, poverty, illiteracy." But, he noted, the same could be said of coverage of whites. The difference is that the media cover a much broader range of white life than of minority life. Many believe this "narrow, distorted view of ethnic minorities presented in the press strongly influences how whites—and such white-run institutions as the police, the courts and the school system—perceive and treat minorities. The press thus plays a major role in perpetuating the ethnic stereotypes—and fueling the prejudices and ethnic concerns—that polarize our increasingly multicultural society."[31]

A recent study suggested the depth of racial stereotyping. Participants were shown news stories about crimes. Howard Kurtz of *The Washington Post* described the results this way:

> Even when news reports made no reference to a suspect, 42 percent of the survey participants later recalled having seen [a picture of] a perpetrator. And in two-thirds of these cases, they recalled that the nonexistent perpetrator was black.

What's more, researchers used digital technology to change the mug shots of some accused criminals, "painting" black suspects into white ones. Just over half of those who saw the white perpetrator accurately recalled his race, but when the criminal was black two-thirds of those accurately remembered his race.

"I was pretty much blown away," said Shanto Iyengar, a political science professor at the University of California at Los Angeles who conducted the study.[32]

Many believe journalists don't understand the impact news stories can have. "If local TV executives understood issues of race, they would not have five minutes of black men in jumpsuits and chains," said Betty Baye, a columnist and editorial writer for Louisville's *Courier-Journal*. "The media need their own dialogue on race. We need town meetings in our own newsrooms."[33]

Many news organizations are aware of these concerns. They now limit the use of racial identifications in news stories unless race is relevant to the story. They have stopped using racial identifications in sentences like this: "Police are looking for a black male wearing jeans and a T-shirt." These editors and news directors say that hundreds of people fit that description. Furthermore, they note, witnesses' descriptions often prove to be inaccurate and inexact. However, nearly all news outlets use police artists' drawings, photographs and specific descriptions of wanted criminals because these could be helpful to police.

Even in newsrooms where journalists are cautioned to be sensitive to racial stereotyping, incidents still happen. *The Virginian-Pilot* in Norfolk ran a story about safe places to live. Of the two safest areas, one was described as a "crime-free, racially mixed neighborhood." Yet the story was illustrated with two pictures of white homeowners. The problem in this case was not a lack of a diverse staff. The people who worked on the story included an African-American reporter, an Asian-American reporter, a white editor and an African-American photographer. When Lynn Feigenbaum, who writes the paper's ombudsman column, asked the journalists involved, they admitted they had made a mistake. They had not considered the racial implications.[34]

Similarly, *The Philadelphia Inquirer* ran a front-page picture of a black man peering out a window at a murder scene in the city's Cedarbrook section. "Nightmare in Cedarbrook," the headline over the picture read. The initial impression for many readers was that the man in the photo was the killer who was about to be arrested. Only when readers got to the second line of the cutline under the picture did they learn the man was a police officer. Many readers complained. "I saw that picture—and particularly the headline," one reader wrote, "and I understood instantly why African-Americans feel they don't get a fair shake. This is incredibly irresponsible and shows a horrible lack of sensitivity."

The paper's editors explained that when they decided to use the picture, the officer's badge and uniform were clearly visible. However, after the picture was cropped, the badge barely showed, and the uniform was no longer recognizable. "The photo was good," the paper's night editor said. "But our handling of it was not."

Mainstream media are also criticized for emphasizing crimes with white victims while overlooking similar crimes involving minorities. For example, the New York media were criticized for giving heavy play to the rape of a white woman in New York's Central Park and ignoring the rape-murder of a black woman at about the same time.

Also, black-on-white crime tends to get bigger play than black-on-black crime. Jeanette Culpepper, founder of Families Advocating Safe Streets in St. Louis, said, "When a black kills a white, all hell breaks loose. But when it's black on black, it's all right." Culpepper and others accused the media of playing up the deaths of two white college students in a predominantly black area of St. Louis but overlooking the murder of an African-American mother and her infant on the same street.[35]

Other Concerns in Minority Coverage

The news media fail to serve minority communities in other ways. Carolyn Martindale, who has done extensive research on the relationships between African-Americans and the media, observed that media coverage of blacks in the past has concentrated on the global problems facing blacks such as racial discrimination and affirmative action. But, Martindale noted, there is little coverage of conditions in local black communities such as schools, recreation facilities, roads, parks and other aspects of everyday life. As the *Los Angeles Times'* David Shaw suggested:

> If all one knew about real-life blacks and Latinos in particular was what one read in the newspaper or saw on television news—and in our still largely segregated society, that's where most whites do get most of their information about blacks and Latinos—one would scarcely be aware that there is a large and growing middle class in both cultures, going to work, getting married, having children, paying taxes, going on vacation and buying books and VCRs and microwave ovens.

Gilbert Bailon, assistant managing editor of *The Dallas Morning News,* contended that "Many immigrants, especially Latinos, are portrayed in the national media as economic burdens and one-dimensional people." Hispanics themselves often are not quoted in stories about their communities. "Immigrants often are reduced to objects of debate forgotten and overshadowed by the verbal volleys between opposing politicians and advocates."[36]

Many news organizations are aware of this criticism, but they have been heavy-handed in attempts to deal with it. Some have tried setting quotas for the number of minority sources, and a plan was discussed at the *Los Angeles Times* that would have tied the compensation of senior editors to their staffs' progress in quoting more women and minorities. Many reporters objected— not to the idea of including more diverse voices—but to the method of counting. "Do we ask sources about their ethnicity when we interview them?" one reporter asked. "Do we identify sources by ethnicity in order to make the count?"[37]

Another result of these efforts is often a kind of tokenism. "My newspaper editors go overboard in coverage of weekend cultural events and ethnic events in an effort to get pictures and quotes from minorities in the paper," said one journalist. Coverage of ethnic communities becomes centered on events like African-American History Month and festivals like Cinco de Mayo, rather than on broader and more important issues in the communities.

Other editors have tried more elaborate measures to target minority audiences. Some have created minority beats. Melita Marie Garza enjoys covering the ethnic-affairs beat that she developed at the *Chicago Tribune* because "you don't have to park your culture outside the newsroom," she said. When managers at the *Los Angeles Times* recognized that the area had a large Latino population that does not read the *Times,* one suggestion was to do a special Hispanic section.

But many journalists find these measures divisive. "What are minority affairs?" asked Michele Vernon-Chesley, an African-American reporter at the Norfolk *Virginian-Pilot.* She contends that issues, not people, should be the focus of coverage. "When we break up the newsroom like that, we break up people."[38]

In Los Angeles, many staffers signed a petition arguing that it's offensive to base a section solely on ethnicity. They contended that a better way to appeal to Latino readers is to improve the coverage of their communities.[39]

Improving News Coverage

Many people contend that the problems in minority coverage are unintentional. "It's not so much some overt racist plot," Janet Clayton, an African-American journalist at the *Los Angeles Times*, told David Shaw. "It has to do with, obviously, who runs newspapers . . . what the values are of those people, the world that they live in. We all bring to the table what . . . our life experience is." However, DeWayne Wickham, a *USA Today* columnist and past president of NABJ, isn't so sure. "The industry has yet to come to terms with its own racism," he said. "The same attitudes that prevail outside the newsroom exist inside the newsroom."[40]

Most news organizations are trying to remedy this situation. One obvious approach is for the media to hire and promote people with diverse backgrounds. However, Deborah Potter of the Poynter Institute and others believe all journalists should be involved in increasing the diversity in news coverage. They offered these pointers:

- **Get to know your community.** Potter suggested that reporters, editors and photographers should spend time in communities they don't normally visit and develop sources and story ideas. "Don't make assumptions about people different from you. Ask them questions." News organizations should invite people from various communities to come into the newsroom for pizza and conversations. One news organization requires its reporters and editors to visit a different area of town each month. They then discuss what they've learned with other staffers.
- **Don't forget that minority communities are also diverse.** Gilbert Bailon of *The Dallas Morning News* said that many news stories have portrayed the efforts to stop undocumented immigration as a clash between whites and Latinos. Reporters overlook that many Latinos along the Texas border supported the efforts.
- **Learn more about customs and manners of minority communities.** As more Vietnamese moved into one Midwestern community, the paper asked members of the Vietnamese community to speak at a staff meeting. At *The Orange County Register* in California, all reporters are being taught Spanish, and many other papers have Spanish teachers who offer classes in their newsrooms.
- **Since crime coverage is a major point of contention, visit high-crime areas and discuss the news organization's coverage of crime.** When possible, Potter said, journalists should "find out details about victims, perpetrators and circumstances of crimes and include them in reports. Get beyond body bags and crime tape." Bailon suggested that reporters focus on the impact news events have on people.[41]

- **Analyze your own stories.** *The Seattle Times* put together a slide presentation of pictures of minorities that had appeared in the *Times*. The results, according to the *Times'* Gary Settle, were "eye-popping" and helped make the staff more sensitive in photo selection. The *Merced (Calif.) Sun-Star* did computer searches of the sources it used and discovered the same names appeared repeatedly. Reporters began to seek out new sources. The result was not only more minority sources, but that by "casting your net farther in the community, you find people who can add a lot more to the story," according to the paper's managing editor.[42]
- **Don't limit minority sources to stories about minority issues.** When Rep. William Gray was majority whip, he was frequently praised for his political skills and grasp of the issues. Yet a study found that when major news organizations quoted him, the stories were usually about black politics or South Africa. "Apparently, his views were not deemed newsworthy when the subject was not blacks," researcher Linda Williams concluded.[43]
- **Watch your word choice.** When *The Atlanta Journal-Constitution* checked its depiction of women, it found frequent use of words like "bombshell, bimbo, broad, dame, fishwife, hag, sex goddess, sex kitten, sex siren, spinster, tart, temptress, tomato, vamp and wench." The report caused many at the paper to take "a long, critical look" at its coverage of women, according to editors. Other news organizations have found similar stereotyping in the words they choose to use.

  Keith Woods of the Poynter Institute cautioned against using a kind of "racial shorthand." He said words like "inner city," "blue collar," and "exotic" are code words that allow reporters to play on stereotypes without directly referring to race. Similarly, Bailon of *The Dallas Morning News* thinks journalists should watch the label "illegal alien." He said it is "a pejorative with the same connotation as 'wetback.'"

6

Faking the News

Like many 15-year-olds, Ian Rustil spent a lot of time on his computer. But Ian was not playing games or surfing the Web. He was a first-class computer hacker. He had no trouble breaking into even the most well-protected computer systems.

One night his target was a big-time software firm, Jukt Micronics. Once inside its computer system, Ian tracked down employee salaries and posted them for everyone to read. He put pornographic pictures on the company's Web site and left his calling card, "The Big Bad Bionic Boy Has Been Here Baby." On a less playful note, he threatened to continue hacking the firm's computers unless he was given money, a subscription to *Playboy* and a sports car.

When officials of Jukt Micronics discovered Ian's demands, they decided to track him down. But not for the reason you might suspect. They wanted to hire him. They thought his skills at breaking into corporate computers might come in handy in the highly competitive business of software development.

According to the story in *The New Republic* magazine, Ian's case was not unique. So many companies had hired hackers that Ian and other teens now had agents who helped them negotiate secret contracts with major corporations. The practice was so widespread that police agencies had formed the Center for Interstate Online Investigations. One of its agents was interviewed for *The New Republic* article and said legislatures in 21 states were considering a uniform law to make it easier to prosecute hackers. Nevada officials even resorted to public-service advertisements warning kids that hacking was against the law.

When this story, titled "Hack Heaven," appeared on newsstands, editors at *Forbes Digital Tool,* an online magazine, decided to do their own follow-up. However, they quickly ran into problems. First, they couldn't find any listings in business or software reference books for Jukt Micronics, which the article described as a "big-time software firm." When they checked the company's Web page, the only number listed was not for a company switchboard but for a cellular telephone. So editors tried a different approach: They called the police agencies quoted in the article. None of them knew about the problem, and they had never heard of the Center for Interstate Online Investigations. The *Forbes* reporters talked to the Nevada state agency that supposedly ran the public-service announcements. No one there had ever seen such ads.

Eventually, *Forbes Digital Tool* editors called *The New Republic* and told editor Charles Lane what they had discovered. Two days later, Lane fired Stephan Glass, a 25-year-old associate editor of the magazine. Glass admitted that he invented much of the information in the story. To make it more believable, he and his brother created a Web site for Jukt Micronics and rigged a cell phone to answer calls to the number listed on the page. After checking Glass' other stories, Lane concluded that 27 of them were either partly or completely fabricated. Some of Glass' earlier work had been questioned by editors and fact-checkers, but he produced faxes, letters and phone numbers of friends who pretended to be his sources.

Soon other magazines, including *Harper's, Rolling Stone* and *The New York Times Magazine,* were checking articles by Glass. He had written an article for *George* magazine about Vernon Jordan, President Clinton's close friend who helped find a job for White House intern Monica Lewinsky. Glass quoted two anonymous sources who said that Jordan liked younger women and talked incessantly about sex. The publisher of the political magazine apologized to Jordan and said the sources never existed.[1]

Glass' exploits illustrate a sad truth: Some journalists engage in shameful reporting abuses. They fabricate stories, plagiarize, make up quotations or embellish the facts. These kinds of fakery are rare, but that they occur at all is disturbing to those seeking a more ethical journalism.

Fabricating News

In earlier days, newspapers enjoyed manufacturing news for their readers. The most celebrated journalistic hoax was the lengthy account, complete with drawings, of the manlike creatures with wings discovered to be living on the moon. This discovery of "man-bats" and other lunar life was supposedly made by a Sir John Herschel, employing a giant new telescope. This 19th-century version of pure baloney was published in the *New York Sun* in 1835 and was one of the stunts that helped it achieve the largest circulation of any daily in the world. After the hoax was uncovered, the paper's editors told readers it was a slow time for news and they just wanted to brighten their readers' days. The readers apparently were not angered by the hoax; circulation remained high.

News organizations know that today's readers are less forgiving. When journalists are caught making up facts, two things usually happen: They lose their jobs, and they face a kind of social ostracization by other journalists.

Just days after Glass' indiscretions were reported, *The Boston Globe* fired columnist Patricia Smith after she admitted some people she wrote about didn't exist and that she had made up some quotes. Journalists throughout the nation were shocked when they heard of her fabrications. Smith had been a featured speaker at journalism writing conferences and had won the American Society of Newspaper Editors Distinguished Writing Award. She had been a finalist for a Pulitzer Prize the year before. In her farewell column, she explained her conduct: "I wanted the pieces to jolt, to be talked about, to leave the reader indelibly impressed. . . . So I tweaked them to make sure they did. It didn't happen often, but it did happen. And if it had only happened once, that was one time too many."[2] A few months later, the *Globe* asked popular columnist Mike Barnicle to resign when it was determined he too had made up characters for one of his columns.

Other news organizations have also been burned by reporters with overly active imaginations. A few years ago, the Associated Press reported on the California phenomenon called "banzai runs." People in high-powered sports cars would fly down the state's freeways at speeds greater than 200 mph. The AP reporter, who said she rode along on one run, wrote, "Signs along the deserted freeway flip past in a blur and gentle curves become hairpin turns." Police were not a concern for the drivers. Their cruisers couldn't catch the racers.

The AP story got great play in California and Nevada. Then the AP alerted newspapers and TV stations that the story was partly phony and partly plagiarized. The reporter who wrote it had not been on any banzai runs. She also had lifted parts of the piece from an article that had appeared nine months earlier in *New West* magazine. In addition, she attributed statements to a California Highway Patrol officer who denied that he had ever talked to her. The 29-year-old reporter resigned.[3]

Broadcast journalism has also had its fabricators. Jessica Savitch in her book *Anchorwoman* told of a fellow anchor at KYW, Philadelphia, who "always came up with cuter, funnier, more interesting closing pads than I did." She couldn't figure out how she was missing those good items in all the newspapers and magazines she scoured each day. "Finally I begged him to tell me where the hell he was getting his information," Savitch wrote. "I make it up," he said. His tenure at KYW was short, Savitch noted.[4]

Journalists are horrified by stories like these. Fabricating stories not only undermines the truth-telling function of journalism, it also violates the trust between reporters and editors. At most news organizations, editors read copy and do as much fact-checking as they can. But in daily journalism, there is rarely enough time for them to check every fact. They must trust their reporters. The first instinct of most editors is to want to stand behind their reporters. When they discover that trust has been betrayed, some editors fire the reporter immediately. Others hope a severe warning will reform the errant reporter.

Two years before Smith resigned, a *Boston Globe* editor became suspicious of her work. He checked all of her columns and found 27 people that were not mentioned in any public records. *Globe* editors warned both Smith and Barnicle about quoting fictitious people. It was not the first warning Smith had received. Years before while Smith was at the *Chicago Sun-Times,* she was suspected of writing a review of an Elton John concert she had not attended. Her review misstated the songs he had performed and the clothes he had worn. She was also reprimanded for sneaking into the *Sun-Times* computer system and altering copy to shift the blame for a mistake she had made to a copy editor.[5]

Janet Cooke and Jimmy's World

The Washington Post, a newspaper that has been a leader in setting higher ethical and professional standards, ran the most famous hoax of the modern era, a hoax every bit as shocking as man-bats on the moon. The story was a dramatic account of an 8-year-old heroin addict. The writer, Janet Cooke, gave him the name "Jimmy," and her Page One article was headlined "Jimmy's World: 8-Year-Old Heroin Addict Lives for a Fix." Illustrated by a moving drawing of what *Post* artist Michael Gnatek Jr. imagined Jimmy would look like while he was getting a fix, Cooke's article began:

Jimmy is 8 years old and a third-generation heroin addict, a precocious little boy with sandy hair, velvety brown eyes and needle marks freckling the baby-smooth skin of his thin brown arms.

The article went on to paint a dreary and hopeless picture of "Jimmy's world" in Southeast Washington. He lived with his mother, an ex-prostitute, and her lover, Ron, a pusher who got Jimmy hooked on heroin. Jimmy wanted to be a dope dealer like Ron. The article stated, "He doesn't usually go to school, preferring instead to hang with older boys between the ages of 11 and 16 who spend their day getting high on herb or PCP and doing a little dealing to collect spare change." At the end of the article Cooke described Jimmy being "fired up" with an injection of heroin:

Ron comes back into the living room, syringe in hand, and calls the little boy over to his chair: "Let me see your arm."

He grabs Jimmy's left arm just above the elbow, his massive hand tightly encircling the child's small limb. The needle slides into the boy's soft skin like a straw pushed into the center of a freshly baked cake. Liquid ebbs out of the syringe, replaced by bright red blood. The blood is then reinjected into the child.

Jimmy has closed his eyes during the whole procedure, but now opens them, looking quickly around the room. He climbs into a rocking chair and sits, his head dipping and snapping upright again, in what addicts call "the nod."

"Pretty soon, man," Ron says, "you got to learn how to do this for yourself."[6]

The story of Jimmy saddened, outraged and angered many Washingtonians, including the mayor, who ordered a search for the child. The police chief threatened to have Cooke and the *Post* editors subpoenaed if they did not reveal who Jimmy was. *Post* lawyers replied that the paper had a right under the First Amendment to protect its sources.[7] The *Post* withstood the legal challenges, but three weeks later, the managing editor told the city editor to find Jimmy and "take Janet with you." Cooke said she had recently revisited the house and that the family had moved. So that was that. Exit Jimmy.

The *Post* entered the story in the Pulitzer Prize competition, and the jurors—with only the dissenting vote of *St. Petersburg Times* editor Eugene C. Patterson, who called the story "an aberration" that should never have been printed—awarded it the Pulitzer for feature writing. Cooke, who had been on the *Post* staff for a little more than eight months, had won herself a Pulitzer at the age of 26.

But then her house of lies began to crumble. The *Post* had submitted a biographic sketch of her taken from her applications. It claimed she was a Phi Beta Kappa graduate of Vassar College; had worked for two years at the *Toledo Blade,* where she had won an award; and could speak French and Spanish. But when she filled out her own background for the Pulitzer, she wrote that she had earned a master's degree, done advanced study at the Sorbonne in Paris, won six awards while at the Toledo paper, and spoke Portuguese, Italian, French and Spanish fluently.

When the *Blade* decided to do a local-woman-makes-good story about Cooke, it found that biographical information in the AP story didn't jibe with the paper's own records of its former employee. She had attended Vassar for one year but had returned to Toledo and earned her B.A. at the University of Toledo. She studied French in high school and college but was not fluent.

Editors at the *Blade* passed along their findings to *Post* editors. By early the next morning, she confessed to her editors that "Jimmy's World" was a fabrication. She had never encountered or interviewed an 8-year-old drug addict. He was a "composite" of young addicts social workers had told her about. She resigned, and the *Post* gave back the Pulitzer.[8]

Why did she do it? At the time her fakery was discovered, Cooke refused to be interviewed, but about nine months later, she allowed Phil Donahue to interview her on NBC's *Today* show. She told Donahue that after spending about two months looking for the 8-year-old heroin addict her sources told her was out there, her "whole mind-set was in *The Washington Post* mentality: He must be there and it's being covered up; I must find him." She decided to make up an 8-year-old addict, she said, because "the last thing I could do was to go to my editor and say, 'I can't do it.'" Cooke said she did not "excuse what happened: It was wrong; I shouldn't have done it. . . . I simply wanted . . . not to fail." Asked why she lied on her job application, Cooke said she believed she would not have been hired otherwise and felt "a need to be perfect."[9]

Composite Characters

As newspapers and magazines looked for better ways to tell their stories, many writers developed a writing technique of making their news stories read as if they were short stories or novels. Their use of description and plotting made the articles more dramatic and readable. Some called this style New Journalism. Practiced by skillful writers and reporters like Tom Wolfe and Gay Talese, it produced some lively articles and books that have also been truthful.

A few writers have tried to borrow the technique without doing the careful research and reporting needed for truthful portrayals. Some have argued that they should be allowed to embellish their stories because the important truths are the impressions they leave in the readers' minds—not the facts. One reporter described presidential candidate Robert Kennedy as looking incessantly at his watch. The image captured how rushed and perhaps desperate his campaign had become. The problem was Kennedy did not wear a wristwatch. The writer had created a literary device to illustrate a point.

Gail Sheehy did an article for *New York* magazine, detailing the lives and fortunes of a prostitute Sheehy called Redpants and her pimp, Sugarman. Although the article was presented as a news account, these people did not really exist. They were composites she created after interviewing several prostitutes and pimps. Instead of reporting what each of her sources said and did, she expressed the sources' words and actions through Redpants and Sugarman.[10]

Other journalists have carried the search for the dramatic beyond composites. They have written books and articles in which they ascribe thoughts to presidents, judges, convicts and other people in the news. For instance, Robert Woodward, the *Washington Post* writer who gained fame for his role in Watergate, has written books in which he reported the thoughts of President Richard Nixon and various Supreme Court justices, the deathbed comments of former Secretary of State William Casey and what Gen. Colin Powell said to himself during the Gulf War with Iraq in 1991.[11]

These writers contend that they have studied these newsmakers so intensely that they can accurately describe their thoughts. Many people find that argument unconvincing. Haynes Johnson, a columnist for *The Washington Post,* is turned off by this technique. "When Tom Wolfe and the people who call themselves the New Journalists use composite characters and tell us what people are thinking because they've talked to so many of them, well, they're playing God," Johnson said. "I find that pretentious."[12]

Using composites and assuming a reporter can guess the personal thoughts of newsmakers are practices not generally accepted in daily journalism.

Staging the News

One reason people watch TV news is so they can see events as they happen. Newspaper readers also want photographs that capture the event. Sometimes, this demand for pictures pushes the media into ethical quicksand.

TV reporters sometimes practice a small-time deception. They seem to be live at the scene of some news event. In reality, they are standing on the TV station's parking lot with a highway or a fence or a lake in the background, whatever would be appropriate to the story. They give their "live" reports and are interviewed through their earpieces by the anchors sitting in studios perhaps a few hundred feet away.

This technique is not limited to local stations. Careful viewers of network news may notice how similar government buildings appear on the nightly news. Reporters sometimes use a downtown church with large white pillars as a backdrop for stories about Congress, the White House or the Supreme Court to create the illusion of their being at those buildings.[13] Some have been known not to leave the studio in the winter. They don their heavy coats and stand in front of projected images of the appropriate buildings.

Radio news, too, is no stranger to embellishments. When the public hearings began on the crash of a ValuJet plane in the Florida Everglades, the news department of an Atlanta radio station fabricated a tape recording of the final seconds of the flight. *Columbia Journalism Review* reported that the re-enactment was "complete with static and beeps, shouts of 'Fire!' and anguished cries and screams." WGST defended the heavily criticized report by noting that none of the families of survivors had called to complain.[14]

Sometimes journalists resort to less innocent tricks. In the early 1990s several lawsuits were filed against General Motors charging that GM pickup trucks had a design defect that increased the likelihood their gas tanks would explode in crashes. *Dateline NBC* wanted to illustrate the problem. So producers bought one of the trucks, filled it with gasoline and then crashed a car into it. The truck exploded in a sea of flames, while cameras recorded the event from both outside and inside the vehicle.

After the segment ran, GM investigators tracked down the remains of the wrecked truck and bought it from a junkyard. They X-rayed the gas tank and discovered that it had not ruptured, as NBC had suggested. Instead, GM discovered that remote-control incendiary devices had been placed on the truck to make sure that there would be a fire when the car and truck collided. After GM announced its findings at a press conference, NBC officials took the unusual step of having a four-and-a-half–minute apology to GM read during the program. Anchors Jane Pauley and Stone Phillips, who apparently did not know of the deception, pledged that such "unscientific demonstrations" would never again be used on the program.[15]

Unfortunately for NBC, at about the same time GM was challenging that story, *NBC Nightly News* ran a story about the environmental damage caused by the timber industry's clear-cutting of forests. The report showed fish floating belly-up in a river, fish that NBC said had died because of clear-cutting in the Clearwater National Forest. A few days later, NBC acknowledged there were two problems with the report. The fish were not in a stream in Clearwater National Forest. And they were not dead. They had been stunned by forestry officials as part of a fish count in another stream.[16] Shortly after these incidents, Michael Gartner resigned as president of NBC News.

Making reality fit the needs of journalists is nothing new. Don Black recalled that when he was assistant managing editor at the Salem, Ore., *Statesman-Journal,* a photographer at another paper was sent to get a picture of young people smoking in a school lounge. The lounge was empty when he got there. "So he rustled up a couple of kids, gave them some cigarettes and set up the picture," Black said. "The paper got into a big hassle, because one of the kids did not smoke and came from a family strongly against smoking."[17]

Reporters at two TV stations were arrested after similar exploits in the name of journalism. In Minnesota, a TV reporter for KCCO wanted pictures to illustrate a story about underage drinking. When he couldn't find any teens drinking, he bought two cases of beer for six teenagers and then filmed them happily chugging away. When the ruse was uncovered, the reporter and cameraman were not only fired, they were charged with violating state liquor laws. They pleaded guilty and were fined $500, sentenced to 10 days in jail and required to do community service.[18]

In Denver, the NBC affiliate wanted to expose the illegal sport of dogfighting, in which dogs square off in pits while spectators bet on which dog will emerge alive. The KCNC series featured videotape of a dogfight that the reporter said had been mailed to her by an anonymous source. But after an investigation by police, two cameramen for the station pleaded guilty to videotaping the dogfight themselves. The reporter, who at first denied any role in the scheme, was later convicted of arranging the dogfight.[19]

Although no one contends that these stories are typical of TV journalism, many are concerned that the demand to get graphic video causes many producers to forget journalism ethics. Syndicated columnist Richard Reeves wrote that the new generation of TV journalists "don't think of themselves as reporters or producers, but as 'filmmakers' with little interest in words, and heavy interest in dramatic effect."[20]

More troublesome, incidents like these often lead the public to believe that all news reports are filled with dishonesty. A few months after NBC News rigged the GM truck fire, the *Los Angeles Times* asked people how common fakery was in the news media. Surprisingly, 56 percent said they thought it was common.[21]

Plagiarism

When Steve Lovelady first joined *The Philadelphia Inquirer* as an associate editor after reporting for *The Wall Street Journal,* he started searching through *Inquirer* clips to learn who the good and not-so-good writers were. He was very impressed with one article he found, but something about it seemed familiar. Then he figured it out. It was his article—one he had done for the *Journal*—that an *Inquirer* reporter had plagiarized. Such dishonesty is serious enough when a college student does it, but it can be career smashing for a professional writer. The *Inquirer* reporter got off with a warning that time, but he was dismissed about a year later when *Fortune* magazine informed the *Inquirer* that one of its articles had been picked up verbatim by the same writer.[22]

Some newspapers react more quickly to cases of plagiarism. Shortly after *The Boston Globe* fired columnist Patricia Smith for making up stories, it suspended popular columnist Mike Barnicle, a 25-year veteran of the newspaper, for repeating jokes without attributing them to a new book by comedian George Carlin. Barnicle at first told editors he had never read Carlin's book. However, a local TV station replayed Barnicle recommending the book during a TV appearance.[23]

The *St. Petersburg Times* obtained a resignation from a reporter after she passed off as her own about a third of an article on credit cards from *Changing Times* magazine. She put a letter on the newsroom bulletin board the day she resigned that read:

> Twelve years of dedicated journalism down the drain because of a stupid mistake. I am writing this public explanation for a selfish reason. It will be easier for me to live with myself knowing that the truth is known. But I hope my mistake will serve as a lesson to others. I have let the *Times* down. I have let myself down. But most of all, I have let the profession down. And for that I am truly sorry.[24]

These examples may represent a surprisingly widespread problem. John Seigenthaler, former publisher of the Nashville *Tennessean* and editorial director of *USA Today,* said: "I'm confident plagiarism happens with a lot more frequency than any of us knows. Part of it is new technology, but more of it is just plain misunderstanding and absence of sensitivity. And sometimes it's a total lack of ethics."[25]

Broadcast journalists also engage in plagiarism. Stephen Isaacs, a former producer at CBS News and associate dean of the Columbia School of Journalism, told *The Boston Globe,* "Hundreds of incidents of plagiarism have taken place that I know of."[26]

Some small TV and radio stations have been known to read stories from local newspapers without crediting them. Reporters and editors at the Reading, Pa., *Times* and *Eagle* got so angry they persuaded management to sue a local station for stealing stories. Most radio news executives are ashamed of their colleagues who rip and read from the local paper. Scot Witt, news director at WDCB in Glen Ellyn, Ill., said, "Any radio newsperson worth his or her salt will provide the proper credit." But, he added, understaffing and the loss of many veteran reporters to other media have "placed the editorial pen in the hands of unqualified folks."[27]

Technology has made it easier to acquire stories from other news organizations quickly. A reporter can tie into the Internet or databases like Nexis and read the offerings of newspapers, broadcast stations and wire services throughout the world. The *Chicago Sun-Times* dropped a columnist after he admitted that he had used information in his columns that he had not reported himself but had gathered through a computer database search. He had credited the newspaper's librarian who helped him with the search but not the newspapers that created the material, according to *Editor & Publisher* magazine.[28]

Not all examples of plagiarism are that clear-cut. "In its worst forms, plagiarism is a sickness," said *Newsweek* media writer Jonathan Alter. "In its lesser forms it's a kind of carelessness that I think every journalist sweats over." He contends that all journalists borrow, "so it's just a question of how much you borrow and what kind of credit you provide."[29]

Sometimes writers accused of plagiarism say the real crime they have committed is sloppiness. David Hawley, the drama critic for the *St. Paul Pioneer Press* for nearly 10 years, resigned and apologized to readers after he copied part of a *New York Times* review. Before a play opened in Minnesota, Hawley read the review that appeared in the *Times* six years earlier when the play opened in New York. He said that he unintentionally "commingled" his notes with parts of the *Times* review.[30]

Plagiarism does not always involve copying parts of another writer's prose. Some reporters recycle quotes. They see a good quote from a source in another newspaper or on television. They then use that quote in their own stories without acknowledging the work of the original reporter. A 13-year veteran of the Fort Worth *Star-Telegram* resigned after it was discovered that he lifted quotes from the New Orleans *Times-Picayune* and TV news reports without crediting them. About the same time, the paper disciplined an editorial writer for repeating several paragraphs from an opinion piece in *The New York Times*.[31]

Both *The New York Times* and *The Washington Post* have had to punish reporters for lifting quotes. A *Times* reporter took quotes from a *Boston Globe* story, ironically enough, about a university dean who was accused of plagiarism. A reporter in the *Post*'s Miami bureau lifted quotes from *The Miami Herald* and the AP.[32]

Tactics used by some reporters to sidestep ethical questions about recycling quotes worry journalists like Eleanor Randolph of *The Washington Post*. Some will call the person who gave the great quote to the other publication, ask whether it was accurate and then use it without crediting the original reporter. She also wonders about the ethics involved when a small paper scores a major scoop and then other media send their own people in and report the story under their own bylines—without mentioning the paper that originally broke the story.

Randolph suggests that if these activities aren't plagiarism, they are awfully close to it. She would prefer that the reporters and news organizations credit their colleagues who originated stories or got the quotes in the first place. She wrote: "The easiest way to avoid plagiarism is to give credit. But the average journalist enjoys giving credit about as much as your local 7-Eleven."[33]

Quote Tampering

Most editors believe that quotation marks are supposed to say to the reader, "What's inside here are the exact words of whoever is being quoted. Verbatim." And most of the time what we read in the press inside quotations marks is a fairly accurate facsimile of what the source said. Careful writers do not use direct quotation unless they are sure they are presenting the exact or nearly exact words of the speaker. If they are not sure, they use indirect quotation, paraphrasing what the speaker said.

Although handling quotations may seem pretty straightforward, journalists often encounter some difficult decisions in dealing with them. For instance, most journalists "clean up" quotes when they are ungrammatical or difficult to understand because they believe it is more important to convey the person's thoughts clearly than it is to confuse the reader. The question becomes, How much cleaning can you legitimately do?

For a *CJR* article, Kevin McManus asked two journalists how they deal with quotes. He quoted one verbatim as saying:

We have an informal policy which is a, uh, policy that's, uh, not un-common in newsrooms around the country, which is, uh, that if you, uh, uh, uh, uh, put a sentence, uh, between quote marks, uh, that ought to be what the person said.

The other journalist told McManus he edited quotes in "certain inoffensive ways." When asked what they were, the journalist said:

Well, ways that, uh, you can, for instance, uh, if the language is, um, horribly ungrammatical and, uh, makes the speaker—as spoken language sometimes is—makes the speaker look like a complete idiot, you can, quote, correct his or her grammar slightly, or make the person agree with the verb. The noun agree with the verb, something like that.[34]

McManus wondered how much you can "clean up" quotes like those and still use quotation marks.

A few journalists contended in a *Washington Journalism Review* article that it is not their job to clean up quotes to make sources sound better. Famed Texas reporter Mollie Ivins argued that "people stand up on the floor of the Texas Legislature and make jackasses of themselves all the time. It is not my responsibility to make them look good."[35] Similarly, *Chicago Tribune* reporter Timothy McNulty told McManus that he believed that changing a quote to make a person sound better is like altering a photo to change the way the person dresses.[36]

But some sources ask reporters "to make that proper English," and many journalists are willing to oblige. "Don't quote what I said, quote what I mean," the late Richard J. Daley, longtime mayor of Chicago, used to demand of reporters. Daley was famous for his fractured English. John Drury, who covered him for WLS-TV, recalled that Daley once told reporters: "The policeman isn't there to create disorder, he's there to preserve disorder." Chicago's print journalists reported what he meant, while the electronic replayed the quote the way he said it.[37]

When President Reagan didn't have a script or TelePrompTer in front of him, he also could bewilder reporters who tried to quote him verbatim. For example, tape recordings indicated that he predicted he would win the 1980 presidential election because the voters were changing and, in his exact words, "uh . . . it's kind of encouraging that more of the people seem to be coming the same way, believing the same things." The AP "cleaned up" the quote to read: "It's re-markable how people are beginning to see things my way."[38]

Sometimes quote tampering gets even more serious. Wayne Thompson, associate editor and veteran reporter for the Portland *Oregonian,* was suspended without pay for eight weeks when he fab-ricated some quotations from an interview with Washington Gov.

Dixy Lee Ray. The nightmare that occurs to all reporters who use tape recorders became reality for Thompson when his recorder malfunctioned without his knowing it during an hour-long interview with the governor. He could make out parts of the tape when he got back to his office, but most of it was a hum.

Because his paper had already promoted the upcoming interview with Ray to its readers and because he could make out about 15 quotes clearly, Thompson decided to try to reconstruct other quotes from his notes and his tape. That was a mistake. The governor complained, sending the paper a transcript of the interview from her own taping. The transcript showed that many of his quotes were inaccurate and some were complete fabrications. The *Oregonian* ran a retraction and punished Thompson, who at the time had 28 years of reporting experience.[39]

Probably the most discussed incident involving supposedly doctored quotes involved a feature profiling psychoanalyst Jeffrey Masson, written by Janet Malcolm for *The New Yorker* magazine. Masson claimed that Malcolm had libeled him by making up quotes that made him appear unscholarly, irresponsible, vain and dishonest. For instance, Malcolm quoted Masson as describing himself as an "intellectual gigolo," but a tape recording indicated he said nothing like that. During the trial, she acknowledged that she had rearranged words within quotation marks and that what she had presented as a single conversation over lunch was really several lengthy interviews she had had with Masson over several months.[40]

The suit put many journalists in a bind. Many were shocked when the evidence suggested that Malcolm had doctored the quotes. Few agreed with what she had done. Yet many journalists feared that if Malcolm lost the libel action, reporters all over the country would be sued if their quotes were not letter-perfect. The U.S. Supreme Court decided it was possible for reporters to libel people by deliberately fabricating or doctoring a quote in a way that damages the reputation of the speaker. But the court preserved protection for writers who make honest errors or who deliberately change quotes in ways that do not materially change the speaker's message.[41] A jury in 1994, 10 years after the article appeared, found that Malcolm had not libeled Masson, and in 1996 an appeals court upheld that decision.[42]

Cleaning up "Dirty Words"

Although movies, recordings and even daytime TV shows are becoming very graphic in their use of four-letter words, newspapers remain almost prudish protectors of their readers' modesty. Often they change the quotations, pictures and sometimes even the facts to avoid offending. David Shaw, media writer for the *Los Angeles Times,* said that a headline in his paper in the 1970s once called a 69-car crash on a freeway a "70-car pileup" to avoid "titillating or offending readers." At about the same time, the paper removed the genitals from a picture of a male lion at the zoo because editors were afraid children might see them.[43]

Although those cases are extreme, reporters occasionally must decide how to handle quotes by sources who sprinkle their conversations with off-color words. They and their editors consider many things when deciding how much of their language will be quoted verbatim. The prominence of the person involved is one major consideration. "If the president of the United States says 'fuck,' I'm going to quote him," observed Benjamin Bradlee, when he was executive editor of *The Washington Post.*[44] That was probably the reasoning when newspaper editors and network news producers quoted President Reagan exactly when he called reporters "sons of bitches." (A spokesman the next day said Reagan didn't recall using that phrase but thought he might have said, "It's sunny, and you're rich.")[45]

Editors also consider the nature of the story and may allow the use of graphic language if it is needed to make a point. In a story about racist and sexist attitudes among Los Angeles police officers, reporters and editors at the *Los Angeles Times* disagreed over how much of the crude language used by cops should appear in print. The top editors decided to use the word "tits" but substituted the phrase "a four-letter vulgarism for vagina" in place of a word the officers used to refer to women. The woman who wrote the story and many editors at the *Times* argued that the vulgarism should have been used because otherwise the story would "fail to accurately portray the severity of the officers' demeaning attitudes toward women."[46]

Editors at other publications are uneven in their decisions about vulgar language. *Newsweek* found that its editors had allowed the use of the word "fuck" three times in 16 years, but during the same time period had also substituted f__k, bleep, F'ing and motherf__.[47] When an editor at the *Los Angeles Times* assigned David Shaw to write an article about newspapers' use of vulgarism, he was told he could use the words in his examples. But when Shaw submitted his story, the editor changed his mind and deleted most of them, including words that had appeared in the *Times* more than 17 years earlier.[48]

Many editors are concerned that euphemisms for vulgarities may give readers a false idea about what was really said. For example, when Jimmy Carter was running for president, he agreed to be interviewed by Robert Scheer for a feature in *Playboy.* Carter, whose image was that of straight-and-narrow Baptist from rural Georgia, used the words "screw" and "shack up" and admitted that he had "lusted" after women in his heart. Carter's comments were reported by most newspapers.

However, editors at *The New York Times* considered the word "screw" too raw for a family newspaper. They substituted the phrase "a vulgarism for sexual relations." The next day editors recognized that readers might assume he had used the "f-word" instead of "screw." So they printed a clarification that Carter had used "a common but mild vulgarism for sexual relations." As Shaw pointed out, it took the *Times* "eight words to clear up the confusion originally caused by having used five words to replace one word."[49]

Occasionally newspapers substitute a more acceptable word and hope that quotation marks or brackets will alert readers to the change. After mechanical failures forced driver Tony Stewart out of the Indianapolis 500 race in 1998, a TV reporter asked him the how-do-you-feel question during a live network broadcast. Stewart responded, "All my life this is all I've wanted to do. And every year I get shit on. How would you feel?" But *USA Today* quoted him as saying, "All my life this is all I've wanted to do. And every year I get 'dumped' on. How would you feel?"

The constantly changing meanings of slang can create problems for editors. The Minneapolis *Star Tribune* ran a story about a writer who balked when a TV network asked him to be part of a six-member script-writing team. The paper quoted him as saying, "If I ain't writing it all, I ain't writing it at all . . . Six people to write a sitcom. No wonder they all suck." The copy editor headlined the three-paragraph brief, "Why Sitcoms Suck." Readers wrote the paper complaining about the word "suck."

Lou Gelfand, the paper's ombudsman, agreed: "At the fore of this discussion should be respect for readers. I'm persuaded that lots of them find the slang meaning of 'suck' offensive. Its use in the locker rooms and by youth who have heard it on television doesn't make it the common, everyday language of ordinary people." Editors at the *Chicago Tribune* and *The Philadelphia Inquirer* told Gelfand that they too discourage use of the word. For it to appear in *The Boston Globe* requires the approval of the managing editor.[50]

Manipulating Photographs

When newspapers first began to print photographs, the combination of poor reproduction and lack of concern over ethics made it possible for many papers to pass off phony pictures as real. Some papers even pasted photographs of newsmakers onto pictures of actors to recreate the news event. The expressions on the faces were rarely suited for the situation, but readers could not tell because printing quality was so bad.

Texas Monthly revived this stunt in the 1990s, according to *Wired* magazine. The magazine twice electronically pasted the head of Gov. Ann Richards on pictures of models. One seemed to show Richards dancing with her opponent in the gubernatorial race, and the other showed her astride a Harley-Davidson motorcycle. Richards said the models had such nice bodies, she could hardly complain. But many readers did. *Texas Monthly*'s editors said the covers had hurt the magazine's credibility so badly that they stopped using any manipulations that might fool readers.[51]

Few news outlets stage pictures so blatantly. Most limit staging to rather benign practices, such as photographers asking a person to pretend to be talking on the telephone or to stand in front of a picture or a building. Editors assume the public will recognize that these are posed pictures. More troublesome is when photographers alter reality in ways that might deceive the public. In 1981 the *St. Petersburg Times* attempted to liven up routine coverage of a baseball game between Eckerd College and Florida Southern. He asked a barefoot student in the stands to print "Yeah, Eckerd" on the soles of his feet. When his editors found out, he was fired. A *Times* editor explained, "One of the cardinal sins of a journalist is to tell a lie."[52]

A British reporter was accused of committing that cardinal sin twice. While promoting one of his documentaries, he said that he had spent a "nerve-shattering" year trying to arrange an interview with Fidel Castro and that finally he was given "rare access" to the Cuban leader. After the program ran, the Cuban government denied Castro had ever been interviewed by the reporter. Later it was learned that the reporter had pieced together archived footage of earlier Castro interviews and edited out the original reporters. The same reporter was accused of faking interviews in a documentary on the Cali drug cartel in South America. That report won several awards, and parts of it were shown on *60 Minutes*.[53]

But this kind of manipulation pales when compared with what photo editors can do with computers. They can rearrange images so competently that even experts cannot separate real from faked photographs. In one infamous incident, staff members of *National Geographic* magazine had a great picture of a camel in the foreground and a pyramid in the background. But the picture couldn't be cropped so that both the camel and the pyramid would be on the magazine's cover. So they used a photo-imaging computer to move the pyramid so it would fit.

Similarly, the *St. Louis Post-Dispatch* used computers to remove a Diet Coke can from a front-page photo because the editors thought it detracted from the image.

The Orange County (Calif.) Register had a more noble purpose in mind when it altered a picture one of its photographers had taken. After the picture was processed, editors noticed that a young man's pants were unzipped. A technician zipped them up for the man using the paper's photo-imaging software. Other papers have protected the modesty of people in photos by enlarging gymnasts' costumes and softball players' uniforms.

Editors at the Louisville *Courier-Journal* also had modesty in mind when they manipulated a photo, but their efforts were ridiculed on local radio stations and received a dart from *CJR*. Because of a mix-up, editors used the wrong picture to illustrate a front-page story on the city's adult entertainment district. The paper printed a picture of a stripper wearing a baggy sweater and a black G-string and performing a high kick. After the first editions of the paper were printed, editors realized that many readers might think she was bottomless. For later editions, editors digitally added several inches of material to her sweater so that the tops of her legs were covered.[54]

For less understandable reasons, a designer at *The Atlanta Journal-Constitution* used PhotoShop to manipulate a travel photo of the house where Romeo's Juliet supposedly lived. He removed "a cheesy looking woman" from the balcony. The paper's editor, Ron Martin, was not happy. "Our credibility is at stake," he said. The paper adopted a policy of putting the label "illustration" on any photo manipulations that might fool readers.[55]

Some photo manipulations do more than trick readers. They anger them. When football player O.J. Simpson was arrested in the murder of his ex-wife, both *Time* and *Newsweek* had the same cover: the mug shot police took of Simpson at police headquarters. But, sitting side by side on the nation's newsstands, the magazines looked considerably different. The Simpson on the *Time* cover appeared to be much more sinister than *Newsweek*'s. *Time* had darkened his face and made subtle changes to his features. James R. Gaines, the magazine's managing editor, claimed his staff had turned the police station mug shot into an image that better told the story. He pointed out that the picture was called a "photo-illustration" on the magazine's contents page. But many were offended that the magazine would tamper with reality in covering such a volatile story. Some saw racial overtones in the handling of the photo, a charge that Gaines strongly denied.[56]

At first, manipulations like these were limited to still pictures. But technology in use at all four network TV news organizations makes it possible to do all kinds of fancy tricks with moving pictures. Tom Pettit of NBC News said, "With the highly sophisticated editing of video tape, we can reshape reality with great ease." Similarly, Victor Porges, vice president of news practices for ABC, said, "Fifteen years ago, I could not put on my newscast something that I had not heard or seen or recorded, unless it was something that an artist might have sketched. Now I can create pictures and sounds . . . that never happened. And that opens up all kinds of ethical problems for everybody."[57]

Thomas Wolzien, a former senior NBC News vice president, doesn't think American news networks would create phony video. But he does worry about video the networks purchase. "The sources of this 'video river' range from state-run broadcasting organizations to stringers, and it can be very difficult to determine where a video image has come from—let alone whether it has been altered."[58]

Even before computer manipulation of video was common, the networks learned the danger of buying videotape on the international market. After a nuclear power plant near Chernobyl in Russia had a near meltdown in 1986, ABC showed dramatic footage supposedly taken inside the structure. Later, the network apologized when the pictures turned out to be the work of a con man who had doctored pictures of a cement factory in Italy.[59]

Many news organizations are trying to establish policies to deal with the ethics of photo-imaging technology. Some have outlawed any manipulation of news pictures, while others require editors to explain any alterations in the cutlines. The *Chicago Tribune*'s policy is succinct: "We do not alter editorial photos, period." *The Dallas Morning News* takes a similar stand. The Associated Press Managing Editors organization was even more blunt. In a report on electronic imaging, APME stated, "This is supposed to be about electronic photo manipulation, but it's really about lying. The more we mess with pictures, the more we mess with our credibility."[60]

But not everyone thinks the ethics of this new technology can be dismissed that quickly. Deni Elliott, Mansfield Professor of Ethics at the University of Montana, distinguishes between the manipulation of pictures and deliberate deception. "If the manipulation of images creates a false depiction of reality or if the manipulation fails to disclose some relevant piece of reality, the manipulation is deceptive," she has argued.

She believes *The Orange County (Calif.) Register* did nothing wrong when it made the sky bluer in its pictures of the explosion of the space shuttle Challenger because the intent was not to deceive the public but to show the sky more as it had appeared on television. (The *Register* had been accused of making the sky bluer so the colors of the exploding shuttle would be more vivid.) However, she does not approve editing out people in the background of a picture because that would be changing reality to suit the desires of the picture editor.[61]

Some scoff at the concern over the new equipment. Lou Hodges, a professor of professional ethics at Washington and Lee University, has contended that the only reason people get upset about technology is that they believe the myth that photographs objectively portray an event. No photograph captures "what really happened." Instead, the photographers have already imposed their subjectivity onto the image when they decide to take a picture or not take one. "And once the noteworthy event has been chosen and the photographer is on the scene," Hodges stated, "other crucial value judgments follow: What aspect of the scene is most important and how can I capture it? What angle, background, framing, light, distance, moment to shoot?"

Hodges also pointed out that even in a traditional darkroom, photographers routinely use techniques like burning and dodging to emphasize parts of the picture and then in the cropping process remove elements that do not contribute to the photograph's major emphasis. In his view, the real challenge of using PhotoShop is to learn to use it to produce better pictures.[62]

The National Press Photographers Association agrees that computers may be used ethically to improve some pictures. The association's code of ethics allows some manipulation—lightening a football player's face in a contrasty photo, for example. More serious manipulations would need to be discussed with newsroom officials before publication. The code bans manipulations that deceive readers.

Researchers at the University of Wisconsin surveyed news photographers and found that about 29 percent of them said they would remove telephone wires from a picture if they detracted from the image, 27 percent said they would close a zipper, and 19 percent would combine two photos to produce a better image.[63] Other photographers would like to see the American media adopt a system like the Norwegians have. The media there agreed to put a warning logo on all altered photographs, even if the alterations are relatively minor.[64]

Time's handling of the O.J. Simpson mug shot was criticized by both of its competitors. Richard Smith, *Newsweek*'s editor in chief, said: "We don't mess around with news pictures." He said *Time* had not changed the picture enough to make it clear it was an illustration.

The editor of *U.S. News & World Report* agreed. He said most readers would never have known it was an illustration if *Newsweek* had not used the same cover.[65]

Polls show that the public is already convinced that the news media are not to be believed. And that's sad. Most reporters and photographers strive to get every detail correct. Yet it takes only a few bad examples to prove to many that the work of all journalists is suspect. When columnists make up quotes, reporters steal stories from other reporters, and photographers create reality to suit their needs, they hurt everyone in the profession.

3

Reporting the News

7

Reporters and
Their Sources

Caroline Lowe, the police beat reporter for WCCO-TV in Minneapolis, had just returned from vacation. While she was calling her usual sources looking for stories, a police officer gave her a tip. He said the public would be shocked to see what happens on Hennepin Avenue at night. He said drug dealing, urinating in the streets and fighting were every night occurrences.

Lowe and photojournalist Nancy Soo Hoo placed a camera in the area and soon discovered the tipster was right. But instead of doing a story about the lawlessness, she wondered why the cops had not done something to stop it. She checked with other sources, including some police officers. They told her the problem was with the police officers assigned to the area. So Lowe and Soo Hoo expanded their probe. Soon they discovered officers sleeping in a movie theater while an assault was happening in the lobby. They videotaped patrolmen hanging out in strip joints and a supervising officer working an off-duty job in the middle of a regular shift.

Clearly, it was a great story. But Lowe faced a problem. If her report was broadcast, she might lose many of her police contacts. Those relationships had allowed her to beat the competition on some highly publicized murder cases and to break major stories, including one about drunken pilots on a Northwest Airlines passenger jet. "Sources are a beat reporter's bread and butter," she explained. "I spent 15 years developing sources in the criminal justice system and I've worked hard to earn the trust and loyalty of my police sources. And I knew the story on the downtown foot patrol could threaten some of those relationships."

Her news director told her that she could give the story to other reporters if she wanted. That way, the story would be broadcast, but she could avoid being blamed for it. But Lowe decided to do the story herself for three reasons. "The first was my strong belief that the story should be told," she said. Second, she felt "ownership" of the story; she wanted to play a role in how it was reported. Also, Lowe wrote, "I knew that I would have to live with the story no matter who did it." If sources are angry enough at a particular news outlet, they often refuse to talk to any of its reporters.

Lowe and Soo Hoo's report was aired over two nights. City leaders reacted immediately. The police unit was reorganized, four veteran officers and the head of the unit were fired or suspended, and the City Council called for extensive reforms. Police reactions to Lowe came just as quickly. Many officers gave Lowe dirty looks or hassled other cops who were friendly to her. "I expected such reactions, but they still hurt," she recalled. "At least one encounter left me in tears."

But most of her best sources stood by her. "Many voiced a similar sentiment: They were embarrassed by the story and frustrated that the department hadn't cleaned its own house," Lowe said. "But they understood why I had done the story and didn't hold it against me. Some even thanked us." Lowe wrote that to her surprise, after the story aired, she was called by new sources offering tips and information.[1]

Lowe's experience highlights the human and ethical problems reporters frequently encounter. Reporters and their sources have "an inextricable interdependence," according to Jeremy Iggers, a reporter of the Minneapolis *Star Tribune*. He wrote that reporters "are keenly aware that future access to information depends on how they handle today's story." At the same time, however, sources are also trying to cultivate reporters so they can present their ideas and spins to the public.[2]

Relationships with Sources

Reporters know that they must have good sources. Good sources take care of reporters, feed them news tips, point them toward other sources and provide background information that makes their stories more authentic. That's why good reporters, especially when they are first assigned a beat, spend lots of time getting to know as many people on their beats as possible. Those minutes spent schmoozing with a source can pay off later in solid information and leads to stories.

Mary Murphy, a veteran police reporter, said she tries to maintain friendly relations with police officers. She shoots guns with them at the police department's pistol range, shares jokes and gossip, and doesn't back away when she encounters them in social situations. She believes this camaraderie helps her on the job. "It's a lot easier when you arrive at the scene and you already know some of the cops," she said. Other reporters have had similar experiences. A reporter assigned to cover courts baked cookies and pies for the bailiffs and clerk's staff. When a heated confrontation flared in a courtroom, one of the bailiffs alerted her. She turned the tip into a solid story.

Although reporters need good relationships with sources, sometimes these relationships can compromise the reporting. A mutual back-scratching pact can easily develop. When reporters need some background, a lead to a story or a good quote, they know who will help them. When that person gets into the news, it's payback time.

Reporters occasionally step over the line and develop friendships with their news sources, seeing them socially as well as professionally. It is understandable how such friendships occur. Reporters and their sources often have a lot in common and share an interest in many things. It is no wonder that politicians and political reporters, police and police reporters, and coaches and sports reporters become friends. And in smaller towns, reporters and their sources are more apt to see one another after work because the social network offers fewer opportunities for them to avoid one another. Friendships can easily spring from the church dinners, softball games and the other everyday contacts.

Murphy believes reporters can avoid this trap. "You always remember that you are a reporter and they really aren't your friends," she said. Murphy has managed to convey this relationship to her sources. Stoney Lubins, a sergeant in a police department that Murphy covered, said: "We like Mary, but we know she's a reporter and she has a job to do and we have a job to do." The key to developing this kind of relationship, Murphy said, is to treat the officers fairly every time. "You burn them one time and they will never help you again."[3]

When your sources are also your friends, sometimes it's easy to forget when they are friends and when they are sources. Ellen R. Findley, a reporter for *The Advocate* in Baton Rouge, La., called an attorney "who was a very good friend" to ask him about the mayor's race. She was interviewing him for a story, but he thought they were talking as friends. When her story appeared, she said, "we both got a lot of flak—me from him, him from the politicians he offended."[4]

The possibility of friendships presents problems for editors and news directors. They appreciate beat reporters who have covered the same beat for many years. They know these reporters have a deep understanding of the area they cover and have developed strong relationships with sources. They also know that these long-term relationships can become too cozy. Occasionally, reporters can begin to identify too closely with the people they cover. Sportswriters begin to talk of "we" when they refer to the team they cover. At one newspaper, the police reporter began to carry a phony badge and applied for a permit to carry a gun.

To get around these problems, some editors and news directors rotate reporters on beats. Other editors don't want to lose the expertise of an established beat reporter. So they will assign another reporter to do a special or negative story that the beat reporter could not do without losing prize sources.

Some reporters go overboard at trying to avoid personal relationships with sources. They treat them all as enemies. They believe an adversarial relationship is necessary if the press is to be a true watchdog of government and other important institutions. They keep their distance from officials and their subordinates. Worse, they may discount every word officials say as being self-serving. The result may be that sources will become defensive in talking with reporters and the public will not learn as much about their ideas. Also, if reporters treat most public officials as crooks or potential crooks, they will not only be wrong in that assessment, but their copy is likely to reflect this bias.

That doesn't mean reporters should let their sources use them. Many sources must be approached with caution, not because they may be covering up some vital information, but because they have their own agendas and want to see their ideas presented positively. They may be willing to flatter and manipulate the reporter if it serves their ends. There are times when journalists must ask the hard questions and be firm when sources begin to avoid questions or to talk around the issues. To get at the truth, sometimes reporters play tough. But to play tough all the time, with experienced sources and everyday people, is probably a role better left to old-fashioned Hollywood detectives.

Beyond Friendship

Occasionally, reporters are drawn to their sources in ways that go beyond journalistic enterprise. Perhaps one of the more notorious of these relationships involved Laura Foreman and Henry "Buddy"

Cianfrani. Foreman at the time was a 34-year-old political reporter for *The Philadelphia Inquirer,* and Cianfrani was a 54-year-old state senator and south Philadelphia political leader. Cianfrani was one of Foreman's sources, and she helped cover his political campaigns. They were also lovers. During their affair, he gave her a fur coat, a sports car and other expensive gifts. They shared an apartment. When her supervising editors at the *Inquirer* heard rumors about the relationship and questioned her, she feigned innocence and said she was the victim of idle gossip by reporters who were envious of the stories she was breaking.

Foreman's professional problems began in earnest when she took a job with *The New York Times* in its Washington bureau. Editors at the *Times* apparently knew nothing of her involvement with Cianfrani until FBI agents questioned her as part of their investigation of Cianfrani on income tax evasion charges. At about the same time, the *Inquirer* broke the story of the Cianfrani investigation and included details about his relationship with Foreman and the fact that she had accepted the expensive gifts while she was covering politics.[5] *Times* editors took a hard line when they learned what Foreman had done. They forced her resignation.

Many people were not convinced that a man would be treated as severely. However, Eleanor Randolph, who was then a reporter with the *Chicago Tribune* and later became a *Washington Post* columnist, stated that if a man had committed actions similar to Foreman's, he would also have some explaining to do to his editors, but for different reasons. A man would have "to explain why he took $20,000 from a person he wrote about—love or no love." She wrote, "As for sleeping with the subject of stories, however, there is little doubt that until very recently a male reporter who took a female source or subject to bed had simply scored with more than a good story."[6] Foreman and Cianfrani eventually married—after he served out a prison sentence for mail fraud, racketeering and conspiracy.

Relations with Sources Shape Stories

Many things can shape the coverage of a major story. One of them is how reporters interact with sources and how they size up their sources' truthfulness. An extreme case of this happened to two Florida newspapers. The case involved a crime story that had all the ingredients of a made-for-TV movie. An 18-year-old medical clerk was raped and murdered. Her body had been discarded in a dump near Orlando. By the time it was found, it was too decomposed to determine the cause of death. Nearby, the body of another woman was found, also badly decomposed. The murders were big news in Central Florida. The public's interest in the case no doubt grew when police called in a psychic who held the woman's skull and offered advice on how to proceed with the investigation.

Eventually, police charged Joseph Spaziano with the crime. If this were a movie, he would be the perfect villain. His nickname was Crazy Joe, and he was a member of the Outlaws, a nasty band of bikers with a reputation for gang rapes and general mayhem. The star witness against Spaziano was Tony DiLisio, a troubled teenager who had worked at his father's business with Spaziano. While DiLisio was being held in juvenile detention, police and his father persuaded him to visit a hypnotist. After several visits, he remembered Spaziano taking him to the dump, where Spaziano showed off his kill.

At the murder trial, the teen testified that Crazy Joe had described in horrifying detail how he had mutilated the young woman's genitals with a knife before he killed her. Prosecutors had circumstantial evidence against Spaziano, but DiLisio was the only witness who could directly tie Spaziano to the crime. That was enough for the jury to convict Spaziano and a judge to sentence him to death. Twenty years later, after a series of appeals, Spaziano was still on death row.

That's when two of Florida's leading newspapers entered the picture. Both papers got deeply involved in Spaziano's case, assigning several reporters each to the investigation. These reporters pored over trial testimony, newspaper clippings and public records and tracked down dozens of people involved in the case. Top editors at each paper oversaw their work.

The Miami Herald concluded that Spaziano was the victim of justice gone awry. Its stories suggested that police work had been shoddy and that hypnosis-induced testimony—no longer allowed in Florida's courts—was no better than witchcraft. When a judge issued a stay of Spaziano's execution, the headline on a *Herald* editorial read, "Justice Awakens."

The Orlando Sentinel, however, saw the story differently. Its investigation led editors to believe that police had the right man and that Spaziano was indeed a brutal misfit who told members of the Outlaws that sex was better after a killing. When his stay of execution was issued, a *Sentinel* editorial was headlined, "Justice Clearly Cheated."

How could two first-rate news organizations come to such different conclusions? David Barstow, a reporter at Florida's *St. Petersburg Times,* studied the reporting and concluded: "The coverage was shaped by forces unseen by readers. The newspapers pursued different questions and were driven by different ideas about the proper role of journalists. Their coverage was molded by ego and instinct. Stories were affected by reactions to what the other newspaper was writing, and by the manipulations of a few key sources."7

Although the crime happened near Orlando, *The Miami Herald* was first to re-examine the Spaziano case. One of Spaziano's lawyers tipped the *Herald*'s Gene Miller, who had won two Pulitzer Prizes for exposing miscarriages of justice. The lawyer said there were problems with the way the Spaziano trial was handled. One problem caught Miller's attention: The hypnotist who had interviewed the teen was the same man whom Miller had discredited in another murder case. So Miller decided to do some checking. He read the court documents and conferred with an outside expert. Finally, he concluded that Spaziano's lawyers might be right: An innocent man might be facing execution.

In his critique of how the papers handled the story, Barstow wrote:

> To Miller, the reporter's mission is to find the truth and then persuade others to do something about it. When the clock is ticking on a man's life, that can mean stepping outside Joe Friday "just the facts, ma'am" journalism. It can mean taking a side. It can mean lobbying a governor in person, or lining up legal help for the condemned. [As the story unfolded, *Herald* reporters lobbied the governor in Spaziano's behalf, and the *Herald* helped pay his attorneys.] To those who say journalists should remain neutral, he responds simply: "A man's life is at stake. I think I'm doing the right thing."

The *Herald* sent reporter Lori Rozsa to interview Tony DiLisio, who was then 37. Dilisio shut the door in her face and threatened to call police. However, on her fifth try, she got the interview. DiLisio said that at the time of the murder he was just a scared kid who made up a story to please police and his domineering father. He never saw the body; he never heard Spaziano confess. Rozsa believed him, and her story ran on the *Herald*'s front page. The governor of Florida immediately called for an investigation.

At *The Orlando Sentinel*, editors were in an awkward position. A rival newspaper, 200 miles away, had scored a major story from their own backyard. They decided to play catch-up and assigned eight reporters to the coverage. Editor John Haile wanted his paper to approach the story differently. He explained later: "As the *Herald* set out to free someone its reporters and editors believed to have been wronged, the *Sentinel* set out to find out when the key witness was telling the truth—or even if he can still remember the truth about this murder case. Who is this guy and what is he about?"8

The *Sentinel* sent reporter Mike Griffin to interview DiLisio. "I caught the guy in the first 15 minutes in a half-dozen lies," Griffin said later. For example, DiLisio told Griffin he had been "Christian and clean" for more than a decade. Griffin knew DiLisio had been arrested twice for drunken driving and twice for hitting a former girlfriend. The inconsistencies led Griffin to wonder if DiLisio was also lying when he recanted his story.

Editor Haile agreed with Griffin: "Were we skeptical of his story? Absolutely." Haile stated that the *Sentinel* began to chase several leads. Reporters found people who said they had heard DiLisio tell of the murders before he underwent hypnosis. "What we didn't find was anyone to support his change of heart," Haile said. The *Sentinel*'s investigation found holes in DiLisio's credibility. The paper reported his recent brushes with the law and quoted friends and relatives who said DiLisio was a compulsive liar.

Clearly, the *Sentinel*'s stories did not sit well with Spaziano's attorney. Believing the stories would hurt Spaziano's chances of escaping the electric chair, he labeled the *Sentinel* "an accomplice to murder." He refused to talk to its reporters and ordered his client to do the same. DiLisio also stopped talking to the *Sentinel*. However, both men continued to talk to the *Herald*, which the attorney called his "investigative partner." The *Herald*'s coverage continued to be sympathetic to Spaziano's cause. (At one point, the lawyer wrote Spaziano, "With the help of God and *The Miami Herald,* we'll cross the finish line together.")

As might be expected, law enforcement officials saw the stories differently. John Gordy, the agent in charge of reinvestigating the crime, was angry at a *Herald* story suggesting he had botched the investigation. So Gordy and other law enforcement officials answered questions from *Sentinel* reporters but often were less forthcoming with reporters from the *Herald*. They saw the *Sentinel* as a paper that would "set the record straight" about Spaziano.

Because reporters from the *Herald* and the *Sentinel* saw their roles differently and because they developed such different relationships with the principal sources, their coverage was different. Barstow wrote, "The *Herald* found in Spaziano a pathetic victim of injustice. The *Sentinel* found a 'dead-eyed' rapist-killer."

Spaziano eventually pleaded no contest to a reduced charge of second-degree murder. As part of the plea deal, he was given a 23-year sentence, which is how long he had been held on the murder conviction. He maintained he did not commit the murder but wanted to save his family the trauma of his possible execution. He remained in prison on a life sentence for an unrelated rape.

Secret Sources

Reporters at *The Seattle Times* presented executive editor Michael R. Fancher with a difficult news decision. They said that eight women had told them that they had been sexually abused by one of the state's U.S. senators. One woman even claimed the senator raped her. The reporters said they had confirmed as many of the details given by the women as possible, but they couldn't confirm the key charges themselves since they happened in private.

The problem was that the women did not want to be identified. They were all Democrats who earned their livings as lobbyists and full-time employees of the Democratic Party. Their careers would be over if it were known they caused the downfall of one of the party's elected officials. The reporters explained that they had tried for years now to get the women to let their names be used or at least be identified to the senator. But the women had staunchly refused.

They asked Fancher to make an exception to the paper's policy against using accusations made by anonymous sources or sources who will not confront the people they are accusing. Fancher's decision was made all the harder because the senator was involved in a re-election campaign. If the paper printed the story, some would charge the story was politically motivated. If the story was not printed, others would say the paper covered up important information.

Fancher decided to use the story about Sen. Brock Adams and to print a front-page message explaining his reasons for violating his paper's policy against printing anonymous charges. Fancher told readers that the paper had been working on the story for more than three years and that it involved "abuses of power and women" over a long period. He said he decided to print the story while the campaign was under way because he believed the voters had a right to hear the allegations and because the story's development had reached "critical mass," meaning the paper had enough information from enough people to believe the story was true. "The bottom line is that we thought the basic choice we had was to withhold an important story we believed to be true or to tell the story without named sources, and it was a reluctant choice," Fancher said.[9] Once the story appeared, the paper's ombudsman said she received more than 200 phone calls, most of them against the paper's conduct.

Journalists are worried about the use of anonymous sources. Some would not have used the Adams story, even with the precautions the *Times* took. "We'd need papal dispensation to use one anonymous source in any story," said Madelyn Ross, managing editor of the late *Pittsburgh Press.* "In all cases, we demand on-record information to maintain our credibility with readers."[10] Some other papers have similar bans on anonymous sources. *San Diego Union-Tribune* editors said they didn't want to second-guess Fancher's decision but noted the Adams story would run afoul of its policies, which discourage reporters from repeating criminal charges made by anonymous sources if they have not taken them to proper authorities.[11]

But a great many editors agreed with Fancher's decision. *St. Petersburg Times* editor Andrew Barnes said his editors argued about whether they would use the story if it had happened in Florida. "I came away thinking I would twitch a lot and then do it," he said.[12]

Editors Growing Wary

Most editors understand Fancher's reluctance to use unnamed sources. They fear (1) that too many reporters are using unnamed sources just because they are too lazy to find on-the-record sources, (2) that there is too great a risk of reporters making up things and passing them off as comments by unnamed sources, and (3) that information from unnamed sources is often either inaccurate or self-serving.

Some editors have had firsthand experience with lazy reporters who do not press to get information on the record. William J. Small, former president of United Press International and NBC News, said he wished he had a dollar for every time a reporter had called him and said, "'Look, why don't we do this off the record?' They're always shocked when I said I never talk off the record."[13] Nancy Woodhull recalled that when she was editor of the Rochester, N.Y., *Democrat & Chronicle,* one of her reporters turned in a story without any specific identification of his sources. Asked about this, the reporter said, "Well, gee, I didn't think they'd want their names used."[14]

But other editors have a more serious concern. They fear that some of the material attributed to anonymous sources may have been the product of reporters' creativity. Several major publications including *The Boston Globe, The New Republic* and *Chicago Tribune* have had reporters quote sources who didn't exist. The most notorious case of phony unnamed sources involved Janet Cooke, a *Washington Post* reporter who wrote a gripping tale of a child drug addict. After the story won a Pulitzer Prize, she admitted that she had made the whole thing up. (This case is discussed more fully in chapters 6 and 11.)

Although deception on that level is rare, editors acknowledge that they suspect reporters have spiced up their stories with fictitious sources. Robert Greene, who was a top investigative reporter and editor at *Newsday,* said he knew reporters who tried to pass off their own ideas by attributing them to anonymous sources.[15] Mark Washburn, an editor at *The Miami Herald,* reacts to anonymous sources even more strongly. He commented, "Anytime I see 'sources said,' the hairs go up on the back of my neck and I want to say 'Oh, bullshit, you made it up.'"[16]

Many editors argue that readers will be less likely to believe stories with unnamed sources. But research suggests that readers are no more likely to distrust a story with anonymous sources than one with named sources, and one study found that they believe stories with no attribution more than ones with named attribution.[17] Even major media mistakes, like the saga of Atlanta bombing suspect Richard Jewell, seem not to have lessened the public's acceptance of information based on anonymous sources. However, when pollsters ask readers directly if they approved of the use of anonymous sources, more than half said no.[18]

If editors are more skeptical of unnamed sources than the public appears to be, it may be because editors have seen too many stories based on unnamed sources turn out to be wrong. *The New York Times* apologized to its readers after one of its reporters used information from an "unnamed corporate official" in stories about negotiations involving the New York *Daily News.* When everybody involved told *Times* editors one of its stories was wrong, the editors asked the reporter who this "corporate official" was. The reporter admitted that he didn't know. He said he had based the stories on an anonymous phone caller who seemed to have inside information about the talks.[19]

The New York tabloids and some of the Florida media got into a no-holds-barred hunt for news when a woman accused members of the New York Mets baseball team of gang-raping her during spring training in Port St. Lucie, Fla. The papers used stories based on unnamed sources who supposedly had ties to the prosecutor's office or the sheriff's office. Many of those stories were dead wrong, according to a follow-up story in the *St. Petersburg Times.* Papers reported erroneously that the woman had been to the hospital after the alleged rapes, that she had submitted a lengthy statement to police in Florida and that the players had been interrogated at the stadium by police.

But the biggest scoop was scored by the *New York Post* when it named three Mets and said they would be charged with the crime "within the next few days." When several days passed without any charges, the *Post* reported that the investigation had hit a snag. No charges were ever filed in the case, and officials later told the *St. Petersburg Times* that there was never a time when they thought they were even close to bringing charges.

The *Post*'s editor was not overly troubled by his paper's mistakes. "Inaccuracies happen on all kinds of stories, in plane crashes and rapes," editor Lou Colasuonno told the St. Petersburg reporter. "But this was a very hot story, a very sexy story, and very fast moving. I'd rather be a little aggressive on something like this than a little timid."[20]

But other editors argue that the likelihood of inaccurate information causes them to be very cautious when allowing the use of unnamed sources. "When people's names aren't attached to a story, it becomes much easier for them to say things that aren't necessarily true," said *USA Today* editor Peter Pritchard. "They're protected. A lot of savvy people will use that protection to float stories that aren't true or that embarrass someone else."[21]

Single, Anonymous Sources

Many journalists were deeply embarrassed by the numbers of mistakes that were made by reporters at usually respectable news outlets during the early coverage of the Monica Lewinsky story. As Tom Fiedler, political writer at *The Miami Herald*, wrote, "instead of this being a banner period for political journalism, our credibility (and claim to responsibility) is at its lowest point since our forebears helped William Randolph Hearst start the Spanish-American War to sell newspapers."

While Watergate reporters had been bound to a two-source rule, reporters madly chased after any source in the Clinton-Lewinsky coverage. *The Dallas Morning News* had to pull a story out of its first edition and replace it with a retraction in the second edition. The reporter had relied on one anonymous source who had only second-hand information. The paper's editor said he would never again stray from the paper's policy of requiring at least two independent sources for every story.

The Dallas paper was far from the only news organization to use poorly sourced stories.

A study conducted for the Center for Concerned Journalists found that in the first six days of the Lewinsky story, just 1 percent of the stories cited two or more sources by name to back up information. Only 25 percent cited a single named source. Thirty percent of the stories cited anonymous sources, and 41 percent of the information was classified as speculation or analysis by journalists. "No wonder we've been so wrong," Fiedler concluded after reviewing these statistics. "The problem here, however, is that 'scoops'—even in the few times that they may be accurate—are fool's gold, utterly valueless in terms of public significance."[22]

The Dark Side of Secret Sources

When most people think of anonymous sources, they envision disgruntled employees who want to tell about the shenanigans of their bosses or public-minded individuals who are fed up with waste and wrongdoing. But not all anonymous sources are even that pure of heart. Eleanor Randolph wrote in *The Washington Post* that "a leak from a high-level official is more often a strategic move to help formulate or further a policy, and many journalists fear that they are being used as part of the process rather than as disinterested reporters relaying facts to the public."[23]

Perhaps the classic perversion of the use of secret sources is the "trial balloon"—a bogus story floated by political leaders to test which way the wind of public opinion is blowing. For example, a city official might tell a reporter, on a not-for-attribution basis, about one of the mayor's plans. Once the story appears in the paper or is broadcast, the official listens for reactions from the public. If there are no complaints, the city might go ahead with the plan. But if the plan is attacked, the mayor might announce that there was no truth to the news report whatsoever and assure voters that such an awful idea would never even be considered.

Prosecutors and defense attorneys sometimes use similar tactics. They may leak details of an investigation even when they do not have enough evidence to bring charges. They hope that the news accounts will put pressure on the people under investigation or encourage more witnesses to come forward.[24] A prosecutor in California acknowledged that people in his office "vastly overstated" when they told reporters about alleged child abuse at a day-care center. For instance, reporters were told that the children had been used in millions of child pornography pictures and films. When the case came to trial, it became clear that police had found no pictures or films at all.[25]

Trial balloons like these are all-too-common ploys, but reporters say there is little they can do to keep from being caught up in them. When President Clinton was formulating his economic package, the administration used trial balloons to test reactions to many of its provisions. "We probably have been used as much as anybody in this," Albert Hunt, *The Wall Street Journal*'s Washington bureau chief, told *Washington Post* reporter Howard Kurtz. "There are days when I pick up the paper and cringe. But if you say we're not going to participate in this, they float it to someone else and you wind up chasing it the next day."[26]

Others leak information so that if things go wrong, they won't be blamed. Kurtz wrote that when James Baker took over President

Bush's re-election campaign, he started leaking stories to key re-porters that the campaign was "in shambles." As Baker had hoped, their stories reported the mess and suggested that if Bush lost, it wouldn't be Baker's fault.

And some people leak stories to avoid risking confrontation with their colleagues. Several Democratic congressmen were unhappy with their leader, Speaker of the House Jim Wright, but they did not want to ask him face-to-face to resign. Instead, they leaked anonymous sto-ries to the news media, according to David Rosenbaum in *The New York Times*. Wright got the message, and the congressmen didn't have to risk alienating him.[27]

Sometimes insiders leak information when they disagree with a decision. Several people in the Reagan White House leaked their con-cerns about a controversial budget proposal because they did not think their objections were getting a fair hearing by Reagan's top ad-visers. After almost daily leaks reporting information contrary to Reagan's economic assessments, the budget proposal was modified.[28]

Stephen Hess, who studies press-government relations, adds an-other variety of leakers to the list. He said that some people will leak stories to get on the good side of a reporter they think can be helpful to them.[29]

Other times, government officials will leak information to just one reporter because they know news outlets tend to play up stories that they have exclusively. Shortly before a State of the Union address by President Clinton, his press secretary leaked different portions of it to reporters from *USA Today, The New York Times* and ABC's *World News Tonight*. The result? "Marginal stories that would barely rate a mention on television were pumped up by virtue of being exclusive," according to *Spin Cycle,* a book by Kurtz on Clinton's media relations.[30]

Occasionally, even seasoned Washington observers can't figure out the motives of people in what Kurtz called the "shadowy world of unnamed sources." He used as an example a *New York Times* story that claimed Gen. Colin Powell was so upset with President Clinton that he might step down as chairman of the Joint Chiefs of Staff. The story, which appeared shortly after Clinton became president, attrib-uted the information to "several close associates" of Powell. The morning the story appeared, Powell appeared on all four network news shows to deny the account. Kurtz wondered if the *Times* had been duped by people who wanted to embarrass Clinton during the early days of his presidency—or if Powell had leaked the story to give himself a forum to show his support of his new boss.

If reporters know that using unnamed sources can lead to these kinds of games, why don't they refuse to play along? One reason is the competitive urge of reporters to score good stories. R.W. Apple Jr., Washington bureau chief of *The New York Times,* told Kurtz: "Ours is a competitive business, and if someone with an authoritative voice says to us a decision has been made to do X, and we check it a couple of other places, we run it. So does *The Washington Post.* So does the *Los Angeles Times.* You're going to be used on occasion. You do your best to get around being used by figuring out motivation and checking the story out from a number of angles."[31]

Sometimes reporters play along because they figure a secret source is better than no source at all. NBC's Timothy Russert noted that reporters covering some criminal investigations may have no other way to get news than to rely on leaks.[32] Similarly, reporters covering fighting in Central America interviewed U.S. embassy people but attributed the information to "Western diplomats" because that title would "inspire confidence in readers" and because they did not want to risk losing access to Embassy sources, according to Frank Smyth, who covered El Salvador for several years.[33]

Occasionally, reporters and news organizations have tried to reduce their use of secret sources. James McCartney, longtime Washington correspondent for Knight-Ridder newspapers, argued that the best thing "that could happen in the journalistic community would be if every reporter were required to take an oath that he would walk out of the office of any official who insisted on talking to him off the record."[34]

Deciding When to Grant Anonymity

Many journalists in the United States believe that certain kinds of information cannot be obtained unless reporters extend confidentiality. "I don't think we can function without it," said Robert M. Steele, director of the ethics program at the Poynter Institute for Media Studies in St. Petersburg, Fla. "It's an essential tool to use at the right time and in the right place."[35] But deciding the right time and right place— and the right amount of secrecy to grant—is no simple matter. Claude Sitton, former editor of the Raleigh *News & Observer,* said at his paper these decisions weren't made until he, the reporters involved and other editors had "prayer meetings" that sometimes included the paper's libel lawyer.[36]

Journalists consider several factors before cloaking a source's identity, including

- **The importance of the story.** Probably the most famous secret source in journalistic history was "Deep Throat," the name that Robert Woodward and Carl Bernstein gave to the anonymous insider who helped them break the Watergate cover-up for *The Washington Post.* Deep Throat was only one of many secret sources used to develop the stories that contributed to the eventual resignation of President Richard Nixon.

- **The motives of the source.** As indicated earlier, sources have lots of reasons to ask for anonymity. Some are good, some are understandable, and some are unacceptable. Most reporters try to figure out the sources' motives before they decide to grant them anonymity. If they suspect they're being fed a trial balloon, they may skip the information. However, many argue that reporters do not do enough to alert readers to sources' motives.

  "It's not immoral to use anonymous sources, but only a small fraction of the time do reporters describe the allegiances or potential biases of the sources," said Tom Rosenstiel, director of the Project for Excellence in Journalism. "We're cheating readers in some ways."[37]

- **Reasons for anonymity.** Sometimes editors must assess the hazards that sources might encounter if their names were used. Some sources might lose their jobs if they are identified. In a few cases, sources might even be physically harmed or even killed. That's the reason Larry Lough, editor of the Muncie, Ind., *Star Press,* gave to explain why his paper—just months after adopting a no-secret-sources rule—used anonymous sources in a story about undercover police officers.[38]

- **Lack of other sources.** Editors are also more likely to bend the rules if regular sources are being unreasonably closemouthed. During the Gulf War, the U.S. military tried to limit press coverage. As a consequence, the number of stories using anonymous sources increased in many newspapers.[39] Other times reporters say they don't have time to find sources who will talk on the record. "You're operating on deadline and you need the information," so the sources are able to demand that their names not be used, said Nina Totenberg of National Public Radio.[40]

- **Matching the competition.** For better or worse, some newspapers soften their ethical policies when they're competing with other news organizations on major stories. Editors at the *St. Petersburg Times,* a paper strongly committed to ethics, said competition combined with tight-lipped officials led them to break their explicit written guidelines about unnamed sources during their coverage of the mutilation murders of five female students at the University of Florida. *The Florida Times-Union* in Jacksonville maintained its policy of requiring reporters to confirm with other sources all information that came from unnamed sources, and editors acknowledged that their coverage wasn't as good as papers with fewer restrictions.[41]

But sometimes the urge to protect sources can lead to difficult decisions. *The San Diego Union-Tribune* quoted anonymously lawyers and judges who called a candidate for district attorney "a dangerous man." An unnamed source said, "I'd hate to see him get into a position of power in the DA's office." The assistant metro editor thought this case was an appropriate use of anonymity. He said it was the paper's "responsibility to reflect what people are saying about the candidate" and the lawyers and judges had an understandable reason not to talk: They feared retaliation from the candidate if he were elected. But the candidate said it was not fair. He thought he should be able to face his accusers. The paper's readers' representative agreed: "This is never any justification for allowing such an attack. It is the epitome of unfairness."

A reporter at the Fort Worth *Star-Telegram* was also taken to task by that paper's ombudsman after she used an anonymous source critical of a minister she was profiling. The source, another minister, had wanted anonymity because she did not want to violate "a generally accepted 'code of silence' that says one minister does not publicly criticize another."[42]

Many papers require reporters to explain in their stories why sources were granted anonymity. That allows readers to draw some conclusions about how credible secret sources are. It also reduces the number of secret sources because reporters know they will have to justify their decisions.

Rituals of Confidentiality

Journalists and their sources have invented a variety of labels to apply to various degrees of confidentiality, such as "off the record," "without attribution," "on background" and "on deep background." One problem is that not all reporters mean the same things when they use these terms, and many sources are understandably confused. Sometimes reporters and sources use the phrase "off the record" to mean what others would call "without attribution."

"Off the record" usually means that reporters will listen to the information but promise never to use it. For that reason, many reporters never go off the record. But other reporters have found that some off-the-record information has kept them from writing stories that are mistaken or incomplete. More frequently, reporters accept off-the-record information in hopes of finding another source who will go on the record. But this tactic has one major drawback: The reporter may burn the source without meaning to. If the reporter seems to know too much about what's going on, other officials may recognize that someone has leaked information and they may guess who it was.

Many reporters will not take off-the-record information unless the source understands that they will try to verify it elsewhere. Without that provision, reporters are afraid they will hear a lot of great stories they will never get to write. Anonymous sources used only to confirm information are called "deep background sources," a term invented by Woodward and Bernstein during their Watergate investigation for *The Washington Post.* "Deep Throat" was a deep background source.[43]

When sources ask to go off the record, most reporters try to talk them into staying on the record. Reporters have found that many people who approach them with information really want to get things off their chests and will decide to talk on the record. But if they refuse to go on the record, some reporters will ask the sources to let them use the information without attaching their names to it. "Without attribution" is the normal label for this agreement.

Occasionally, at the end of an interview, reporters are hit with a tricky request. The source will ask, "You're not going to quote me, are you?" Before reporters answer that question, many take into consideration how media smart the person is. If the person deals with the media regularly and if the reporters made it clear they were talking with the person to get information for a story, most reporters believe the interview is on the record and feel justified in using the information and the person's name. But many reporters temper that rule if their source is not used to dealing with reporters. Business writer Gary Ruderman wrote that if he is convinced the source is not "playing dumb," he may consider using the quotes but not using the person's name.[44]

A reporter for the student newspaper at the University of Missouri–St. Louis was handed a similar belated request for confidentiality. At the beginning of a well-publicized speech on campus, NBC sportscaster Bob Costas announced that his comments were off the record. He then made several biting comments critical of NBC and its sports coverage. The student editors decided to honor his request and did not run the story. The paper's adviser was surprised by Costas' request: "If anyone else did what he did, I can see him rising up in righteous indignation. I find what he did to be astonishing." Costas later told *Editor & Publisher* that he had decided not to make any more off-the-record public appearances.[45]

The phrase "on background" is used by journalists in two ways. Sometimes it is used much as the name suggests: Sources offer reporters background information that will give them a better understanding of complicated news events. Ruderman said that he considers backgrounders essential when he is working on stories about complicated topics. He wrote that if he were assigned a story on the "intricacies of floor and ceiling guarantees on the London Interbank Offering Rate," he would call a banking source for a "fast course" on "how it works and what are the pitfalls." He could then begin reporting the story with more expertise.[46] Since much of the information he received would be common knowledge to the industry, he probably would not attribute it to his source.

Other times, background sessions are meetings between reporters and government leaders—sometimes at breakfast—for free-form discussions of the issues. The participants agree in advance whether the information will be on or off the record. Journalists are divided on the usefulness of such meetings when they are off the record. Some say it is a good opportunity to get an understanding of the thinking of key officials. Others believe it provides officials with opportunities to plant stories without being accountable. A *New York Times* reporter attended a backgrounder in the White House Map Room with six other reporters and found it to be of little value. If the meetings had been on the record, he said, the reporters would have asked Clinton tough questions and written front-page stories. However, "there was no point in asking tough questions, since it would just piss off the president and you couldn't use it anyway."[47]

The "backgrounder" has evolved its own style of attribution in Washington. Often the understanding is that the information and opinions expressed can be used, but they must be attributed to "a senior White House official," a "State Department adviser," a "key congressional aide" or some other designation. When Henry Kissinger was Richard Nixon's secretary of state, he often gave interviews in which he was to be identified as "a high State Department official traveling on the secretary of state's plane." Most readers soon figured out who the source was.[48]

Press aides for Clinton created another way of masking attribution. After off-the-record meetings, reporters can ask press aides if some of his comments can be used. Often they were told to attribute them like this: "Clinton has told friends that . . ." Other times Clinton held what some called "psychic backgrounders." Reporters could use the material, but they had to write it as if it were their own musings about what the president must be thinking.[49]

Breaking Their Promises

On rare occasions, reporters and their editors get so bothered by their dealings in this shady business of leaks and clandestine sources that they decide to expose their "secret" sources.

One such incident involved Oliver North, a Marine colonel who played a key role in several secret international dealings during the Reagan administration including supplying weapons to guerrilla forces in Central America. When he was charged with lying to Congress, he admitted that he had not told Congress the truth about his activities. But, he testified at hearings, he lied because he could not trust Congress to keep the information secret. North then cited some specific cases in which he believed his work had been hindered by leaks from Congress.

Many journalists were stunned by North's allegations. They knew it was North himself—not members of Congress—who had leaked the information in those specific cases. *Newsweek* editors believed this violation of trust was so great that they broke their pledge of confidentiality and identified North. "Given these unusual circumstances, we felt an obligation to point out to our readers that North himself was a frequent source of administration leaks," *Newsweek*'s editor said.[50]

Sometimes reporters decide to break confidences because they believe that informing the public of what the source said is more important than keeping their word. That was the decision Milton Coleman made when he was covering politics for *The Washington Post*. When Jesse Jackson was running for the Democratic nomination for president, he said to Coleman, "Let's talk black talk." Coleman, who is black, had heard Jackson use the phrase before and understood it to mean that the conversation was off the record. "Jackson then talked about the preoccupation of some with Israel," Coleman wrote. "He said something to the effect of the following: That's all Hymie wants to talk about is Israel; every time you go to Hymietown, that's all they want to talk about." Coleman claimed he had never heard Jackson use those words before, and he made a mental note of the conversation.

Although Coleman did not write a story about the remarks himself because he felt there was no context for them in any of his stories, he passed Jackson's comments to another *Post* reporter who was doing a story about Jackson's difficulties with Jewish voters. The 37th paragraph of his 52-inch story read: "In private conversations with reporters, Jackson has referred to Jews as 'Hymie' and to New York as 'Hymietown.'" The comments seemed to go unnoticed at first until the *Post* published an editorial calling on Jackson to explain his use of those "degrading and disgusting" words. Jackson, after first insisting he could not recall using them, finally conceded that his remarks were "insensitive" and denied that what he said "in any way reflects my basic attitude toward Jews or Israel."[51]

Coleman said he thought he was right in repeating Jackson's racist remarks because Jackson "was presenting himself for the highest elective office in this land" and "he had said something that appeared to at least stereotype if not . . . denigrate a group of American electors. That statement ought to be brought to the public's attention." He argued that "the convention of background and nonattribution has never been intended to hide remarks that would denigrate a particular group of people."[52]

Many journalists supported both Coleman's and *Newsweek*'s decisions to violate their pledges to sources. But other journalists vehemently criticized them. Many *Newsweek* staffers let it be known that they opposed their editors' decision in the North case. These journalists worried that incidents like these may persuade other sources to refuse to provide needed information because they believe that they can't trust reporters' promises. Sources for information might dry up. Besides, many journalists find the whole idea of not keeping their word distasteful.

A Supreme Court ruling in 1991 gave journalists another reason to abide by pledges of confidentiality. The court ruled that a pledge of confidentiality is a binding contract between the reporter and the source. The case grew out of stories in the Minneapolis *Star Tribune* and the *St. Paul Pioneer Press*. A Republican politician gave reporters copies of documents revealing that the Democratic candidate for lieutenant governor had been convicted of shoplifting 12 years before. The man passed out his copies a week before the election with the understanding that he would not be identified as the source. All the newspaper and broadcast reporters agreed, and none of the reporters used the man's name in their stories.

But editors at the two Twin Cities newspapers weren't so sure that keeping the source's name secret was a good idea. At the *Star Tribune* about 15 editors debated the story. Many thought the 12-year-old conviction itself was not news. The real story, they thought, was the use of dirty tricks by the Republicans. After having another reporter confirm that the only person who had checked out the court file on the case in several years had ties to the Republican politician, the *Star Tribune* decided to print his name despite the pledge the reporter had made. Editors at the *Pioneer Press* came to a similar conclusion. John R. Finnegan, vice president and editor of the St. Paul paper, accused the politician of "trying, in the most blatant way, to manipulate the Twin Cities media for maximum exposure with no risk to himself or his party."

When the story broke, both reporters were angry. And so was the source. The bad publicity cost him his job with a public relations firm. He sued the papers for breach of contract, misrepresentation and fraud and won.[53]

Secret Sources, Reporters and Jail

Virtually all journalists who grant sources anonymity keep their names secret when they write their stories. The touchier decision sometimes comes after the stories are printed. Prosecutors, defense lawyers or lawyers in civil cases may read the stories and demand that the reporters reveal their sources. These attorneys contend that unless these sources testify in court, innocent people may go to jail, guilty people may walk free, or injured parties won't receive just settlements. They ask judges to order reporters to name their sources or be held in contempt of court.

Many reporters have had to make that decision. Tim Roche, a 24-year-old reporter, was sentenced to 30 days in jail in 1993 for refusing to reveal sources he used in stories he wrote about a child-custody battle he covered for *The Stuart (Fla.) News*. The child's foster mother said his initial stories on the case may have helped save the life of the child who was going to be returned to an abusive home.[54] And Timothy Phelps of *Newsday* and Nina Totenberg of National Public Radio were threatened with contempt of Congress when they refused to identify sources they used to reveal Anita Hill's claims of sexual harrassment by Supreme Court Justice nominee Clarence Thomas.[55]

Once in a while, reporters are saved from jail when their sources identify themselves to authorities. Susan Wornick, a reporter for WCVB-TV in Boston, had been ordered to three months in jail by a judge after she defied his order to name the sole eyewitness to a drugstore burglary. Wornick told the judge that she had promised confidentiality to the eyewitness because he feared retaliation by police. The burglary was allegedly committed by members of the Revere, Mass., police force. After the man came forward and testified before a grand jury, the judge withdrew his contempt ruling against the reporter.[56]

Not all stories that can land reporters in jail are the kind that save children from abuse, protect people from corrupt police officers or question the integrity of a Supreme Court nominee. The first reporter in modern times to go to jail to protect a source was Marie Torre, radio-TV critic of the old *New York Herald Tribune.* In 1958, she refused to identify the CBS executive she had quoted in her column to the effect that Judy Garland, the actress who played Dorothy in *The Wizard of Oz,* was being dropped from a TV program because she was too fat.

Many news organizations believe anonymous sources are so basic to journalism that they have sought laws to shield reporters from having to identify their sources. About half the states have shield laws, which vary greatly in effectiveness. In states without shield laws, judges have applied either common law or provisions in state constitutions to give some protection to journalists.[57]

But still, the sight of a subpoena being served in a newsroom is not a rarity. About 3,000 subpoenas are issued each year, ordering news organizations to turn over news articles, photographs, videotapes and reporters' notes. Most of them are complied with because the material had been printed or broadcast. But media contest about a third of the subpoenas, and shield laws quash a small percentage.[58]

Using secret sources can create other legal problems, too. News organizations may have trouble winning libel suits if the sources will not testify in court. At some newspapers, editors consult with libel attorneys before using sensitive stories based on anonymous sources. An Associated Press Managing Editors committee has suggested that if reporters can't get sources to go on the record, they ask them to agree that the paper will keep their identities secret unless there is a libel suit.[59] *The Seattle Times* took this step when it decided to mask the identity of the women who accused Sen. Brock Adams of sexual harassment.

Paying Sources for Information

While not common among American newspapers, paying sources for information, photos or interviews—exclusive or otherwise—is accepted practice in other countries. "The British tabloids are notorious for buying their 'scoops,' and the juicier the scandal, the higher the price," Tamara Jones, a *Los Angeles Times* foreign correspondent, discovered. Throughout Europe, government officials often demand "honorariums" before they grant interviews. Sports stars like Boris Becker, Steffi Graf, and some soccer players often receive large amounts of money before they will talk with European reporters.[60] In Moscow, interviews with law enforcement officials can cost as much as $400, an interview with death row inmates can be arranged for

$1,000 and getting guards to allow picture taking inside the Lenin Mausoleum can cost $5,000.[61]

Checkbook journalism on that level has not come to the United States although there have been notable exceptions. CBS once paid $100,000 for an interview with H.R. Haldeman, Richard Nixon's top White House aide, and then several years later gave Nixon himself $500,000 for a 90-minute interview.[62] The editor of the *Los Angeles Times* admitted his paper paid a court official "quite a bit" of money for sealed court documents during the investigation of the Manson murders in California in 1969.[63]

Both CBS and the *Times* were heavily criticized for their activities, and each has since adopted a formal practice against paying for information. Few mainstream news organizations pay money for interviews.

The debate over paying for interviews was rekindled in the early 1990s by talk shows like *Donahue* and *The Jenny Jones Show* and by tabloid TV news programs like *Hard Copy* and *Inside Edition*. These programs were often willing to buy interviews in hopes of scoring bigger ratings. When a religious cult in Waco, Texas, had a shootout with federal officers and touched off a siege at the cult's compound, one tabloid TV program paid the mother of the leader of the cult, David Koresh, for interviews. The rush for ratings is so great that several programs got into a bidding war to interview a group of high school boys whose claim to fame was that they formed a club that awarded points for sexual conquests of girls at their school.[64]

The mainstream media often smirk at such antics, but they are not entirely virtuous. During the 1992 presidential campaign, *Star,* a grocery store tabloid, paid Gennifer Flowers (reportedly $150,000) for her account of an affair she said she had with Bill Clinton. Although most American dailies would not stoop to paying Flowers, nearly all of them repeated her unsubstantiated allegations once the *Star* announced its coup. (This episode is discussed further in Chapter 8.) The *Star*'s stories touched off a media hunt to find more women willing to tell stories about Clinton. *The Washington Times* reported that a British tabloid was offering $500,000 to anyone who could confirm Flowers' story. Michael Hedges, a *Times* reporter, was told several women were willing to invent stories of affairs with Clinton if the price was right.[65]

Why Not Pay for Interviews?

One argument against checkbook journalism is that some people will lie or exaggerate if it puts bucks in their pockets. *Newsweek* magazine learned that lesson. For a story on the spread of AIDS, reporters for *Newsweek* found a prostitute who said she had AIDS but continued to work the streets. The magazine paid her $60 for her story. After the article appeared, the woman told authorities and other reporters that she had lied to *Newsweek* to get money to feed her heroin habit. Police were unable to determine if she had AIDS and did not press charges.[66]

Legal and media scholars are bothered by the growing number of cases in which news organizations offer payments to jurors before they render their decisions in highly publicized trials. Just before testimony started in the trial of Bernard Goetz for the shooting of a would-be mugger in a New York subway, the *New York Post* arranged to buy the comments of one juror for nearly $5,000, while the *Daily News* gave another $2,500. What troubles people in the legal community about these payoffs is the fear that these jurors may try to make verdicts more sensational in hopes of getting more money.[67]

Many also worry that people in high-profile cases may "embellish" what they know in hopes of getting the attention of a tabloid. In the O.J. Simpson case, some potential witnesses were not called to testify after they sold their information to tabloids. Prosecutors feared their testimony had been tainted by payoffs. Shortly after the Simpson trial, the California legislature passed measures making it illegal for witnesses to accept money from the media. Those laws are being challenged in the courts.[68]

A second argument against checkbook journalism is that many people will withhold information unless they are paid for it. Reporters have been hounded for payoffs by eyewitnesses at crime scenes and tragedies. Some have even been threatened. A reporter and a photographer with the *Detroit Free Press* said they feared a drug addict they were interviewing "might become violent if he wasn't given any money." The reporters at first refused to fork over cash but then agreed to buy a portable radio and a sausage from the man. When editors found out what they had done, they were suspended without pay for a few days.[69]

The Los Angeles police officers on trial in the Rodney King beating stopped talking to reporters in the middle of their second trial. They had decided to peddle interviews to the highest bidders. The *Donahue* show paid two of them $25,000 each, while *A Current Affair* paid one, Stacey Koon, $10,000.

When gang violence in Los Angeles became a national story in the early 1990s, a county government official with ties to the gangs often helped arrange interviews but told reporters that the gang members would want money.[70] "The money is not buying a story," he argued. "It is showing respect" to the gang member.

Many TV news shows have had trouble getting people to appear on their shows without being paid. A producer for ABC's newsmagazines, which do not buy interviews, said it now takes "a lot more persuasion" to get people to appear on ABC's news programs.[71]

Some of the "persuasion" newsmagazines use is even less ethical than paying money, according to *60 Minutes* executive producer Don Hewitt. Some producers promise that if people appear on their programs they will be asked only soft questions. Hewitt said that the extensive discussions with press agents and book publishers about what will and will not be asked is not healthy for journalism. Hewitt also criticized programs that agree to show book covers if authors will agree to be interviewed.[72]

But making promises appears to be standard practice when the networks try to land newsworthy interviews. When two babies were switched in a Virginia hospital, the media hustled to arrange interviews. The family said that a CBS reporter promised one mother that if she appeared on his network, she would be interviewed by anchor Dan Rather. ABC's *20/20* upped the ante. Barbara Walters personally called her and asked her to appear on *20/20*. The mother said later, "She's a very nice woman. She told me her heart breaks for me." The mother turned down CBS but appeared with the baby's maternal grandparents on *20/20*. (The families also got plenty of offers of money. *Star,* a grocery store tabloid, reportedly offered $50,000 for a pictures of the babies.)[73]

Recently news directors have run into another problem: people wanting money for their amateur video of news events. Marci Burdick, news director at KYTV in Springfield, Mo., said, "Even at this level, around the 80th [largest] market, it is an increasing trend. People are shopping their home video and trying to get us into a bidding war." George Bagley, a former news photographer for a Salt Lake City TV station, has seen that happen. When he arrived at the scene of an avalanche, an amateur photographer offered to sell him photos. When he hesitated, the man began to hawk the pictures to other news crews. One of them bought the pictures.[74]

A third argument against checkbook journalism is that it may lower the quality of the reporting itself. If a TV program or tabloid newspaper has paid big bucks for an interview and has promoted it in order to get higher ratings or street sales, the people doing the interview may be less likely to push the source with tough questions and to expose inaccuracies in the information. A *PrimeTime Live* producer noted that since the programs pay for the interviews, "they also script them, so it's not really real."[75]

A fourth argument is purely financial. News organizations fear that if they begin to pay for interviews they will be required to shell out a constant stream of cash.

Is Information a Commodity?

Some reporters see contradictions in outright bans on checkbook journalism. John Tierney, a reporter for *The New York Times* who wrote a series of stories about street people in New York, stated that many of them asked him for payment in exchange for being interviewed. "Sometimes I explained that I couldn't pay them, but that I could buy them a meal during the interview," he wrote. "Things would go well until we sat down in a restaurant and the person announced: 'I'm not hungry now. Just give me the money and I'll eat later.'" Tierney claimed it is difficult to explain why it is "ethically superior to buy a homeless man a $30 dinner than it was to give him $10 in cash."

To learn about the drug culture, Tierney once paid a drug user to give him "a tour of shooting galleries and crack houses." He stated that he considered the fee much like paying an interpreter or guide in a foreign country. But Tierney balked when his "tour guide" offered to take him to a crack-driven sex party the next day. When Tierney asked what time the party would begin, the guide told him to name a time. Tierney wrote that it was obvious that his money was going to be used to arrange the event.

Tierney contends some interviews would be easier if there was a cash transaction between source and reporter because it would clarify the relationship. Then sources would understand that he was neither a friend nor an advocate. They would know he was a reporter who had paid them for information for his stories. But Tierney cautioned that he did not believe all sources should be paid. When they are paid, he believed readers should be given details of the deal.[76]

Some media people argue that some stories are important enough to pay for. Appearing on ABC's *Nightline*, Phil Donahue, a pioneer of the TV talk show format, said, "I think checkbook journalism is here. We operate in the marketplace." Donahue said that if Adolf Hitler were to be discovered alive today, he doubted many news organizations would refuse to interview him because he demanded $100 in advance.[77]

Others contend that information in our society is commonly bought and sold. Jack Landau, a journalist and lawyer who directed the Reporters Committee for Freedom of the Press, has said he can't understand why newspapers willingly buy photographs of news events if their own photographers were not there and pay columnists for their ideas but then balk at paying eyewitnesses and experts.[78] Others note that news organizations make their profits selling information. Why shouldn't the people who are interviewed—and therefore are the original sources of the information—share in the profits?

But journalists remain overwhelmingly opposed to checkbook journalism. In one poll only 17 percent of journalists said they thought paying for an interview would ever be justified.[79] Polls have found that the public, too, opposes the practice. Fewer than a third of them believe checkbook journalism is ethically acceptable.[80]

8

Privacy

When 15-year-old Grant Hussey was reported missing from his job at a grocery store in Eden Prairie, Minn., the community reacted with alarm. Only a few days earlier, another child had been abducted. Residents of the Minneapolis suburb plastered more than 40,000 fliers about the missing teen on trees and in storefronts, and 500 people rallied at City Hall to help publicize the boy's disappearance. Even the local Chamber of Commerce got involved and promoted a "white ribbon" campaign. The boy's disappearance and the community's re-action were, of course, news. But deciding how to cover this story be-came a "gut-wrenching" test of the ethics of reporters, editors and news directors.

The same day Grant Hussey disappeared, a 30-year-old neighbor also was reported missing. Stephan Eastburn, who lived across the street from the teen, had gone fishing with Grant and his father, and the family had allowed Grant to go on an overnight hunting trip with Eastburn. Reporters wondered among themselves if the two disap-pearances were related. Their suspicions intensified when, at a tearful news conference, the boy's father did not want to talk about any pos-sible connection between them. "We just want to focus on getting [Grant] home, that's all we're thinking about," he said.

Reporters quickly learned some troubling background. About a week before Hussey was abducted, Eastburn had called the boy's par-ents and confessed that he had sexually molested their son. Eastburn told them he wanted to kill himself. When the parents looked out their window and saw Eastburn in his garage pointing a gun at his head, they called police. While being questioned by detectives, Eastburn admitted he had sex with the boy while they were on the hunting trip. According to police reports, he said he "could not understand why he would hurt someone whom he cared about so deeply." Eastburn was charged with criminal sexual conduct. A judge released him on a $5,000 bond and ordered him to stay away from the boy.

When they learned of this, editors and news directors faced the first of a series of ethical tests. Most news outlets have rules against naming the victims of sex crimes. Initially, one TV station decided to follow that rule and only hinted at a relationship. But most of the Minneapolis media reported that Eastburn had confessed to molesting the boy. The *Star Tribune* provided this additional detail: "Eastburn then told investigators in a taped statement that he had first molested the boy when they were camping on Saturday night and that the next morning he tied his hands and feet, then loosened the ties and sexually assaulted him."

Following these reports, the Husseys and Eastburn's aunt appeared together in a televised news conference. "Stephan and Grant, we are very concerned about both of you; we want you safely to return," the teen's mother said. "We do not blame either of you. We are praying for your safety. Grant, I miss you so tremendously." The aunt addressed Eastburn: "I know I can depend on you to do the right thing. I am with you 100 percent; I would never turn on you. I look forward to talking to you."

As the coverage continued, editors at the Minneapolis *Star Tribune* had an even tougher decision. A reporter had been tipped that the teenager had been to Alternatives, a gay counseling and antiviolence center, with questions about his sexuality. His visits were weeks before he was assaulted by Eastburn. When the reporter called the parents to get their reactions and comments, they begged the paper not to print the story.

Later that day, while editors were still discussing whether to run the counseling story, the bodies of Hussey and Eastburn were found in a car near where they lived. Police concluded that Eastburn kidnapped Hussey and drove straight to a remote section of a wildlife preserve. There he shot Hussey with a rifle and then killed himself, probably within an hour of the abduction. TV stations interrupted their programming to report the discovery of the bodies. It was the lead story in the next day's *Star Tribune*. Along with the main story, the *Star Tribune* printed the story about Hussey's visit to the gay counseling center.

That same day, editors at the *St. Paul Pioneer Press* also had a decision to make. One of their photographers took an aerial photo through the windshield of Eastburn's car. The legs of the man and the teen could be seen with the teen in the passenger seat and Eastburn behind the wheel. Between Eastburn's legs was the rifle. Neither their faces nor any blood was visible. Editors decided to illustrate the story with this powerful picture.

The Hussey story was the major topic on talk radio shows and in conversations among friends for days and days. Although some people discussed the failure of the criminal justice system in this case, most thought the real villains were the news media. They wondered why newspapers and TV stations had reported so many details of the teen's life and of the murder-suicide. They thought it was insensitive and sensational. And many were appalled that the *Star Tribune* would print a story reporting that a teen had been to a counseling center. They argued that there was no need to "out" the teen and that such visits should be confidential.

Questions about whether a journalist should reveal intimate details about the lives of people are privacy questions. Some people think of privacy as a legal issue, involving lawyers and standards set by the courts. They are partly right. Several famous and not-so-famous lawsuits against the media have involved questions of invasion of privacy as the law has defined it. But the privacy decisions that journalists usually face are more ethical than legal: not whether it would be legal to seek out and report certain private information, but whether it is ethical.

Much of the information published and broadcast in this country is regarded by some of the people involved as private information. A political candidate may consider it a private matter that he was disbarred for mishandling clients' money, or a drunken driver may not welcome news accounts about an accident in which he killed a child. The question for journalists is not whether to invade privacy but when and how much. At what point does an invasion of privacy pass from reasonable to unreasonable? The public believes the media do it far too often. Surveys by the Pew Foundation found that 80 percent of the respondents were fed up with what they consider the media's invasions of people's privacy.

Three Conflicting Obligations

When making many tough ethical decisions, *Pioneer Press* editor Walker Lundy said rules and guidelines aren't much help. His paper has an ethics code with rules that ban freebies and misrepresentation. "But to try to draft a rule that would help you in the case of the Grant Hussey picture," he said. "There was a lot of debate that night, and the way we make most controversial decisions like this in the newsroom is not a single person saying, 'We're gonna do it,' but a lot of people getting involved—photo people and word people and editors together—and talking about it at some length."

At the *Star Tribune* the process was similar. Doug Smith, an assistant city editor, said editors had heated discussions. "It was a gut-wrenching evening."

Decisions involving privacy often require journalists to balance three sometimes conflicting obligations:

- To get the news out
- To show compassion
- To educate society

To Get the News Out

Journalists know that they have an obligation to get the news and report it to their viewers and readers. As *Pioneer Press* editor Lundy said, "The foremost issue for us is our job, which is to tell people what we know. They hire us: They pay us a quarter a day not to keep things from them but to tell them what we know, and that's what we do." Of course, Lundy said, there are stories that he would not print. "But there has to be an overriding reason to withhold anything from our readers."

Star Tribune editors and reporters struggled to figure out if they should report that the teen had been sexually molested by Eastburn. "I haven't seen a case like that before," Smith said. "We went counter to policy, naming a juvenile victim of sexual abuse when we ran the charges of molestation of Grant Hussey by Eastburn. It didn't make a lot of us feel good to lay it out there in public—we never do that—but this time it was an important element of the story."

For similar reasons, editors decided to report that Hussey had sought counseling. They believed the information "gave a more complete picture of the crime and what may have led up to it." *Star Tribune* Editor Tim McGuire was concerned that readers might believe that Grant was "a kid standing on a street corner who was randomly selected." Instead, McGuire said, there was a complicated relationship between Grant and Eastburn. "Without that information [about the earlier molestation and the teen's questions about his sexual identity], readers were left with only half a picture. It is our job to enlighten readers, not to withhold information." That night Bob Schafer, assistant managing editor, said editors were asked, "Was the story relevant? Did it provide greater understanding of the events surrounding the youth's death?" He said the consensus among the editors was yes.

To Show Compassion

Most people who have been in the news business very long know of facts that weren't reported because they would have brought unnecessary harm to people. At a reception with hundreds of people and many TV crews, a man lifted himself out of his wheelchair when introduced to President Clinton. Unfortunately, the man's pants fell down. Only cable's Fox News Network showed the incident, and it digitally distorted the man and his private parts. In the 1980s, news organizations from around the world carried stories about the "bubble boy," a child born in Houston who had an immune deficiency that forced him to live in a germ-free bubble. But none of the stories gave his complete name—he was called only David—or hinted at where he lived so that his family could live as normal a life as possible. Most newspapers do not print the names of rape victims for similar reasons.

Many readers thought Grant Hussey deserved that same kind of compassion, and they let the paper know it. Readers complained about the paper's reporting that the boy was the victim of a sex crime. "If Grant is returned, it's going to be a real tough thing to live with," one reader wrote. The boy's father was also angry. He called the stories "very insensitive, irresponsible and unnecessary." He said, "I don't think it was protecting the legal and moral rights of a juvenile."

Star Tribune ombudsman Lou Gelfand and editorial writer Jennifer Juarez Robles agreed with some of the criticism. Juarez Robles wrote, "For the *Star Tribune* to have withheld certain controversial details of Hussey's life would have meant abandoning journalism's public service mission. Yet the newspaper might have lessened the harm by postponing the story for a day [and] by explaining quickly and in greater detail its decision to publish."

To Educate Society

On occasion the media's invasion of people's privacy has helped knock down stereotypes and undermine stigmas that contribute to public ignorance and bigotry. Alcoholism, prescription drug abuse, various cancers and AIDS have received detailed news coverage that has raised public understanding and lowered the secrecy that once surrounded these conditions.

Some editors at the *Star Tribune* hoped their coverage of Grant Hussey might have a positive effect. One editor thought "the story brought greater understanding to the difficulties that 15-year-old youths face and that it was worthwhile to publish if it somehow might help other youths who were struggling with questions of sexual identity—and help their parents as well." Assistant managing editor Schafer said that comment was key in the decision to go ahead with the story. McGuire said he saw heavy traces of homophobia in some objections to his paper's stories. Some used words like "embarrassing," "distasteful," "ugly" and "not fit to be printed." McGuire said that if the paper had not printed the stories for those reasons, "we would have been buying into the premise that teen struggles with sexuality are something to be hidden and are, in fact, shameful. I could not get comfortable with that."

However, Juarez Robles believed the paper could have found a better way to educate society about the problems of teens and sexual identity. She suggested reporters might have used the Hussey case for a story that would have looked into the larger issues surrounding teen sexuality. Juarez Robles conceded that it's not easy to weigh the public benefits of publication against the anguish caused to the Hussey family. But, she hoped, "Maybe some of the futility and pain of Grant's very public death will help create an environment where young people won't feel the need to struggle in secret."[1]

Privacy of Ordinary People

Cases as complicated as the Hussey murder-suicide do not happen often. Yet ordinary people get involved in newsworthy events every day. At least for the moment, the news media usually treat these people like public figures. Some of them, such as marchers, protesters and criminals, take actions that thrust themselves into the news. Others, such as victims of crime or tragedies, suddenly find themselves in the media spotlight. Many journalists worry about hurting ordinary people who, often through no design of their own, find themselves being interviewed and photographed for display in newspapers and on news broadcasts.

Names, Addresses and Ages

In earlier times, the rule was clear. Reporters were supposed to get the exact names including middle initials of people in the news, their exact ages and their exact addresses. It was argued that full identification saved the reputation of innocent people. If the story said John G. Smith, 62, 1234 Primrose St., was charged with drunken driving, then John L. Smith, 24, 1252 Primrose St., would be off the hook.

However, full identification can also create problems. Many papers have stopped using exact addresses because printing this information may endanger residents. One small-town editor said that when her paper reported that a gun had been stolen from an address, other burglars would target the home because they knew the family kept guns and would most likely replace the weapon. Similarly, burglars have been known to read obituaries to find out when families will be at funerals so they can loot their empty homes. Also, many editors say that not using complete addresses eliminates embarrassing errors caused either by sloppy record keeping by officials or by criminals who give wrong addresses to police.

The Charlotte Observer found that publishing a name and address even in a routine feature story can sometimes spur harassment. The *Observer* ran an interesting but fairly standard photograph on its front page showing a mother strolling her 6-year-old daughter to the first day of classes at her elementary school. The caption under the photo identified the mother and daughter and gave their address. Four days later, the mother called the paper to complain that she had received more than 100 telephone calls, some obscene, some threatening, some from men in jail, some from men who wanted to meet her, others from men who wanted to meet her daughter. "Do you realize that hundreds of sick people know who I am and where I live?" she asked city editor Greg Ring. The calls and letters stopped after about two weeks, but the mother's anger continued long after that. "Newspaper editors need to pay attention to what they're doing to innocent people," she said.[2]

Many editors got the message. Some newspapers no longer use exact addresses in any stories, and the majority no longer use them in crime stories. Often exact addresses are replaced with block numbers (1200 block of South Primrose Street) or less specific identifications.[3]

Using exact ages is another kind of problem. If people's ages appear in the paper, it is unlikely to increase the chances that they will be burglarized or harassed. But for many people, age is a very private matter. Some editors believe ages should be used only when they are relevant to the story. They contend that ages of people who speak at governmental meetings usually add little to a story. But other editors aren't so sure. Although *The Dallas Morning News* has a policy of using ages only when they are relevant, "age seems always to be relevant," John Davenport, assistant to the managing editor of the paper, told *Presstime*.[4]

Diseases

Americans have traditionally been squeamish about diseases that cause death. Once the word "cancer" was spoken only in whispers. News accounts would not say someone died of cancer but of a "lingering illness." It took several public-education campaigns to get cancer recognized as a disease and not a moral failing.

Early on, doctors did not know what AIDS was and how the disease was spread. Eventually scientists learned that many gay men had acquired the disease during anal intercourse. But many newspapers saw themselves as family-oriented and would not print those words. As Daniel Lynch, managing editor of *The Times Union* in Albany, N.Y., noted, papers used euphemisms such as "exchange of bodily fluids" or "intimate sexual contact."

Lynch wrote that this shyness in reporting the way the disease is spread contributed to two misunderstandings. First, many people incorrectly guessed what kinds of "intimate sexual contact" spread the disease. Second, because the media were not forthcoming in reporting the way the disease was spread, many people developed mistaken ideas. Media gave so much attention to people who had received the disease through blood transfusions that many believed that was the most common way to acquire it.[5]

The AIDS discussion also opened the media to the use of the word "condom." Bill Wheatley, former executive producer of *NBC Nightly News,* recalled that in the mid-1980s, staffers at NBC had a lengthy debate over whether America was ready to hear that word on a network newscast.[6]

Many readers believe some body parts are just too private to be shown in the media. Many newspapers and TV stations have received complaints after using pictures and illustrations with stories that explain how women can check themselves for breast cancer. One woman wrote a letter to one paper asking if the paper would illustrate a story about prostate cancer with similarly explicit pictures.[7]

Naming Crime Victims

The news media's treatment of victims of crimes has been criticized by many, including some journalists who themselves have become the victims of crime. Thomas Oliphant, a columnist for *The Boston Globe,* wrote: "I got mugged the night before last, a humiliating opportunity to be reminded that the allies of crime victims are the cops, not the press. Any crime, of course, is humiliating. Most cops understand this and treat crime victims as people. Most journalists don't understand this and treat us as subjects."

Oliphant wrote that after the crime he was pulled in two directions. He wanted to call the police in hopes the mugger would be caught. Yet he knew that by dialing 911 he would give up his privacy. He knew that some people would wonder what he was doing walking where he was that late at night. And others would chuckle that a liberal columnist had been the target of street crime. "What infuriates me as a crime victim," he wrote, "is that the press would insist that it alone can decide when I lose my privacy, and that my recourse to contest that decision is virtually nonexistent."[8] Other victims of crime have also complained that news reports made them the subject of ridicule or the center of attention about an event they would just as soon forget.

A handful of news organizations will not name victims of crimes. But in most newsrooms, reporters and editors decide whether to use the name on a case-by-case basis. Typically, if the name appears in the police log, journalists are likely to use it unless the crime is likely to cause embarrassment. When a recently widowed woman in her 70s was bilked out of $300,000 by a psychic, TV stations in Orlando agreed to use only her first name and to blur her face so she could not be recognized. The local newspaper, however, printed her full name and the community in which she lived. In a story about dishonest repairmen who prey on the elderly, *The Washington Post* decided to avoid embarrassing the victims and used only their first names.[9]

Naming People Suspected of Crimes

When people have been formally charged with a crime, most news organizations feel free to use their names. Three-fourths of editors surveyed said they will use the names of suspects who are in custody but not formally charged. However, only a fifth of them will name suspects not yet arrested or charged.[10]

This split was seen in the coverage of the gang-related killing of an 11-year-old boy in a drive-by shooting in Minneapolis. The investigation into the shooting bogged down, reportedly because people in the community did not want to talk to white detectives. Eventually, police settled on a suspect. A reporter with good sources in the police department was given the suspect's name. However, her station, WCCO-TV, did not report her scoop. It has a policy against naming suspects until they are charged. Other Minneapolis media were not so reticent. By the next day, most police-beat reporters had been tipped, and TV stations

and the Minneapolis *Star Tribune* used the suspect's name and photograph. Three days later, police released the suspect, saying they did not
have enough evidence to charge him. The WCCO reporter was proud
that her station had held firm to its policy: "You can always add to a
story, but you can never take something away from it."[11]

Perhaps the most notorious case of naming a suspect was the
Richard Jewell affair. Jewell's name was leaked by law enforcement
officials as their prime suspect in the bombing at the Olympic Games
in Atlanta. *The Atlanta Journal-Constitution* checked out the tip and
confirmed that police and FBI agents were following Jewell and maintaining 24-hour surveillance of his apartment. Confident the tip was
correct, the paper named Jewell as a suspect. CNN then reported the
story, attributing it the *Journal-Constitution*. Soon Jewell's name and
picture were indelibly linked to the bombing. For the next three
months, the public learned all about his job failures and his social life.
Journalists who had never met him became pop psychologists analyz-
ing him. Then law enforcement officials determined that Jewell had
no role in the bombing.

Many journalists think the *Journal-Constitution* was right in
printing the story. They point out that the bombing and the search for
the bomber were international news. Also, the paper's story was
truthful: Jewell clearly was a suspect in the crime. The paper's publisher wrote, "We honored our obligation to the public and accurately
reported on the status of the investigation."[12] Once Jewell was
cleared, the media immediately reported that story and emphasized
his innocence. What troubles many about the Jewell affair was how
no detail of his life had gone unreported. CNN President Tom
Johnson said, "We are guilty of more of a frenzy than is justified."

The news media have also been grappling with so-called "Megan
Laws," named after 7-year-old Megan Kanka, who was sexually molested and killed by a neighbor who had served a prison term for a sex
crime. Megan laws require governments to notify communities if released sex offenders live there. Although some newspapers and TV
stations have used the names, others haven't. *The Sacramento Bee*
was concerned that the information "has the power to create unnecessary panic and to keep punishing people for crimes they've already
paid for."[13] When California officials issued lists of names, newspapers found that some names and addresses were wrong. The lists also
named people who had committed crimes more than 20 years ago
and had not been in trouble with the law since.

Other papers unabashedly use publicity as punishment. The *Lake
Worth Herald,* a weekly paper in suburban West Palm Beach, Fla.,
prints the name, mug shot, marital status, occupation, address and

other personal information about anyone charged with soliciting prostitutes. Editors have devoted as many as three pages in some issues to Project Harlotry, as they call it. According to *Editor & Publisher*, the *Herald* reports only the arrests and does not follow up on cases. "Why should we?" the paper's editor asked. "They're obviously all guilty." He believes the program has reduced the number of prostitutes working in the area.[14] Similarly, a paper in Kentucky prints pictures of every person charged with drunken driving.

Naming Juvenile Offenders

While news organizations may be softening their stand on naming suspects, most are taking a harder line on naming juvenile offenders. In the past, when people under 18 were arrested, they were tried in juvenile courts, which were closed to the public and the media. Usually the punishment handed out by these courts was less severe than adults would receive for similar crimes. The hope was that these youths could turn their lives around and become law-abiding citizens.

However, as the seriousness of teen crime grew, many prosecutors and judges became more willing to try juveniles in adult courts, which are open to the public. As the names became part of the public record, journalists were free to use them. According to a survey, most editors do. That's particularly true in cases that are serious or represent a threat to public safety. Dave Long, editor of the Logansport, Ind., *Pharos-Tribune,* told *Presstime* that his staff talked to juvenile-court judges and prosecutors before deciding to identify youthful offenders. "All agreed that juveniles should be held accountable." Managing editor Joseph T. Stinnett of *The News & Advance* in Lynchburg, Va., argues that people in the community have "a right to know that a kid has been charged with murder even if he is just 16, or even 14."

But other editors disagree. Executive editor Keith Moyer of *The Fresno Bee* said his paper was reluctant to use teens' names: "You never know when a kid might still lead an honorable, productive life but would have a much tougher time doing so if his or her name were publicized."[15] The *Chicago Tribune* held to its policy of not naming offenders under 17 until two boys, 13 and 11, ambushed their classmates in Arkansas. The paper used the names and decided to review its policy.[16]

Details of Crime

As recently as the 1970s, many newspapers thought the word "rape" was too explicit a description of the crime and banned its use. A reporter could write that a woman may have been "criminally assaulted" or "molested," but not "raped." One Houston paper even changed a woman's direct quote. Instead of yelling "Help! I'm being raped!" she was quoted as yelling "Help! I'm being criminally assaulted!" Few news organizations today are that squeamish. Papers and TV stations reported graphic accounts of the mutilation of the bodies of female students at the University of Florida who were found murdered in their apartments near campus. And many people were given more details of Milwaukee killer Jeffrey Dahmer's cannibalism than they really wanted.

Journalists disagree on how graphic these accounts should be. When a jogger was gang-raped in New York's Central Park, the gruesome details of the crime and intimate information about her previous sex life were part of the court record and were available to reporters. Many papers printed much of this information. Some journalists told *Newsday* they had no problems with the explicit coverage. John Corporon, vice president for news at New York's WPIX-TV, said, "It's a tragedy on top of a tragedy she already suffered, but I don't think the media can turn their backs on a story to protect her privacy." And Thomas Mulvoy, managing editor of *The Boston Globe,* argued that the story transcended considerations of privacy. "It's more of a symbolic story than it is about one person's privacy," he said. "It has to do with what's happening in society."

But other journalists were bothered. When *Newsday* managing editor Howard Schneider read his own paper one morning, he found a verbatim account of the rape as contained in a videotaped confession. "I was stunned," he said. "It really troubled me. I thought, 'My God, this is incredibly explicit.'" He learned at work that day that the story had been approved by the paper's editor. Veteran reporter Gabe Pressman of WNBC-TV in New York said he too believed the media coverage of the rape of the jogger was an "outrageous violation" of her privacy. "I think there's a kind of prurient or scatological tendency in the press and television these days," he said. "Unconsciously, we like to use those little morsels. We know we're titillating people by giving them some of the raw details of the crime."[17]

Why Some Media Name Rape Victims

As we saw in the opening of this chapter, some of the most intense debates about privacy are sparked by the media's treatment of victims of rape and abuse. Some journalists believe that society is served best if news media deal openly with these crimes. Charles Houser was executive editor of the Providence, R.I., papers when they named a woman who was gang-raped on a pool table in a New Bedford, Mass., tavern. "Any time we are suppressing public information, we are deciding what is good for society, for the public, for an individual," he said.[18] Similarly, Irene Nolan, managing editor of the Louisville, Ky., *Courier-Journal,* argued: "It's basically wrong to treat rape differently from other violent crimes. I know people who've gone through this, and I've seen the horrible agony they go through, but we're not doing anything to help."[19] (The *Courier-Journal,* however, follows a policy of generally not naming rape.)

Alan Dershowitz, a professor at Harvard Law School, put a different spin on the get-the-news-out argument. He contended that if the news media name the accused man (who is presumed innocent until proven guilty), they should name his accuser. "In this country there is no such thing as anonymous accusation," he insisted.[20] Some advocates contend that in some cases, naming the accuser has prevented wrongful prosecutions by leading people to volunteer information to the police.

The potential for false accusations concerns many editors. Michael Gartner, former president of NBC News and now editor of *The Daily Tribune* in Ames, Iowa, cited a case in which a local basketball player was accused of rape. After lots of media coverage naming the man but not the alleged victim, the charges were dropped. "So is that fairness?" Gartner asked. This may not be an unusual occurrence. Nationally, about half the rape cases do not end in convictions. About one in eight editors reveal the accuser's name when the suspect is found not guilty.[21]

Many people, including some feminists, have another reason that victims should be named. They contend that by not reporting these crimes fully, the news media are reinforcing the stigma attached to them, as did earlier generations of journalists when they hid the fact that people died of cancer. They argue women might be better off if the media treated rape just as they do other serious felonies. Isabelle Katz Pinzler, director of the Women's Rights Project of the American Civil Liberties Union, has said: "There are feminist arguments why it might not be a bad idea to name the victims. It might be a step toward destigmatizing and, by making rape less of a faceless crime, it brings home the horror."[22]

Editors at *The Des Moines Register* wanted to give the public a better understanding of rape and its aftermath. They assigned reporter Jane Schorer to write a series of stories about a rape in a rural Iowa town. Since the *Register* usually does not print the names of rape victims, the paper found a woman willing to volunteer. Schorer used her name and gave explicit details of the crime. During the police investigation and subsequent trial, Schorer talked to the woman about her feelings. The series was criticized by some and became a hot topic on call-in radio talk shows in Des Moines. But most people who called the paper expressed appreciation that the veil of secrecy had been lifted from the crime. Schorer, who won a Pulitzer Prize, stated that she hopes the series will "mark the point where society at large first showed itself as ready and willing to listen" to rape victims and their problems.[23]

The media have also been hesitant to report domestic abuse cases. Some contend that this reticence has led our society to misunderstand domestic violence and underestimate how frequently it occurs. Ellie Dixon, managing editor of the *Caledonian-Record*, a small daily in northeast Vermont, wrote that her paper started using names after the staff was shocked at how much abuse was taking place in the community. "Domestic battering was real," Dixon wrote. "Who were we to hide it from our readers? In fact, if we addressed the subject with real names and real instances, could we lessen the horrific instances of domestic violence in our community?" She wondered if the policy might have headed off some abuse cases that escalated into murders. Dixon said that many townsfolk support what the paper is doing, and some victims have told her that publishing the names helped family and employers understand their situations.[24]

Occasionally a news outlet will name victims for less noble reasons. The *New York Amsterdam News*, a black-oriented newspaper, named a jogger who was raped and beaten in Central Park. The editors wanted to protest the fact that the media were withholding the white victim's name while using names and pictures of the six African-American youths, ages 14 to 16, accused of attacking her.[25]

Reasons against Naming Rape Victims

The arguments for naming rape victims don't wash with more than 90 percent of editors and news directors. They rarely use victims' names—usually out of compassion. Many argue that publishing rape victims' names makes them victims twice, once when the crime is committed and again when the story is reported in the media.[26] Rape, they say, is different from other crimes. As Robin Benedict, a Columbia University journalism professor, wrote: "As long as people have any sense of privacy about sexual acts and the human body, rape will, therefore, carry a stigma—not necessarily a stigma that blames the victim for what happened to her, but a stigma that links her name irrevocably with an act of intimate humiliation."[27]

One problem with trying to make decisions based on what will be best for society is that it is difficult to predict how people will react to the stories. While some argue that printing names might lessen the stigma attached to these crimes, others maintain that naming names will hurt society. They fear that if names are printed, fewer women may be willing to press charges against their assailants. They cite an opinion poll that found more than two-thirds of women surveyed said they would be more likely to report sexual assaults if there were laws against disclosure of their names.[28]

Editors who name victims contend that has not happened in their communities. Ellie Dixon, whose paper names victims of spouse abuse, said the number of women filing abuse charges has increased since the paper began the policy. She thinks the media attention made them more aware that they could take control of their situations.

Joe Doster, publisher of the Winston-Salem, N.C., *Journal,* said naming rape victims had not slowed the number of complaints filed in his county. He said more rapes are reported in his county than in the more populous surrounding counties, where the news media do not name victims.[29] However, the victims themselves don't like the paper's policy. When researchers from Iowa State University questioned women whose names had been used in the *Journal,* most were angry at the paper's policy, and many said it worsened the feelings of embarrassment and shame. A few said they thought being named in a rape case had made them targets of offensive comments and insensitive phone calls.[30]

The ban against naming rape and domestic-abuse victims is not absolute at most news outlets. Nearly all of them use names if the victim was also murdered, according to a study by professors at Texas Christian University. Also, most will name victims who decide to go public about the crime and agree to have their names used. Nearly half will name the victim if the person is well-known nationally, but only 7 percent if the person is well-known locally. Other editors bend the rules if other media name the victim, if a wife charges her husband with rape or if the victim was abducted.[31]

These exceptions can lead to controversies. A small-town daily reported that a woman had been kidnapped, and it used her name. Later, when police found the woman and arrested the man, he was charged not only with kidnapping but also rape. The editor continued to name the woman although his paper was attacked in the community for doing so.[32]

The Washington Post, which normally does not name victims, and many other news organizations were criticized for using the name of a 14-year-old girl who had been sexually assaulted by David Koresh, head of a cult in Waco, Texas. She spoke publicly to a congressional

committee investigating the handling of the siege of the cult's compound by law enforcement officers. The *Post*'s ombudsman agreed
with the decision to print the name because the girl's appearance was at
a public forum. However, others wondered if a 14-year-old can give
"informed consent" to reveal such personal information.

The ethical problems for the media intensify when the abuser is
the parent or spouse of the abused. If the abuser is named, readers can
figure out who was abused. Editors at the *Wabasha County Herald,* a
weekly in southeastern Minnesota, were faced with a such a call.
When a father was charged with sexually abusing his daughter from
the time she was 8 until she was 16, the paper decided not to print the
story to avoid embarrassing the girl. The father was found guilty but
was sentenced to only one year in jail. The editor decided the community needed to know about the "lenient" sentence and ran a story
naming the father and describing the case. The girl was mortified and
appealed to the Minnesota News Council. She told the council:

> I then gave a statement at my dad's [sentencing] hearing and I felt a
> huge weight lift off of me. I said to myself, "I can finally move on."
> Until a week later when I saw the article on the front page. It totally
> tore me apart knowing that I had gone so far, and for what? To have
> the whole town know detail by detail what my father did to me?
> Because of the article I feel that everybody is looking at me and isn't
> seeing me . . . but somebody who had sex with her father.

The girl's therapist, Sandy Garry, said that the story had hurt her
because she had not yet accepted the fact that she wasn't to blame for
the abuse and had no control over the situation. Garry said the editor
should have talked to people about the girl before he decided to run
the story. The therapist said at least he should have warned the girl
that the story was going to appear. The news council agreed that the
paper had been insensitive.

However, Garry believes there are times when naming victims is
appropriate. She told the news council that some victims will heal
more quickly if their names and details of the crime are printed, especially those victims who have resolved that they bear no blame. These
victims take the attitude: "I took all this abuse, now I'm going to give
some back."[33] (The problems of dealing with victims and their relatives are also dealt with in Chapter 11.)

Identifying Gays and Lesbians

Two events in the 1970s have played a role in discussions about how
the media treat gays and lesbians. One involved Oliver W. Sipple, a

33-year-old ex-Marine. He became a national hero when he grabbed the arm of a would-be assassin and stopped her from shooting President Gerald Ford as he left the St. Francis Hotel in San Francisco. Soon after the incident, Harvey Milk, a San Francisco politician, and other gay rights activists said they were proud that "one of us" had saved the president's life. They claimed that Ford was slow to honor Sipple because he was gay. The activists asked the Bay area media, which had made no reference to Sipple's personal life during the first two days of coverage, to acknowledge that Sipple was gay in hopes it would help break the stereotype.

But Sipple himself did not answer reporters' questions about his lifestyle directly. "My sexual orientation has nothing at all to do with saving the president's life," he said, "just as the color of my eyes or my race has nothing to do with what happened in front of the St. Francis Hotel." He told reporters he had never told his employer, his mother or his family about his lifestyle and wanted to keep it that way.[34]

Although most news organizations were slow to use the story, Herb Caen, a widely read columnist for the *San Francisco Examiner,* reported the remarks of Milk and the activists. Then a *Los Angeles Times* reporter wrote a story that was picked up by the national wire services. Although the story quoted Sipple as being unwilling to discuss his sexual orientation, the reporter was told by gay activists that Sipple had participated in well-publicized activities within San Francisco's gay community.

The exposure of Sipple's personal life had one result that the reporters and gay activists had not anticipated. When the *Times* story appeared in Sipple's hometown newspaper *The Detroit News,* it was read by his parents, who were stunned when they discovered their son's lifestyle.[35] Sipple and his mother, who died four years later, never spoke again. Sipple sued the newspapers. However, the courts ruled that the stories did not meet the legal understanding of invasion of privacy.

The media's awkwardness in handling homosexuality was also apparent when Washington's two daily newspapers covered a fire that killed eight men at a gay-oriented, X-rated movie theater in 1977. Editors at the papers made different decisions on whether to print names of the victims, which included an Army major, an aide to a congressman and a former pastor. Editors at *The Washington Post* decided not to name them. They said their "main motivation in not using the names was compassion for the wives and children of the men."

But George Beveridge, ombudsman of the *Washington Star,*

wrote that "the identity of the victims in a local tragedy as substantial as this one was so vital an element of the story that the printing of the names never arose" as an issue in the minds of *Star* editors who handled the story. He argued that being in a gay-oriented theater didn't prove the men were gay and that whether they were gay didn't matter to the story. While "it is hard to imagine that anyone fails to share the *Post*'s compassion for the families of the fire victims," he wrote, "the *Post*'s failure to identify the victims of the disaster amounted "to a sort of double standard of press responsibility that is much easier started than stopped."[36]

Times have changed since these incidents. As one editor said, "We look at sexuality a lot differently from how we did 10 years ago, because the media have been willing to talk about it. There've been homosexual relations since the beginning of time, but if you look at the newspapers of the 1950s, '60s and '70s, they didn't exist. In the last 15 years we've started talking about it and attitudes have started to change."

Some gay groups continue to pressure the media to engage in "outing," a term given to exposing gays and lesbians who have not gone public with their lifestyle.[37] In the early 1990s there were even magazines devoted to "outing." Media ethics scholar Deni Elliott wonders if the ploy may not backfire. In a column she wrote shortly after Sipple died in 1989, she claimed stories that make a big deal of the fact that a hero is gay may contribute "to the idea that there was something bizarre about a man who is both heroic and homosexual."[38] And even if these stories might contribute to a better understanding of gays and lesbians, Fred Friendly, former president of CBS News and journalism professor emeritus at Columbia University, asked, "Whatever the cause, do we as journalists have the ethical or moral prerogative to strip away anyone's privacy, unless there is an overriding and prevailing justification?"[39]

By and large, the media have answered Friendly's question with a resounding no and have resisted efforts to get them to out gays. In 1991 a free-lance writer reported that while the Pentagon was enforcing a ban on gays and lesbians in the military, there was a high-ranking Pentagon official who was gay. Many news organizations carried stories about the allegations, usually in the context of the larger question of "outing." But only a handful, including *The Detroit News, The Patriot* of Harrisburg, Pa., WPIX in New York and CNBC, a cable news channel, used the man's name.[40] However, many editors who refused to identify the Pentagon official did print stories acknowledging that a conservative columnist who had frequently taken anti-gay positions was himself gay and had died of AIDS.[41]

Invasive Photos

Freshman Travis Roy skated onto the ice to play his first shift in the season opener for the Boston University hockey team. The Terriers were a preseason pick to be a contender for the national championship, and Roy was expected to play a role in their pursuit of the title. Moments later, Roy was injured. His spine was badly damaged, leaving him paralyzed.

Months after the injury, Roy held his first news conference in an Atlanta hospital's spinal clinic. More than two dozen TV crews and several newspaper reporters showed up. Roy told them, "I am still the same Travis Roy I was before the accident. I haven't changed as a person; only my body doesn't react the way it used to." *The Boston Globe* printed Roy's courageous statement along with a picture. It was the picture that aroused the ire of many Bostonians. *Globe* reporter Peter S. Canellos described the uproar like this:

> The image was both tender and tragic: paralyzed Boston University freshman Travis Roy, his blond hair trimmed in a boyish cut, weeping in his wheelchair as his girlfriend gently wiped away his tears.
>
> For many Boston readers, though, it was more than just a powerful glimpse at the physical and emotional consequences of a spinal-cord injury—it was journalistic exploitation of a young man's pain.

Hundreds of people called the *Globe*'s ombudsman and complained that the photo had stripped the young man of his dignity. Editors and news directors, of course, pick pictures that will help tell the story. Often pictures can illustrate the impact of events more clearly than words. However, because pictures can have such a strong emotional impact, readers and viewers often are more likely to complain about them than the stories they accompany. And the closer to home the pictures are, the more likely they are to complain. Although hundreds of Bostonians complained when the *Globe* ran the pictures, Georgians were not troubled when the same photos were in *The Atlanta Journal-Constitution*.

Shocking Pictures

When deciding whether to run strongly emotional pictures, editors and news directors often balance the ability of the pictures to help tell the story, the importance of the public seeing the pictures and the need to be compassionate toward the people in the pictures and the public.

The need to tell the story is, of course, fundamental. *The Sacramento Bee* received many complaints when it ran a large color picture showing a Haitian man slashing another man to illustrate a report that the CIA continued to arm Haitian death squads. An editor said, "I can understand why many readers were disturbed about this photo, but the article was also shocking, and the photo helped to corroborate that."[42]

Some photographers believe the news value alone can justify most pictures. Pottstown, Pa., *Mercury* photographer Tom Kelly used a similar explanation for printing a series of photos that he described as "shocking and very emotional." They showed a blood-stained young man who had gone berserk and killed his wife, stabbed his daughter in the eye and seriously injured his 71-year-old grandmother. Kelly did not hesitate to publish the pictures. He said he did not believe the press "should hide what's going on. It's life. It happened."[43]

Others reject Kelly's argument. They contend some aspects of life are too gruesome for the news media to cover. They point out that reporters often leave out unneeded details of violence and that many papers and TV stations avoid pictures of death and nudity.

Just as news stories have increased understanding of alcoholism or AIDS, photojournalists contend that some pictures do more than just show the world as it is. They believe these pictures are critically important for people to understand the news. That's the reason many editors and news directors used powerful pictures of an American soldier being dragged through the streets of Somalia. They knew the pictures would be shocking, but they also thought they gave insights into the problems American forces were having as they tried to intervene in the Somalian civil war.

Many believe pictures taken by press photographers and TV news crews swayed attitudes toward the war in Vietnam. Americans were stunned by images of a small girl who had been burned by napalm, a Vietnamese officer shooting a civilian in the head, Buddhist monks setting themselves on fire and American forces facing sniper fire. As gruesome as they were, they showed Americans what the war was like to the people who were living it.

And pictures of actor Rock Hudson, gaunt and weak, put a face on the then-mysterious disease of AIDS.

Occasionally, editors and news directors use the good-for-society defense on other kinds of pictures. For example, the managing editor of *The (Bakersfield) Californian* defended a picture of the lifeless body of a 5-year-old boy surrounded by his distraught family; it claimed that it might remind parents to be more careful when their kids are swimming.[44]

Some journalists push this argument to its limits. The editors of the *New York Post* ran a front-page picture of the crushed body, un-

A family's anguish: As the weeping father kneels over the body of his young son, a rescue worker (*left*) tries to console the drowning victim's brother and other family members. The editor who ran this picture said he wished he hadn't.

(Photo courtesy of The Californian, *Bakersfield, Calf.)*

covered and face up, of a 4-year-old boy who fell to his death from a 53rd floor window of an apartment building. The boy was the son of guitarist Eric Clapton. The paper claimed that it used the picture, not because the victim was Clapton's son, but because the paper wanted to warn people of the dangers of children playing near open windows in high-rise apartments.[45]

This "the public needs to be reminded" argument doesn't impress journalism professor George Padgett. "Despite the good intentions, the prevention justification simply does not hold up." He contends if newspapers were truly dedicated to promoting safety they could do more than publish an occasional photograph.[46]

Pictures of Grief

Pictures of war and major disasters stir readers' passions. But perhaps the most commonly criticized pictures are those of grieving people at the scenes of tragedies. A free-lance photographer for *The Orange County Register* in California snapped a picture of a woman just as a police officer confirmed that her husband had died an auto accident. Readers protested that the photo was insensitive and irresponsible. Pat Riley, the *Register*'s ombudsman at the time, said, "It mirrored emotional reality in a powerful way and aroused our empathy. It did not, in my view, hold the woman up to ridicule. It showed her expressing natural understandable suffering, and we could all feel it."[47]

But others believe that pictures of grief are overused and that readers and viewers don't need to see more pictures to understand that relatives of victims suffer. When *The Boston Globe* ran a picture of a man grieving over his slain brother, ombudsman Mark Jurkowitz called it "gratuitous." He also criticized a picture of mournful grandparents after two boys died in a fire. He said he was more troubled by that picture than by "the sight of [hockey player Travis] Roy's tears."

Minneapolis *Star Tribune* ombudsman Lou Gelfand thought two pictures in his paper invaded people's privacy. One was of a man falling to his knees and crying after he had learned his daughter had died, and the other was of a young man weeping after hearing that a friend had been killed in a car crash. He contended that "newspapers can show compassion without compromising their mission. Denying the readers this view of someone's grief would not have shortchanged the news report."[48]

Jurkowitz put together some suggestions on how the media might handle such pictures:

> **Contact families:** When the *St. Paul Pioneer Press* ran a photo of a child's bike crushed under the wheels of a truck, the grieving mother told the paper that her only complaint was that she had not been forewarned. Now, that's the paper's policy. Before using a photo of a 15-year-old gunshot victim lying in a parking lot, the *Daily Press* of Newport News-Hampton, Va., approached his family. They [gave

approval] but asked the paper to publish a picture of the boy when he was alive. The photos ran together. (Family reaction can be surprising. The mother of the lifeless baby in the famous Oklahoma City bombing picture was reportedly relieved to know that someone had cared for her child to the end.)

Make the stories meaningful: Controversial photos go better with stories about something more complex than the sensation of the moment. "The best reporters tell us not only how it happened, but why it happened and what it means," writes Bob Steele, director of the Ethics Program at the Poynter Institute for Media Studies, in an evaluation of "Journalists and Tragedy."

Explain yourself: Before running the photo of the dead U.S. solider being dragged through Somalian streets, the managing editor of Norfolk's *Virginian-Pilot* wrote a lengthy memo explaining how difficult it was to publish the picture in a military community and admitting frankly: "There was no unanimity. There was no consensus." Such self-disclosure is good for the soul while trying to reassure readers that such decisions are not taken lightly.

John Long, a former president of the National Press Photographers Association, suggested the following questions can help separate images that need to be used from the merely sensational: "Does the event have an impact on the community in general? Is there an overriding societal interest in the event? Does the photo further our understanding of some aspect of our community and help us make informed choices as a community?"[49]

TV news crews often face even tougher ethical challenges. Because of the cameras, lights and microphones, their actions often seem more intrusive than press photographers'. Michael Sherer, a professor at the University of Nebraska at Omaha, wrote that most TV news photographers "are sensitive to the feelings of those caught in tragic moments." But they also know that television demands closeup images. "Getting in tight for the most dramatic, emotional and compelling images means that photojournalists must make instant ethical decisions."[50]

Invading Privacy to Get the News

Most older journalists have stories about times when they or their cohorts secretly listened in on conversations they knew they were not supposed to hear. More recently, some TV and radio news crews have used long-range microphones to eavesdrop on police officers and politicians who are having discussions out of earshot of the news media. Although these kinds of antics were at one time considered acceptable, some journalists are becoming more leery of them.

During the early part of the crisis after the Three Mile Island nuclear power plant breakdown in 1979, two *Philadelphia Inquirer* reporters pretended to be bickering lovers so they could stay in a hotel corridor to eavesdrop on a meeting of public relations executives for the utility. Each time a motel official or some guest would come by, the two reporters would strike up a lovers' quarrel—which is a great way to get people to look the other way.

Although reporters often use what they overhear while eavesdropping only as ideas for stories, these *Inquirer* reporters reported what they heard through the hotel room door and explained to readers how they got their information. The reporters said that they had tried for days to talk to the officials inside but were always told that the head of public relations for the utility was too busy discussing the "nuclear question." But when the reporters listened through the door, they heard that the conversation inside "was about the press question, about how to get us off their tail. They had lied to us."[51] Although the reporters were obviously angered by the use of deception by the utility's public relations people, they were not troubled by their own use of deception and their eavesdropping to get the story. Eugene L. Roberts Jr., *Inquirer* executive editor at the time, said: "We have to have high standards, but we can't get so finicky about ethics that we use them as excuses for not doing our jobs. . . . There's no ethics in being docile and the pawn of whoever wants to prevent you from getting the story."[52]

Getting caught while eavesdropping is embarrassing and not in keeping with the image most journalists like to project. Two reporters for the high-minded Louisville, Ky., newspapers embarrassed their news bosses when they got caught eavesdropping on a police meeting in 1974. The reporters were arrested after police found one of them lying on the floor while the other had his ear to the door of a room in which the local Fraternal Order of Police was holding a closed meeting. Charges against both reporters were eventually dropped. What prompted them to eavesdrop? They were doing a story about the police chief's bugging squad cars to check on police misbehavior.[53] Michael Davies, managing editor of one of the reporters, said "the resultant publicity was awful." The papers' publisher issued a statement trying to justify the reporters' conduct, but, Davies recalled, the statement "didn't sit well with anyone outside the papers." Davies said he opposes eavesdropping: "We should conduct ourselves the way other people do."[54]

Journalists are divided about how far they should go to get information in closed meetings. Philip Meyer, a former journalist and now a journalism professor at the University of North Carolina, asked newspaper editors and reporters to respond to a hypothetical case in which a just-nominated presidential candidate is meeting with advisers to pick a vice presidential running mate. A reporter asks a person who will attend the meeting to carry a briefcase and to leave it there to be picked up by someone else. Unknown to the person, the briefcase contains a tape recorder. About 45 percent of the editors and news staff said they believed the reporter should be admonished and the story killed, 29 percent would admonish the reporter and use the story only as background for other reporting, 7 percent would admonish the reporter but use the story, and 20 percent would reward the reporter.[55]

How often do journalists engage in eavesdropping? There probably is no firm answer. When editors were asked how often their papers engaged in a variety of questionable reporting practices including false identity, stolen documents, concealed recording and eavesdropping, 28 percent said their papers never did any of these things. Only about 8 percent said that any of these activities happened at their papers as often as once a month.[56]

Foraging for News

In the past it was rather common for journalists to enter private property after a fire or a crime or some other human tragedy, unless the police stopped them. Jerry Thompson, a reporter for *The Tennessean* in Nashville, once beat the police to the scene of a celebrated murder case. He went into the house just before police arrived and was inside when he heard a police sergeant order the house sealed so that no journalists would be allowed in. Thompson quickly found a picture of the dead woman in an upstairs room and threw it out the window. Fortunately for him, the picture landed safely on some shrubbery, and Thompson was able to retrieve it. He was proud that his paper was the only medium to have a photo of the dead woman for three days.[57]

Sometimes such escapades blow up in the reporters' faces. When police charged a man with New York's notorious Son of Sam murders, the next day three journalists were arrested after they broke into his apartment. In another case a newspaper reporter, who went on to become a network news anchor, broke into a house to get a photograph only to learn later that he had gone to the wrong address.

The days in which journalists also double as cat burglars and thieves are fading. A reporter for the old Rochester, N.Y., *Times-Union* thought he had scored an exclusive story when he went to the house where police had rounded up a group of suspects. He found two envelopes containing information that apparently had been dropped by the police. He took them back to the newsroom and used the information in his stories. When editors asked him about some unattributed details in his story, he told the editors what he had done. He justified his actions by saying he had seen reporters do that in the movies. The editors weren't impressed, and he lost his job.[58]

Although most journalists are now wary of breaking into people's homes as a method of getting news, some don't object to sneaky methods being used to get information from government files. Reporters in Anchorage, Alaska, searched through a grand jury's trash for information about an investigation of the governor.[59] And a good many reporters would probably acknowledge that at one time or another, they've glanced at documents on desks in the halls of government.

Les Whitten, who was a senior investigator for the Jack Anderson column for 12 years, admits he once committed a felony by taking some papers out of a U.S. senator's files, copying them and returning them the next day. He had help from a person he would not name who unlocked the office for him and told him the letter of the alphabet he should seek in the files. "It was a hell of a story that helped prevent a multimillion-dollar insurance fraud, and I couldn't resist it," he admitted.[60] Although most journalists would not themselves steal documents, they might be willing to use documents stolen by other people. One editor said that if he were given documents that showed Lee Harvey Oswald, the man accused of killing President Kennedy, worked for the CIA, he would use it "no matter how it got in my hands."[61]

Computers and Privacy

The ethical question of using stolen information became very real during the summer of 1998. *The Cincinnati Enquirer* published an 18-page investigative report contending that a Cincinnati firm, Chiquita Bananas, had engaged in several unlawful practices. The report triggered an investigation by the federal Securities and Exchange Commission and by authorities in South and Central America where Chiquita does business. About a month later, the *Enquirer* retracted the story and paid the company more than $10 million.

The *Enquirer* said it took the action because the reporter, Mike Gallagher, had lied about how he had gotten some of the information. Gallagher contended that a high-ranking officer in the company had given him copies of phone messages left on the company's phone-mail system. However, editors at the *Enquirer* decided that Gallagher had in fact stolen the records, perhaps by breaking into the company's phone-mail computer. Steven G. Warshaw, Chiquita's president, said, "Our business and my personal privacy were violated in the most extreme way. I mean, my children leave me messages. I don't want the world to know their grades."

Editors at the *Enquirer* agreed and fired the reporter. He later pleaded guilty to felony counts of unlawful interception of communications and unauthorized access to computer systems. In its apology, the paper stated, "We want to send a strong message that deception and unlawful conduct have no place in legitimate news reporting at the *Enquirer*." The Society of Professional Journalists decried the reporter's conduct and praised the paper for retracting the story.

Others were less convinced that the *Enquirer* should have retracted the story so quickly and so totally. Many noted much of the story was gathered by traditional reporting techniques. *The New York Times* checked some of the information and concluded that the story had raised legitimate questions about the banana company. Yet readers were left with no way of knowing how much, if any, of the report was true.

"Doesn't the paper owe it to its readers to explain what was and wasn't true in the article?" *Newsweek* magazine asked. "Enquiring minds still want to know: What should we make of the banana story?" A *Wall Street Journal* columnist pointed out that "A true story, even if dishonestly come by, is different from a false story."

Media ethics scholar Lou Hodges also thought people were too quick to judge. Assuming the story was true, he wondered if the ethical problem was one of balancing the greater good (exposing a corrupt international company that was endangering people's lives) with the lesser evil (stealing documents). One investigative reporter told Cincinnati's *CityBeat* magazine that "Gallagher should have been proud of his voice-mail scoop. That's very aggressive reporting." The reporter acknowledged that "there's a line between aggressive and illegal, and I'm not sure where it is. This case will help define that line, I suppose."[62]

However, the paper's editor and publisher indicated they wanted to wash their hands of the whole mess. "This deceitful, unethical and unlawful conduct has undermined the entire project and jeopardized the *Enquirer*'s reputation," they wrote. "The reporter betrayed his co-workers and his newspaper. His misconduct has no place in journalism, and the *Enquirer* wants no part of it." They did not accuse him of making up information or getting the story wrong.

The *Enquirer* case underscores some the privacy concerns that are raised as reporters forage for information in the electronic era. Massive amounts of information are stored in a variety of databases, including information the owners have probably never told their best friends. Adept computer operators can find personal information: people's age, height and weight as they are listed on their drivers licenses; their home addresses and phone numbers; and their neighbors' addresses and phone numbers. They can find out if people are married, if they've been involved in any sticky divorce proceedings and if they've been sued or have sued someone for any other reason. They can also learn how much people paid for their homes, whether they own other real estate and whether they have any ties to major corporations. They may be able to track down driving records and the types of cars owned. They can probably find out which political party people prefer by checking voter registration records and if they have contributed any large sum of money to candidates for federal offices. Even some health records may be accessible.[63]

To test their ability to do this, writers at one magazine in 1993 used computer databases to acquire much of this information—along with credit data and biographies—about many movie stars, sports figures and political and civic leaders.[64] Writers for another magazine found even greater access to information in 1998.[65]

For many investigative reporters, a mouse and a spreadsheet are replacing the notepad and shoe leather as their primary tools. *The Seattle Times* has won two Pulitzer prizes using computer-assisted reporting. For one report, the paper processed a 40-foot pile of documents to determine that 737 jetliners made by Seattle-based Boeing had potentially fatal flaws. The other prize-winning report involved systematic analysis of federal housing grants to Indian tribal leaders. It found that top Indian officials were buying expensive houses while 100,000 native Americans remained in need of basic shelter.

As governments begin to rely on computers, they will create even more databases with information that will be available to people who can tie into them. These databases can provide a gold mine of important stories. *The Atlanta Journal-Constitution* searched through 5.4 million computer files to track down 43 drivers who had at least 15 drunken-driving convictions. Many of them had repeatedly renewed their driver licenses.[66] And the *St. Petersburg Times* used computers to identify substitute teachers who had criminal records, some for sex offenses. In states with strong public-records laws like Florida, courts have ruled that most data on government computers are public, although it's up to the media to find ways to get at the information.[67] In other states, legislators are passing laws limiting access to much of this information, and some bureaucrats are finding their own ways to make access difficult.

But information in databases and on the Internet can also be misused. The irony is that as journalists expose how personal information is readily available to telephone solicitors, nosy neighbors and salespeople, legislatures have passed laws that keep journalists from getting valuable information for news stories that are in the public interest. In several states, access to driving records and auto registration information has been restricted, and some Web sites have voluntarily closed.

Privacy for Political Leaders

An outgoing president is unhappy with the way he was treated by the media. In his early drafts of his farewell address, he attacks the news media and calls them "savage." Perhaps he is reacting to rumors reported in some newspapers that he is sexually impotent.

Or maybe he is reacting to the media's treatment of his secretary of the treasury, an accomplished politician who some had hoped might succeed him. Many papers had reported juicy details about a love affair this man had with a married woman. According to the reports, the woman was down on her luck when she had asked the wealthy politician for help, and he had obliged her by giving her some money—that night, in her bedroom. The affair continued until the woman's husband found out. He tried to blackmail the politician, who then ended the affair, leaving the woman heartbroken and suicidal, according to newspaper accounts.

But don't think this politician's chief political rival was given a free ride in the media. His moral standards were attacked too. After newspapers reported he was having an affair with a woman and that he was the father of some of her children, he was so angry he told the press that he would not dignify their stories with a response.

When many Americans hear stories like these about the media invading the private lives of political leaders, they wonder if the Founding Fathers wouldn't roll over in their graves if they saw what the press was doing. But the Founding Fathers didn't have graves when those stories were printed. Those stories were *about* the Founding Fathers. It was George Washington who thought press coverage was "savage,"[68] Washington's secretary of the treasury, Alexander Hamilton, who eventually admitted to the affair with the married woman,[69] and Thomas Jefferson, who was reported to have fathered the children of one of his slaves.[70]

Newspapers during the early days of our republic were highly partisan. Some received the bulk of their money from political factions, and they were quite willing to print rumors and gossip about the private lives of opposition candidates. Often they weren't too concerned about the truth—or even consistency—of the rumors. Washington was accused by some papers of being impotent and by others of fathering dozens of illegitimate children, including one who grew up to be a member of his own cabinet.[71]

Few political leaders escaped the newspaper rumor mill, according to John Seigenthaler, former publisher of *The Tennessean* in Nashville. Andrew Jackson was accused of convincing Rachel Robards to leave her husband and move in with him. Martin Van Buren was said to wear women's corsets that made it "difficult to say whether he is a man or woman." William Henry Harrison was depicted as senile and mentally failing. Henry Clay was reported to spend his days gambling and his nights in brothels. Franklin Pierce and John Fremont were alleged to be heavy drinkers.[72] Abraham Lincoln's wife was called a Confederate spy,[73] and Lincoln himself was reported to be a "Negro."

The partisan press began to fade from the scene in the mid-1800s, but papers continued to have a field day exploring the private lives of the candidates. For example, in 1884 most observers thought Democrat candidate Grover Cleveland had little chance of winning the presidency. His hopes were further dimmed when the newspapers reported that Cleveland had fathered a child out of wedlock while he was the sheriff of Buffalo, N.Y. The woman reportedly had other lovers too, but Cleveland, the only bachelor she was seeing, accepted responsibility and had faithfully paid child support. When these payments were disclosed during the campaign, the *New York Sun* called him "a course debauchee who might bring his harlots to Washington . . . a man leprous with immorality."[74]

Most Republicans thought those stories would clinch the election for their man. But then another scandal made the front pages. Papers reported that the first child of Republican candidate James Blaine was born only three months after Blaine and his wife were married. Blaine announced that it was all a misunderstanding. He contended that he and his wife were actually married twice—six months apart. His message apparently failed to convince many voters, and Cleveland became the only Democrat to be elected president between 1861 and 1912.[75]

The Era of the "Lapdog"

In the 20th century, the press went from being a watchdog of candidates' morals to a lapdog, according to Professor Larry Sabato in his book *Feeding Frenzy*. The press looked the other way as candidates and political leaders engaged in drunkenness and carousing. Some of them were so drunk that they had to be carried off the floors of the House and Senate, but the voters back home would never read about it.[76]

These reporters were adhering to a gentlemen's agreement that political leaders' private lives were off limits. Sabato, a professor of government at the University of Virginia, contends that this informal agreement intensified during Franklin Roosevelt's presidency in the 1930s and 1940s. The press took the position that if Roosevelt's polio did not affect the way he handled his duties, it would not be reported. The news media deliberately avoided doing anything that might show the president was physically disabled. Of the 35,000 photos taken of FDR, only two showed his wheelchair. When Roosevelt was seeking his fourth term as president in 1944, he was desperately ill, yet many publishers—even those who supported Roosevelt's opponent—chose not to run pictures that hinted at how sick he was.[77]

But the press did not limit its discretion to Roosevelt's health problems. Roosevelt was all but estranged from his wife and had a long-term relationship with his secretary, neither of which was ever reported.[78] The lack of interest in such stories was not limited to Roosevelt. His Republican opponent in 1940, Wendell Willkie, openly kept a mistress both before and during his bid for the presidency, but it was not a story to the press of that era.[79]

Even if a politician's public image bore little relation to the truth, reporters would not write about it. President Dwight Eisenhower's quick temper and salty language were never mentioned. Instead, the media in the 1950s portrayed him as a kindly, soft-spoken grandfather figure. Albert Hunt, a *Wall Street Journal* reporter, told Sabato about a married congressman who left his family in his home district and lived with another woman while he was in Washington. Yet every two years the man would run for re-election, and his campaign would feature pictures showing him as an upstanding family man with a wife and four kids. "I never wrote about it, though today . . . I surely would," Hunt said.[80]

The heaviest criticism of the news media's willingness to look the other way came when the public learned of President John F. Kennedy's many affairs. Kennedy has been linked romantically with actresses, an airline attendant, one of his secretaries, even the girlfriend of a Mafia chieftain—all while he was serving as president. Even before Kennedy became president, many journalists were aware of his amorous adventures. They were so legendary that the press corps covering his presidential bid joked that his campaign slogan ought to be changed from "Let's back Jack" to "Let's sack with

Jack." However, not one newspaper or TV reporter did a story during the campaign or Kennedy's term in office that hinted at his extramarital exploits. "Not only did the media not want to dig for the unpleasant truth, they willingly communicated a lie, becoming part and parcel of the Kennedy public relations team," Sabato wrote. "In the press reports, Jack Kennedy, champion philanderer, became the perfect husband and family man."[81]

Some contend that Kennedy got such special treatment because he was well liked by the press. But history suggests that explanation may not be valid. The press also overlooked indiscretions in the personal lives of at least three presidents who preceded Kennedy and the one who followed.[82] Seigenthaler pointed out that it was historians and biographers, not journalists, who revealed the relationships between Warren Harding and Nan Britton, Franklin Roosevelt and Lucy Mercer, Dwight Eisenhower and Kay Summersby, and Lyndon Johnson and Alice March.[83]

This see-no-evil agreement probably was one reason people had more respect both for politicians and for reporters than they do now, according to Ellen Hume, executive director of a center that studies press and politics at Harvard University. "The news was much more upbeat in the 1940s and 1950s when [the] nation's political leaders were treated by the journalists with deference and respect," she told the *Los Angeles Times*.[84]

Growing Concerns

Some believe the event that triggered reporters to include more honest coverage of candidates' personalities was Watergate, the name given to the investigation of President Nixon's role in a break-in at Democratic offices during his 1972 campaign. The probe ultimately cost Nixon many of his supporters and led to his resignation. The criticisms of Nixon had more to do with character issues (suspicions that he lied and was meanspirited and foulmouthed) than with his political policies.

Sabato argues that the move away from a lapdog press began earlier. He contends that by the time of Watergate, reporters had already begun to reconsider their responsibilities. In 1969 Sen. Edward Kennedy, who had a considerable reputation for drinking and womanizing, waited until the next day to report an auto accident at Chappaquiddick in which a young woman riding in his car was killed. "Kennedy had been too flagrant, his actions too costly for one young woman, and his excuses too flimsy and insulting to the many perceptive minds in the press corps," Sabato wrote. "Good reporters were ashamed of, and the press as a whole was severely criticized for, the process of concealing Kennedy's manifest vices that had preceded the senator's own cover-up of the facts surrounding the accident."[85]

Other reporters believe that it was neither Chappaquiddick nor Watergate that led to journalism's new candor in reporting politicians' private lives. Seymour Topping, who was assistant managing editor of *The New York Times* during the 1970s, argued that changes in society like the sexual revolution of the 1960s allowed newspapers "to explore things that we wouldn't explore in the past." And Richard Wald, the president of NBC News at the time, noted that politicians themselves were more open in the 1970s, admitting to alcoholism and talking publicly about their divorces.[86]

For whatever reason, news coverage of the private lives of political leaders became even more intense in the mid-1970s. Stories of abuses by congressmen began to appear. But none of those stories made a bigger splash than the ones about the carryings-on of Wilbur Mills, the Democratic congressman from Arkansas who headed the powerful Ways and Means Committee. Reporters who had covered Mills knew he was a heavy drinker and appeared to be drunk at some committee meetings, but they would not pursue the story because they did not think they should invade his private life.

Then one night in 1974 Mills was stopped by police for speeding and driving with his headlights off. A young woman climbed out of Mills' car and jumped into the Tidal Basin, a body of water near the monuments in Washington. The passenger was Fanne Foxe, a striptease dancer who billed herself as the Argentine Bombshell.

Now Mills was named in a police report, and his drinking was no longer a private matter. Stories about Mills' problems began to appear in the media. A few days later, a drunken Mills climbed on stage while Foxe was performing at a Washington strip joint. This action prompted many more reporters to shed their adherence to the boys-will-be-boys notion of privacy for public officials. "The guy was falling down drunk, but the press in general portrayed him as one of the great legislative leaders in American politics," David R. Jones, then national editor of *The New York Times,* said later. "Now, he himself says that his drinking affected his job."[87] After undergoing treatment for his drinking, Mills admitted that sometimes he had to ask aides what had happened and what he had said at committee meetings he had chaired.

Neither the Watergate controversy nor the Mills affair led to an "anything goes" mentality among reporters. The old gentleman's agreement may have been weakened, but it was still the rule of the day, as *Newsweek* reported in 1975: "There is hardly a journalist in

Washington who cannot identify at least one alcoholic or philandering congressman. Such behavior only becomes news when it either interferes with the congressman's duties—say, by preventing him from voting on an important measure—or lands him in trouble with the law, as happened in the Mills case."[88]

However, more and more journalists were wondering if they should not write about these "character issues." As Ben Bagdikian, a journalist and media critic who would later become dean of the journalism school at Berkeley, said in 1975, "Since Richard Nixon, there has been a growing feeling that the character of leading politicians is important—and that you've got to know something about their private lives to understand their real character."[89]

The "Piranha Press"

Just as the privacy pendulum began to swing from the gentlemen's agreement of earlier years to a more probing kind of reporting, Gary Hart stumbled into the media spotlight. Hart, a Democrat, attempted to run for president in 1984 but lost support when he gave inconsistent explanations as to why he had changed his last name (from Hartpence), subtracted a year from his age and changed facts in his official biography.

When Hart decided to try again for the presidency in 1988, rumors about his womanizing were already rampant. Even his campaign workers and big campaign contributors were concerned, and he promised them that he would mind his manners and make sure his sex life was not a campaign issue. In meetings with reporters and political columnists, he assured them he was doing nothing wrong. Hart was so insistent in his denials that he may have invited his own downfall. In an interview with a *New York Times* reporter, he said: "Follow me around. I don't care. I'm serious, if anybody wants to put a tail on me, go ahead. They'd be very bored."

Not surprisingly, someone took up his challenge. Two *Miami Herald* reporters staked out his home in Washington that weekend. Instead of being bored, they watched as a young woman entered the town house and apparently spent the night. Hart at first tried to explain away the story. (The reporters, he said, had missed seeing her leave, and the reporters admitted that they had not kept constant watch on both doors, making it possible that she had left unseen.)

But then came reports that a few weeks earlier, Hart and the woman, a model named Donna Rice, had taken an overnight cruise to Bimini on a yacht called, of all things, *Monkey Business*. When one of Rice's friends sold the *National Enquirer* snapshots of Rice sitting on

Hart's lap, Hart's efforts to explain away the reports became more difficult. The final straw came when *Washington Post* reporters told him they had evidence of other affairs. Hart decided to drop out of the race.[90]

Although many journalists were uncomfortable with the idea of reporters acting like two-bit private eyes, many justified the story on the grounds that it raised questions about Hart's honesty and about his willingness to engage in risky behavior. The *Herald* reporters were honored by the SPJ.

The times had changed. President Kennedy's affairs had some impact on his job performance. Sabato noted that occasionally his trysts required him to be out of touch with the military command at a time when the Cold War demanded that the president always be accessible in case of a Russian sneak attack. Seymour Hersh, a Pulitzer Prize–winning reporter, wrote that top military officials with urgent requests would not interrupt Kennedy when they suspected he was with a woman. Hersh wrote that even confirmation that the Russians had missiles in Cuba was delayed until the next morning.[91] Kennedy also opened himself to blackmail, and some argue that then FBI director J. Edgar Hoover used his knowledge of Kennedy's affairs to gain more power for himself and autonomy for his department.[92]

But, by the standards of reporters of that era, Kennedy's affairs were his private life. Associated Press reporter James Bacon told Hersh that actress Marilyn Monroe had given him a firsthand account of her relationship with Kennedy. "She was very open about her affair with JFK," he said. But he didn't write the story. "Before Watergate, reporters just didn't go into that sort of thing." Bacon said there was no conspiracy to hide Kennedy's philandering. "It was just a matter of judgment on the part of the reporters."[93] Twenty-five years later, Hart was not to receive that courtesy.

The public has had trouble making up its mind about how far the press should go. Polls done during the Hart-Rice controversy found that about 70 percent of the public thought the reporters had gone too far.[94] Only a few years earlier, news organizations had been criticized for covering up President Kennedy's affairs.

The often-heated debate over whether the media had treated Hart fairly did not cause some reporters to back off the "character issue." Early in the 1992 presidential campaign, Democratic candidate Bill Clinton had refused to answer questions about his personal life. Then the *Star*, a grocery-store tabloid that usually prints gossip about actors and singers, paid Gennifer Flowers—reportedly $150,000—to tell about a 12-year-long affair she said she had with Clinton. (Paying for information is discussed in Chapter 7.)

To many, her allegations were important news. Phil Donahue, host of a popular talk show, noted that both campaigns were emphasizing "family values" and "character" as key issues. Donahue wrote in *The New York Times* that the media should report such stories even if the majority of people do not care about the marital fidelity of the candidates. He contended such information might make a difference in some voters' choices.[95] In many elections, a shift of only a few percentage points can determine the winner. During the 1992 elections, some polls reported that 14 percent of the public said the revelations about Clinton's affair might sway their vote.

Other writers believe candidates' past indiscretions can provide a clue to the kind of people they are. Thomas Reeves, author of a biography of John F. Kennedy, wrote, "Sexual indiscretions, particularly if they are prolonged and varied, can reveal much about a person's integrity, fidelity, prudence and other qualities that make up character."[96]

The news media's transformation from lapdog to attack dog may have had one unintended side effect. Harvard's Ellen Hume argued that the news media's coverage "doubtlessly feeds the public's cynicism and distrust of its political leader—and of the piranha press corps which seems willing to devour anyone, at any time, for frivolous infractions as well as serious ones."[97] Polls indicate that Americans are becoming more cynical, and many believe the news media are one of the causes.

Are Politicians Still Fair Game?

When Bill Clinton ran for president in 1992, he faced a barrage of news reports about sexual exploits while he was governor of Arkansas. Finally he quelled some of the criticism by confessing on *60 Minutes* that there had been problems in his marriage. His wife, Hillary, was by his side. He went on to defeat incumbent George Bush. During the 1996 elections, many voters admitted to pollsters they did not trust Clinton and doubted his honesty and morality—but they said they planned to vote for him. Nor were voters bothered by reports in the *National Enquirer* and the New York *Daily News* that 1996 Republican presidential candidate Bob Dole had an affair in 1968 while he was married.

By the middle of Clinton's second term, the nation was gossiping about whether he had an affair with Monica Lewinsky, a White House intern about the age of his daughter. Yet Clinton was receiving some of his highest popularity ratings. While the FBI was testing Lewinsky's dress for semen stains, 63 percent gave Clinton a favorable rating although 60 percent said he was lying about the affair.[98] *Washington Post* columnist David Broder suggested that if Clinton would have confessed ("I foolishly let myself become involved with this young woman in a way that is deeply painful to my family and embarrassing to all of you"), the American people would have forgiven him and the special prosecutor would not have pursued the case.[99]

This lack of moral outrage may not signal that Americans are getting less serious about morality and marital fidelity. A survey found that 78.5 percent thought extramarital sex was "always wrong."[100] However, surveys found that more than half of the voters didn't think a candidate's marital fidelity is an important issue. Some noted that three of the most popular presidents of the 20th Century (Roosevelt, Eisenhower, Kennedy) cheated on their wives.

Clinton and Dole aren't the only candidates to have benefited from the public's new attitude. In Mississippi, Republican Kirk Fordice won two elections for governor by campaigning as a strong supporter of family values. During the Clinton-Dole race, he called Clinton a "philanderer" and a "congenital liar." Then, one November day, while his wife was in France, Fordice told his security guards to take the day off. That afternoon he was seen holding hands with a woman during an intimate lunch in a quiet restaurant. Later that night, as Fordice was driving alone on a Mississippi interstate, his car flipped, and he was seriously injured.

The events of the day became big news in Mississippi. The waitresses were interviewed, positively identifying the governor and describing his rendezvous. Fordice's staff gave conflicting accounts of his day. Fordice himself had nothing to say for nearly two months. Then, he told a press conference that the accident had caused him to suffer memory loss. He could not recall anything that had happened beginning shortly before he had lunch that day. He couldn't remember where he had gone, whom he had seen, what he had done or how the accident occurred. Besides, he said at a press conference, "even a governor is entitled to some private time." Despite these developments, public support for Fordice remained steady and he was considering running for another public office. (Mississippi limits governors to two terms.)

"Before Clinton, that kind of personal stuff just killed you," a Democratic political consultant told *U.S. News and World Report.* "Now, it's been relegated to a factor in the political equation. The attitude is, 'Yeah, sure, but I like what he did on welfare.'" In Fordice's case, a newspaper poll found that about 75 percent of Mississippians were satisfied with Fordice's story of short-term memory loss. "But satisfied doesn't mean they believe him," *U.S. News* reported. "Some who said they've heard enough also suspect the governor of hypocrisy, faking amnesia, or worse. They just don't think the whole business amounts to much."[101]

Novelist Thomas Mallon sees this sentiment as becoming more widespread in America. He suggested to *The New York Times* that Americans at one time pretended that they didn't know such things happened and then seemed shocked when confronted with them. Today, Americans are now "much more willing to admit things go on."[102]

Other political observers note that in many European nations, voters are less concerned about candidates' private lives. Italians elected to Parliament a woman who had appeared in adult movies. During his last term in office, French President François Mitterand acknowledged that he had a daughter by a mistress. The mistress, their daughter and his wife stood together at his grave as he was buried.

Many people, both in and out of journalism, hope the news media find a way to allow political leaders some time out of the spotlight, what former *Washington Post* ombudsman Joann Byrd called a "privacy zone where what happens is absolutely nobody's business."[103] Political scientist Joel Silbey told *The New York Times,* "Watching some of these press briefings over the past weeks [during the Lewinsky affair], you get the idea that nothing is sacred. Nothing is out of the arena of discussion, and maybe some things should be." As things stand today, *Times* reporter John Broder wrote, "Anyone contemplating a run for public office must weigh the prospect that his or her morality will be debated on cable television by sex therapists, jury consultants and dime-store philosophers."[104] Some wonder if such scrutiny is good for the republic.

Relatives of Politicians

Just as candidates come under increasing scrutiny from the press, their relatives are often seen as fair game, and many both in and out of journalism are troubled by this. A *New York Times* columnist chided the press for some mean-spirited humor about the clumsiness of Chelsea Clinton, the president's then 12-year-old daughter. And Mona Charon wrote in *The Atlanta Journal-Constitution:* "Scrutiny of presidential candidates is one thing. Even attention to candidates' spouses is legitimate. But let's have mercy on the kids."[105] By and large, the media stayed out of Chelsea's life during Clinton's first six years in office. She got some attention when she enrolled in Stanford

University in California, but nearly no coverage once the school term was under way.

Even at the height of the Lewinsky scandal, most news media limited coverage of Chelsea to pictures taken at public events with her parents. A few magazines and tabloids, however, did capitalize on her. *People* magazine was attacked by many after it ran a cover story psychoanalyzing Hilary and Chelsea Clinton. "If [Chelsea] were a Kennedy kid who had been caught drugging it up or accused of raping a date or—to be petty—had mouthed off to somebody in a public place, that's one thing. But Chelsea hasn't proven to be that way," syndicated columnist Myriam Marquez wrote. "The personal may be the political, but to this mom, Chelsea's privacy outweighs the public's right to gawk."[106]

Journalists occasionally disagree on the limits of mercy for political leaders' children. In 1991 the 20-year-old son of Oklahoma Gov. David Walters was charged with a misdemeanor, possession of drug paraphernalia, after a pipe and other drug-related items were found in his room. Newspaper coverage was low-key. Ed Kelley, managing editor of *The Daily Oklahoman* in Oklahoma City, told *Presstime* that his staff considered these facts in deciding the amount of coverage to give the story: Walters' son was not a public official himself but had participated in the campaign, and he was the son of the state's highest elected official. Kelley said the paper ended up running five or six short stories—none of them on Page 1.

TV news directors saw it as a bigger story. They gave the arrest and subsequent court hearing at which he pleaded no contest extensive coverage. Six weeks after the trial, the young man took his life by overdosing on prescription drugs. The governor argued that the media had driven his son to suicide.[107]

The Philadelphia Inquirer was criticized when it ran a story that the daughter of the mayor of Philadelphia was about to marry a convicted bookmaker. Steve Lovelady, who was then associate executive editor of the paper, argued that it was news and said that if the top editor of the *Inquirer* had become engaged to a bookmaker, the paper would report that too.[108]

Other journalists are not as sure as Lovelady of the need for such stories. Brit Hume, former ABC News reporter, said he regrets a story he did back in the early 1970s when he was working for columnist Jack Anderson. Hume tracked down the son of then Vice President Spiro Agnew in Baltimore and confirmed that he had broken up with his wife and moved in with a male hairdresser. He said he is "more ashamed of that story than anything I've done in journalism. I'm sorry about it to this day. We ought not make relatives public persons by extension."[109]

Perhaps no other name in America seems to draw as much attention as "Kennedy." The press's hounding of the Kennedy family reached a low point in 1984 when David Kennedy died of a drug overdose at the age of 28. He was the son of Robert F. Kennedy, who was assassinated while campaigning for the presidency. The heavy coverage of David's death was questionable, but the attention paid to the family wake and burial seemed ghoulish.

Eric Schmitt, a young reporter who covered the wake for *The New York Times,* claimed it made him ashamed to be a journalist. "Instead of what should have been a private moment for the family, the press declared the sad gathering of Kennedys a newsworthy event." He asked, "Why were three dozen journalists at Hickory Hill chasing hearses, interviewing priests and cornering family friends as they left the house?" He rejected the notion that the coverage was justified because it was the Kennedys. "Who was David Kennedy other than the son of the late United States senator?"[110]

The name "Kennedy" brought notoriety to two previously private people when William Smith was accused of rape in 1991 while vacationing with his uncle Sen. Edward Kennedy at the Kennedy compound in Palm Beach, Fla. Because a Kennedy relative was involved, this incident mesmerized the nation. (To make sure no one would forget his bloodlines, the media usually referred to him by his full name, William Kennedy Smith.)

Not only was Smith given national exposure, the woman who accused him was also the subject of media attention. At first she was named only by two of the least savory members of the press—an American supermarket tabloid and a British scandal sheet. But soon, several other publications, including *The New York Times* and NBC News, used her name. The *Times* even printed a lengthy story about her lifestyle and background, including the number of traffic tickets she had accumulated.

After days of new revelations about Smith and his accuser, particularly on TV shows like *Inside Edition* and *Hard Copy,* parts of the trial were broadcast on television and radio. These broadcasts included graphic details of the incident, which Smith described as consensual sex and the woman called rape. Technicians tried with only moderate success to block out the woman's face with a large blob as she testified. Lawyers, of course, spoke her name, which occasionally made it over the public airways, and eventually the woman gave the media permission to identify her. The jury found Smith not guilty of rape, but many Americans believed the media were guilty of violating both Smith's and the woman's privacy.

Privacy of Celebrities

Celebrities, of course, get more public attention than do ordinary folks. They put themselves in the limelight. Many hire publicists to attract media attention. They court the media to keep their names—and thus their careers—fresh in the minds of the public. But occasionally they get more media attention than they want. And journalists must wrestle with questions about when to grant them privacy and when to report the details of their lives.

For the paparazzi and free-lancers who pester celebrities in hopes of getting a photo or a story they can sell to a grocery-store tabloid, the answer is easy: If there's a market, they will supply the goods. But the mainstream American media want to hold themselves to a higher standard. They will not purchase such sleaze. Unfortunately, once the story or picture is splashed on the front page of the *National Enquirer* or is the lead story on *Hard Copy*, respectable news outlets can't resist repeating it—often with a shame-on-the-tabloids tone.

A more fundamental concern involves celebrities who are part of legitimate news stories and would rather not have their involvement reported. Actor Bruce Willis accused *The Wood River Journal* of Hailey, Idaho, of using his fame to draw attention to stories about a company Willis owned that built cabins in the forest. The paper contended the U.S. Forest Service was not charging the company enough rent. When the paper printed a picture of Willis' cabin in Sawtooth National Forest, the actor said the picture invaded his privacy and jeopardized the safety of his family by letting people know which cabin was his. He stopped advertising his bar, restaurant, theater and ski resort in the paper.[111]

The Grand Forks (N.D.) Herald also encountered a famous person who did not want to be named. The community was devastated when the Red River flooded the area in 1997, leaving many people homeless and businesses destroyed. Then word spread that an anonymous person was giving $15 million directly to flood victims. Most residents, including some *Herald* reporters, received $2,000 checks. Using airport records, *Herald* reporters discovered that the benefactor was Joan Kroc, widow of the founder of the McDonald's hamburger chain. The paper decided to publish her name against her wishes. "It wasn't a decision we took lightly," said Jim Durkin, managing editor. But everyone in the newsroom agreed that the story should be printed. "The principle of us holding onto a story and suppressing it, we could not live with," *Herald* publisher Mike Maidenberg said.

However, the news director of an area TV station made a different call. He said his reporters also tracked down the name, but the station decided not to name Kroc. The paper was criticized by many in town who feared that exposing the names of benefactors might keep other people from donating money.[112]

Privacy and Sports Figures

A pollster once asked school children in Chicago to name the person they admired most. Tied for first place were Chicago Bulls forward Michael Jordan—and God. Clearly sports figures are bigger than life to many. The news media have had a major role in creating these heroes. Yet reporters sometimes struggle with deciding how to report the misdeeds of the stars.

"In the past, reporters almost always kept quiet about a player's off-field behavior," Jonathan Rowe wrote in *Christian Science Monitor.* "Babe Ruth's libidinous adventures were well-known to writers who traveled with the Yankees, just as John F. Kennedy's were to 'the boys on the bus.'"[113] Those days are over in political reporting, and they're fading fast in sportswriting. Bill Lyon, a sports columnist for *The Philadelphia Inquirer,* said that until the 1960s every sports department "was a 'homer'—an arm of the local team's public relations staff." But he believes that "if Babe Ruth played today, you'd know he was a heavy drinker and a womanizer."[114]

Often athletes' off-court indiscretions become news only after they become legal cases. The *Boston Herald*'s Michael Gee told the *Christian Science Monitor* that it was no secret that Boston Red Sox star "Wade Boggs was one of the biggest chasers around." His mistress often tagged along on road trips. But it wasn't news until the mistress sued him for $12 million and told her tale in *Penthouse* magazine. Boggs' libido immediately became a story in nearly every newspaper and sports broadcast. *The New York Times* even analyzed Boggs' batting statistics and discovered he hit better when his mistress traveled with him. Boggs later told a news conference that he was addicted to sex.

Most sports pages now seem to contain as much news about crime, drugs and paternity suits as they do win-loss records. As one might expect, most athletes believe these stories get too much attention. Gene Policinski, former managing editor of sports, *USA Today,* said athletes think too much is expected of them. They complained to him that "It's not enough just to be good at what you do on the field, you have to be a good spokesman, a good communicator, a good role model. Never get mad. Never make a mistake. And never, even in the locker room, have fun."

Many in the sports establishment, however, are not sympathetic to this viewpoint. They see these expectations as the price professional athletes have to pay. Dallas Cowboys owner Jerry Jones reminds his millionaire athletes that they make so much money because the media have created so much interest in football.[115]

It's not just the professional athletes who get scrutinized by the media. When a star football player at a major university is caught shoplifting, cheating or abusing his girlfriend, it's national news. Even high school athletes draw media attention. Shortly before an important football game, a high school coach suspended five players for drinking. Without these star players, the game was a rout. Editors at the *St. Cloud (Minn.) Times* printed a story that named the suspended players and explained what they had done. The editors believed the suspensions were newsworthy because they involved a public activity and had an impact on the game.[116]

The Arthur Ashe Case

Few sports stories have created as much controversy and divided the journalistic community as passionately as the coverage of Arthur Ashe, the revered tennis player. Ashe won nearly every major tennis title but was forced to retire early from the game because of heart problems. However, he stayed in the public eye. He became a tennis commentator for HBO and ABC, wrote columns for several major publications and coached the U.S. Davis Cup team. He also remained active in social causes, raising millions of dollars for several groups, giving countless speeches and even being arrested during an anti-apartheid protest at the South African embassy.[117] One sportswriter said Ashe was "a good tennis player, but an even better man."

After receiving a transfusion of blood that had been tainted with the HIV virus, Ashe developed AIDS. Many sportswriters learned of Ashe's illness and decided that the need to show compassion outweighed the pressure to publish this information. Some had known about Ashe's condition for several years but had not reported the story, as one national sports correspondent explained, "out of respect for Arthur Ashe."[118]

Then a reporter at *USA Today* got a tip about Ashe's illness. Policinski, sports managing editor, called Ashe and told him what his reporter had heard. He said that unless Ashe denied the story, the paper would keep investigating but would not run any stories until the rumor was confirmed by someone with direct information about Ashe's medical condition. Believing the newspaper was about to break the story, Ashe called his own press conference so he could tell his story rather than having *USA Today* tell it. He said he would have preferred to have waited and made the announcement when his 5-year-old daughter was older and could better understand. He also said he feared she might be taunted and shunned by her classmates at school once they knew her father had AIDS.

Ashe's revelations at his news conference were reported in nearly every newspaper and TV newscast. But journalists were divided on the ethics of the way *USA Today* pursued the story. As do many discussions of privacy issues, the debate about the Ashe story centered on trying to balance three basic pressures (discussed earlier in the chapter): the obligation to get the news out, the need to show compassion and the desire to educate the public about social issues.

Many journalists argued that the story was news and therefore it was their obligation to print it when it was confirmed. For example, *USA Today* sports editor Policinski called it "a significant news story." The paper's editor, Peter Pritchard, supported him. "Journalists serve the public by reporting news, not hiding it," he said.119 Top editors at the *San Jose Mercury News* and *The Star* in Kansas City told *Washington Journalism Review* that they agreed. "With the level of interest about AIDS and the level of interest about Ashe, you have a powerful story," said Arthur Brisbane, *The Star*'s editor.120

Exposing Ashe's condition was also justified by the argument that printing the story educated the public about AIDS. Pritchard contended, "By sharing his story, Arthur Ashe and his family are free of a great weight. In the days ahead, they will help us better understand AIDS and how to defeat it."121 Others defended the story on the grounds that it taught the public a lesson about how AIDS is spread, or, in this case, not spread. Many papers printed sidebars explaining that health officials have changed the procedures used in handling blood to make transfusions safer than when Ashe received contaminated blood. Some have suggested that the Ashe story may have helped break down the stereotype that AIDS is mostly a gay men's disease. People, it is argued, may become more sympathetic to the need for better AIDS treatment when they read of cases like Ashe's.

Jonathon Yardley, a *Washington Post* writer, disputed the claim that the story served a larger societal need. "No public issues were at stake," he said. "No journalistic 'rights' were threatened. The fight against AIDS will in no way be hastened or strengthened by the exposure to which Ashe has been subjected."122 Similarly, William Rubenstein, director of an AIDS project for the American Civil Liberties Union, said that if the media wanted to do something about AIDS, there were much better stories than whether Arthur Ashe had the disease. They could report on the inadequate health care available to people with AIDS and the discrimination against them, he said.[123]

Many other journalists and members of the public argued that the need to show compassion to Ashe and his family outweighed the need to get the news out or any benefit to the public gained by reading Ashe's story. Randy Shilts, the late newspaper columnist who wrote two books about AIDS, acknowledged that the Ashe story made people more aware of AIDS. "As a person who cares about AIDS, this is good for [informing people about] the epidemic. But as someone who cares about the human condition, this guy deserves some privacy."[124]

Stephanie Salter of the *San Francisco Examiner* said that most reporters she knew would have experienced a "sickening feeling" if they had been asked to call Ashe and ask him about AIDS. "That sickening feeling, I contend, is our basic human knowledge that what we are about to do is wrong."[125] And Floyd Abrams, a constitutional lawyer and champion of First Amendment rights, said if the rumors had been about a presidential candidate, he would have supported *USA Today*'s actions. But in this case, the potential for harm was so great and the information it provided so little, "I find even the concept of such a story abhorrent."[126]

Ashe himself spelled out the ethical question journalists faced. "Are you going to be cold, hard, crass purveyors of the facts just for the sake of peoples' right to know, under the guise of freedom of the press—or are you going to show a little sensitivity about some things?" he asked. Ashe conceded that if the story had been about someone who was in a position of trust—"from the president down to the conductor of the subway"—the public should be informed. But, he said, "I would hope that the so-called newsworthiness of that story will be tempered with sensitivity."[127]

9

The Government Watch

A man who said he was a private detective called the police reporter at the *Hattiesburg (Miss.) American.* He told her that some men were trying to hire a hit man to kill a Hattiesburg businessman. At first, she and her editor decided the caller was some kind of nut. But when he called again eight days later, she got worried. After talking with her managing editor, she notified police. When the man called a third time, she persuaded him to talk to the authorities.

A few days later, the reporter and her editor received an urgent call to come to a cabin owned by the U.S. attorney. When they got there, they were met by the attorney, the district attorney, some police detectives and the police chief. Soon they were joined by the local TV station manager, who had been a reporter and the station's news director.

The law enforcement authorities told the journalists that they believed the hit was on the level. They said an undercover officer had been offered $35,000 to commit the murder. However, police could not make an arrest until the officer met the people. Over the phone, they told him they would pay him when they saw news stories stating the businessman was dead.

The authorities had a plan. They would smear blood on the businessman's pickup truck and abandon it along a county road. Then they would "discover" the vehicle, hold a press conference and announce that the businessman had been kidnapped and probably murdered. They wanted the TV station and the local paper to give the murder full coverage for the next few days. They would then arrest the money men when they paid the undercover officer.

Cliff Brown, station manager of WDAM-TV, decided to go along. That evening his station showed pictures of the bloody pickup truck. The reporter said that police believed a struggle had taken place and that Oscar Black III had disappeared and was probably murdered. For three days the station continued to report false details of the police investigation of the murder-kidnapping. The newspaper, however, played the story much differently. It printed only a one-sentence item in its police roundup: "Police are seeking information concerning suspected foul play directed toward Oscar Black III." That was the paper's only mention of the crime.

The hoax finally ended when police announced that their plan had failed. The money men had sensed something was wrong and had gone into hiding.[1]

This case illustrates how difficult it is for journalists to come to grips with conflicting values. As citizens, they want to help government and law enforcement. Yet they must maintain enough distance that they can serve as critical, independent observers and maintain their role as truth-tellers.

Government Cooperation and Secrecy

Journalists report about most areas of American life, including business, sports and entertainment. But it is the city, county, state and national governments that have traditionally gotten the most intense and vigorous surveillance. Three key reasons for this are

- Government controls many aspects of our lives. It can take away freedoms, imprison people, regulate businesses, impose taxes and tariffs, and even send citizens to war.
- Government runs on tax dollars. When the government wastes money, it is money collected from citizens.
- Citizens can make a difference. By voting, attending public hearings and voicing their opinions, people in a democracy can influence their government. But first they must be alerted to what's going on.

Most elected officials understand why reporters scrutinize the government so closely. But many do not like it when that scrutiny is directed toward them. Often with the best of intentions, they would prefer to conduct the public's business out of sight of the public. "Every government has an interest in concealment; every public, in greater access to information," philosopher Sissela Bok wrote. "In this perennial conflict, the risks of secrecy affect even those administrators least disposed at the outset to exploit it. How many leaders have not come into office determined to work for more open government, only to end by fretting over leaks, seeking new, safer ways" to keep information about government actions from the public?[2]

Government secrecy was tested in 1998 by reporters from seven newspapers in Indiana. They went to local government offices and asked to see documents that were open to the public under Indiana law. Instead of helpful civic servants who gladly provided them with the information, many were met with hostility. In some cases, the officials ran record criminal and financial checks on the reporters. One reporter was taken aback when a county sheriff asked her, "Why aren't you driving your own car?" In more than half the counties, reporters were unable to get police incident reports and crime logs. In many counties they were denied minutes of school board meetings, death certificates and the salary figures of high school coaches—all of which are public record in Indiana. When one official was shown the Indiana statute, the response was "Go get a court order, and then you can have your public record."[3]

Some governments try other methods to limit reporters' access. The police department charged *The Dayton (Ohio) Daily News* $5 per page for copies of electronic records, while other city departments asked for only a nickel a page.[4] A small-town newspaper was told that its request for public records would cost more than $30,000.

Other reporters have run into city councils and school boards that make their decisions secretly. Before their regularly scheduled meetings, the members hold conference calls, luncheons or "executive sessions," where they debate the issues and vote. Then at the official meeting, they go through the formality of passing measures unanimously with no discussion and no dissent. The public is not allowed to hear the reasoning of their elected officials.

Members of the Lorain, Ohio, school board tried to avoid some of the controversy involved in closing one of the city's three high schools. "The school board had several meetings behind closed doors. They kept arguing they didn't have a quorum and that it wasn't an official meeting, but serious discussions took place," Kevin F. Walsh, publisher of *The Morning Journal* in Lorain, said. Ohio has open-meeting laws, but Walsh said they "have no teeth. Very little, if anything, happens if laws are violated and officials know that." Walsh said he tells reporters to write stories each time they're denied access.

In many states, open-meeting laws do have teeth. But even then, it's left to journalists to keep officials honest. Often that means lawsuits. The publisher of one small paper said that the legal bill to get access to one set of court records cost his paper $20,000, money he planned to use hiring a reporter.[5]

Government Spin Control

As governments grew in size and complexity during and after World War II, it became obvious to government leaders that they needed to communicate effectively with citizens. American business had already discovered this and had turned for help to a new breed of specialist— the public relations expert. Government soon followed suit, adding scores, then hundreds, and finally thousands of such specialists to the public payroll.

Today, in both government and the private sector, no major enterprise is without public relations counsel. From the largest federal commissions to the local school system, public relations experts play a key role. Often their expertise has proved helpful. Government agencies began to find better ways to assemble and package information that the public needed. And reporters often ask these public-information officers to help them find facts inside the bureaucratic mazes. But occasionally, their expertise is used to manipulate information. Today, image making and spin control are instruments of government strategy.

The American people and most American journalists were slow to catch on to this development. In 1960 the Soviet Union accused the United States of flying sophisticated spy planes over Moscow and other Soviet territory. President Eisenhower denied it, and the American people—and many in the press—believed the accusation was just another Soviet lie. Then the Soviets announced that one of the spy planes had crashed deep inside Russian borders. The U.S. government continued to deny the plane was spying. If a plane had crashed in Russia, it was on a training mission and may have mistakenly entered Soviet airspace. By and large, Americans believed that was what happened. Unfortunately, the Soviets produced CIA agent Francis Gary Powers, who admitted that he was piloting the plane on a spy mission. Eisenhower's lie was exposed. As strange as it may seem today, Americans were stunned that the government would deceive them.

On the national level, officials justify deception and concealment in the name of national security. Howard Simons, former managing editor of *The Washington Post,* said it was impossible for journalists in Washington to do their daily jobs "without bumping into a secret." He noted that about 4 million bureaucrats have access to classified information and estimated that 20 million government documents are classified as secret each year. Simons said he was amazed that government officials "can remember what is secret and what is not secret."

Sometimes they can't. A National Security Agency deputy was arguing to a judge that the U.S. government was justified in stopping *The Washington Post* from publishing the Pentagon Papers, the U.S. military's then-secret history of the Vietnam War. The deputy brought along a top-secret document that he said was contained in the Pentagon Papers. To drive home how secret the document was, he had sealed it in several envelopes in a double-locked briefcase. He said if the *Post* printed this information, the lives of American soldiers would be jeopardized. The judge ordered him to open the document. Fortunately for the *Post,* the lawyers had brought along George Wilson, respected Pentagon reporter for the paper, who remembered that the material had been read before an open hearing of the Senate Foreign Relations Committee. And Wilson had the transcript to prove it. As Simons added in telling this story, "That clinched that for the *Post.*"[6]

The courts allowed the *Post, The New York Times* and other papers to print the Pentagon Papers. Philosopher Bok believed they made the right decision. The papers contained information about the war that "should never have been secret in the first place," she stated. "This information was owed to the people, at home and abroad, who were bearing the costs and suffering of the war; keeping them in the dark about the reasons for fighting the war was an abuse of secrecy."[7]

Secrecy in War

During World War II, American journalists routinely wore military uniforms, and many accepted the honorary rank of captain. In many ways, they were part of the military establishment. Often they were told in advance about military troop movements and overall strategies. Their reports were subject to censorship. "Nevertheless, the nation's news organizations eventually provided the American public with comprehensive coverage of the war," concluded Frank Aukofer and William Lawrence in a study of military-media relations.

Relations were somewhat less friendly during the Korean conflict, which did not have the same level of support from Americans as World War II. Censorship in Korea extended well beyond security concerns. Aukofer and Lawrence wrote, "A story could be released only if it was accurate, did not disclose military information, would 'not deteriorate morale' and would not 'cause embarrassment to the United States or its allies.'" Gen. Douglas MacArthur broadened the provisions to rule out any criticism of American military commanders or soldiers.[8]

Relationships between reporters and military leaders soured even more as the American military was drawn into the quagmire of Indochina. The rift between the news media and the military was not caused by reporters giving away military secrets. There were no reported cases during the Vietnam War of the news media revealing secret plans or troop movements. The problem was more basic. The military expected the media to support the war effort as had been done during World War II, while reporters believed they should send back truthful reports even if they were negative. Soon government officials and reporters in Vietnam "settled into a more or less permanent state of confrontation," according to Malcolm W. Browne of *The New York Times*.[9]

Since Vietnam, the military has tried to control the flow of information. In October 1983, Caribbean radio stations and newspapers issued stories stating the United States was about to invade Grenada. When reporters asked about it, White House press secretary Larry Speakes, after checking with a member of President Reagan's national security staff, labeled the stories "preposterous." The invasion took place the next day. Within hours after Reagan announced at a press conference that the landing had occurred, more than 400 American journalists had flown to Barbados, about 160 miles northeast of Grenada. But many of their journeys ended there. For the first time since the Civil War, the government had denied frontline access to journalists in military engagements. Some reporters and photographers rented boats or planes and tried to reach Grenada on their own. At least two boats and a plane were turned back by American warships and aircraft.

Two days after the invasion, the military agreed to fly a pool of 15 journalists to Grenada, but the pool was delayed in returning to Barbados. The reports based on what the pool had seen missed the big network newscasts that night. Somehow, though, the films taken by military camera crews made it back in time. This prompted *The Washington Post* to describe the invasion as "the first official war in the history of the United States, produced, filmed and reported by the Pentagon, under the sanctions of the president."

By the time journalists were allowed to travel to the island, it became clear that the president and Pentagon had issued a lot of misinformation. To make the raid seem more justified, the Pentagon had reported there were at least 1,100 Cubans there, all "well-trained professional soldiers." These Cubans were supposedly planning a military takeover of the island. But the State Department later confirmed that only about 100 of the Cubans were soldiers. The rest were construction workers, working on an airport.

Protests from nearly all major news organizations and journalistic associations apparently pushed the Pentagon to agree to a press-pool arrangement for future Grenada-type military operations. When military aircraft bombed Libya in retaliation for terrorism in 1986, a pool of eight journalists was allowed aboard the USS *America,* an aircraft carrier from which attacking planes were flown.[10]

In press-pool coverage, the pool journalists cover the story for the entire press corps by sharing their reports and photos. Very few journalists like press or media pools. They prefer to have some reporters and photographers present during military operations. However, most agree pool coverage is better than no coverage at all.

Pools Become Tools

Unfortunately for journalists and the public as well, the media pools after the Libyan operation did not work well. When U.S. troops invaded Panama in late 1989, a pool of reporters and photographers was flown to Panama by the Pentagon but was prevented from getting anywhere near the military action. The military said it had to protect the journalists. Instead of covering the invasion by American troops, the pool journalists were kept in windowless rooms at the airport. Once the fighting was over, they were led by their military handlers on tours of deposed dictator Manuel Noreiga's various hideaways. They were shown cocaine, firearms, skin magazines and a Hitler portrait, which were found in Noreiga's lairs.

The military handlers apparently hoped that their reports about these items would cause Americans to support the invasion, which ended with the arrest of the dictator on drug charges. The pool journalists rightly felt they were being used as propagandists.[11] The pool never got near the major stories that came out about six months later: More than a dozen U.S. soldiers were killed or wounded by friendly fire, and the number of casualties among residents of Panama was much higher than originally suggested.[12]

Pool reporting was similarly abused by the military in the 1991 Persian Gulf War. Stanley W. Cloud, Washington bureau chief of *Time* magazine at the time and former Vietnam War correspondent, called it the "worst-covered major U.S. conflict in this century." Not only did the Pentagon restrict Gulf War coverage to rigidly controlled pools, the pool reporters had to agree to submit their reports to military censors for "security review," Cloud noted. Five years before the war started, the media had agreed to allow pool coverage of the initial stage of any U.S. military action. But because "journalists naively failed to insist on binding rules about how and when it would operate, the national media pool quickly became a tool for government control of the press," Cloud stated.[13]

A few Gulf War correspondents like Chris Hedges of *The New York Times* broke out of sole reliance on pool reports and official military briefings. Hedges, who speaks Arabic, wrote later about how he did it:

> For two months several colleagues and I bluffed our way through roadblocks, slept in Arab homes, and cajoled ourselves into (military) units. Eventually, following armored battalions in our jeeps through breached minefields to the outskirts of Kuwait City, we raced across the last stretch of open desert and into the capital before it was liberated. Our success was due in part to an understanding of many soldiers and officers of what the role of a free press is in a democracy. These men and women violated orders to allow us to do our job.[14]

Despite the work of correspondents like Hedges, many in the media played along with the government. Because there was little original video coverage of the war, TV newscasts repeatedly showed the video-game footage of U.S. missiles blasting away Iraqi strongholds. Newspapers too were caught up in the glitz of the war. Many featured elaborate graphics showing how the various high-tech weapons worked. The news reports seemed to indicate that America was waging a clean war with pinpoint-accurate missiles hitting only military targets. Later the military admitted the accuracy of the missiles was considerably less than had been portrayed.

That Hedges received help from soldiers in the field is not unusual. The disagreements between the military and the media are often not between reporters and soldiers, but between reporters and military and political officials who want to control the news. In one 1995 survey, more than half the military officers said they thought the media should be able to report without censorship, and 82 percent agreed that the "news media are just as necessary to maintaining the freedom of the United States as the military." Among members of the news media, 76 percent opposed censorship but acknowledged the need for guidelines.[15]

Working with Police

The relationship between reporters and the police is a complicated one. Police reporters often need lots of detailed information quickly, and the police are their best—and sometimes only—sources. To make this relationship work, many journalists believe that some cooperation between police and reporters is appropriate. Robert Greene, retired managing editor of *Newsday,* noted: "All the cops are required to give a police reporter are the basic skeleton details on the blotter report. But they give him more, plenty of background. They volunteer that information." To keep the information flowing, Greene said, reporters sometimes help police. The ethical question is how much cooperation between the news media and law enforcement can be tolerated without threatening the independence and credibility of the press.

Matthew Waite, a young reporter at Little Rock's *Arkansas Democrat-Gazette,* was tested shortly after he was assigned the police beat. A police source tipped him that the drug unit was planning a large-scale crackdown on cocaine. The reporter arranged to ride along with the police jump teams as they stormed into crack houses ahead of other officers. "Great fun," he said. "High speed chases, deadly force situations, resisting arrests, all within feet of my eyes."

The raids were so successful that police rounded up more suspects than they could handle. They asked Waite to help out by moving a truck. He agreed, "Probably because my parents raised me to always be helpful." But when he returned to his newsroom, his editors weren't happy. "My bosses weren't against being helpful, but they were concerned about crossing that line between observer and participant and about liability issues." They told him not to do it again, or he would face formal reprimand.

Veteran police-beat reporters were divided on the ethics of his conduct. Robert Short, police reporter at *The Wichita Eagle,* believed Waite was behaving as any citizen might. "If the cop needed you to call 911 or hand him his shotgun to save or defend someone's life, would you do that? Of course you would." However, other beat reporters thought it was important to maintain the line between being a reporter and a participant—even in cases like moving a truck. "What happens when you take a step away from your standards, get caught in the middle, then suddenly try to become a reporter again?" asked Kathryn Sosbe of *The Colorado Springs Gazette.* "You really can't waffle back and forth without causing harder feelings. It's better to stand your ground." Sosbe said that when reporters maintain a consistent pattern of integrity, police officers will respect them for their professionalism.[16]

In some well-known examples, reporters have worked directly with law enforcement. The *Chicago Sun-Times* bought and operated the Mirage Tavern to expose shakedowns by city inspectors. Some reporters posed as owners of the tavern. Every day they made reports to the Illinois Department of Law Enforcement, identifying inspectors who took bribes. The reporters had an understanding with the police that no arrests would be made until the end of their project. The reporters were criticized for two reasons: for their use of deception and for being an arm of the law instead of reporters covering a story. (The Mirage series is also discussed in Chapter 10.)

When reporters develop close relationships with police, their reporting can suffer. David Shaw, media critic at the *Los Angeles Times,* wrote a series which concluded that had happened at his paper. The paper was so intertwined with people who wanted to make the police seem effective and the city seem like a good place to visit that it became "a patsy—a press agent—for the police," one judge said. All the while, the *Times* was missing important stories.

Shaw reported that the Los Angeles police department had been understaffed for years because voters and politicians wanted to keep taxes low. To keep the city under control, many police officers felt they needed to show they were tougher than the criminals. Minorities in particular were targets. The mainstream media were blind to the story, even after a commission looking into the riots in the Watts area of Los Angeles concluded that "a resentment, even hatred, of the police [was] a fundamental cause for the riot."

According to Shaw, the *Times* coverage underwent a major shift when David Rosenzweig became city editor in 1979. He moved the paper away from its traditional cops-and-robbers coverage. He wanted coverage that would emphasize the "process" of policing.[17] Other papers have also expanded their coverage to include the conduct of their police departments. *The Dallas Morning News* won a Pulitzer Prize for a series documenting that Texas police had been "investigated and prosecuted more frequently for beating, torture, coerced confessions, rapes and needless deaths than police in any other state."

These stories can lead to tense relationships between police and reporters. In Los Angeles, police complained that the *Times* was "out to get the LAPD" and said their good work was often overlooked while their misdeeds were heavily reported.

In Minneapolis and Portland, Ore., relations between the media and police became so strained that police officials and journalists held meetings to resolve their differences. Minneapolis police complained that journalists used "dirty tricks" to get information that police did not want released. They also objected to being called every 20 minutes by interns wanting to know if there were any developments in their cases. For their part, journalists said that information stored in computers was being kept from them and that police treated reporters as nuisances at crime scenes. After the meetings, the media agreed to call the officers less frequently, and the police bought software that gave reporters easier access to computer records.

In Portland, TV stations used helicopters to broadcast live pictures of a raid by a SWAT team. Police said the pictures could have cost the lives of officers if the suspects had been watching television. After a series of meetings, police officials and news directors agreed to a set of rules that limited how close the helicopters could come to police scenes and what the stations could broadcast live (but not after the event). Police, in turn, promised to provide more information during their tactical operations.[18]

Holding Stories, Reporting Untruths

In the opening of this chapter, journalists in Hattiesburg, Miss., were asked to play along with a hoax. Frank Sutherland, who was managing editor of the paper and president of the Society of Professional Journalists at the time, defended his paper's handling of the situation. He said he had approved of the reporter's cooperating with police when she told them about the murder plot. "You can't hide behind a journalistic shield" when crimes are about to be committed. But he and the paper's publisher thought police wanted too much when they asked them to play along with the hoax. Publisher Duane McCallister explained, "An important principle was at stake—you just don't lie to your readers." Cliff Brown, the manager of the TV station, said he too abided by journalism's commitment to truth. But when a person's life was on the line, "I realized there are few absolutes in the world."

Other news organizations have also been asked to cooperate with officials. *Newsweek* reporter Michael Isikoff was ready to break the story that Monica Lewinsky had said she had sex with President Clinton. Special prosecutor Kenneth Starr begged the magazine to hold the story because he wanted to verify Lewinsky's story by having her wear a hidden microphone. "You want to report what you know," Isikoff told *Brill's Content* magazine. "But you don't want to influence what happens." *Newsweek* editor Richard Smith said that Starr's request was one reason that he decided to delay publication.[19]

Other editors have also cooperated with police by holding stories. When Patty Hearst of the famous newspaper family was kidnapped in 1974, police asked the news media in the San Francisco Bay area to hold the story for 12 and a half hours. All of them did, except for *The Oakland Tribune*. Its publisher insisted on publishing the story because, he said, it was no ordinary kidnapping, many people heard the gunfire when she was abducted, and a story that big could not be kept quiet.[20] Afterward, most journalists joined police in condemning the *Tribune.* When the Professional Standards Committee of the Associated Press Managing Editors association asked 328 editors if they agreed that the story should have been held, 260 said yes, 40 disagreed, and 28 were not sure.[21]

Several news organizations in Florida also wrestled with a request from police to hold a story. Police asked them not to report the kidnapping of a young boy for fear the stories might spook the kidnapper and perhaps cause him to kill the boy and run. All the news media agreed. On the second day, reporters on their own were able to learn some details of the abduction and the name of the boy's father. The FBI added to what was known by releasing a photograph of the child, but it asked that his name not be used. Many journalists were reluctant to publicize a photo without a name, but authorities convinced them that if the name were publicized, every "kook and crazy" in South Florida would make crank calls to the family and interfere with ransom instructions from the kidnapper. Going along with the embargo "was the responsible thing to do," said Bill Dunn, then managing editor of *The Orlando Sentinel.* Police eventually arrested the kidnapper, and the boy was found unharmed.[22]

An even tougher embargo was asked of news media in El Paso, Texas, when two small boys were abducted from their townhouse. Because the kidnappers told the family they would kill the children if any stories about them were printed or broadcast in the first 36 hours, the news media agreed to hold the story that long. They also held the story when the FBI asked for an extension of the news blackout. Two and half days after the kidnapping, the embargo was lifted when the kidnappers told the family they could find the boys in an abandoned car across the river in Juarez, Mexico. They were safe.

"With the FBI telling us that two lives were at stake, it was an easy decision not to run the story," Paula Moore, then co–managing editor of the *El Paso Times,* told readers in an article about the media blackout. "We're not accustomed to withholding news from the community for any reason, but people's lives are certainly more important than an immediate story. We knew we could tell the full story later."[23]

Occasionally police decide that they don't trust the media to play along. In Orlando, Fla., a murder suspect was fleeing police. He had robbed two convenience stories to fuel what police called "a cocaine binge." Then he broke into a home and held two small children hostage. Police surrounded the home, beginning a three-day standoff. At press briefings, police said the man was treating the children well, playing with them and keeping them calm. However, after a SWAT team broke into the house and killed the man while he was asleep, police told a different story. They said the man was a violent sociopath who had shown no kindness toward the children. In negotiations with them, he had coldly threatened to kill them. Why the different stories? Police knew the man watched TV news continuously. "We were trying to help build a bond between him and the children," the chief negotiator said. "Sometimes the press uses us, sometimes we have to use the press."[24]

Pack Journalism

Journalists flock to major news events. As many as 15,000 reporters cover the Democratic and Republican national conventions, and 375 journalists tagged along when President Clinton visited China in 1998. It is estimated that reporters covering Congress outnumber senators and representatives three to one. Even a high-profile crime story can attract hundreds of media people.

With so many journalists covering most major events, one might expect that stories in various newspapers and TV broadcasts would have considerably different angles on and approaches to the same information. But often they don't. Why do so many stories have the same spin? David Shaw of the *Los Angeles Times* calls it "consensus journalism." Others call it "pack" or "herd" journalism. Several reasons have been offered by Shaw and others for such uniform interpretations:

- Journalists, particularly the more than 4,000 covering the national government in Washington, tend to use the same sources and call the same experts. As noted in other chapters, journalists come to depend on sources who sound authoritative and speak in quotable sound bites. When journalists find good sources, they use them over and over.
- News organizations follow the lead of other news organizations. The major print media such as *The New York Times, The Washington Post, The Wall Street Journal, Time, Newsweek* and the Associated Press influence news judgment. For example, each night the wire services carry a list of the stories slated to appear on the front page of *The New York Times* the next day. Many editors and news directors check this list when deciding which stories they will use. If a story is on the *Times* front page, they are more likely to use it. On the other hand, television often provides quick analysis of breaking events. If the president gives a speech, TV reporters and their sources will analyze it immediately. Their comments often become the conventional wisdom that other journalists adopt.

- Journalists may like to think of themselves as iconoclasts and risk takers, but they aren't. They may have been in an earlier day, but most contemporary journalists are "more serious, more formal—both more corporate and more conformist," Shaw wrote. "Journalism is now a Profession, with codes of ethics, pension plans and newsrooms that look more like insurance offices than the cluttered city rooms of generations past. . . . [T]hose in the press are now more inclined toward responsibility than sensationalism, and with responsibility often comes respectability and caution." Normal Pearlstine, former *Wall Street Journal* editor and *Time* magazine executive, adds that much of the conformity is caused by journalists themselves having similar educations, backgrounds and economic statuses.[25]

Some believe the Internet will create less conformity in the media. With little financial backing, people can create Web sites that are visited by tens of thousands of readers. One of the most prominent in the late 1990s was Matt Drudge. Using an aging 486 computer and working out of a small apartment, Drudge drew as many as a million visitors to his Web site some days.

Drudge distanced himself from mainstream journalists. He saw the Internet as an entirely new information system where the public will not need to rely on journalists for news. "Clearly there is a hunger for unedited information, absent corporate considerations," Drudge told the National Press Club in Washington. "Every citizen can be a reporter."

However, many argue that this opens the doors to lots of bad journalism. Although Drudge has broken legitimate stories, some of his most famous scoops have been unsubstantiated rumors that later turned out to be wildly inaccurate. Drudge wasn't overly bothered by his errors. He contended that his job was to relay information that the professional media missed. "All truths begin as hearsay," Drudge said. "Some of the best news stories start as gossip. At what point does it become news? This is the undefinable thing."[26] Drudge's notoriety earned him a talk show on the Fox News network in 1998.

Many Internet news outlets, particularly those with ties to major newspapers, magazines or TV news departments, maintain traditional journalistic standards. Other Web sites report stories from political viewpoints. Many of them can't afford to do original reporting, so they interpret events using information from several news outlets. A few play the role of media watchdog, exposing what they consider to be biased, inaccurate or underreported stories in the mainstream media. As the use of the Internet grows, these Web sites may help rein in the power of pack journalism.

Are Journalists Biased?

Americans tend to think that reporters should keep their opinions out of their stories. But poll after poll shows that the American public believes there is bias in the news. Surveys in 1996 by the Pew Foundation found that 74 percent of the public believed the media are politically biased.[27] The criticism that the media are biased is so widespread that when the Fox cable news channel began in 1996, it promised "something Americans believe is all too rare in journalism: full, fair and balanced coverage of news events." Although occasionally people attack the media as a tool of big business, most people who see bias in the news believe the media are liberal and favor the Democrats. In the 1992 presidential election, for example, more than half thought journalists wanted Clinton to win, while only 17 percent thought they favored Bush.[28]

Many journalists, however, argue that by and large they do keep their opinions to themselves. If they don't, their editors and publishers will see that they do—especially if they try to paint stories with liberal overtones. Everette Dennis, director of the Gannett-supported Freedom Forum Media Studies Center, wrote in *The American Editor* that conservative owners and advertisers wouldn't allow liberal bias because "biased journalism is bad for business."

Political Leanings of Journalists

Surveys have shown that those who complain that journalists aren't like the rest of Americans are right. By and large, journalists aren't representative of the population. They're more likely to be white, male and college-educated. According to surveys, the religious background of journalists is about the same as the rest of the nation: about 60 percent Protestant, 27 percent Catholic and 2 percent Jewish.[29] Yet they were less likely to say they were strongly religious. About 42 percent of the journalists—but only 18 percent of the public—said they were "nonpracticing" in terms of religion.[30]

Journalists also tend to be different from the public on social and political issues. Surveys have found that journalists tend to be more liberal—or at least less conservative—than the population on most social issues. But on economic issues, they tend to be more conservative than the public.

The *Los Angeles Times* surveyed newspaper journalists' opinions on social issues. It found journalists were

- More likely to favor abortion than the general public (82 percent to 51 percent).
- More likely to favor government help for people who are unable to support themselves (95 percent to 83 percent).
- More likely to support employee rights for homosexuals (89 percent to 57 percent).
- More likely to support affirmative action for blacks and other minorities (81 percent to 57 percent).
- More likely to support stricter handgun controls (78 percent to 50 percent).
- More likely to support government regulation of business (49 percent to 22 percent).
- Less likely than the public to support prayers in the public schools (25 percent to 74 percent).
- Less likely to favor the death penalty (47 percent to 75 percent).

Professor David Croteau of Virginia Commonwealth University surveyed Washington-based journalists' opinions on economic issues. He found that they were more conservative than the public on issues such as corporate power, foreign trade, Social Security and Medicare, health care, and taxes. For example, journalists were less concerned about the power of giant corporations. In Croteau's poll, 43 percent of the journalists did not believe corporations were too powerful. The public is much more fearful, with 77 percent saying corporations had too much power. Similarly, journalists were much more satisfied with the economy than the public.

The accusation that journalists are liberal is often based on the perception that they seek out liberal sources for their articles. However, Croteau found that when Washington-based journalists looked for sources for their articles, they were more likely to turn to government and business officials than to liberal sources like labor union officials or consumer activists.

In Croteau's study, most journalists called themselves "centrist" in their political orientation. The minority of journalists who do not identify with the "center" are more likely to identify with the "right" when it comes to economic issues and the "left" when it comes to social issues. Croteau suggested these findings explain why journalists tended to vote for Bill Clinton in large numbers. Clinton's centrist "new Democrat" orientation combined moderately liberal social policies with moderately conservative economic policies.[31]

Of course, these findings alone do not prove that the news itself is slanted by reporters to suit their political leanings. A University of California sociologist suggested the possibility that "many reporters, inclined to be Democrats themselves, bend over backwards to avoid the appearance of being unfair to Republicans" and end up being more critical of Democrats.[32] Also, most journalists work for large corporations and therefore do not have the final say on the content of their stories. Many contend that the corporate culture keeps reporters' personal views out of their copy.

Editorial Pages Tell Another Story

If journalists tend to be liberal on so many issues, one might expect newspaper editorial pages—traditionally the pages where opinion is supposed to be expressed—to strongly advocate liberal positions and routinely to endorse liberal Democrats and attack conservative Republicans. That is not the case.

On their editorial pages, newspapers have been strong supporters of conservative presidential candidates. The majority of newspaper endorsements preferred conservative Republican Ronald Reagan to middle-of-the-road Democrat Jimmy Carter in 1980, Reagan to liberal Democrat Walter Mondale in 1984 and conservative Republican George Bush to liberal Democrat Michael Dukakis in 1988. Conservative Republican Richard Nixon got more endorsements than any of his three liberal Democratic opponents, including John F. Kennedy. Nixon was endorsed by 57.7 percent of the papers, Kennedy by 16.4 percent.

The conservative leanings are so strong that since 1936, when records of such things were started, newspapers have endorsed 13 of the 15 Republican presidential candidates by overwhelming margins. For instance, in 1940 Republican Wendell Willkie won the endorsement race, 59 percent to incumbent Democrat Franklin Roosevelt's 19 percent, and in 1948 Republican Thomas Dewey was preferred to Democrat Harry Truman, 79 percent to 10 percent.

The only exceptions to this Republican landslide in newspaper endorsements were in 1964 when Democrat Lyndon Johnson edged Republican Barry Goldwater, 440 endorsements to 359, and in 1992 when Democrat Bill Clinton got 183 endorsements to George Bush's 138. An overwhelming majority of papers chose not to make an endorsement in that race, and a handful endorsed Ross Perot.[33]

So if journalists are so liberal, why do newspapers endorse so many conservatives? The explanation to this seeming paradox is that most working journalists—liberal or otherwise—have little say in the editorial policy of the newspapers they work for. These decisions are usually made by the top editor and an editorial board, and these top editors tend to be more conservative than their reporters. In the *Times* poll, 35 percent of the top editors said they were conservative compared with 17 percent of the rest of the news staff. On many political and social issues, top editors were more like the general public than they were their news staffs.

Moreover, the majority of the top editors answer to general managers and publishers, most of whom are employed by large corporations to run the paper. At about 60 percent of the papers, these executives play a direct role in the direction of the editorial pages, and often they are even more conservative than the top editors. One survey found that 72 percent of the top editors at chain-owned papers and 68 percent at nonchain papers believed they were more liberal than their publishers or general managers.

That means that sometimes the top editors of the paper may not agree with the positions taken on their editorial pages. These top editors said that nearly a fourth of the time they do not vote for the candidates their papers endorse. Sometimes the number of editors who disagree with their papers' endorsements is striking. For instance, 65 percent of them said their papers endorsed Reagan over Mondale, but only 35 percent of the editors said they voted for Reagan.[34]

Many newspapers have also stopped making presidential endorsements. In 1996 nearly 70 percent of editors responding to a poll by *Editor & Publisher* magazine said they would not make an endorsement in the Clinton-Dole race. That's up from about two-thirds who did not make endorsements in 1992. In 1940, when *E&P* first tracked presidential endorsements, only 13.4 percent stayed neutral. Editors offer many reasons for no-endorsement policies. Many fear that if their paper endorses a candidate, people will believe that the paper's news content will be slanted toward that candidate.[35]

Few TV and radio stations make endorsements, and most carry no editorials at all on a daily basis.

Does the News Have a Liberal Slant?

Does the news have a liberal slant? That's a question that has dogged researchers for years. There is no easy way to answer it. For one thing, it is difficult to know what is going on in a reporter's mind. A story that seems unfair may be an indication that the reporter was biased—or that the reporter was incompetent, failed to understand the issues or was rushed to meet a deadline.

Even trying to define words like "fairness" and "balance" can create problems. People can, in good faith, disagree on their meanings. Some researchers measure "balance" and "fairness" using an "equal-time" formula. They measure the time or space given to each candidate. The assumption is that if the media are fair, each candidate should get the same amount of space in the paper or time on TV newscasts.

Yet measuring column inches or timing TV segments will not take into account the substance of the coverage. For instance, researchers studied a TV news segment in which the reporter was doing a voice-over. His words were unfavorable to a candidate. However, while the reporter was talking, stock video favorable to the candidate was being shown on screen. Viewers tended to remember seeing the positive images but didn't recall the negative words. Research has shown that camera angles can have an impact on how viewers react to a candidate and that people may react differently to close-up photos than to medium and long shots.[36] None of these characteristics is counted when researchers rely on an "equal-time" formula.

Some have another concern about using equal time or space as the basis for fairness. They contend that if the news media try to give equal time or equal space, they may not provide voters with the best coverage of the campaign. For example, front-running incumbents often follow a "Rose Garden" strategy. To avoid making mistakes, they stage only "safe" appearances and stay away from discussions of controversial issues and debates. Challengers, on the other hand, may be raising important issues and running event-filled campaigns.

Some say that a better way to determine fairness and balance is to use an "equal opportunity" formula. Under this notion of fairness, reporters follow the candidates' activities with equal diligence. Then they make news judgments about what goes into the paper or on the nightly news. If the incumbent visits a veteran's hospital and the challenger unveils a major tax proposal, the challenger is likely to get more coverage. However, the "equal opportunity" formula is not easy for researchers to apply. The analysis requires researchers to judge the accuracy, judgment and motivations of the reporters.

Not only is defining "fairness" difficult, people often perceive different things in the same reports. Longtime CBS newsman and commentator Eric Sevareid observed that there was plenty of "biased reading and hearing." By that he meant that many people see bias in the media when the facts in a story do not jibe with the way they would like the world to be. This is especially true for true believers in a cause or a candidate.

Los Angeles Times media reporter David Shaw ran into this when he reviewed two books critical of the media—one written from a liberal perspective and one from a conservative viewpoint. He stated that reading the books back-to-back "is a bit like listening to two people's accounts of a football game in which each rooted for the opposite side." One author saw liberal bias in the same news accounts that the other author saw conservative bias.[37]

Even people with similar political leanings can interpret the same information much differently. As researcher Michael Robinson has pointed out, some people said that Ronald Reagan won a landslide victory in 1984 despite hostile coverage by network television. Others said that his campaign received a major boost from the TV networks because their "superficial, picture-oriented coverage fit perfectly with his masterful media management."[38]

Finally, even if research concludes beyond a doubt that one candidate received considerably more bad press, that may not indicate that the reporting was biased. As a journalist once suggested, sometimes when reporters say it's raining, it really is raining. Politicians can make mistakes or run poor campaigns. News coverage will reflect these problems.

Also, reporters today believe that they should do more than report the event. They should try to explain why things happen and who is affected. This can lead to coverage that seems to favor one candidate. If a candidate wows a bloc of voters, does well in the polls or wins a primary unexpectedly, reporters will produce stories that explain these successes and will reflect positively on the candidate. On the other hand, when a candidate makes gaffes, takes unpopular positions, or does poorly in polls and primaries, reporters will write about them too. To supporters, the media may seem to be ganging up on their candidate.

Academic researchers are aware of these problems, and they've tried to find ways of overcoming them. As one might expect, with so many factors to consider, their studies have not been conclusive. In the 1980s and 1990s, about half the studies found media bias and half didn't.[39] For example, a study that used one approach concluded that the media gave Clinton more favorable coverage than Dole in the 1996 election. But other researchers using different methods found "remarkably balanced media coverage."[40]

After studying three campaigns, Michael Robinson and his colleagues at George Washington University concluded: "Ideological bias is one of those mistakes that the network news doesn't make. In the 1980 primaries CBS treated 'liberal' Ted Kennedy worse than it treated 'middle-of-the-roader' Jimmy Carter, and in the general-election campaign CBS treated Carter worse than Reagan."

In the Reagan-Mondale race, they found that there were 10 times as many negative things about Reagan as positive things and seven times as many negative things about him as there were negative things about Mondale. They pointed out, however, that the bulk of the news about the candidates was neither positive nor negative. They concluded that "overall the biased pieces were so few and the bias so weak in implication that real issue bias hardly existed at all."[41]

Robinson's studies concentrated primarily on story content. Other researchers, like Doris Graber, have made efforts to include the impact television's pictures and graphics might have on voters in the same election. She found that the words reporters spoke were more favorable to Mondale, but that a disproportionate share of Reagan's coverage dealt with traits favorable to him, like his personableness and good looks.[42]

If academic researchers have so much trouble finding bias, why is it that so many people believe that coverage is routinely slanted? Researcher Mark Watts and his colleagues believe they may have an answer. Their research found no significant bias in the coverage of the presidential elections in 1988, 1992 and 1996. However, two other phenomena were at work. First, many candidates, especially conservative ones, were accusing the media of bias. Then the media repeated their claims, and reporters and talk shows began to discuss "the liberal media." Many in the public could not themselves cite any specific instance of bias, but they were convinced the bias was there. The researchers pointed out this irony: Because of their belief in fairness and objectivity, the media report politicians' claims of bias, yet these stories may contribute to many people not trusting the fairness of the news.[43]

Studies like these are of interest to journalists and political scientists, but they are unlikely to have much impact on the public's impressions of the media. As Robinson observed: "Can anyone other than a Democrat conclude that political reporting is unbiased against Republicans and conservatives? Perhaps not. Nor will these data persuade many true believers that over the long haul the national press is biased against everybody, but in near equal proportions."[44]

The Tilt toward Bad News

Michael Robinson's contention that the media are "biased against everybody" is a frequent criticism of news organizations. Robinson saw so much negativity in newscasts that he described the news as a "cacophony of carping and criticism." His research found that bad-news messages outnumbered good ones 20 to one, although most of the news was neutral. In 100 days of watching all three network news broadcasts, his researchers found only 47 positive statements by correspondents.[45] This trend was also evident in the 1996 elections. Researchers found that while the coverage was chiefly objective, it contained few positive stories and a high percentage that were negative. When motives were attributed to the candidates, they were "almost exclusively categorized as self-serving."[46]

Some believe the real problem with the media is not that reporters favor the liberals or the conservatives. Instead, they fault journalists for their bias toward bad news. James Squires, the former *Chicago Tribune* editor who became Perot's press spokesman in the 1992 presidential campaign, said he did not believe the media attacked Perot because the reporters disagreed with Perot's politics. He believed they attacked Perot because it was the best way to advance their careers. Squires argued that reporters are so intent on getting a front-page story that they stoop to "hit-and-run journalism." They know that reporting negative news about a candidate will get more play for their stories than if they report positive news. So, Squires said, journalists will report rumors and break promises to sources because "simply taking the story to a new level and creating controversy does more for a reporter's career today than the more mundane truth ever could."

Squires is not a Johnny-come-lately critic of journalists' preference for bad news. When he was editor of the *Chicago Tribune,* he criticized young reporters at Chicago's city magazines by saying: "They go out of their way to bash the big institutions. . . . They're not going to attract any attention if they have a very positive kind of story." He explained:

> If you go to *Chicago* magazine and say, "Boy, the *Tribune* sure has changed in the last seven years; it's a great newspaper now," there's not any interest. If you go into them and you say, "You know, I hear there's great conflict of interest in the editor's office at the *Tribune* and he had a temper tantrum the other day and wet on his desk," then they say, "Jesus Christ, that's a great story; let's get that."[47]

Other journalists have come to the same conclusion about the press's penchant for bad news. Reluctantly, they have begun to agree with Spiro Agnew, who was Richard Nixon's vice president until he had to resign amid a bribery scandal. Agnew once described reporters as "nattering nabobs of negativism."

Many people mistake this negativism for bias because they just do not understand the "dynamics of the journalistic process," according to the *Los Angeles Times'* David Shaw. He explained, "They don't understand that good news isn't news, for example, or that the bias most reporters have is not political but journalistic: They are biased in favor of a good story, a juicy, controversial story that will land them on Page 1 or on the network evening news."

Shaw acknowledged that reporters may get more pleasure out of writing negative stories about candidates they don't like. "But," he wrote, "almost every reporter I've ever known would rather break a really juicy story exposing the wrongdoing of a politician he agrees with than do a routine story making that same politician look good. Does that make us ghouls? Nattering nabobs of negativism? Yes. Is that good? Probably not. But it sure as hell doesn't make us ideologues or cheerleaders for the left."[48]

Syndicated columnist Richard Cohen said it more pointedly: "Liberal or conservative, a reporter is a primitive being who would go after his own mother if he thought that was a good story." *Time* magazine concluded an article on bias in the media with this observation:

> Some of the toughest stories about Clinton have emerged from the liberal *New York Times* and *Los Angeles Times.* Bush's two most ferocious critics, syndicated columnists William Safire of *The New York Times* and George Will of the *Washington Post,* are staunch members of his own party. That summarizes the deepest objection most politicians have to journalists—not that they are liberal, nor that they are conservative, but that they are stubbornly individualistic and persistent.[49]

While the *Time* writer presented journalists' leanings toward negativity in almost heroic terms, polls show that the public doesn't like the media's emphasis on bad news. Two-thirds of the respondents in one survey complained that the media were too negative.[50]

Columnist William Raspberry suggested that reporters need to consider a different approach to covering the news. When Raspberry speaks to groups of reporters, he begins with a question: "What's happening in this community that especially pleases you? What activity or program or individual do you find exemplary, worth letting readers across the country know about?" Raspberry said that no matter where he is, he always gets the same answer: dead silence. Raspberry said that reporters know positive things about their communities. "Our training, the news values we inculcate, the feedback we get from our editors," he said, "all encourage us to look for trouble, for failure, for scandal, above all for conflict. This is not to say that news outlets should stop covering conflict. But if they cover conflict to the exclusion of stories that reflect efforts to build community, they risk breeding general cynicism."[51]

10

Deception

Imagine that you are executive editor of a metropolitan daily newspaper. A veteran reporter on your staff has been doing an exhaustive study of the prison system in the United States. He has spent months investigating American prisons and jails, inspecting dozens of them and interviewing scores of prisoners and experts on the penal system. Still, he does not believe he could truly describe the psychological effect of being inside just from talking to prisoners. He wants to pass himself off as a criminal and spend a few days in some big state penitentiary to find out what it's like from the inside. This, of course, will mean that he will have to deceive some people because if the warden knows who he is, he will get special treatment, and if the other inmates know who he is, his life may not be worth a nickel. Nevertheless, the reporter believes he can arrange to get himself incarcerated without the people at the prison knowing he is really a journalist.

Do you approve of your reporter posing as a criminal for a few days, assuming that his security can be assured? Are you concerned that he will not identify himself as a reporter? Does it bother you that the people will assume they are having private conversations with a fellow inmate when in reality they are being interviewed for a newspaper story? Will the information he will learn in jail justify all the deception needed to pull off his scheme?

Those are the kinds of problems that confronted the editors of *The Washington Post* in 1971 when Ben Bagdikian wanted to get inside the Huntingdon State Correctional Institution in Pennsylvania as an inmate. His editor decided to allow him to do it. Bagdikian arranged his incarceration through the state attorney general's office and assumed a false identification, a false name and a false history. The warden and Bagdikian's fellow inmates did not learn his true identity until five weeks after his release when they read about his experiences inside Huntingdon in the second of an eight-part series called "The Shame of the Prisons."[1]

When Bagdikian ran into the warden at a conference on prisons several months later, the warden accused him "of unethical behavior, of coming into his prison under false pretenses." Bagdikian tried to explain, but the warden was too angry. "No warden or administrator likes to think he was spied upon for public use," Bagdikian said.[2]

Ironically, the editor who approved Bagdikian's posing as a convict later began to reconsider his paper's use of deception and came to a conclusion much like the warden's: He no longer could justify using "false pretenses" to get a story. Bagdikian's editor was Benjamin Bradlee, who played a key role in the *Post*'s Watergate probe. Bradlee began to believe that if the news media were going to criticize other people for lying and using dirty tricks, reporters should not lie and trick people either.[3] Bradlee's change of heart coincided with the growing belief among newspaper journalists that honest reporting rarely needed to begin with dishonesty.

However, as newspapers began a full-scale retreat from the use of deception in the 1980s, TV news began to adopt it with gusto. The ethics of deception can still stir heated debate among serious-minded journalists.

The Three Faces of Deception

What Bagdikian did in passing himself off as an inmate is often called "undercover" reporting. That term creates an exciting picture in people's minds of reporters pretending to be Klansmen and criminals. However, not all undercover reporting fits this image. Even when journalists merely pose as members of the public, their motive is still to get a story. They are misrepresenting their intentions. All undercover reporting involves deception. This deception takes three forms:

- Active deception, in which reporters stage events so they can expose wrongdoing.
- Passive deception, in which reporters appear to be just members of the public so they can gather information without people knowing reporters are present.

- Masquerading, in which reporters misrepresent themselves as other people.

Active Deception

When most reporters do stories about cheats, charlatans and governmental fraud, they interview victims, police and prosecutors; talk to experts who work for public-interest groups or at universities; and search public records for verification of the allegations. But that's not enough documentation for some journalists. They believe they must take an active role in arranging events so they can uncover wrongdoers and get the most accurate and complete story.

For example, producers from CBS's *60 Minutes* had heard that owners of clinics were receiving illegal kickbacks from the laboratories that processed their medical tests. The practice was costing Medicare and Medicaid millions of dollars a year and was growing. After a citizens-action group, called the Better Government Association, told *60 Minutes* that the scheme was widespread in Chicago, *60 Minutes* rented office space there and announced that a new clinic would soon open. Members of the citizens group posed as staff while a camera crew hid behind one-way mirrors. Soon a salesman from a laboratory came in and offered to pay kickbacks. After hearing the offer, *60 Minutes* reporters popped out of a back room and confronted the salesman. He told them kickbacks "were a way of life in inner-city Chicago."[4]

An even more dramatic example of active deception was carried off by the *Wilmington (N.C.) Morning Star*. In 1983 America was mourning the loss of 241 Marines who were killed when terrorists drove a truck loaded with explosives up to a U.S. Marine barracks in Beirut and set off the bombs. Reporters at the *Morning Star* wondered if terrorists could do the same thing at nearby Camp Lejeune. They decided to find out by staging their own terrorist assault. One team of reporters drove trucks filled with boxes that could have contained explosives into the base; another team entered the base by boat. Once inside, they roamed the base taking pictures of their trucks outside buildings that terrorists would probably have targeted, like barracks and communication offices. A couple of the reporters were even able to get inside base headquarters and the base commander's house simply by asking to use the rest room. They left notes pointing out that if they had been terrorists, they could have planted bombs inside those buildings.

The Marines later said that they knew in advance that the reporters were coming and used their assault to practice counter-terrorist drills. However, after the raid, security was tightened, and the base's two top officers were reassigned.[5]

Passive Deception

No staging or setting up of sting operations is required for passive deception. Reporters using this approach simply do not identify themselves as reporters. They let others assume they are just members of the public. Perhaps the most benign use of passive deception is when restaurant critics fail to inform their waiters that they are dealing with a journalist or when reporters doing consumer stories pose as customers to check the honesty of repair shops and other businesses.

A more elaborate example of passive deception was provided by Neil Henry, a reporter from *The Washington Post*. He was working on a story in 1983 about the exploitation of jobless and often homeless men in Washington. He learned they were offered jobs picking vegetables in the South with promises of good pay and good living conditions. But what they encountered after they were hauled to the fields was backbreaking work, filthy bunkhouses and overpriced meals featuring delicacies like pig ears. Sometimes after a day's work, they had earned only enough to pay for their meals and a night in the bunkhouse.

Wanting to get a first-hand taste of this treatment, Henry decided to hang around soup kitchens in Washington. As he had expected, one day a recruiter asked him if he wanted a job. The reporter answered all the recruiter's questions honestly—he used his real name and Social Security number—and said he was willing to work. He did not volunteer that he was a reporter, although he carried his press card. After working in the fields but before writing his story, he returned to the farm as a *Post* reporter and interviewed the operator of the camp. He also talked to the man who had recruited him and others who knew about the legal and illegal harvesting of crops in that part of the world.[6] Henry contended that to understand "this particular subculture," he had "to become, as nearly as possible, one of these people, to suffer as they do, to yearn as they do. The only way to really get the story was to become part of the story."[7]

A similar use of passive deception earned reporter Tony Horwitz of *The Wall Street Journal* a Pulitzer Prize in 1995. Horwitz worked at a chicken-processing plant and then wrote about the degrading routines of the workers. According to *Columbia Journalism Review,* Horwitz did not falsify his work history on his job application but listed his employer as Dow Jones, the corporate owners of the *Journal.* Plant managers apparently mistook the name as "Don Jones," a large poultry wholesaler.

For many journalists, passive deception is a harder call than active deception. James Squires, when he was editor of the *Chicago Tribune,* acknowledged that passive deception can be as "deceptive as lying." Nevertheless, he said, "I'm more comfortable if I can be deceptive by silence and not deliberately lie and misrepresent myself."8 Editors at *The New York Times* apparently take a similar position. They approved reporter Jane Lii's request to go undercover for a story. However, they reminded her that she "was under express instructions to do nothing misleading." This order presented no problems for her. When the managers of a garment sweatshop saw a young woman who looked Asian, they immediately offered her a job that required brutal 15-hour days with only 15-minute lunch breaks.9 Rules at *The Washington Post* no longer allow a reporter to pose as a prison inmate, but they are less clear on the ethics of passive deception.

Masquerading

Tales are often told about Harry Romanoff of the old *Chicago American* who would pose as a police officer, a coroner or even a governor to get a story.10 He once got the mother of mass murderer Richard Speck to talk to him by telling her he was her son's attorney.11 Romanoff died in 1970, but his techniques have lived on.

Many older journalists have known reporters who made calls from the press room in police headquarters and introduced themselves this way: "Hi, I'm Mike Jones. I'm calling from police headquarters." The ploy often worked; people assumed they were talking to a police official.

Some journalists have not just masqueraded as someone else, they have developed elaborate plots. Robert Greene had an illustrious career as an investigative journalist for *Newsday* and a founder of the Investigative Reporters and Editors organization. According to a *Quill* article, Greene was having no luck getting information about a man involved in heroin trafficking in 1974. So Greene called the man's wife and told her he was an attorney who represented an estate. Her husband had been left $8,000 in the will. However, before the woman could collect, Greene explained that he would need some information about her husband so he could feel sure he had found the right family. To complete the masquerade, Greene had phony business cards printed, wrote a seven-page will and had another reporter play the role of his secretary. Greene's ploy was so convincing that the man's wife not only provided Greene the information he wanted but gave him a picture of her fugitive husband.12

Other journalists have used equally successful disguises. When Lester Piggott, the great English jockey, was riding in a race in Florida in 1992, his horse fell, throwing him to the ground and shattering several of his bones. Although hospital employees had been told to keep visitors away from the jockey because he needed rest, they allowed a priest, a mortician and a laboratory technician to enter his room. But they weren't the people they appeared to be. They were reporters for British tabloids, wanting to get pictures of the jockey and maybe even a quote or two.[13]

American journalists have also posed as hospital employees to eavesdrop on conversations they were not supposed to hear. When Eugene L. Roberts Jr., former editor of *The Philadelphia Inquirer,* was covering a murder case as a reporter for the Raleigh *News & Observer,* he picked up a stethoscope from a desk in a hospital and walked nonchalantly into the emergency room where police were questioning a suspect. No one stopped him as he went into the interrogation room and heard the suspect confess to police. Years after the trick, Roberts still believed he was justified. "I didn't lie to anyone," Roberts said. "We're not obligated to wear a neon sign."[14]

But some reporters believe that telling people who you are is important, even to the point of wearing signs. David Halberstam, who won a Pulitzer Prize for his reporting from Vietnam for *The New York Times,* stated that when he was in Vietnam, he and Horst Faas of the AP "got these little tags that we sewed on our fatigue jackets that said 'Halberstam, New York Times' and 'Faas, AP.' Most of the reporters began to do this. We didn't want anyone to speak to us with any misimpression of who we were."[15] Surveys suggest that most journalists today agree with Halberstam. Seventy percent of those polled said claiming to be someone else could never be justified. Almost the same percentage of the public told pollsters they feel the same way.[16]

Although news organizations may require reporters to identify themselves, some reporters do not believe it is necessary to identify themselves immediately. Veteran police reporter Mary Murphy of the *Portland (Maine) Press Herald* has found that many people shy away from reporters. So when she goes to the scene of a crime, she will often strike up conversations with people without telling them who she is. "But not a word they say before I identify myself will be used in my story," she explains. "If they don't want to talk to a reporter, I find someone else."[17]

From Nellie Bly to Diane Sawyer

For nearly 100 years journalists used variations of these three kinds of deception and rarely gave the ethics of them a second thought. When

Bagdikian asked Bradlee if he could pose as a prisoner, Bradlee's "chief concern was security not the ethics of it," Bagdikian stated.[18]

Undercover reporting goes back at least to the 1890s when Nellie Bly (her real name was Elizabeth Cochrane) pretended to be insane to find out how patients were treated in Blackwell's Island Insane Asylum. Her three articles for the old *New York World* were headlined "Ten Days in a Mad-House."[19]

The heyday for undercover reporting by newspapers was in the 1930s, perhaps because most cities had two or more papers battling for dwindling depression dollars. Nellie Bly's inside report on a mental institution was repeated by the old *Chicago Times* in 1933. Silas Bent's story was headlined "Seven Days in a Madhouse." Bent acknowledged that his undercover report caused the *Times'* circulation to go up considerably "but that was of minor importance in comparison with a drastic cleanup of the institution."[20]

When journalism historian Frank Luther Mott started publishing collections of the best news stories each year, undercover reports were mainstays. The best news stories of 1934, for example, included an exposé of the Drake estate swindlers by a *Milwaukee Journal* reporter who pretended to be a prospective investor and a story by an *Omaha World-Herald* reporter who posed as a transient and spent a night in a shelter for homeless men.[21]

Undercover reporting by newspapers continued into the 1960s and 1970s. Even Nellie Bly's madhouse story had a copier in 1975. Annapolis *Capital* reporter Doug Struck conned his way into the Crownsville, Md., Hospital Center, a mental institution, and wrote about the jail-like conditions he found during his six days as a patient there.[22] A Pulitzer Prize was given to William Jones of the *Chicago Tribune*, who took a job as an ambulance driver for a story about collusion between police and ambulance companies in 1971. The *Tribune* also won Pulitzers for stories done by reporters who posed as election judges to uncover vote fraud in 1973 and worked in hospitals to document patient abuses in 1976. The New York *Daily News* got a Pulitzer in 1974 after a reporter and photographer posed as Medicaid patients with the knowledge of New York Medicaid officials and exposed doctors who were cheating the system.

Turnaround on the Mirage

To find out about reported shakedowns of small businesses by government inspectors, the *Chicago Sun-Times* went into the tavern business. Reporters Pamela Zekman and Zay N. Smith posed as a couple from out of town and bought a tavern they called the Mirage. With help from Chicago's private, muckraking Better Government Association, Zekman and Smith rigged the tavern with obvious plumbing and electrical problems. They also built little hideaways where photographers could snap pictures as dozens of electrical and building inspectors solicited bribes to overlook the deficiencies. Zekman and Smith allowed state officials to set up a special auditing team in the bar to uncover tax fraud by accountants who specialized in taverns, restaurants and other cash businesses.

The *Sun-Times* exposé rocked Chicago with four weeks of exciting, dramatic stories and pictures. Scores of electrical and building inspectors were indicted for soliciting bribes. Ralph Otwell, who was then editor of the *Sun-Times,* called the series the most successful undercover investigation the paper had done for 40 years. Otwell said that "it documented something that had always been a truism in Chicago but yet had never been documented by anybody to the extent that we did it."[23] Journalism schools sought out Zekman and Smith as guest speakers.

Although the series attracted attention around the nation, it did not attract another Pulitzer Prize to the *Sun-Times'* display case.

Why no Pulitzer for such an enterprising piece of reporting? Like *The Washington Post's* Bradlee, many editors were growing concerned about the ethics of using deception. Eugene C. Patterson, a member of the Pulitzer advisory board in 1979 and 1982, said the Mirage series caused a debate on the board. Many believed that by honoring undercover reporting, they were endorsing it. Patterson, then chief executive officer of the *St. Petersburg Times,* said he was among those opposed to giving the Mirage series a Pulitzer. He called undercover reporting "a fashionable trend I don't like to see encouraged." He said he believed "that the press as a whole pays a price in credibility when a newspaper that editorially calls for government in the sunshine and candor in business shows itself disposed to shade the truth or mask its motives." Patterson said undercover reporting should be limited to "extraordinary circumstance that would require a policy decision by the editor."[24]

When the Pulitzer board did not give the *Sun-Times* the prize for the Mirage in 1979 and then rejected another undercover story in 1982, most newspaper journalists began to reconsider the ethics of undercover reporting. Many editors decided to limit the use of deception by reporters. The *Sun-Times* has since stopped the practice.[25]

Undercover Reporting Rebounds on Television

By the early 1990s, most newspaper editors were showing disdain for deception and misrepresentation. However, hidden cameras and phony identities were becoming standard tactics of many TV news programs. Tabloid TV shows like *A Current Affair, Hard Copy* and *Inside Edition* were getting large ratings with their mixture of hidden-camera exposés, re-enacted news events and frequent stories on top-less dancers and sexy murders. Meanwhile, network news-magazine programs like ABC's *20/20* and *PrimeTime Live,* CBS's *60 Minutes,* and similar programs on NBC were using hidden cameras to uncover insurance fraud, auto-repair rip-offs and poor treatment of children in day-care centers.

That's not to say that television had not done undercover report-ing before. *60 Minutes* has a long history of using hidden cameras, and before he became a talk-show host, Geraldo Rivera did serious undercover reporting for ABC. Local stations like WBBM in Chicago developed reputations for their investigative work, which occasion-ally made use of undercover techniques. However, in those days the use of undercover reporting on TV was relatively rare. Now hardly a day goes by that a viewer can't see hidden cameras at work on one of the tabloid TV shows, a network newsmagazine or the local evening news.

Perhaps the biggest flap over a TV undercover story was created by Diane Sawyer's report on ABC's *PrimeTime Live* about Food Lion supermarkets.[26] A labor union that was trying to organize Food Lion workers tipped the show's producers about unsanitary practices in some of the chain's stores. Union organizers gave the producers a list of employees to interview. After talking to the employees, *PrimeTime* decided to have one of its researchers get a job at a Food Lion store and take along a hidden camera. At first the researcher couldn't get hired. So producers had to step up the level of deception. Union mem-bers gave her a crash course in how to wrap meat, created a phony work history for her and supplied her with a glowing recommenda-tion from her "previous boss" at an out-of-state grocery. She wrote on her application that "I really miss working in a grocery story, and I love meat wrapping." She said she hoped to have a career with Food Lion.

Once on the payroll, she began videotaping her fellow employees as they gave her advice on how to do her job, including ways to sell old meat and deli products as if they were fresh. They sometimes would douse old meat in barbecue sauce and sell it at a premium price since it was ready to grill. She did not witness the most striking claim made by employees. They said that some meat-counter em-ployees would soak outdated meat in bleach and then repackage it. ABC invited Food Lion to answer the charges, but officials rejected the offer.

Public response to the segment was dramatic. Food Lion sales dropped immediately, and the value of the company's stock fell. Officials delayed expansion plans and closed some stores, causing layoffs. The company fought back with TV ads emphasizing the cleanliness of its stores and pointing out that the chain had an "above average" rating from state health inspectors.

The chain sued ABC. It did not accuse ABC of libel nor did it claim the story was false. Instead, Food Lion accused ABC of committing fraud when the researcher lied on her application. A jury agreed and awarded Food Lion $5.5 million in 1997. A judge reduced the award to $315,000. ABC's appeal of the decision was still pending as this was written.

A Controversial Method

For at least 30 years, people both in and out of journalism have been debating whether the news media's use of undercover reporting is justified. The debate often centers on these questions:

- Are the hidden cameras being used purely to hype the story?
- Do the ends—uncovering wrongdoing—justify the means—using deception and possibly violating laws?
- Are there privacy concerns?
- Are hidden cameras the best way to get the story?
- How significant and widespread is the issue under investigation?

Hype or News?

Undercover reporting with hidden cameras can yield legitimate news stories that capture the attention of the audience. But many worry that the hidden cameras are being used only for the hype. "Nothing matters anymore, except the competition for audience," Reuven Frank, former president of NBC News, told a *Chicago Tribune* reporter. "Everybody in the spectrum is fighting everybody else for audience, so you're getting a mushing up of [ethical] standards. Standards are fine, if they don't lose audience."[27]

Many journalists say the quest for higher ratings is not an acceptable reason to go undercover. *60 Minutes* reporter Mike Wallace would agree. "You don't like to baldly lie, but I have," he said. "It really depends on your motive. Are you doing it for drama or are you doing it for illumination?"[28]

There's little question that some stations have used hidden-camera reports to create drama and boost ratings. During one sweeps period, KENS-TV in San Antonio broadcast a report on homosexual activity at a public park, promoted as "Perverts in the Park." According to *CJR,* the station showed hidden-camera video of "men explicitly, graphically, unmistakably engaged in oral sex" twice during the report. The anchor later apologized to viewers, explaining, "I think it's probably the result of a continued attempt to get ratings."[29]

Ends Versus Means

When journalists discuss the ethics of deception, they often get embroiled in a controversy that's been around since the time of Plato: Do the ends justify the means? Or, as Valerie Hyman, a former TV journalist and ethics teacher at the Pointer Institute, phrased it, "If truthtelling is one of the values we hold dear as journalists, then we have to think awfully hard before we decide to be deceptive in our pursuit of telling the truth."[30]

Don Hewitt, *60 Minutes* producer, believes the ends often justify the means. "It's the small crime versus the greater good," he argued. "If you catch someone violating 'thou shall not steal' by your 'thou shall not lie,' that's a pretty good trade-off."[31] However, former *Washington Post* executive editor Benjamin Bradlee concluded: "In a day in which we are spending thousands of man hours uncovering deception, we simply cannot deceive. How can newspapers fight for honesty and integrity when they themselves are less than honest in getting a story. When cops pose as newspapermen, we get goddamn sore. Quite properly so. So how can we pose as something we're not."[32]

Others point out that when journalists go undercover, they often break the law. People are not allowed to sneak onto restricted military bases, lie to school officials or apply for passports under phony names. Yet journalists have done these things without being arrested or punished. Jurors in the Food Lion case sent a clear message that they did not think ABC's researchers were above the law. They thought the journalists had committed fraud by lying on job applications and should be treated like everyone else.[33]

Privacy Issues

Reporters working undercover also face the charge that they are violating people's privacy. The argument is not that undercover reporters are necessarily breaking any privacy laws. Most news organizations have attorneys who guide them through the maze of state laws and court rulings. The concern is that reporters invade privacy in an ethical sense: People think they are talking privately to fellow employees or new acquaintances. In reality, what they are saying may be repeated to thousands of readers or broadcast to millions of people watching television. "I just think it's wrong," Tom Goldstein, dean of the journalism school at the University of California at Berkeley, told *The Washington Post.* "Journalists should announce who they are. I'm uncomfortable living in a world where you don't know whom you're talking to."[34]

The Wall Street Journal was criticized when it allowed reporter Beth Nissen to get a job in a Texas Instruments plant to see how that company tried to keep its workers from forming a labor union. The reporter deliberately talked about the union to her fellow employees.[35] Critics pointed out that by openly engaging fellow employees in talk about anti-union activities, she may have jeopardized their jobs. "People don't know who you really are when they bare their souls to you, and then you smear them by invading their privacy," Lawrence O'Donnell, *Journal* associate editor at the time, said.

The Albuquerque Tribune in 1983 allowed one of its young-looking reporters to enroll in an Albuquerque high school, claiming her family had just moved to town. She realized that the Albuquerque high school would request a transcript from her old school. So she called her old school and, posing as a school official, told them to disregard Albuquerque's request for a transcript because it was a bureaucratic mistake. After spending 11 days as a student, she wrote a series of articles. "Students, teachers, parents and school administrators reacted with shock and anger, not to the meat of the articles but to the ethics of the method," the reporter later confessed. "They felt violated, intruded upon and tricked into trusting an individual who lied for no good purpose." The reporter believed her conduct was justified because it was the only way she could get the trust of high school students. Her editors, however, decided against using the method again "because of the obvious questions about their credibility and fairness."[36]

These questions led editors at the *San Francisco Chronicle* to define strict ground rules before they allowed a reporter to pose as a high school student in 1992. Not only was she required to get permission from school officials before beginning the project, but she had to check with every student and teacher mentioned in her stories and delete anyone who did not want to be included.[37] A similar requirement was made by editors at the *Star Tribune* in Minneapolis when one of their reporters enrolled in a college course for a story about academic rigor in women's studies programs.

Best Way to the Truth?

Perhaps the most fundamental question is whether deception is the best way to get the story. Zekman, one of the Mirage bar reporters, thinks it always is. She said undercover reporting is "a much more valid way to get at the truth of things than any other technique there is."[38] Others contend deception should be a last resort. Undercover reporting can be "a terrific way to get stories when no other way is possible," said Hyman, the former TV journalist who now teaches ethics. "When the more straightforward, more conventional alternatives have been considered and dismissed for legitimate reasons, and when the story itself is of such import that it must be told, deception is warranted. Our job—as journalists—is to inform, not to conceal."[39]

The problem, of course, is trying to decide when conventional techniques won't work. Zekman contended that having the *Sun-Times* buy the Mirage bar was the only way to uncover corruption in Chicago. She rejected using traditional methods or working undercover in someone else's bar. "You had to own the bar to find out whether businessmen were being extorted by building inspectors," she said. But Eugene C. Patterson, a respected journalist, argued that the *Sun-Times* could have exposed corruption in Chicago without the theatrics of buying the bar. He said that "hard work and shoe leather could have unearthed the sources necessary to do the Mirage story."[40]

A Villain or a Widespread Problem?

Nearly everyone who advocates undercover reporting agrees that there needs to be safeguards built into the technique and that it should be only one part of the investigation. Without adequate research before the undercover project begins, reporters cannot provide enough background. The public has no way of knowing whether the story has uncovered a few bad apples or a widespread, ongoing problem. That's why Bagdikian, the reporter who wanted to go inside a prison in the example at the beginning of this chapter, had already spent a long time researching the problem before he asked if he could go undercover. He had talked to experts, visited prisons and studied the public records that were available. Armed with this information, he knew what he was likely to encounter and knew he could judge whether his experiences in prison were typical of most inmates'. His undercover work was only one story in an eight-part series. Similarly, before *60 Minutes* opened the storefront clinic, the producer knew that illegal kickbacks at medical clinics were a growing problem costing taxpayers millions of dollars and that it was common in Chicago.

Some worry that not all stories are this carefully researched before the undercover work begins. But people both in and out of TV
journalism have some concerns about the *PrimeTime* Food Lion report. "I cannot believe that such a story would be done that way on
any CBS program," Joe Peyronnin, CBS's senior vice president for
newsmagazines, told the *Chicago Tribune*.[41]

The pictures *PrimeTime* had of Food Lion workers were clearly
powerful: Viewers watched as workers appeared to be doctoring meat
and listened to them as they rather smugly discussed other equally unpleasant tricks of the grocery business. It was good television and exposed a serious consumer problem. However, as Russ W. Baker wrote
in *CJR, PrimeTime* may have fallen "into a typical trap—focusing in
on a villain when the problem is systemic."[42] The episode showed a
few workers at a handful of stores in one chain. Viewers were left
with no clue as to how widespread the problem was. Were these practices followed in all Food Lions? In all supermarkets? By focusing on
only one supermarket chain, the *PrimeTime* report may have caused
some people to stop shopping at Food Lion and switch to a market
with even worse practices.

A way to avoid this criticism is to broaden the research. Baker
noted that at the same time *PrimeTime* was preparing its Food Lion
story, a local station in Atlanta, WAGA-TV, was doing a larger-scale
investigation of food safety on its own. The Atlanta station found
that each of the 20 supermarkets it tested was repackaging old meat.
The stores included both national and local chains.[43] Similarly, when
Dateline NBC did a story on adulterated ground beef, reporters collected samples from different stores in several parts of the country.
They then sent more than 100 samples to an independent lab whose
tests showed that what the label calls "100 percent ground beef" may
contain as much as 20 percent pork or poultry.

Two Newspapers, Two Answers

Reporters at *The Miami Herald* and *Newsday,* a Long Island, N.Y.,
daily, had heard reports of racial discrimination in housing. They
knew this was a story that had been done by many newspapers during
the past 30 years, including college newspapers, small dailies, large
dailies and network TV news. But they were convinced it was still a
major problem in their communities, so they began work on how they
would go about documenting the story. Both papers have long histo-
ries of doing first-rate investigative reporting.

The technique selected by the *Herald* in 1986 is probably typical of most of these investigations. Reporters Paul Shannon, who is white, and Larry Bivins, who is black, created almost identical backgrounds for themselves so they would be "ideal tenants—well-dressed, professional, relatively affluent, and no kids or pets." Then they went from apartment office to apartment office using classified ads. The black reporter went in first and the white reporter 10 to 30 minutes later so that they were apt to deal with the same rental agent. Both used their own names but fudged their occupations: Bivins said he worked as a minority recruiter for the *Herald,* which was part of his job, and Shannon said he worked in an office for the Knight-Ridder Corporation, owners of the *Herald.* "No one caught on," Shannon said.

They found both overt and subtle discrimination. One rental agent would tell Bivins that an apartment complex was all filled up and 20 minutes later tell Shannon that he could have an apartment there immediately. The white reporter would be shown such amenities as a swimming pool, sauna and Jacuzzi, while the black reporter was never told about them.

Heath Meriwether, *Herald* executive editor at the time, defended the misrepresentation used to get this obviously important story even though he is very cautious about approving any kind of deception. "There are times," he said, "when undercover reporting with very stringent . . . safeguards, preceded by full discussion, is OK."[44]

Newsday reporters had heard complaints about real estate agents steering whites to white areas of town and blacks to black areas. They wanted to expose this illegal practice. How they went about tracking down this story was described by Marcel Dufresne in a *CJR* article.[45] *Newsday* editors had read several stories about the problem in other papers, and they were troubled by the inconclusive nature of many projects. They noted that reporters in many earlier investigations had tested only a dozen or so salespeople—even though there were hundreds of offices with countless agents in each city. After the stories based on these probes appeared, the companies involved often claimed that the violations could be attributed to individual agents and that the company itself promoted the ideals of equal opportunity. At best, a few agents were reprimanded or fired, but the practice of housing discrimination continued.

Newsday wanted more than that. One plan would have had 20 teams of reporters and trained actors who would visit 200 of the thousands of real estate offices on Long Island. When project editor Joye Brown was convinced the overall project would work, she took the idea to managing editor Howard Schneider. He was not enthusiastic about using undercover reporting. However, Brown and her group still wanted to do the story. They brought in an adviser from Chicago, an expert on documenting racial discrimination who assured them that by using trained testers it would be possible "to show the extent of steering on Long Island with 95 percent accuracy." The expert's presentation was strong enough that Schneider decided to go ahead with the undercover work.

The project team starting looking for ways to guarantee that each of the 20 teams would present themselves to the real estate agents the same way so that differences in body language and nuances of speech would not affect how the agents reacted. Almost 10 months after the idea was first proposed, the *Newsday* team thought the time had come to go undercover and begin testing for discrimination. But then Anthony Marro, the paper's editor, vetoed the idea.

A year later, *Newsday* began publishing a 10-part series, "A World Apart: Segregation on Long Island." The articles were based not on undercover revelations but on interviews with African-Americans who were shown homes only in black neighborhoods, brokers, agents, housing advocates and state prosecutors. Dufresne stated that the series used "moving personal accounts and startling statistics to bring readers face to face with racial segregation." The series, which was nominated for a Pulitzer, described Long Island as a place where many black residents were "trapped in neighborhoods beset by drugs and crime, where the police are unresponsive, and where the schools are inferior."

After the project ended, Brown was asked whether she believed the story would have been better if they had gone undercover. "Did we need the test? The truth of the matter is no, we didn't," she replied.

Both newspapers discovered a serious problem in the community. The *Herald*'s story showed that racial discrimination was occurring in the city's rental offices. The story could be done rather quickly. *Newsday*'s story was a thorough documentation of the extent of the racism in housing and its impact on the communities involved. But the series required a team of reporters at a newspaper known for its willingness to invest in investigative reporting.

Improving the Profession

In its handbook *Doing Ethics in Journalism,* the Society of Professional Journalists suggested these guidelines for deciding when deception by a journalist is justified:

- When the information obtained is of profound importance. It must be of vital public interest, such as revealing great "system failure" at the top levels, or it must prevent profound harm to individuals.
- When all other alternatives for obtaining the same information have been exhausted.
- When the journalists involved are willing to disclose the nature of the deception and the reason for it.
- When the individuals involved and their news organizations apply excellence, through outstanding craftsmanship as well as the commitment of time and funding needed to pursue the story fully.
- When the harm prevented by the information revealed through deception outweighs any harm caused by the act of deception.
- When the journalists involved have conducted a meaningful, collaborative, and deliberate decision-making process in which they weigh:
  a. the consequences (short- and long-term) of the deception on those being deceived.
  b. the impact on journalistic credibility.
  c. the motivations for their actions.
  d. the deceptive act in relation to their editorial mission.
  e. the legal implications of the action.
  f. the consistency of their reasoning and their action.

The SPJ handbook also suggested some criteria that *cannot* be used to justify deception:

- Winning a prize.
- Getting the story with less expense of time and resources.
- Doing it because "others already did it."
- The subjects of the story are themselves unethical.[46]

CHAPTER

11

Compassion

A Marine from Colorado was among those taken hostage when Iranians seized the U.S. Embassy in Tehran. Months later, his family received word that their son might soon be freed. The release of the 52 hostages, coming after months of tense negotiations and even a failed rescue attempt by American military forces, was big news. Reporters from throughout the state scrambled to be there when the family received word their son was coming home.

Ramon Coronado, a reporter for *The Coloradoan* in Fort Collins, described what happened while the mob of journalists was waiting to capture the joy of Billy Gallegos' parents:

> The media camped in the sloped front yard, an area no bigger than two spaces in a parking lot. Electrical cords, telephones, television sets, radios, tape recorders, microphones, cigarette butts, coffee cups and paper from fast-food restaurants blanketed the ground. In the back, the alley was filled with television news trucks manned with technicians.

About three dozen reporters and photographers were allowed inside the small home, while the rest had to stay outside. As those inside jostled for better positions, one journalist knocked a ceramic plate off a wall, Coronado reported. Photographers stood on furniture, breaking one table. A reporter from Colorado Springs was caught looking in the family's mail. In summing up his experience, Coronado wrote that "the press lost sight of the fact the Gallegoses were not just a story but are people. People with feelings and the need for privacy."[1]

In California, a teenager was killed in a freak accident during track practice at school. Friends and officials warned his family to be prepared for the media. The "tough questions and persistence [of the reporters] may be intrusive and uncomfortable," family members were told. It wasn't long before a TV reporter called. The family decided reluctantly to meet with her. "We really wanted to share our story with our city, so we braced ourselves and waited for the reporter to arrive," they explained.

But instead of the unfeeling ogre they had expected, they discovered a reporter who was "gentle and loving" and a photographer who promised to pray for their son. Soon a newspaper reporter visited them. "What a special lady," the family said later. "Yes, she got the story, but with love in her heart. She never pushed or intruded or tried to develop a bigger story than it was. She reported the news." During the next few days, TV and print reporters from both large and small news organizations interviewed the family. "The media often take a bad hit from the public, but I must say that during our time of grief it was wonderful to be with such caring people," the family wrote in a letter to the editor printed in the *Los Angeles Times*.[2]

It's hard not to be appalled by the reporters in the Colorado incident. When journalists misbehave that badly, it leaves a foul taste in people's mouths and lessens their respect for all journalists. The family in California had a much different experience, one that is probably more common than many people realize. These two incidents highlight the basic question of this chapter: What is the role of compassion in the demands of daily journalism?

Curiously, this discussion of compassion in journalism would surprise both members of the press and members of the public—but for much different reasons. Many journalists would be surprised to see the need for compassion considered an important issue facing journalism. And, according to polls, about two-thirds of the public would be surprised to find out that journalists even know the meaning of the word.[3]

Room for Humaneness?

Many journalists, especially newspaper reporters, shun the notion of compassion. They believe compassion runs counter to objective reporting, which most reporters try to practice despite widespread doubts as to whether it's achievable or even desirable. A tenet of objective reporting is that reporters are spectators and not participants in what they cover. Reporters are not supposed to get involved with the people in their stories; they are supposed to be neutral observers.

Another concern is that compassion will cause reporters to become weak willed and forget their obligations to keep the public informed. Louis Boccardi, president of the Associated Press, recalled that when he was a young reporter covering courts, he was asked many times not to put certain things in the paper. He feared that if compassion became too prevalent in journalism, reporters would agree to these requests and legitimate news stories would not be printed.

Competitive pressures are another reason some journalists believe they must suppress compassion. Ginger Casey, when she was a reporter for KQED-TV in San Francisco, was covering a shooting at a playground. She did not want to interview any of the children who might have seen the tragedy and make them revisit its horror. Yet she knew that dozens of reporters were swarming around the neighborhood, looking for angles for their stories. If one reporter interviewed a child, she would have to. "You don't want your competition to have any angle you don't have, and crying kids on camera were powerful images," she wrote. "If having your voice heard at a news conference scored points, so did interviewing a child. Your boss would tell you that you 'kicked ass.' Your resume tape would look terrific."[4]

Casey's observation suggests another reason some journalists feel they must shed feelings of compassion: They don't want compassion to get in the way of a big story that will impress their editors or news directors. This search for a career-making story may be why so many younger reporters advocate questionable reporting tactics. When researchers showed journalists a list of tactics including badgering sources for information and deceiving people, younger journalists were more likely to say they were justified than were their more seasoned colleagues.[5]

Does Compassion Improve Journalism?

Many editors do not believe compassion lessens the quality of the work a journalist does. They believe compassion makes for better reporting. Geneva Overholser, former editor of *The Des Moines Register,* argues that the notion of journalist-as-machine has made so much newspaper writing boring, dull and meaningless. In her view, journalists should write stories that make readers "laugh, weep, sing, hope and wonder how people can go on." That kind of writing can be achieved only if journalists have feelings and are concerned about the people and issues they write about. She said it cannot be done by journalists who spend their time "polishing up their value-free journalism skills."[6]

Journalists often want to write stories that go beyond the bare facts. They want to humanize social problems and even provoke a sympathetic response in their readers. To do this, they must become involved with people who are experiencing the problem, interview them with sensitivity and describe their conditions with care and compassion.

Jacqui Banaszynski wrote a series of stories called "AIDS in the Heartland" for the *St. Paul Pioneer Press.* The stories portrayed the final months of the life of man with AIDS. She visited the man and his partner frequently and interviewed friends and family. Sensing that the relationship was going beyond a traditional reporter-source one, she started reminding the men that she was a reporter and told her editors to be extra diligent in editing her copy. Because friends and family members were so open with her, she read the quotes she planned to use back to them to make sure they were accurate. Her honest and compassionate reporting led to sensitive stories that gave readers a deeper understanding of the AIDS crisis. Her efforts were rewarded with both a Pulitzer Prize and a Distinguished Service Award from the Society of Professional Journalists.

Are Journalists Con Artists?

> Every journalist who is not too stupid or too full of himself to notice what is going on knows that what he does is morally indefensible. He is a kind of confidence man, preying on people's vanity, ignorance, or loneliness, gaining their trust and betraying them without remorse.

This accusation by writer Janet Malcolm caused "more newsroom and cocktail-party debate, more belligerent editorializing and more honest soul-searching" than almost any other article on journalism ever had, according to *Columbia Journalism Review.*[7]

Malcolm's specific target was Joe McGinniss and the way he befriended Dr. Jeffrey MacDonald, who was on trial for the murder of his wife and two children. The doctor came to regard McGinniss as a confidant and allowed him to be with his legal team throughout the trial. But when McGinniss' book, *Fatal Vision,* was published, there was no doubt that McGinniss thought the doctor was a cold-blooded killer. Malcolm accused McGinniss of tricking the doctor so he could get material for the book.[8] Many journalists began to ask themselves if they tricked their sources into talking and then betrayed them when they wrote their stories.

Tricks of the Trade

Columbia Journalism Review asked a selection of the nation's top writers and journalists about Malcolm's opening paragraph. One of them, novelist and screenwriter Nora Ephron, saw little wrong with Malcolm's observations. She said, "Some of the best journalism I've read happened after what Janet is describing as 'betrayal' or as 'immoral.'" Ephron thought the public needed to learn "that journalists are not their friends."

Some journalists denied they deceive sources but acknowledged they use "tricks." Mike Wallace, known for his hardball interviews on CBS's *60 Minutes,* said, "As a journalist, you do some role playing. You don't turn all your cards face up." To get sources to cooperate, he said he sometimes used persuasion. "And as long as it's done honestly, as long as no promises are made which are then broken, then it seems to me perfectly reasonable to 'sell' the object of your scrutiny on the wisdom of cooperation."

This gamesmanship troubles some journalists. In an article in the *San Francisco Examiner,* Casey, the former KQED-TV reporter, wrote, "I knew all the tricks. I had learned to hide my excitement when I found someone naive enough to share their pain with me. And I swallowed the shame of knowing that their tragedy would be a good career move for me."[9] John Tierney, a reporter for *The New York Times,* knows how Casey felt. He believes it is a common feeling among reporters. They worry that they exploit their sources because, to get them to talk, the reporters must allow them to believe that their ideas will be presented favorably. Yet the reporters know that they may not be.[10]

Some journalists have been less than honest. *Dateline NBC* representatives told officials at a trucking company in Bangor, Maine, that they wanted to do a story that would display "the positive side of trucking." The company agreed to allow a TV crew to ride along with truck driver Peter Kennedy as he drove his big rig on a coast-to-coast run. During the long trip, the journalists talked to Kennedy about life on the road. He told them that government regulations required him to take more sleep breaks than he thought he needed. He referred to the log book in which he recorded his rest breaks as the "joke book."

However, Kennedy's friendly passengers were not after a positive story. Earlier, when they had pitched the story to *Dateline NBC* producers, they promised an exposé of safety violations by truckers. When their report aired, it proclaimed, "American highways are a trucker's killing field" and included tape of Kennedy saying he drove more hours than the law allowed. Later, Kennedy and the trucking company, claiming misrepresentation, sued NBC and were awarded $525,000 in damages.[11]

Sources Feel Betrayed

A mother called *The Ann Arbor (Mich.) News* and told a reporter that she believed he should write a story about the untimely death of her 17-year-old daughter. The woman said her daughter was at a New Year's Eve party where kids were drinking automobile antifreeze to get high. Her daughter drank too much and died. The mother said she hoped the reporter would write a story to alert students and the community to the hazards of drinking antifreeze.

The reporter interviewed the mother, who described her daughter as a good girl who died because of a high school fad. Then the reporter checked with school authorities, drug experts and police. He found no evidence to back up the mother's belief that drinking antifreeze was common in Ann Arbor. He also talked to people who knew the girl and learned that her life had not been exactly the way her mother described it.

Instead of writing a warning about teens drinking antifreeze, the reporter wrote a story based on what he had discovered about the girl's life and death. When the story appeared, the mother complained that the paper had made her daughter look "wild and crazy," portrayed her as the only kid in school drinking antifreeze and hinted she might have committed suicide. The mother said that when she called the paper, she hoped the paper would print "a tribute and a warning." Instead the reporter wrote a news story. "Maybe I was naive to expect anything else," she said. The reporter told the paper's ombudsman that he was not surprised the mother was upset. He said he recognized during the interview what she wanted a tribute, but he knew he could not write what she had in mind.[12]

Reporters know that many of their sources will be unhappy when they read the stories. "It is natural for a source or subject to feel betrayed when the story comes out and the subject doesn't like everything in it," Ken Auletta, a former New York *Daily News* columnist, said. "But that doesn't mean the accusation of betrayal is justified. In journalism your loyalty is to the truth as you perceive it, not necessarily to your subject."[13]

While most journalists would probably agree with Auletta, many also believe journalists should remain sensitive to the feelings of their inexperienced sources and perhaps remind them of how the news game is played. When the Ann Arbor paper's ombudsman wrote about the mother's complaint, he did not criticize the story. But he re-

gretted the way his paper handled her. "Reporters do not write trib-
utes," he wrote. But he stated that the girl's mother "did not understand that when she called the *News*. I wish someone would have
told her."[14]

A more sensitive reporter might have been frank with the woman.
He might have explained that he could not write a tribute and that
before he wrote the story, he would check with other people and
would include in his story what they had to say. The mother might
then have understood the procedures. And as it became clear that the
woman's fear of an antifreeze craze in the high schools were un-
founded, the reporter might have called and explained that.

Some might ask, "If the reporter had explained how he would
handle the story, would the mother have backed out of the interview?" She might have. The newspaper would have lost a story about
an isolated event by an apparently troubled young woman, a story
that served only to satisfy the curiosity of readers. If the story had
been about a real threat to the community, the reporter would have
had to balance the desire to show compassion with the need to get the
news out. But even then, he could have attempted to explain to the
mother why the story was important before it was printed.

As Joann Byrd, former ombudsman at *The Washington Post,* has
said, if reporters and photographers would take the time to call people involved in their stories and pictures, it would lessen the hurt
when the stories appear. She told *Quill* that she believes those phone
calls are essential and compassionate and might help the journalist
sleep at night.[15]

Treating Sources Fairly

Many journalists say they take great pains to make sure they treat
their sources fairly. Long before the tempest over Malcolm's remarks,
Bob Greene, the popular columnist for the *Chicago Tribune* (not to be
confused with the former *Newsday* investigative reporter of the same
name), wrote about the interviewing style he uses for his columns that
often portray the lifestyles of private people and the quirkiness of
everyday life. Greene admits that he uses tricks to get people to talk,
"to make an interview subject feel so comfortable and so warm that
he cannot conceive of being betrayed by this nice fellow who is asking
the questions and making the notes." He continued:

> As often as not, though, the person I'm with has never been inter-
> viewed before. He is wary at first; it takes a while to make him under-
> stand that this is not a surgical procedure. There are tricks to that, too;
> I will stumble around in my conversation. I will make my questions

sound exceedingly dumb; if he is having a few too many drinks, I will drink right along with him. I may or may not be a likable person in real life, but I can be a likable person in an interview situation; it's just another trick I have learned. . . .

I decided a long time ago in situations like those, I had the obligation to help protect a person even if he didn't know enough to protect himself.[16]

Greene stated that one way he has protected interviewees is by offering not to use their names even if he knew they would be willing to be named. He wrote what the source "doesn't know is that the sight of his words and his world in cold print, in front of hundreds of thousands of strangers, is going to jar him."

Greene is not the only reporter who is concerned about dealing with people who are unaccustomed to being interviewed. Mike Feinsilber, who was Washington news editor for the AP, said that he did not want to take advantage of inexperienced interviewees, so he would remind them, "Don't tell me anything you don't want in the newspaper." Feinsilber also gave news sources a chance to collect their thoughts. He would call them, tell them what he wanted to interview them about, and then offer to call back in 10 minutes or so. "I find I get better information and better quotes that way, and people appreciate it," he said.[17]

Other reporters take steps throughout the interview to make sure sources know that they may be quoted. Barry Michael Cooper, who writes for *The Village Voice* in New York, will stop an interview "when I think subjects could be hurting themselves inadvertently." He'll remind them that the interview is on the record and ask them if they want to continue.[18] A few editors take this courtesy a step further. If unsophisticated sources call reporters later and say they said something during the interview that they don't want printed, reporters are required to remove those comments, even if doing that spoils the story.

Covering Tragedies

Donald Nibert lost his 16-year-old daughter in the 1996 TWA 800 explosion off Long Island. At a journalism conference months later, he described reporters who stalked grieving families, yelled questions at surviving relatives and lied to gain access to restricted areas. He said, "The national news media and the local coverage were terrible. They magnified the sorrow we had to endure. For what purpose? To increase ratings? To sell newspapers? To sell magazines? To increase personal status? I don't know. But I wonder if this can be justified considering the pain they caused the families—maybe permanent pain."[19]

While Nibert and others have felt as though the media were hounding them, relatives of other victims have become angry when reporters did not contact them. Donna Witherspoon, a Dallas attorney, criticized the coverage of the slaying of her mother. She said that reporters were content to talk to neighbors who "hardly knew her. . . . The media never talked to anyone who really knew her." She described her mother as "an incredible human being with a lot of accomplishments that were never mentioned by the media."

Witherspoon's desire to talk to the media is not uncommon. Like the California parents described in the opening of this chapter, many people involved in tragedies want to share their experiences with their communities.

Yet the image of intrusive reporters at tragedies is well-entrenched in our society. Many in the public see reporters as vultures even when reporters are on their best behavior and when people agree to be interviewed. Reporter Rene Stutzman, then with United Press International, was covering the collapse of a walkway in a Kansas City hotel that killed more than 100 people. She approached a victim's family sitting in the lobby of a nearby hotel and asked if she could interview them. "If they had made the slightest indication they did not want to be interviewed, I would have stopped," she said. But family members asked her to sit down and began to talk. "Then people in the lobby came up and started calling me names, and I had to leave."[20]

Jack R. Hart, a senior editor at *The Oregonian* in Portland, is not surprised by the public's attitude. He believes there is an inevitable conflict between a community that is shocked by a tragedy and the reporters who are covering it. "News coverage is intrusive, and grief demands privacy," Hart told a journalism seminar on covering tragedy. "Just the fact that [media representatives] are there is offensive to the community."[21] Add to this understandable suspicion the fact that major events attract a horde of reporters, and almost unavoidably there are going to be problems.

Still, serious crimes, plane crashes and the like are news. Journalists must cover them and their aftermaths; readers and viewers expect to find these stories. The key, many experienced reporters say, is to treat victims as fellow human beings. Reporter George Esper, who has covered wars and mass suicides for the AP, told the seminar, "We should frame our questions with respect and research. We must be sensitive, but not timid."

Sensitive reporting helped Rick Bragg of *The New York Times* Atlanta Bureau win a Pulitzer Prize for his coverage of the bombing of a federal office building in Oklahoma City. Bragg's first interview at the scene was with a rescue worker who had just assisted in surgery on a little boy whose brain was "hanging out of his head." Bragg said, "We looked at each other and stared. I said what was on my mind, which was, 'I can't believe this.' I asked him what he'd seen, and he told me. We only talked a few minutes. It was enough. He smoked his cigarette and moved on."

Bragg handled the interview with humanity and simplicity. Unfortunately, the conduct of some journalists falls far short of Bragg's. The brother of a freshman player on the University of California—Davis basketball team was killed in a plane crash. The student was crushed by the loss of his brother, who had played with the Phoenix Suns in the NBA. Once the season started, the player continued to have problems dealing with his brother's death, was hesitant to board airplanes and found it difficult to talk about his problems.

At first, writers at *The Sacramento Bee* decided not to interview him, "recognizing that he was still in grief and shock." Then the sports information officer at the school sent a memo to reporters who covered the team asking them not to interview "the young man relative to the recent tragedy in his life," adding that after-game interviews with him about his play in that night's game could be arranged. When *Bee* sportswriters got the memo, one of them asked team officials if the player himself had been asked whether he minded discussing his brother's death with reporters. The sports information officer acknowledged that they had not directly asked him. So a *Bee* reporter contacted the player, asked him for an interview and pointed out that he could say no. The player agreed to be interviewed but broke down after the subject of his brother came up. The reporter later acknowledged that all the interview revealed was what he already knew: The player was not handling his brother's death well. However, the reporter went ahead and wrote the story.

After the story ran, the player's family, team officials and fans scolded the paper for its conduct. Team officials said his play suffered after the interview. The sports information officer said he thought the story could have waited until at least the end of the season. Another person charged that the paper "seemed intent on proving that no one can tell *The Sacramento Bee* what to do, and if it hurts people and causes them anguish, what the hell."

The paper's ombudsman stated that he thought the paper deserved the criticism. He noted that coaches and team officials were supposed to know their players' feelings. "I could discern no urgency to the story. It could indeed have kept. As it was, because [the young man] apparently could not bring himself to articulate his personal pain, the finished story was thin gruel containing only one quote from him, the rest from three teammates and a coach." The ombudsman concluded his column: "A great newspaper is known for many things, among them insight, vigor and courage. But also for its ability to see clearly where the line between privacy and public interest should be drawn. It's called compassion."[22]

Interviewing Victims and Their Families

Many journalists simply do not know what to say when they interview people involved in tragedies, and they end up blurting out the wrong thing. William Coté and Bonnie Bucqueroux of the Victims and Media Center, Michigan State University School of Journalism, tell of an unfortunate encounter between a young reporter and a man who had just lost his daughter. "I know how you feel," the reporter said. "I remember when my dog died." The remark added immensely to that father's pain, according to Coté and Bucqueroux.[23]

Editor Sandra Rowe of the Portland *Oregonian* agrees that reporters need to draw on their own life experiences when they cover tragedies. "There are too many reporters and editors who haven't been there to have the empathy they need. Perhaps they haven't lost anyone. They need to think it through enough to say, 'If I were in this person's place, how would I feel? What questions would I be able to handle? What would be offensive?'"[24]

After studying the treatment of victims by journalists, the Victims and Media Center put together the following tips for reporters:

1. Grant victims and their families a sense of power and control. They are suffering from horrific stress that has robbed them of their sense of mastery. Ask them to tell you when they want to say something that they do not want in the paper. Give them your phone number and tell them that they can call you to discuss the story or just to talk.
2. Discuss issues of privacy and confidentiality at the beginning of the interview. This can prevent misunderstandings and establish trust. Explain what you need, with whom you plan to talk and for how long. Make sure to encourage the victim to ask questions.
3. Prepare for the possibility you will be the first to deliver the bad news. Often reporters telephone or appear on a family's porch looking for quotes about a victim, only to find that no one had yet been informed. Organize your thoughts before you call or ring the doorbell.
4. Ask permission. This is particularly important whenever you approach the victim's physical "zone of intimacy." Even caring

gestures can be misinterpreted or seen as threatening or out of bounds. Approach them without your notebook in hand and then ask if you can take notes. Ask if you can use a tape recover. It is better to say, "Would you like a tissue," than to thrust the box at them.

5. Fans of the TV show *NYPD Blue* know that the detectives always say, "Sorry for your loss." To our ears, the phrase may begin to sound trite and artificial, but using a canned phrase that strikes the right note is far better than using the wrong words. A former police commissioner who became a therapist suggests that at least one of these sentiments will always be appropriate: "I'm sorry this happened to you"; "I'm glad you weren't killed"; and, because people in tragedies often blame themselves, "It's not your fault."

6. Don't say, "I know how you feel." Even if you think you may have suffered a similar victimization, no one can really understand what's going through a person's mind during and after a tragedy.

7. Be accurate. Accuracy is the overarching goal in all reporting, but the stakes are much higher when dealing with victims and the family of victims. A local paper recently ran a correction when it misquoted a minister at a funeral as saying the man "put himself before others" instead of "put others before himself." The mistake was not minor to the friends and families involved.

8. Be especially sensitive in placing blame. If you mention that the victim had been drinking, does it imply that he or she was drunk? Reporting requires more than emptying your notebook, and editors should always fix their antennae to spot any inadvertent suggestion that the victim was at fault.

9. Be alert to the special impact of photos, graphics and overall presentation. Occasionally, a sensitive and respectful story is undercut by a tasteless picture or a headline that misses the nuances the reporter put in the story.

Patsy Day, director of Victims Outreach in Dallas, adds a couple of other points, according to Phil Record, ombudsman of the Fort Worth *Star-Telegram*. She reminds reporters that people react differently to tragedy. Journalists should be careful not to guess how people feel based on their external appearance or behavior. Some may be suffering from shock or post-traumatic stress disorder, yet on the surface, they may appear very "businesslike" as they go about dealing with their loss. Some become stoic. Others cry a lot.

Day also suggests that reporters arrange interviews with victims and their relatives just as they would in other circumstances. "If you were covering the hostile takeover of a bank, you wouldn't knock down the bank president's door. You would call his office and ask for an interview. So why can't you call a crime victim and ask for an interview?"[25]

Getting Involved in the Story

For three months, while working on a story about the lives of drug-addicted mothers, reporters from the *Los Angeles Times* witnessed dozens of horrifying episodes of children being mistreated. They watched as a mother with AIDS and bleeding gums used her own toothbrush to brush her 3-year-old daughter's teeth. They saw a mother who worked as a prostitute lay her baby on a bed wet with semen and urine. They talked to young children who were fed one bowl of rice a day and were beaten regularly by their father. Although they were shocked by what they saw, they did not intervene. They did nothing to stop the abuse nor did they call authorities. The children stayed in those surroundings for at least four more months until officials tracked them down.

The *Times* reporters said they were abiding by one of the traditional dictates of journalism: Reporters are not to get involved in their stories. They are supposed to watch the fortunes and misfortunes of others, write about them and move on to their next story. The series' editor explained to *American Journalism Review,* "We wanted to tell a story that was real, that held up this big, giant mirror to society and said, 'Take a look at this! This is real serious stuff. And it's a world you've never been in before, and we're not going to tamper with the world.'" Another *Times* editor said, "If you decide to go to authorities when you witness abuse, you'd have to call off the story before getting started. The result is there'd be no investigation, the kids would still be in danger and the public wouldn't know about it."

But other journalists were outraged. Jane Daugherty, who was a Pulitzer Prize finalist for her stories on child abuse in *The Detroit News,* said, "If you sit there for three months and watch, what you're saying is that what you have to document at length is more important than those individual children." Daugherty said that when she was an editor at the *News,* a reporter working on a story similar to the *Times* series also saw child abuse. She said she called authorities, "myself, that day, the minute I found out about it." The paper then wrote about how long it took authorities to react. Daugherty contended the paper got a compelling story and saved the children.[26]

Michael Nicholson, a journalist for Britain's Independent Television News, also decided to abandon the fly-on-the-wall concept of journalism. He was assigned to cover the civil war in Bosnia and became attached to a 9-year-old girl in Sarajevo, a city under constant shelling at that time. Wanting to get her out of the war zone, he illegally added her to his passport. She was then able to travel to London, where his wife was waiting to meet her.

Some journalists applauded his conduct. "It's ridiculous to say journalists don't have feelings. You can't expect journalists to be machines," Robin Knight, *U.S. News & World Report* senior European editor, told *CJR. Los Angeles Times* European correspondent William Tuohy agreed. He said he appreciates objectivity, but "one must do what has to be done."

However, Nicholson's action horrified other journalists. Some said he had sacrificed his impartiality. "By revealing his cards, he is blaming the Serbs for ruining this girl's life, for invading her country," Ian Bremner, news desk assistant at ABC News in London, said. Others thought his conduct would tarnish all journalists. "If you get that involved personally, it affects your judgment and it allows people to dismiss journalists, to dismiss their objectivity," explained ABC News' Paul Cleveland. Some argued that Nicholson should decide whether he wants to be a journalist covering the civil war or a social worker trying to save children from the war. He can't be both, in their judgment.

Nicholson said he understood the complaints, but he contended that saving a child's life was not taking sides. "To be partial politically is wrong. But if you act as any decent person would act, then it is okay," he said.[27]

On Saving Janet's Jimmy

Jimmy lived for almost seven months. He was created on the front page of *The Washington Post* by Janet Cooke. "Jimmy" was what she called the 8-year-old heroin addict she wrote about—and he died almost seven months later when she confessed she had made him up. (An account of this fakery and its aftermath appears in Chapter 6.) The two ethical issues that received the most attention right after the fakery was disclosed had to do with the deception itself and the use of anonymous sources. But to Charles Seib, retired ombudsman for the *Post,* the more serious question was: "Why were the *Post* editors so willing to let Jimmy die?" Seib noted editors had expressed deep concern over Cooke's safety after she claimed Jimmy's dope-dealing guardian had threatened her. "But not a thought for Jimmy."[28]

Seib was not alone in his feeling that the *Post* should have tried to help Jimmy, assuming that he did exist. Thomas J. Bray, then associate editor of the editorial page of *The Wall Street Journal,* asked "Why didn't the *Post* scrap the story and insist that the reporter report this pathetic case to the authorities? Was the story in this instance really more important than 'Jimmy'?"[29] John Troan, retired editor of the *Pittsburgh Press,* wondered why somebody at the *Post* had not said, "Hey, let's get this kid out of his horrible predicament, get him the help he needs—and then run the story. That way we might not only win a prize but—even more important—save a life."[30]

Benjamin Bradlee, then executive editor of the *Post,* explained the thinking of *Post* editors. "We talked ourselves into the position that we were focusing on a social problem and would do the community more good by focusing on it than by going to the cops with a story we thought would put our reporter in physical jeopardy."[31] Other *Post* editors were not satisfied with that answer. Robert Woodward, one of the Watergate reporters who by then was assistant managing editor in charge of the metro staff, thought the *Post* was in a "morally untenable position" of having witnessed a crime and saying "to hell with" the 8-year-old victim.

Pity the Shooters

News photographers for print and television frequently get into ethical difficulties because they must respond quickly to tragedies, sometimes arriving at the scene ahead of the authorities. When covering breaking stories, they may have only one opportunity to take the picture. Many shoot first, think later. Newspaper photographers have one advantage over TV news crews. They can follow the axiom: "Get the pictures, let the editors decide what to do with them later." TV photographers may not have that luxury. Their images are often being broadcast live. But both print and TV photographers share one dilemma: They occasionally have to choose between their journalistic responsibility and their desire to be compassionate.

A classic case illustrates this ethical problem. It involved a photographer for the old *Oregon Journal* named William T. Murphy Jr., who was driving across a Columbia River bridge when he spotted a man and a woman struggling near the railing. He stopped his car and instinctively grabbed his camera. By then the man was standing on the outside of the bridge railing, and the woman, who turned out to be the man's wife, was on the inside, desperately trying to stop the man from jumping into the swirling river 100 feet below. "At first they didn't notice me," Murphy said. The wife was screaming and pleading with the man. Murphy took one picture and then another one just as a boy on a bike pedaled within a few feet of the woman. Cars on the bridge slowed when they saw what was going on, but none stopped.[32]

Murphy tried to remember how suicide prevention experts had dealt with jumpers. "One thing was for certain," Murphy said. "I didn't want to try to rush the guy because I thought he'd jump for sure. I got within 10 feet when he noticed me." Murphy started talking to the man, and when a van stopped, he told the driver to go to the police at the end of the bridge. But time ran out. The man "leaned out and was gone." Murphy took a picture of the man falling away from the bridge. He took a total of only five pictures. About then, he noticed that the van driver had gotten out and was standing about 50 feet away watching the man jump.

After his pictures were published in his paper and were carried by a wire service to other papers around the nation, angry letters and phone calls started coming in. "Don't the ethics of journalism insist that preservation of human life comes first, news second?" asked a woman in Philadelphia. "He let a man die for the sake of a good photograph," a New Yorker wrote. Murphy was in agony. He had taken his pictures, but he had also tried to help the man. "Why didn't someone else stop?" he asked. "I don't know what I could have done differently. I am a photographer and I did what I have been trained to do. I did all I could."[33]

It is difficult to assess Murphy's actions. No one can be sure how a distraught man might react if he saw Murphy photographing him or saw Murphy approaching him with cameras around his neck. Some have suggested that Murphy should have gone for the police and then photographed the scene with a long lens. Others contend that if he believed he could talk the man out of jumping, he should have left the cameras behind.

But the point in telling Murphy's story is not to imply that he should have done anything differently or that anyone else would have been able to handle the bridge suicide any better. His experience illustrates the frustrations that journalists face when they have to decide whether to help people or to go for the story or picture. Or to put it another way, when they have to decide whether to substitute compassion for dispassion.

Murphy Case Sparks Change

Murphy's case had a major impact on news photography in this country. Many editors and photographers began to worry about being thought of as cold-hearted, uncaring human beings. They didn't like the image of putting pictures above human life. Murphy himself told of two occasions after the bridge jump tragedy when he used his first-aid training to help auto accident victims. In each case, he waited until ambulance crews arrived and the people were OK before he took pictures.[34]

A suicide leap. This is the scene photo-journalist William T. Murphy Jr. found when he stopped his car on a bridge connecting Washington and Oregon.

"That's not the right thing to do, pal," Murphy said he shouted at the man struggling to free himself from his wife's weakening grip. The unidentified bicyclist did not stop.

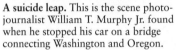

The man jumped to his death in the swirling Columbia River nearly 100 feet below. Murphy then noticed that the young woman he had asked to go for the police was still on the bridge watching the suicide.

(Photos courtesy of William T. Murphy Jr., Portland Oregonian.)

Other photographers have chosen to help victims rather than take their pictures. Bill Perry, photo editor for Gannett News Service, was on assignment in Yosemite National Park. Suddenly, a woman rushed toward him screaming that a car with children in it had gone into the river. Perry drove quickly to the scene to find a partially submerged car jammed against a tree trunk out in the icy Merced River. Two women and three young children, about 7, 5 and 3, were perched, terrified, on the car's roof.

A nonswimmer with no emergency gear in his car, Perry shouted to the stranded five that he could go for help. He raced his car to the nearest campground office, where he called for help and was assured that park rangers were on the way. After speeding back to the desperate scene, Perry for the first time pulled out his cameras. Shooting with a long lens, he saw that there were no longer five people on the car, but only the older of the two women. She was soon rescued by a park ranger in a wetsuit, who attached himself by rope to a tree on the bank and went out into the raging waters to bring her ashore. The other woman and two of the children had drowned. Some passers-by with ropes had saved the third child.

"I know I couldn't have found help any faster than I did," Perry said afterward. "I know the rangers got there as fast as they could. I

Rescued from a flood. The news photographer who took this photo first went for help. *(Photo courtesy of Bill Perry, photo editor, Gannett News Service.)*

know that three people would still be alive if they had waited for professional help. I don't think I'll ever forget those five terrified faces."[35] Perry apparently would agree with his colleague, William Sanders, former president of the National Press Photographers Association, when he said he "would give up a picture to help somebody in trouble" because "you're a member of the human race first and a journalist second."[36]

Other photographers have made the same decision. On his way to lunch, Chris DeVitto of *The Lima (Ohio) News* came across an accident. A woman was trapped in her overturned car and was dangling upside down, being held in place by a seat belt. "My first instinct was to render aid to the victim," DeVitto said. He rushed to the car without his cameras. When he saw that the woman was not badly hurt and after being told that paramedics had been called, DeVitto got his camera and took some pictures. Later the paper received phone calls and letters "claiming I was no better than the paparazzi that allegedly caused Princess Di's death."[37]

Don McCullin of the *Sunday Times* in London was photographing guerrilla fighters in El Salvador. He put aside his camera when he

Dangling by the seat belt. Before taking the photo, the photographer ensured that the woman was not badly hurt and paramedics were called.

(Photo courtesy of The Lima [Ohio] News.*)*

and a *Newsweek* reporter asked guerrilla leaders, victorious for the moment, for permission to carry wounded enemy soldiers to a hospital truck. McCullin rode along to the hospital and carried one man in.

Photographer Robin Moyer of the Black Star agency accompanied 150,000 malnourished Cambodian refugees as they listlessly staggered across the Thai boarder. "Bullets killing people is one thing," Moyer told Liz Nakahara of *The Washington Post.* "But watching people die of malnutrition is much more terrible." Moyer put down his camera and helped carry people out of the hills.[38]

Death and the News

Police reported that a man was sitting in a pickup truck parked along a Los Angeles freeway shortly before rush hour. He had a gun. KCBS-TV dispatched its helicopter to the scene. When news executives at KTLA-TV saw the police blockades causing traffic to back up for miles, the station interrupted a children's program and began to broadcast live images. Soon six other Los Angeles TV stations were also covering the story.

There was a moment of drama when the man unfurled a banner criticizing health maintenance organizations. But then he got back into his truck and sat with his dog. Some stations cut back to normal programming. "He could have sat in that truck for 10 hours," Cheryl Kunin Fair, KABC news director, said. Other stations stayed with the news event.

In a few minutes, the truck erupted in flames. KCBS ordered its camera to pull back. "We were very concerned that he was going to come out of the cab totally on fire," news director Pat Casey said. Some stations didn't respond as quickly, and they showed the man as he threw himself out of the cab with hair and clothing on fire. *The Orange County (Calif.) Register* described the scene: "Writhing in pain, the man rolled on the ground, pulled off his burning pants and underwear, then climbed onto an overpass sidewall as if to jump."

Then he held up his hands. More stations went to longer shoots at this point. But KTLA news director Jeffrey Wald thought the man was surrendering, so KTLA stayed with tight shots of the live action. Then he pulled a shotgun from his truck. At that point, KCBS ordered its camera to pull back even more. But KTLA was caught off guard, and viewers could see the man blow his brains out.

Stations received heated complaints from viewers. "I've never seen someone commit murder or suicide, and I don't want to," said one viewer who was watching Rosie O'Donnell when KNBC broke away. "Is this real reporting, or is this sensationalism?" Others wondered if the incident merited live coverage on eight TV stations. "This wasn't a presidential assassination or anything that would affect many lives in the city," one said. Many were bothered by the timing. Most stations broke away from programming popular with children. "Nobody at the station had the forethought to switch cameras or do a damn thing but make sure all the small children at home could witness such despicable broadcasting," one said. Another agreed: "In your quest for 'news,' you traumatized countless viewers who turned their channels a second too late." One mother said she didn't have time to switch channels before her child saw the man rolling in flames.

The coverage was also challenged by media critics. Ken Waters, a journalism professor at Pepperdine University, saw the broadcast as another example that the profit incentive has pushed stations to present news as drama—and thus entertainment. "If you make that decision, that anything that's dramatic we're going to do live, then you have to live with the consequence," he said. Jeff Cole, director of the UCLA Center for Communications Policy, which monitors TV programming, was also troubled by the broadcast. "We're really talking about the technology defining the coverage," Cole said. He said too many broadcast journalists accepted the idea that "We have mini-cams, we have helicopters, therefore we're going to cover it because it's 'neat.'" Others pointed out that the stations had lost editorial control over the images they were broadcasting.

Some journalists and viewers defended the coverage, saying that the TV stations didn't have time to react to the situation. However, Howard Rosenberg, TV critic at the *Los Angeles Times,* timed the broadcasts. He found that 11 seconds passed between the man grabbing the shotgun and then using it. During that time, KTLA veteran reporter Stan Chambers even observed on air: "There he has his gun now." Rosenberg concluded:

> Live coverage of a volatile situation is the equivalent of playing Russian roulette. Sometimes you must play anyway because the story is potentially worth the risk, as when KCOP-TV Channel 13's live chopper pictures probably saved Reginald Denny's life by showing him getting savagely beaten during the Los Angeles riots. Or when the story is as mammoth as the North Hollywood bank shootout last year. But this time, for a story that began as a massive traffic tie-up before it spun out of control?

News directors said they would reconsider their live helicopter coverage. "Of course this is a wake-up call for television news," said KTLA's Wald. Wald said he had nightmares after the broadcast. But he said his station would continue to go live with such stories. Other stations said they were going to find ways to improve communication between the station and the field teams. MSNBC, a national cable channel that picked up KNBC's feed, planned to install a delay mechanism. Two stations apologized on air to viewers. One took the unusual step of having newsroom personnel—reporters, photographers and anchors—return calls from upset viewers. No station replayed the suicide. But none of the station managers said they planned to cut back on live crime coverage.[39]

News executives at KHOU-TV in Houston had to make similar decisions when a woman stole a Houston police cruiser. She used the police radio to tell officers she wanted them to kill her. KHOU's traffic helicopter caught up with the woman when she wrecked the cruiser near a freeway. As the helicopter hovered overhead, police arrived. The woman got out of the car, drew a large kitchen knife and ran toward the officers. They opened fire, knocking her to the ground. The KHOU news director decided not to show the station's exclusive video of the woman being killed. He called it "a relatively easy decision."[40]

For photographers at a small TV station in Alabama, the question was not only whether to videotape a news event but whether they should intervene. WHMA-TV in Anniston dispatched them to nearby Jacksonville, Ala., after a man had called the station four times late one evening to say that he was going to set himself on fire to protest unemployment. The station notified Jacksonville police. The caller, who had apparently been drinking, asked for a reporter and photographer to come to the town square. Once the photographer had his cameras ready, the man doused himself with charcoal starter fluid and applied a lighted match. The photographer filmed the horror for several seconds before his partner rushed forward and tried to beat out the flames with his small reporter's notebook. But the flames got stronger and were not put out until the burning man raced across the square where a volunteer firefighter smothered the fire with an extinguisher. The man survived but spent eight painful weeks in a hospital.

Interviewed after the incident, WHMA news director Phillip D. Cox contended that many people misunderstood the actions of his crew. For one thing, Cox said, his photographers tried to stop the apparently drunken man from setting himself afire, but the man warned them off. "He said 'Stay back!' several times," Cox explained.[41]

However, many believed the news crew should have done more to stop the self-immolation even if that meant not getting the pictures. The man was looking for publicity. If the photographer had refused to film him, the man might have delayed setting himself on fire long enough for police to arrive. *The New York Times* claimed that just by being there, the TV crew was "creating the news."[42] Network television showed WHMA's tapes. The network's stories, as well as those in other national news media, were not about the torching incident so much as they were about the ethics of what the Alabama station did that night.

Some good came out of this awful Alabama incident. A photographer in Middletown, Ohio, specifically mentioned the Alabama case after he helped save the life of a burning man. When an explosion at an auto body shop set a worker on fire, he ignored his camera, grabbed a coat and tried to smother the flames. He said later, "I don't know how you could continue filming. . . . That's what ethics are—you don't just stand by."[43]

Improving the Profession

We've all seen this a time or two. We've been in electronics stores or on used-car lots, and we've watched as salespeople turn up the charm and turn down the honesty in hopes of getting some naive couple to part with their hard-earned cash. Some of us have been disgusted by the unctuous conduct of these salespeople; others have chuckled at their blatant devotion to greed. But we should keep in mind that many people believe that those salespeople live by higher ethical standards than those practiced by most journalists.

Many people see journalists as vultures, floating over the land, looking for someone suffering a misfortune so they can swoop down and snag a front-page story. Getting that story and advancing their careers are their motivations. The First Amendment is just a tool they use to help them win prizes.

It's not hard to understand why many people have that attitude. They read stories like the one that opened this chapter about reporters in Colorado who showed total disrespect for the family of the hostage and trashed the family's home. And they hear of reporters and editors like those at *The Washington Post* who valued getting a story about the 8-year-old heroin addict more than they did helping the child escape that environment. They see pictures of people mourning the death of kin, trying to commit suicide, or even setting fire to themselves, and they rightfully wonder why those picture takers didn't drop their cameras and help the poor people they were photographing. They grow tired of hearing news organizations retract major investigative pieces a day or two after splashing them on the front page or promoting them heavily on newscasts.

Their impressions of reporters are also formed by other incidents, the small ones they hear about in their own communities. They empathize with the mourning mother who wanted the paper to print a tribute to her daughter and instead read a news account of her daughter's wild ways and possible suicide. They don't understand the bravado that would drive a sportswriter to question a college freshman who hasn't been able to come to terms with the death of an idolized brother any more than they can understand a reporter who would force Arthur Ashe to announce he had AIDS. These incidents reinforce the image of the journalist as a callous brute intent on getting the story—any story—no matter who gets hurt.

Fortunately, not all journalists behave this way. And many owe their successes to being able to deal with people honestly and honorably. They have found these traits often win the respect of sources and readers alike.

The push for compassion in journalism is not just to solve a public-relations problem. As Geneva Overholser, former editor of *The Des Moines Register*, explained, journalists who have trained themselves to be devoid of emotion and feeling all too often have produced a journalism that was equally emotionless and frequently dull. Journalists who demand "only the facts, ma'am" miss the nuances of stories that more sensitive reporters include.

As news organizations broaden their definitions of news, reporters are no longer concentrating their coverage on city hall and the police stations. They are covering subjects and issues that have an impact on their communities. These kinds of stories often demand that reporters deal with a variety of people and deal with them compassionately.

None of this is to say that journalists should become weak-kneed fawns allowing themselves to be pushed around by sources. As long as there are stories people do not want to see reported, journalists will have to ask tough questions and push to get information. But it is not too much to ask that the motive for producing stories that cause harm to people be something more than an opportunity for a byline or a front-page story.

No one wants a complaisant press that avoids controversy and allows wrongdoing to go on unimpeded, but that does not mean we cannot have a compassionate press that shows respect for people and avoids causing needless pain.

Conflicts
of
Interest

12

The Business
of News

The war in Vietnam had divided America. To hawks, the war was necessary to stop the spread of communism. Anti-war protesters were unpatriotic traitors who were giving aid to the enemy. To doves and many young people, the war was senseless. They staged massive rallies and sneered at President Lyndon Johnson with the chant: "Hey, hey, LBJ, how many kids do you kill today?"

All the while, deep inside the Pentagon, officials were writing an amazingly candid history of the war, documenting that American military and government leaders had misled and, in some cases, deceived Congress and the American people in an effort to justify escalating the war. This history, which became known as the Pentagon Papers, was classified top secret. Yet a *New York Times* reporter obtained a copy. When the *Times* began publishing his stories, the Nixon administration got a court order forcing the *Times* to stop.

That's when reporters from *The Washington Post* got involved. They tracked down their own copy of the Pentagon Papers. Working in seclusion in executive editor Benjamin Bradlee's Georgetown home, they read the lengthy documents, sized up their key findings and prepared a series of stories. Bradlee wanted it printed as quickly as possible—partly to show unity with the *Times* and partly to help establish the *Post* as a major player in American journalism.

However, many in *Post* management wanted the *Post* to stay out of this battle. The company's lawyers contended that Nixon would undoubtedly find out that the *Post* had copies of the Pentagon Papers and would ask the courts for another restraining order. Once he did, the *Post* would be embroiled in a lengthy—and very costly—legal battle. Further, the lawyers argued, the Nixon administration might seek criminal charges against the *Post* for violating espionage laws. They doubted that the First Amendment would protect reporters from those charges.

There were also business concerns. The Washington Post Co. was changing its status from a family-owned business to a publicly owned corporation. The company hoped to sell more than $1 million worth of stock. Frederick Beebe, chairman of the board of directors, worried that the stock offering would be canceled if the *Post* got involved in a messy lawsuit. Beebe also feared that Nixon might use the Federal Communications Commission to cause trouble for the Washington Post Co.'s TV and radio stations. At that time, the FCC had considerable regulatory powers over broadcasters.

In the middle of all these arguments was Katharine Graham, publisher of the *Post*. After lengthy telephone conversations with Beebe, Bradlee and corporate attorneys, she told Bradlee to go ahead and publish the stories. David Rudenstine, a law professor who wrote the definitive history of the Pentagon Papers, described her decision like this:

> Graham assumed that publication would cause the government to sue the *Post* for an injunction; that there might be difficulties with the stock sale; and that there might also be repercussions for the company's electronic broadcasting stations. But she was deeply worried about the morale and commitment of her editors and reporters and about the reputation of the paper.[1]

The courts allowed both the *Post* and the *Times* to print the Pentagon Papers. The information in the papers changed many people's opinions of the war. The sale of *Post* stock went ahead, but the FCC did scrutinize the *Post*'s broadcast properties closely.

A quarter of a century later, managers of CBS faced a similar decision. *60 Minutes* had prepared a report charging that the top executives of tobacco companies lied to Congress when they testified that nicotine was not addictive. CBS found a former scientist for the Brown & Williamson tobacco company who said that the company's own research showed that nicotine was addictive. *60 Minutes* reporters also learned that tobacco companies knowingly added a cancer-causing substance to pipe tobacco.

Once Brown & Williamson heard that *60 Minutes* was preparing the report, it threatened to sue CBS. The suit would not claim the reports were libelous or that they were false. Instead, B&W attorneys planned to accuse CBS of enticing the scientist to violate a clause in his contract that forbade him from talking about his work.

It was a novel way to sue the media. But media attorneys doubted the courts would allow it. James C. Goodale, who represented the *Times* in the Pentagon Papers affair, said it would be a "slam-dunk win" for CBS. Joseph B. Jamail, an attorney who won a $10.5 billion judgment for a similar claim by Pennzoil against Texaco, told *The New York Times*, "If you've got as much backbone as a banana, you go with that one. I just don't see the damages."

But other issues clouded CBS's decision. One was the relationship between CBS's owners and the tobacco industry. At that time, CBS's parent company was the Tisch family's Loews Corporation. Loews also had an interest in Lorillard, a cigarette company. As CBS News was preparing the *60 Minutes* episode, Lorillard was negotiating with Brown & Williamson to buy six of its brands. Further, Lawrence Tisch, who was CBS chairman at the time, was the father of Andrew Tisch, the chairman of Lorillard and one of the tobacco executives who told Congress nicotine was not addictive.

CBS executives had other things to consider too. CBS and Westinghouse were negotiating a merger. An editorial in *The New York Times* suggested, "With a $5.4 billion merger deal with the Westinghouse Electric Corporation in the works, a multibillion-dollar lawsuit would hardly have been welcome. Some of the executives . . . stand to gain millions of dollars themselves in stock options and other payments once the deal is approved." CBS executives strongly denied that the prospect of monetary gain influenced them.

However, the story was killed. It was not until after *The Wall Street Journal* published a similar story that CBS managers allowed *60 Minutes* to broadcast the episode. When the story's reporter, Mike Wallace, talked to reporters after the broadcast, he was blunt: "[F]or the first time, CBS News and CBS management cared more about the sale to Westinghouse or the difficulties of perhaps defending a lawsuit than they cared about the news. As a result of which, it took us months to finally get a tobacco piece that we wanted, that was carefully reported and was worth putting on the air, to get it finally on the air."[2]

The issues and realities faced by executives at the Washington Post Co. and CBS were, of course, different. Yet one observation can be made: Management plays a key role in the ability of journalists to practice their profession. Graham stood behind her journalists despite the threats to the financial health of the *Post*. CBS did not. As a *New York Times* editorial put it: "The most troubling part of CBS's decision is that it was made not by news executives but by corporate officers, who may have their minds on money rather than public service."[3]

Since the news media are big businesses, they are influenced by the same forces that bear on all American business enterprises. There is nothing intrinsically wrong or illegal about the media following the same economic Pied Pipers that motivate K-mart, Mobil, United Technologies, IBM and Crazy Joe's Used Cars.

However, news businesses differ from other businesses in one important way. Their constitutionally protected freedom is interpreted by most people to mean that they are a semipublic service as well as private, profit-seeking businesses. This dual role of serving the public and making profits for their owners can create ethical problems for journalists. As James C. Thomson Jr., former curator of the Nieman Foundation, noted, this duality creates tension "between greed and idealism." Thomson believes every news organization has "two cultures, or at least outlooks, that are often at odds with each other: on the one hand, reporters and editors, who traditionally see their role as uncovering and disseminating the truth (or some approximation thereof); and on the other hand, owners, publishers, 'management,' who seek to stay in business and make a tidy profit."[4]

Robert P. Clark, former executive editor of the Louisville *Courier-Journal,* fears greed may be taking a bigger role now than ever before. "We in journalism are facing a new ethics problem not addressed in any of our codes: bottom-line journalism." Too many corporations are buying media just to make a buck.[5]

News Makes Money

The news media have made lots of money for their investors. Many corporations, like Gannett and the Tribune Co. of Chicago, own both newspapers and TV stations, two of the most profitable industries in America. Former Gannett president Al Neuharth was once asked whether he pronounced the company's name GAN-nett or gan-NETT. He said he pronounced it, "MON-ey." Gannett's newspapers and TV stations are so lucrative that for 22 straight years, each of its quarterly profit reports was higher than the previous one.[6] In 1996, Gannett's profit margin was nearly three times the average for Fortune 500 companies. Of the major chains, the newspaper division of the Tribune Co. of Chicago was the most profitable with a 27 percent profit margin. Although that profit margin is down from a decade ago, one financial analyst pointed out that "there are lots of industries that do not see 15 percent margins in the midst of their biggest booms."[7]

Newspapers continue to produce torrents of revenue. *Forbes,* a business magazine, reported that $53.2 billion was spent on daily and weekly newspapers by advertisers and readers in 1997. Between 1992 and 1997, spending on newspapers grew at a 4.3 percent compound annual rate.[8]

TV stations, particularly network affiliates, traditionally have made even more money than newspapers. Jon Katz, a former producer at *CBS Morning News,* once quipped, "Nobody but Colombian drug lords makes as much money" as station owners.[9] Profit margins of 40 percent were not uncommon in the 1980s, and big-city stations often made more than $50 million in pretax profits. Although a recession in the early 1990s hurt the TV industry, larger stations with network affiliations still recorded profit margins of 26 percent and average profits of $33 million. But by the late 1990s, profit margins had returned to the 30 to 40 percent range. Sinclair Broadcast Group, which then owned more TV stations than any other company, reported profit margins of more than 50 percent in 1997.

The Changing Ownership of Newspapers

At the beginning of the 20th century more than 98 percent of American newspapers were independently owned, often by local families.[10] Some families owned newspapers to make money; others wanted the power and prestige of newspaper ownership.

Many newspapers flourished under local publishers. Their roots in the community and their commitment to the family-owned business pushed them to produce quality papers. Often these families took such pride in their papers that they willingly poured a large part of their profits back in the newsroom to improve the newspaper.

For example, although *The Washington Post* is today one of America's best newspapers, that has not always been the case. Donald Graham, when he was publisher of the *Post,* recalled a time when the paper was struggling. "In the early 1950s," he said, "the *Post* aspired to be a world-class newspaper; its heart was in the right place, but it just didn't have enough money. There's an old joke around the *Post* that in those days we could cover any international conference as long as it was in the first taxi zone."

He noted with pride that although the *Post* had no foreign correspondents before 1960, it had bureaus all over the world by the early 1980s.[11] Today, the paper has about 25 reporters overseas. With a publisher who spent money to improve news coverage, the *Post* hired topnotch journalists and gave them the time and resources they needed to produce stories that were responsible and complete. They could readily meet the ethical demands of their profession and by doing so made the paper one of the most influential in the country.

The Louisville papers also gained national respect under the Bingham family. "The Binghams published distinguished newspapers," former *Courier-Journal* executive editor Clark stated. "The motive was not primarily money, but public service."[12]

However, not all family-owned newspapers encouraged their staffs to do ethical journalism. Some of these papers suffered under narrow-minded owners who pushed the papers toward one-sided reports and political favoritism. Journalism Professor John Hulteng cited several classic cases of activist publishers, such as conservatives Eugene Pulliam of *The Indianapolis Star* and William Loeb of *The Union Leader* in Manchester, N.H. When Loeb decided to back a candidate in one election, his paper began a crusade that included front-page editorials with misleading quotes from other papers. In one presidential primary, *The Union Leader* devoted twice as much space to Loeb's choice (who was not considered a serious candidate by most observers) as it did to all the front-runners combined. Similarly, when Robert Kennedy was running for president in the Indiana primary, Pulliam's *Indianapolis Star* heaped negative coverage on Kennedy while writing many favorable stories about a "favorite son" candidate who was running only to keep Kennedy from winning the primary.[13]

A recent biography of Robert McCormick, legendary publisher of the *Chicago Tribune,* stated that during his reign, the *Tribune* became "a megaphone to amplify the publisher's caprices." McCormick was so strongly against Franklin Roosevelt that 97 days before the 1936 election, a front-page headline in the *Tribune* read, "Only 97 Days Left to Save Your Country." McCormick liked the phrase so much he had the *Tribune*'s switchboard answer all calls that way, each day counting down to election.[14]

While not all family-owned papers were used this blatantly to promote the political philosophies of owners, many were hopelessly co-opted by "sacred cows," a term journalists gave to the publisher's friends and favored institutions that were to receive preferential treatment. Others engaged in hometown boosterism that required reporters to paint rosy pictures of the city's economy and government.

Newspaper Chains Grow

The number of family-owned newspapers has declined dramatically. Today, chains own 80 percent of the nation's dailies. Most of the remaining independent papers are in small communities and have circulations under 10,000.

Many journalists bemoan the loss of truly local papers. Former *Washington Post* ombudsman and journalism dean Ben Bagdikian worries that the growth of group ownership of the American media will result in less individuality in American papers and the loss of distinct editorial voices.[15] Other journalists believe newspapers may lose their sense of purpose under chain management. C.K. McClatchy, a newspaper editor and owner, once said: "I fear the day when newspaper people are no longer in charge of newspapers. . . . To make a gross generalization, one can say that good newspapers are almost always run by good newspaper people; they are almost never run by good bankers and good accountants."[16]

Some publishers have even taken steps to keep chains from buying their papers. Nelson Poynter gave controlling stock in his highly respected *St. Petersburg Times* to Modern Media Institute. Now the Poynter Institute for Media Studies, it uses its share of the profits from the *Times* to fund studies of journalism and conduct workshops for journalists. Theodore Bodenwein placed his paper, *The Day* in New London, Conn., in a trust that gives any profits not used to improve the paper to community groups. In Peoria, Ill., Henry Slade set up an employee stock ownership plan in an effort to keep the *Journal Star* in local hands. Apparently Slade's deal was too generous. "As employees began to cash out early—many becoming millionaires— the financial burden of buying back the stock became too great," *Editor & Publisher* magazine reported. In 1996, the paper was sold to Copley Press Inc. for $174.5 million.[17]

Unlike the Poynters, the Bodenweins and the Slades, most families decided to sell their papers. Estate taxes caused some to sell. At one time these taxes were as high as 70 percent. If the paper had an appraised value of $1 million, the children had to pay the government $700,000 in taxes to inherit it. The tax in 1998 could reach as high as 55 percent.[18] Many decided to sell the paper rather than scramble to find that much cash. Sometimes the children themselves did not want to be newspaper publishers and sold the paper so they could follow other careers. Occasionally, a family sold because a chain had made an offer that was just too good to turn down. More recently, some families have sold their papers because they believed group ownership was the only way the paper could keep up with the demands of the new electronic era, such as Internet sites and expensive pagination systems. Only on rare occasions did a family sell the newspaper because it was losing money.[19]

The trend toward group ownership took off in the 1980s, a decade when corporate raiders fueled by "junk bonds" took over many major corporations. Investors were drawn to media properties because they had "been able to generate rivers of cash decade after decade," as the national business magazine *Forbes* put it.[20] Many of these investors had little interest in public service. If they saw the value of their shares go down or if annual dividends were not high enough, they pressured executives to turn things around. A Pulitzer Prize might be nice, but high annual yields were even nicer. Sometimes, to keep stock owners happy, these executives pushed editors at respected publications to match the profit margins of lower-quality chains.

The entry of new investors had another effect. Prices for newspapers and TV stations soared to what *Forbes* called "preposterously high prices."[21] Financial observers watched in awe as newspapers sold for prices that were two or three times what businesses with similar earnings in other industries would bring. When the McClatchy Newspapers chain paid $74 million for three small papers in South Carolina, *The New York Times* headline read, "Sale Price Arouses Wonder over Deal in South Carolina."

Larger papers, of course, have sold for much more. In the early 1990s, Gannett paid the Bingham family $307 million for *The Louisville Times* and *Courier-Journal,* Hearst paid $375 million for the *Houston Chronicle,* Times Mirror paid $450 million for the Baltimore *Sun,* and the New York Times Co. paid $1.1 billion for *The Boston Globe.*[22] In 1997 Knight-Ridder paid the Walt Disney Co. $1.65 billion for the Kansas City *Star,* Fort Worth *Star-Telegram* and two smaller dailies. Disney had acquired the papers through a series of mergers. A few months later, the McClatchy chain set a record for a single paper by paying $1.4 billion for the Minneapolis *Star Tribune.*

Between 1992 and 1996, more than 300 of the nation's 1,500 dailies were sold, usually by one chain to another.[23] In 1997 162 dailies exchanged hands. Chains buying out other chains is happening with enough regularity that an investment banker has predicted that all American mass media may eventually be owned by six conglomerates (Tables 12.1 and 12.2).[24]

When a Chain Buys a Paper

What happens to the quality of journalism at newspapers when they are purchased by investors who may have gone deeply in debt to buy them? Are journalists allowed to meet the ethical demands of their profession, or do the business needs of the new owners overrule? Researchers have studied these questions but have found no clear answers.[25] It all seems to depend on what paper is being discussed and what chain bought it.

TABLE 12.1.   Twenty Largest Newspaper Chains

	Daily		Sunday	
	Circulation	*Papers*	*Circulation*	*Papers*
Gannett Co. Inc.	5,984,526	87	6,000,609	70
Knight-Ridder	3,893,639	33	5,512,197	31
Newhouse Newspapers	2,806,016	23	3,602,725	21
Dow Jones & Co. Inc.	2,349,419	20	549,795	14
Times Mirror Co.	2,348,407	9	3,040,125	7
The New York Times Co.	2,263,091	20	3,181,360	16
MediaNews Group	1,427,463	34	1,557,114	14
The McClatchy Co.	1,351,543	11	1,837,415	11
E.W. Scripps Co.	1,337,700	20	1,583,200	17
Hearst Newspapers	1,325,569	12	2,560,098	11
Thomson Newspapers Inc.	1,281,758	62	1,319,629	46
Tribune Co.	1,241,863	4	1,869,347	4
Cox Enterprises Inc.	1,135,972	16	1,596,204	16
Hollinger International	1,025,384	54	849,808	29
Freedom Communications	965,603	28	1,082,999	24
A.H. Belo Corp.	914,998	6	1,277,728	6
Media General Inc.	846,106	20	972,225	14
The Washington Post Co.	830,626	2	1,166,399	2
Central Newspapers	800,334	7	1,052,931	5
Copley Newspapers	789,229	12	866,274	8

Source: Facts About Newspapers, *1998.*

TABLE 12.2.   Twenty Largest American Newspapers

The Wall Street Journal	1,774,888	*San Francisco Chronicle*	484,218
USA Today	1,713,674	*The Dallas Morning News*	481,032
The New York Times	1,074,741	*The Boston Globe*	475,966
Los Angeles Times	1,050,176	*The Arizona Republic*	437,118
The Washington Post	775,894	*New York Post*	436,226
Daily News, New York	721,256	*The Philadelphia Inquirer*	428,233
Chicago Tribune	653,554	*The Star-Ledger,* Newark	406,010
Newsday	568,914	*Star Tribune,* Minneapolis	387,412
Houston Chronicle	549,101	*Detroit Free Press*	384,624
Chicago Sun-Times	484,379	*The Plain Dealer,* Cleveland	383,586

Source: Facts About Newspapers, 1998.

Some chains like Knight-Ridder and Times Mirror have, in the past, willingly spent money to pump new life into mediocre newspapers. For instance, Knight-Ridder turned *The Philadelphia Inquirer,* once a disreputable newspaper, into a well-regarded publication that has filled its trophy cases with Pulitzer Prizes and other top journalism awards. Eugene L. Roberts Jr., executive editor of the paper during the turnaround, said that although Knight-Ridder "doesn't understand losing money," the group wanted "the *Inquirer* to be accurate, reliable, fair, and aggressive."[26] During Roberts' editorship, the *Inquirer* opened foreign bureaus, added to its news hole and encouraged reporters "to go off for months—even years—on massive investigative projects," a journalism review reported.[27]

However, as Knight-Ridder sought to bring its profit margins in line with other publishers, editors felt more pressure to control expenses. Roberts left the paper in 1990 after a series of arguments over the *Inquirer*'s budget.[28] He later became managing editor of *The New York Times* and a journalism professor.

Seven years after Roberts left, another *Inquirer* editor, Maxwell King, resigned. King said, "When I look at big newspaper companies across the board, the question that occurs to me is, 'Are they all too intent on taking profit now and not intent enough on investing in content for the future?'" Knight-Ridder wanted the paper to boost its profit margin from 8 percent in 1995 to 15 percent in 1997.[29]

A similar situation was developing at Knight-Ridder's *Miami Herald*. Publisher David Lawrence abruptly resigned in 1998 after 27 years of service with the company and called the newspaper business "permanently frustrating." A few days later, Tony Ridder, Knight-Ridder's CEO, said the company would sell the *Herald* if its profit margins did not improve. "All we're asking them to do is get to a 22 percent profit margin by the year 2000," Ridder said. The paper's projected profits for 1998 were 18.5 percent.[30]

The Gannett chain has been credited with improving some small-city papers that it purchased. The chain brought in experienced editors and updated the papers' equipment and design. But the chain also is well-known for its concern for the bottom line. In some cases, Gannett doubled the profits of newspapers it purchased by tighter management, volume buying and much higher advertising rates. When Gannett took over *The Asbury Park Press* in New Jersey, it cut the staff from 225 to 180 and told the theater critic there was no money for him to cover plays on Broadway, which is less than 70 miles away. Robert H. Giles edited the two Gannett dailies in Rochester, N.Y., before he became executive editor of Gannett's *The Detroit News*. Giles contended that Gannett wants it both ways: "put out good newspapers and continue to make a lot of money, and you can't always do that."[31]

In the late 1990s, Gannett owned about 90 daily papers including *USA Today* and sold nearly 6 million copies a day.[32] Gannett dwarfed second-place Knight-Ridder, which owned about 30 dailies, with a total circulation of fewer than 4 million. Gannett also owned approximately 35 weekly newspapers, 10 TV stations and several radio stations.

Some publishers are more concerned about making money than producing quality newspapers. These publishers may keep the size of the news staffs small so they can save money and keep profits high. They require their staffs to work long hours churning out stories to fill the paper. To these reporters, some journalistic principles may seem like luxuries they can't afford. They don't have time to check several sources or provide social context to their stories. And to add insult to these injurious conditions, often these journalists are among the lowest paid in the business, barely making a living wage.

For many years, Thomson Newspapers Inc. was cited as a company that put profits ahead of news. Some journalists who have worked for Thomson papers sarcastically quote a statement by the chain's founder, Roy Thomson: "The news is the stuff that separates the ads." At its peak in 1993, this Canadian company owned 156 dailies and 25 weeklies in the United States, more than 40 dailies and about 20 weeklies in Canada, and publications in Great Britain and Australia. Thomson had a reputation for buying papers in small cities and turning them into cash cows.[33]

Richard Harrington, president and CEO of Thomson, explained to *Presstime* how the company accomplished that feat: "We raised rates, cut costs, and made a lot more than 20 percent on margins." Harrington admitted Thomson was "known as a company that didn't put a lot of money into its papers."[34] The result was often a lot of second-rate journalism. Norman Isaacs, who edited daily papers in Indianapolis, Louisville and St. Louis, refused to label Thomson a newspaper chain, preferring to call it a "commercial printer."[35] A Canadian government commission that examined chain-owned papers in that country concluded that Thomson's "small-town monopoly papers are, almost without exception, a lacklustre aggregation of cash boxes."[36]

Similar accusations have been brought against other chains. When Tom White quit his job at the *Lincoln (Neb.) Journal-Star*, he ripped into the paper's owner, Lee Enterprises. A front-page story in the paper quoted him as saying, "I think it's worthy to note that Lee's corporate leadership has no vice president for news, no one with a news background and, in my view, no significant personnel development program for journalists. They're very good business operators and I respect that, but I think the company needs to look at journalism too."[37] Lee owns about 19 daily newspapers, 15 network-affiliated TV stations and several shoppers.

The TV News Business

Anyone with enough money can start or buy as many newspapers as they want. Newspaper chains can own hundreds of newspapers. However, that's not the way things work in broadcasting. A government agency, the Federal Communications Commission, regulates the ownership of radio and TV stations. Until the early 1980s, FCC rules limited a person or company to owning only seven TV stations. As TV stations became more and more profitable, companies jostled to own the seven most lucrative stations they could find. That created a heated market as several companies vied to buy stations in larger, more profitable markets.

Then, in the early 1980s, the FCC decided to allow companies to own up to 12 TV stations as long as they reached no more than 25 percent of the households in America. Many media companies saw the new rules as a chance to own more stations in bigger markets. They borrowed heavily and entered into bidding wars that pushed prices of stations to record levels. For example, just three years after WCVB, a Boston TV station, was sold for $220 million, it was purchased by Hearst for $450 million.

The desire to own American broadcast stations led Rupert Murdoch, an Australian press baron who owned media properties around the world, to become a naturalized U.S. citizen so he could meet FCC regulations that require owners to be Americans. Murdoch soon owned enough TV stations to reach 21 percent of the nation's TV viewers, and he started the Fox network with affiliates in most large markets. In 1993 the FCC gave him special permission to own both a New York TV station and the *New York Post* despite its rules that one company can't own both a TV station and a newspaper in the same town.

The 1996 Telecommunications Act added even more heat to the red-hot demand for broadcast stations. The act eliminated the limit on the number of stations that one company could own. In addition, it raised the coverage cap so that one company's stations could reach 35 percent of the nation's homes. The act also revised the formula for calculating how many homes a station reached. Companies were allowed to discount by half the potential audience for UHF stations (the ones with numbers higher than 13). Applying this formula, a UHF station that reached 500,000 homes would be counted as reaching 250,000. Another provision in the 1996 act allowed companies to enter into "local marketing agreements" that allowed them to control stations they could not buy outright because of FCC limits. These provisions allowed some station owners to reach considerably more

TABLE 12.3.   Twenty-five Largest TV Broadcast Groups

	Homes reached (FCC formula)	Stations owned	Homes reached
Fox	34.9%	23	40.5%
Paxson	30.9%	55	61.4%
CBS	30.8%	14	31.7%
NBC	26.9%	12	27.3%
Tribune	26.5%	19	37.5%
ABC	23.9%	10	24.2%
ChrisCraft/BHC/United	18.7%	10	21.6%
Gannett	16.5%	19	16.6%
USA	15.5%	13	31.0%
A.H. Belo	14.2%	17	14.2%
Univision	13.5%	13	27.0%
Sinclair	13.0%	56	22.4%
Paramount	12.4%	17	24.4%
Telemundo	10.7%	8	21.3%
Hearst-Argyle	9.6%	16	10.9%
Cox	9.6%	9	9.7%
Young	9.1%	15	9.2%
E.W. Scripps	8.0%	9	9.8%
Hicks, Muse, Tate & Furst	7.2%	23	10.0%
Post-Newsweek	7.1%	6	7.1%
Meredith	6.3%	11	7.7%
Granite	6.1%	12	7.9%
Pulitzer	5.2%	9	5.5%
Raycom	5.2%	23	6.0%
Media General	4.5%	13	5.3%

Source: Broadcasting & Cable, *April 6, 1998.*

than 35 percent of the homes. Because Paxson owned many UHF stations and had entered into local marketing agreements with other stations, it reached 61.4 percent in 1998. However, under the formula of the 1996 act, Paxson's reach was calculated at 30.9 percent, well below the act's limit. (See Table 12.3.)

Immediately after Congress passed the act, several large broadcasters announced they were buying other broadcasters. Westinghouse bought CBS. The addition of CBS-owned stations brought Westinghouse's total to 14 stations reaching 32 percent of the population. Westinghouse became the country's largest broadcaster at the time. Shortly after that deal, Tribune Co. bought Renaissance Broadcasting to become the second largest owner with 16 stations reaching about 25 percent of the homes. This trend of one broadcast group buying another has continued. *Broadcasting & Cable* reported that the top 25 TV-station groups owned or controlled 35 percent of the commercial TV stations in 1998, up from 33 percent in 1997 and 25 percent in 1996.[38]

Just as local stations became hot properties in the 1980s and 1990s, all three major TV networks changed owners. In the 1980s, General Electric bought RCA, the owner of NBC, for $6.28 billion. Both Ted Turner, owner of TBS and CNN, and conservative Sen. Jesse Helms tried to acquire CBS until Laurence Tisch of Loews International bought controlling interest in the network. Capital Cities Communication, which already owned seven TV stations and 17 newspapers, bought ABC for $3.5 billion. Then, in 1995, ABC/Capital Cities, as the new company was called, was purchased by Walt Disney Co. for $19 billion, and Westinghouse bought CBS for $5.4 billion. After purchasing CBS, Westinghouse began to sell its industrial units so it could concentrate on its broadcasting properties. It changed its name to CBS Inc.

Television Finds Profits in News

While newspaper companies sell primarily one product (the paper), broadcasters have two kinds of products: news and entertainment programming. In earlier days, station owners and network executives did not expect their news departments to make money. Some station owners neglected their news departments and scheduled only enough news and public affairs programming to satisfy FCC requirements. Other owners believed strong newscasts gave their stations prestige in the community and drew viewers to the moneymaking entertainment programs. So they spent money willingly on their newsrooms. For these stations news was a "loss leader," according to Ben Bagdikian, formerly of *The Washington Post,* who was referring to the grocery-store practice of advertising a few products at below-cost prices in hopes that buyers will fill their shopping carts with more profitable items.

The days of news-as-prestige began to fade when the networks discovered news could make money. Bagdikian places part of the blame on one program: "*60 Minutes* was the best of times and the worst of times. It was the best of times in the sense that it did a lot of serious investigative reporting bigger. . . . But it was the worst in the sense that it was the first public affairs program that made money."

60 Minutes has been rated in the Top 10 among prime-time shows for more than 20 straight seasons and is the most profitable series on television. In the mid-1990s, CBS generated more than $300 million annually from *48 Hours* and *60 Minutes.* Other networks wanted a piece of the pie. ABC cashed in with *PrimeTime Live,* which it combined with its other popular newsmagazine, *20/20*, in 1998. These two programs had added more than $200 million to ABC's coffers in 1997. NBC tried 17 times to create a successful newsmagazine before it finally hit pay dirt with *Dateline NBC*, which now earns about $20 million annually.[39]

Network accountants like newsmagazines because they are cheap. One edition of *Dateline NBC* or *20/20* cost about $250,000 to produce in 1997, which was about a fourth the cost of an hour-long, prime-time drama. And the networks don't have to pay residuals for the reruns.[40] The networks need the profits from newsmagazines. In 1998 ABC and CBS networks operated in the red, and ratings-leader NBC's profit declined from $500 million in 1997 to about $100 million. That probably explains why the networks were scheduling newsmagazines almost every night.[41]

Local stations were a little slower than the networks to look to their newscasts for profits. But today, local news is firmly entrenched as a key profit center. It now generates more than half the revenues at many stations and as much as 70 percent at some.[42] At KXAS-TV in Dallas, the half hour of late news makes almost as much money for the station as the three-hour block of prime-time programming. And in Presque Isle, Maine, advertisers clamor for spots during the news, according to WAGM-TV news director Sara Dyer. Nationally, between 30 and 35 percent of the money spent on TV advertising is targeted at news programming.

Station managers are looking for ways to increase that stream of cash. "What we've learned is that you can certainly make a lot of money in news," one broadcast executive said.[43] In 1995 alone, more than half the stations increased the time spent broadcasting news, and 63 percent added more newspeople to their staffs.[44] Some stations that had shunned news in the past now embraced it.

How Money Affects News Quality

When owners decide how much of a newspaper's or TV station's income should be spent on gathering the news, their decisions will have a direct impact on the quality of work that journalists can do. If these business executives do not hire enough reporters and editors or allow big enough news holes, then news that editors believe the public should know about cannot be covered.

Understaffing has become common. James Squires, former editor of the *Chicago Tribune*, stated that in the 1970s, the average newspaper spent between 13 and 15 percent of its revenue in the newsroom.

Since then, much of the production work—typesetting, pagination and proofreading—was shifted to news personnel.[45] Yet the percentage of revenue spent on the newsroom has also fallen to 8 percent at many papers and 6 percent at some.[46] Over half the journalists in one survey said their newsroom budget had declined in the previous five years, and 71 percent called it inadequate.[47]

In understaffed newsrooms, news desks may struggle to fill the paper by deadline and may trade ethical concerns for expediency. To meet deadlines, copy editors hastily scan the first couple of paragraphs of stories from the AP or another news service. If the first few paragraphs look good and the story will fill the space, the story may appear in the paper without anyone in the newsroom ever reading it in its entirety. Stories aren't edited. They're shoveled into the paper. Similarly, press releases may get only minor editing before going into the paper.

An even more pernicious effect of having an underfunded newsroom is the overreliance on story quotas. To fill the paper each day, many editors require reporters to write a certain number of stories each week. If the newsroom is shorthanded, the editors increase the quota. This practice may lead to ethical problems for reporters. To meet the quota, some may feel pressured to turn in stories before they have had time to gather all the information they need or to check additional sources to provide balance and ensure accuracy. They may produce stories with only one source, often a government official, and bypass important but time-consuming stories altogether. The papers are filled with "quick hits" that reporters can knock out in an afternoon.

Norman Pearlstine, former managing editor of *The Wall Street Journal* and president of Time Inc., said he fears that newspapers will do less investigative reporting in the future partly because newspaper groups may cut newsroom budgets to the point that editors cannot afford it.

At wealthy papers and TV stations, reporters are still given the resources and time they need. In addition to giving a reporting team several weeks to work on one investigative project, the *Los Angeles Times* once spent $10,000 photocopying records the reporters needed and $30,000 to hire people to enter data into their computers so reporters could analyze it. To examine allegations of wrongdoing by the Columbia/HCA hospital chain, *The New York Times* gave a team of reporters a year to work on the story. Their expenses including salary, database searches, travel and clerical help cost the paper about $625,000.[48]

But many editors would have trouble freeing a reporter for even a few days. Michael Pride, editor of the *Concord (N.H.) Monitor* in the early 1990s, said, "I have 14 reporters, down three or four from a year ago, with the same news load. I just can't back off and give someone time to do an investigative report."[49] At some papers, reporters have to get permission to make long-distance calls.

News staffs at many TV stations can understand his plight. "Cost-cutting, technology and tight-staffing and employment practices now dictate how TV stations cover the news," a veteran TV reporter said. Typically, TV stations often hire fewer than a 10th as many reporters as do newspapers in similar-sized cities. Even in the 25 largest markets, the average TV newsroom has 50 reporters, photographers, producers and other staffers. The average for all stations is 30.[50] Although the number of reporters has increased at many stations, the time devoted to news has tripled in many cases as stations add Saturday and Sunday newscasts and back-to-back-to-back newscasts in the early evening.

Trying to fill the local newscast with the work of only a handful of reporters, assignment editors must choose carefully where to send news crews. They must send them to stories that can be covered quickly and will provide good video. "We don't have time to do complex stories," one broadcast journalist in a Top 25 market said. "We have to do the quick stories, the easy stories. What's missing is the relevance."[51] Also missing may be sound decision making, according to Syracuse University Professor Dow C. Smith. He said, "Short-staffing means that overworked people, who are already stressed and tired, are prone to make mistakes in news judgment."[52]

At some stations, "one-person bands" cover the news. Instead of a news crew with a photographer and reporter, one person will be sent to the scene and will send back video. At the station, a writer will edit the video, take a sound bite or two out of the material and prepare the story. "Sometimes they don't even bother to debrief you," one cameraman at a large Los Angeles station said, "or they don't have time. They just turn the cassette over to a news writer and I go out again. I don't get a chance to explain why I concentrated on shooting a particular scene or what it might mean."[53]

Understaffing contributes to another frequent criticism of TV news: its emphasis on crime. "Most of that crime coverage is not editorially driven, it's economically driven," Joseph Angotti, a former vice president of NBC News, said. "It's the easiest, cheapest, laziest news to cover, because all they do is listen to the police radio, react to it, send out a mobile camera unit, spend an hour or two covering it and put it on the air."[54] At most stations, murders, convenience store holdups and traffic accidents fill about a third of the evening newscast. At some stations, it's as high as 60 percent. As a reporter in a

Top 25 market said, "We've become the police blotter." (Crime news is discussed further in Chapter 3.)

Understaffed newsrooms are more likely to rely on public relations people to help fill the news hole. Some newspapers print PR releases without editing them. Because TV news demands video, public relations people and promoters know that they can get their message on the 6 o'clock news by staging media events that promise good pictures. Harried reporters may lack the time to research the issue and to provide balance and depth. The result is that some news segments are shaped largely by the sources, not the journalists. One study suggests that as much as 70 percent of some TV newscasts is coverage of pseudo-events—events created by individuals or groups to draw attention to their activities or positions.[55]

Video news releases are also becoming a common way of filling time. Video news releases are news-like segments that public relations firms develop to promote the interests of their clients. For instance, James B. Beam Distilling Co. can't advertise its whiskeys on television, but many stations used a VNR about the patriotism of the company and its promise to use only American-grown grains. Political candidates also offer VNRs to local TV newsrooms, and nearly two-thirds of the stations are willing to use them.[56]

Viewers probably cannot tell these VNRs from news stories the station has obtained from regular news services. Some VNRs are designed so the station's reporters can appear in the segment, further giving viewers the impression that they are watching locally produced news.

A company that distributes VNRs to TV stations via satellite claims that at least one release is used each week at 78 percent of the stations it surveyed.[57] Randall Rothenberg, who covered advertising for *The New York Times,* wrote that he expects the use of VNRs to continue to grow as TV stations cut back on the number of reporters they hire while expanding the length of their newscasts.[58]

Salaries Often Low

Salaries are almost directly proportional to the size of the paper's circulation or the TV station's market. The Newspaper Guild is a labor union that negotiates minimum salaries for reporters and editors at many papers. At large papers like the *Chicago Sun-Times,* the minimum was $57,252 in 1997; at midsized papers like the *Akron (Ohio) Beacon Journal,* $42,640; and at the *Norwalk (Conn.) Hour,* $18,720.[59]

The salary spread is even wider in broadcast journalism. In the Top

10 markets, a news director at a station affiliated with ABC, CBS, Fox or NBC makes an average of $154,971 a year, a news anchor makes $313,712, a news producer makes $61,776 and a news reporter makes $109,664. In markets smaller than 150th, a news director makes an average of $45,743, a news anchor makes $28,172, a news producer makes $19,237 and a news reporter makes $18,105.[60] Despite television's reliance on visuals, broadcast photojournalists are more poorly paid than reporters. They average $14,000 in small markets and $40,000 at network affiliates in Top 25 markets.[61]

Salaries for beginning broadcast and print reporters are unconscionably low. In 1996, 22 percent of journalists under 25 earned salaries below the official poverty level of $15,141. Reporters at some small news organizations received pay raises in 1997—but only because the government raised the minimum wage. Worse, salaries at small papers often remain low despite the quality of work done by the journalist. When Betty Gray won a Pulitzer Prize in 1989, her small-town paper, the *Washington Daily News* in North Carolina, gave her a $25-a-week raise, pushing her salary to $15,000 a year. Starting salaries at her paper were then about $12,000 a year.[62] After surveying salaries paid to entry-level journalists in Virginia, Steve Nash, a journalism professor, concluded that a beginner had better be prepared to drive a very used car and live on peanut butter sandwiches.[63]

These low salaries contribute to the poor quality of journalism in many small cities and towns. G. Kelly Hawes, former president of the Society of Professional Journalists and an editor at the *Muncie (Ind.) Star,* asked, "Are news outlets attracting qualified applicants for poverty-level wages, or are they settling for what they can get?" Worse, beginning journalists who accept the low salaries often plan to stay at the newspaper or TV station only long enough to get enough experience to move to a bigger, better-paying newspaper or station. At some smaller TV stations, the turnover rate in the newsrooms is as high as 50 percent a year.[64] This can create at least four problems:

- The desire to get to a bigger paper or a bigger TV market may keep new reporters from developing any ties to the community, thus depriving themselves of an opportunity to better understand the community's problems.
- This constant turnover in reporting staffs results in inconsistent coverage and less-than-thoughtful accounts of the day's news as each new batch of reporters tries to learn the workings of the community and to develop reliable sources.
- Some new journalists may bend journalistic ethics in hopes of finding a story that might open doors for them. Surveys indicate

that young journalists are more willing to cut ethical corners than their more experienced colleagues.

- If they can't find jobs at bigger papers or TV markets, many good young journalists may leave the profession altogether. A study by journalism Professor Betty Medsger found that 43 percent of new journalists said they might seek jobs that paid better.

While Hawes was president of SPJ, he urged the organization to join the fight for better salaries. "SPJ has tended to shy away from labor-management issues," Hawes said. "But when our profession ranks dead last in terms of salaries [paid to new college graduates], that's something we ought to speak up about."

The Search for Readers, Viewers

Companies that own newspapers and broadcast properties are hauling in loads of money. Nevertheless, one tough truth haunts both media owners and journalists: Interest in mainstream news media seems to be declining. Newspaper circulation figures have been stagnant for the past 30 years, hovering around the 60 million mark almost every year. While the population of the country has grown from about 106 million in 1960 to more than 186 million today, newspaper circulations have hardly grown at all.[65] For several years researchers have asked people if they read a paper the day before. In 1946, 73 percent of the population said yes.[66] By 1990, only 43 percent said they had.[67] However, this downturn in reading may have bottomed out. The percentage who said they read a newspaper the day before remained fairly consistent throughout the 1990s and was slightly higher in 1998.

Some of the decline in circulation was caused by the calculated business decisions of the publishers themselves. For example, many newspapers raised their prices from 25 cents to 50 cents or more. These increases drove away some readers but produced higher profits overall. Also, many newspapers have begun to reduce the size of their market areas. Publishers believe that selling newspapers in far-flung cities boosts a newspaper's circulation but does not produce enough income to cover delivery costs or help sell advertisements to local merchants. A few newspapers have consciously reduced efforts to sell papers in poorer neighborhoods in an effort to achieve the more upscale audience that advertisers prefer. But the fact remains that the "decline in newspaper reading is evident in almost every consumer segment regardless of age, education, family type, or employment status."[68]

The number of people who regularly watch TV news is also going down. According to Nielsen researchers, the percentage of people watching evening network news shows has dropped from 56 percent to 31 percent in the past 25 years.[69] In the past, six out of 10 Americans watched the nightly network news on either CBS, ABC or NBC regularly. Today, only 38 percent describe themselves as regular viewers. Today's core audience is predominantly older and female. Although people turn to cable news channels when major stories happen, CNN, the nation's dominant cable news network, has also seen its day-to-day audience diminish from a high of 35 percent in May 1993 to 23 percent in 1998, according to studies by the Pew Trust.

The biggest concern for many in print and broadcast journalism is the dramatic decline in the use of media by young adults. In 1965, 67 percent of those under 35 said they read a paper the day before; in 1990, only 29 percent said they had.[70] While about two-thirds of people over 50 told pollsters they considered themselves to be regular newspaper readers, only one-third of those between 18 and 30 said they were. And young adults are less likely to watch TV news. Only 22 percent of men under age 30 watch the nightly network news regularly, compared with 55 percent of women over age 50.

It's not that young people do not like to read. They are more likely than other age groups to read magazines, according to Pew research. And they're the biggest users of the Internet. Fully 38 percent of Americans under age 30 in 1998 said they went online the day before. That's more than said they read a newspaper. Young adults do read. They're just not attracted to newspapers and TV news.

This decline in interest in mainstream news outlets does not bode well for journalists—and democracy. A democracy depends on its citizens being informed enough about the issues to make wise decisions. Unless the media can interest Americans in the news, voters may not be able to meet these expectations. Many newspapers editors and TV news producers are experimenting with ways to make the news more compelling for the public, particularly younger Americans. But in some newsrooms, the search to attract more readers and viewers has clashed with the basic assumptions of what ethical journalism ought to be.

Marketing and the News

The use of marketing techniques to shape the news product is nothing new at most TV stations. Newscasts are often judged by the same standards as other programs, namely ratings. If the ratings are down, consultants may be brought in to find out why viewers aren't watching. Depending on their findings, the station may build new sets, add new features to the newscast, order new hairdos for its on-air people, or fire its anchors and hire some new ones.

Some print journalists point to the news content of local TV news to show what's wrong with using marketing surveys to make news decisions. For instance, surveys in many markets indicate that viewers have little interest in politics and don't care about candidates and their policies. The consultants say viewers want stories about the weather, the environment, the economy and especially crime. So station managers demand that those things be emphasized on their newscasts. Viewers see so much crime news that many are now convinced their communities are much more violent than they really are.

The tradition in print journalism was much different. Editors and reporters decided what was news. They envisioned an impregnable wall between news operations and business departments. The business side delivered the papers and sold the ads; the news side made all the decisions about the news content of the paper. Symbolic of this relationship, at one time elevators that carried advertising personnel to the *Chicago Tribune*'s business offices could not stop on the floor where the newsroom was.

However, at many papers like *The Arizona Republic, Houston Chronicle, Chicago Tribune* and Fort Lauderdale *Sun-Sentinel,* the barriers were lowered as journalists and advertising and circulation staff work together on committees that study declining readership and revamp certain sections, such as the paper's TV or entertainment guides.

At the Knight-Ridder's *Bradenton (Fla.) Herald,* reporters and editors get "business literacy" training so they will learn all facets of the *Herald*'s business operations. They join people from advertising sales and circulation on committees that plan the paper's marketing strategies. Advertising and circulation executives also sit in on news decisions but do not dictate them. "They know where the line is," the paper's publisher said.

The wall between editorial and business was lowered even more when former General Mills executive Mark Willes became CEO of the Times Mirror Co. and publisher of the *Los Angeles Times.* Willes decided the *Times* needed some serious reorganizing. He saw problems everywhere.

- The paper was reaching only about 28 percent of the homes in its circulation area, less than half the penetration of *Newsday* (64 percent), the Times Mirror paper on Long Island, and considerably less than its Baltimore *Sun.* Circulation was particularly weak among small-business owners and Latinos.

- Although the circulation was growing, 85 percent of new subscribers stopped taking the paper within 12 months.
- Although the newsroom was producing Pulitzer Prize caliber journalism, a defeatist attitude permeated the newsroom. One editor told *Columbia Journalism Review* that "the prevailing attitude was that newspapers were dead." That feeling is common in many newsrooms. Surveys have found that many journalists describe newspapers as dinosaurs and have advised their children not to enter the profession.

Willes believed that changes were needed to make the paper "more compelling to our current and potential readers." Willes' solution was to overhaul the entire organization. No longer would the newsroom be separated from the business department. As Willes explained it in a memo to *Times* staffers:

> Advertising, promotion, circulation and so on will all become key elements in the strategic plans that will be developed for each section [of the paper]. Each of these elements will have measurable objectives associated with them. This does not mean every section must earn a profit— some clearly will not. But it does mean that every section must have a measurable plan that will result in improved performance as measured by growth in readers and by growth in revenue relative to costs.

Willes contended that serious journalism would not suffer at the *Times* because news is necessary for the business success of the paper. Readers expect the paper to give them the truth in depth and in context. "[T]he worst thing we could ever do from a business point of view is break faith with our readers," Willes stated. "Advertisers spend money with us because we effectively reach our readers. If we ever broke trust with our readers, we would lose them and all the dollars our advertisers direct to them."

At one of his first meetings with *Times* staffers, Willes ordered a revamping of the paper's features section. The problem was not a shortage of readers. Research showed it was one of the best-read parts of the paper, a section that people read all the way through. The problem that Willes saw was that the section lacked focus and did not attract advertisers. *American Journalism Review* recounted this exchange:

> After an hour, one reporter gingerly asked what everyone in Life & Style really wanted to know. "If we don't get the section fixed," she inquired, "would you close it?"
>
> "I wouldn't rule it out," Willes replied. End of conversation.

Other sections also changed. Rather quickly, two features were added to the paper's business section. Kelly Ann Sole, that paper's national advertising sales manager, noticed that the paper got few advertisements from mutual fund companies, even though they were advertising heavily in other media. So she phoned business editor Bill Sing. According to *AJR,* she told him, "We don't get any mutual fund advertising. Why don't we create an editorial vehicle to demystify investing? It would be a logical home for financial advertisers. This marketplace is starved for investment education." The editor said he too had been thinking about adding a mutual fund package. After the conversation, the paper added a package called "Wall Street California." Another package was added to the business section when market research found small-business owners were not reading the paper.

After these changes, financial advertising went up 40 percent, and Sole was named general manager for the business and health sections. The new position, she said, means that she and the business editor "will regularly sit down and talk about how to make the product more compelling." Business staffers concede that some features were added to increase ad sales. However, on the whole, associate editor Narda Zacchino said, "If everyone always thinks of the reader first—and that's the first question we ask and the last question we ask—then we don't have a problem."

Editors at other papers have also welcomed more cooperation. Rich Oppel, editor of the *Austin American-Statesman,* told *CJR* that he worked closely with advertising and circulation executives. "I think we're a team. There is a lot of mutual respect." However, Oppel is reluctant to allow his reporters to get too involved with the business department. "I'd be wary of that kind of thing," he said. "Reporters and copy editors should stick to the task of journalism." He said news executives can maintain the respect of their news staffs if they push "traditional public service journalism with vigor and clearly value it highly."

Many journalists, however, are worried. They point out that not all newspapers have top-quality news staffs like the *Los Angeles Times'* or dedicated editors like Oppel. They suspect that at some newspapers the news content will be unduly influenced by business-side managers. They worry about editorial decisions made by section editors who have been promised bonuses if advertising and readership increase in their sections. They also wonder how many important stories will never be written because reporters were too busy working on special sections or too afraid of offending business interests.

Many believe these fears are quickly being realized. "When I first became an editor at Knight-Ridder, the editors were lions, they were rambunctious," John Carroll, editor at the Baltimore *Sun,* told *Los Angeles Times* media writer David Shaw. "When they had their annual editors meetings, the corporate brass would speak to the editors and the editors would definitely speak back. There was no trepidation. . . . You don't find as many editors who behave that way now. The culture doesn't seem to encourage it."

This change in attitude is being felt in newsrooms. Sandra Mims Rowe, editor of *The Oregonian* of Portland and former president of the American Society of Newspaper Editors, told the ASNE convention in 1998 that reporters "wonder whether their editors have sold out journalistic values for business ones. They long for the inspiration provided by leaders with abiding passion for the gritty world of journalism."[71]

Broadcast journalists are also concerned. John Lansing, news director at WXYZ-TV in Detroit, said the wall between news and business has completely disappeared at most local stations. "The business of television is not independent from the newsroom. It is absolutely a part of the newsroom," he said. "So the people in charge of newsrooms realize that they are going to be judged every day on their ability to turn that number up and win the game. That by itself, I think, describes the dilemma of local TV news. The way our industry measures audiences—the overnight rating service and the larger profit margin expectations—are combining to squeeze the trust level out of the everyday product that we create."[72]

"Softer News"

Long before Willes became publisher of the *Los Angeles Times,* marketing was beginning to influence the news pages of many papers. *USA Today* was the first major American daily to be conceived with the help of marketing experts. While journalists generally praised the paper's design and graphics, they mocked its short, "quick read" stories that often emphasize "soft news" about lifestyles, entertainers and happy events. The paper avoided "hard news" about government and tough social issues and tried to simplify complicated problems so they could be told in a few paragraphs. Former *Washington Post* ombudsman and journalism dean Ben Bagdikian charged that the paper selected stories "not because of their inherent importance but on the basis of their potential for jazzy graphics."[73]

Other newspapers began to call in small groups of readers and ask them about their papers' coverage. These "focus groups" began to play a larger role in deciding what was news. *The Wausau Daily*

Herald in Wisconsin adopted a reader-driven format that devoted news space to grade-school awards and bowling scores. The paper's editor told a *Washington Journalism Review* writer, "We do less government, to the point where the mayor calls and complains."[74]

Perhaps the most extreme example of a newspaper opting for soft news occurred in Winnipeg, Canada. Editors at that city's *Free Press,* then a Thomson chain newspaper, put the 1992 Los Angeles riots on Page 56 in the fourth section of the paper. They reserved the front page for stories about edible golf tees and local residents' good deeds. The paper's ombudsman wrote a column calling the editors' decision an example of the paper's "not so subtle" shift away from hard news to softer features.[75]

In Boca Raton, Fla., *The News* became a testing ground for ways to appeal to young adult "baby boomers." The Knight-Ridder chain spent $3 million researching reader interests before revamping the paper. The new *News* ran more "soft news" about Pets of the Day, Heroes of the Day and other lighter topics. When space was tight, government stories were the first to be dropped, according to Lou Heldman, who headed the Knight-Ridder project team.[76] The paper's editor, Wayne L. Ezell, acknowledged that the pressure to produce more features, graphics and business stories left his staff little time to do real investigative reporting.[77] Once the experiment was over, the paper backed away from most of the changes because the graphics and features proved too expensive. Knight-Ridder sold *The News* in 1998.

The shift to softer news is not limited to small-city newspapers, according to a study by the Center for Excellence in Journalism. More than half the stories on prime-time newsmagazines have to do with people and celebrities, lifestyles and "news you can use." About a fourth of them are about crime and justice. Only 8 percent of the stories cover the combined areas of education, economics, foreign affairs, the military, national security, politics and social welfare issues.

The network nightly news has also changed. Stories about scandals have soared from just one-half of a percent in 1977 to 15 percent in 1997. The first survey was taken *during* the Iran-Contra scandal, while the 1997 survey was *before* the scandalous stories about Monica Lewinsky and President Clinton. Also, the number of human-interest and quality-of-life stories has doubled—from 8 percent of the stories that appeared in 1977 to 16 percent in 1997.

Newspaper front pages have changed too, but not as much as network news. In 1977, 60 percent of the stories were straight news accounts; in 1997, 30 percent were. Researchers concluded: "If you combine stories that emphasize human interest, quality of life, the bizarre, personality, and public fear into a broad category of features, they rose from accounting for just 8 percent of newspaper front-page stories to nearly 25 percent today. Very possibly, newspapers included some of these types of stories deeper in the paper in 1977, but by 1997 they had become front-page material."

The movement to softer news does not sit well with many journalists. According to nationwide surveys, most print journalists see the duty of journalists as investigating government claims (66.7 percent said this was very important) and informing the public quickly (68.6 percent). Considerably fewer journalists saw their role as to appeal to the widest audience (20.2 percent) or to entertain (14 percent).[78] Yet many journalists fear that changes in the news content suggested by marketing studies will shift the emphasis of their profession. They fear that they will be expected to find ways of entertaining a wider audience at the expense of covering the serious news of the day.

David Shaw of the *Los Angeles Times* said that use of focus groups and the push for softer news has rekindled a larger debate within the journalistic community:

> Is a newspaper essentially a consumer product, like a new car or a box of cereal, in which case survival depends on giving the customer what he wants? Or is it a professional service, like medical care or classroom instruction, in which case the provider—journalist, doctor or teacher—should offer what his experience and expertise suggests is necessary, regardless of what the reader/patient/student says he wants? After all, as Barry Glassner, a University of Southern California sociologist who takes the latter view, puts it, "We would all criticize a dentist who told a patient, 'Sure, I understand you don't want me to pull those bad teeth and you'd rather have candy, so, here, have a handful of chocolates.'"[79]

Does Quality Pay?

Consultants, journalists and professors have all argued that the owners of news organizations need to worry more about quality. They contend that in the long run, quality will pay off with higher circulations and more advertising. Newspaper stock analyst John Morton has urged the news media to make "strategic investments" in "higher pay, bigger staffs, bigger news holes, more and better journalism, more and better market research and promotion."[80] An academic study by journalism professors Stephen Lacy and Frederick Fico concluded, "Papers that cut quality as a short-run cost-saving device may end up paying in future circulation."[81]

Some news media companies have found that quality journalism does pay. *Forbes* magazine praised officials of the A.H. Belo Corp., stating they did not just acquire newspapers and TV stations. "They add value, with heavy emphasis on news coverage. That's clearly what people want—and what advertisers respond to." The magazine noted that for the past three years, Belo's *Dallas Morning News,* with a circulation base half as big as *The New York Times'*, has run more advertising linage than the *Times* or any other paper in America.[82] Belo also owns *The Providence (R.I.) Journal-Bulletin,* the Riverside, Calif., *Press Enterprise* and 17 TV stations. Each of its TV stations is first or second in local ratings.

Publisher Howard Bronson also discovered that quality paid off. His paper, *The Mobile (Ala.) Register,* had a miserable reputation. It was nicknamed "Cash Register" because about all the paper did was generate money for its owners. Some journalism professors admitted to looking to the *Register* whenever they wanted a bad example. In 1992 Bronson hired Stan Tiner as editor and began to pour money into the newsroom. The staff grew from 80 to 130. Tiner and Bronson "staked the *Register*'s future on vigorous reporting, fresh writing and a defiance of the status quo," according to *American Editor* magazine. The result has been impressive both editorially and financially. The paper has been a finalist for a Pulitzer Prize and has won prestigious awards for investigative and environmental reporting. And its circulation increased even though the paper doubled its newsstand price.[83]

Perhaps the most surprising paper to benefit from an infusion of quality is *USA Today.* When the paper began, it was a thin publication that emphasized flashy design and quick-read stories with little depth or flair. The paper's own editor later joked that *USA Today* was "the newspaper that brought new depth to the meaning of the word shallow." For its first 10 years, it lost money for Gannett. In 1992 it reported its first profits and now is a moneymaker. Gannett executives think they know why things changed. "It has been the quality of journalism," said Tom Curley, *USA Today*'s publisher. "When the journalism improved, the advertising cascaded. It has been the improvement of the product that has brought in advertising." The paper hired more journalists and expected them to produce stories with depth, original reporting and enterprise.[84] The paper's front page is no longer dominated by celebrity news and lifestyle pieces. Its mix of hard and soft news is now about the same as the mix on the front page of *The New York Times.*

Some research has suggested that newspaper managers are being simplistic when they group people as "readers" and "nonreaders" and believe they have to choose between hard or soft news. A large-scale project for the ASNE found people's attitudes toward newspapers fell into four distinct groups. One group consisted of die-hard readers who depended on their newspapers each day. Another group was made up of people who would never read a newspaper no matter what was in it. Between these extremes were two groups who might be enticed to become regular newspaper readers. One group would prefer a paper that was easier and quicker to read. These people "would rather have the news presented to them than read it themselves." The other group wanted a paper that gave them greater depth and insight into the news.[85]

If this research is right, the challenge to newspapers may be to find ways to appeal both to readers who want the "quick reads" that *USA Today* originally promised and to readers who want more. Some newspapers are trying to find that mix. The *St. Paul Pioneer Press* has experimented with a "Read-It-Fast, Read-It-Slow" format. For time-conscious readers, the paper has summaries on many of its stories and lots of news outlines. Yet the stories themselves are thorough accounts of the news and would appeal to readers looking for depth.[86] Other papers, like the *Portland Press Herald* in Maine, have also tried to appeal both to readers looking for a quick read and to readers wanting depth.

Clearly these are lessons that many news outlets already knew. Many papers, both large and small, field teams of reporters who have the time and resources to do good journalism. Many TV station owners are also committed to quality journalism. Although the average news staff at a Top 25 station has about 50 people, some stations have more than 100 reporters, producers and technicians in their news departments. WFAA in Dallas, KCRA in Sacramento, WBBM in Chicago, WSMV in Nashville, WPLG in Miami and WCCO in Minneapolis were cited by *CJR* as stations whose owners provide above-average funding for news.[87]

Corporate Owners Cause Conflicts

Concerns over corporate control of the media have grown significantly in the past few years. Not long ago, media companies owned mostly media properties. Gannett, for example, owned lots of newspapers and TV stations, but it did not manufacture jet fighters, operate amusement parks or supply parts to nuclear power plants. Today, business conglomerates are buying newspapers and TV stations, and news media companies are branching into non-news areas.

Ed Bishop of the *St. Louis Journalism Review* looked at the holdings of four media conglomerates in 1996. At that time, General Electric owned NBC and 11 TV stations; Time Warner owned CNN, Turner Broadcasting, *Time* and *Sports Illustrated;* Walt Disney Co. owned ABC and 11 TV stations; and Westinghouse owned CBS and 14 TV stations. Bishop found that "[These four conglomerates] own companies that touch almost every aspect of the lives of everyone in the United States and most people in the world. They own companies that manage hazardous, radioactive and toxic waste. They own bookstores and movie studios, sports franchises and cable networks. They produce plastics, home appliances, whiskey and children's programming."[88]

Bishop and many others worry about these conglomerates and their control of the news. "Conflicts of interest between the public's need for information and corporate desires for 'positive' information have vastly increased," Ben Bagdikian wrote.[89] Journalists who work for conglomerate-owned media are also troubled. "Any news division is quite rightfully suspect when reporting on the interests of its corporate parent. It's a significant concern," David Marash, an ABC reporter who covered the Disney-ABC merger for *Nightline,* told *AJR.*[90]

Occasionally, these concerns are realized. Shortly after GE bought NBC, the stock market took a big dive. It was a major story for most news organizations, including NBC's. GE's chairman complained to then NBC News President Lawrence Grossman that NBC's coverage was too negative and that reporters should stop using terms like "Black Monday." The GE executive feared the reports might frighten investors away from the stock market, causing the value of GE's stock to go down even more. Grossman stated that he never told reporters about the call. But he was bothered that a corporate official "felt no qualms about letting his news division know" how he thought news should be covered.[91]

On other occasions, NBC's corporate ties with GE have shown through. The news staff on NBC's *Today* decided to make a key omission in a report on dangerously substandard bolts in airplane jet engines—the fact that GE built them.[92] At about the same time, a guest on *Today* who was discussing consumer boycotts was warned not to mention a boycott against GE. NBC later said that the producer was using her own judgment.[93]

Some journalists say they've been pressured into writing puff. When the f/X cable network went on the air, the *New York Post* devoted a full-page spread to the story. "Not only did we run a splashy story on the day they debuted," *Post* TV writer Steve Bornfeld said, "but we ran a splashy story on the day after they debuted about a network that no one in the five boroughs of New York could see." The

Post ran the phone numbers of local cable companies so readers could demand that f/X be added. The *Post* did not point out that both it and f/X are owned by Rupert Murdoch's News Corp. Bornfeld told *American Journalism Review* that he did not want to write the pieces. "My choice was to write the stories or be fired. . . . There was no shame about it at the *Post.*"[94] Both *TV Guide,* another Murdoch publication, and the *Post* were used to promote *Party of Five,* a TV program produced by Murdoch's Fox Network. Murdoch is not the only media giant engaged in self-promotion. Disney has also been criticized for using ABC to publicize its movies and theme parks.

Fortunately, such antics are not common. Most journalists who work for conglomerate-owned media say they have experienced little or no corporate pressure. *Time* magazine movie reviewer Richard Schickel said he's never been forced to give favorable reviews to Warner Bros. movies even though *Time* and Warner Bros. are part of Time Warner.[95] Andrew Heyward, president of CBS, doubts that kind of pressure would ever be exerted. "I know it sounds like boiler-plate," he said, "but I can't imagine a scenario where we would be embarking on a story on nuclear power and someone from Westinghouse [which then owned CBS and manufactured power generators] would say, 'Don't do that.' It's an outlandish proposition."

Nancy Woodhull, a founding editor of *USA Today,* said that's probably not how corporate influence would happen. She expected the pressure to be more subtle. She wondered if an editor who is about to receive a big bonus from a corporation would encourage an investigative report of another company owned by that corporation. And she worried that editors might be more prone to employ people who will bend to corporate culture. Although Woodhull doubted that major media outlets would yield to such pressures, she was less confident about small- and medium-sized organizations, which hire many young journalists who may not understand the importance of journalistic independence.

Former NBC news president Grossman also suspected that corporate culture rather than direct censorship would influence coverage: "It's not really the simple thing of 'You print what I like or you're fired.' It's an environment that's set up, a corporate environment where people with odd views are not encouraged and tend not to be hired." Some cite what happened to a reporter at *The Phoenix Gazette* as an indication of the way corporate pressure might work. The reporter broke a series of stories about maintenance problems at America West airlines. When Phoenix Newspapers merged the *Gazette* with *The Arizona Republic,* he was among those let go. At the time, the chairman of the airline was also on the board of

Phoenix Newspapers, and in the past the newspaper company had financial dealings with the airline. America West was later slapped with the second largest fine for maintenance problems in the FAA's history.

Internet news and information sites are also feeling corporate pressures. MSNBC, a joint project of Microsoft and NBC, has been accused of playing down stories critical of Microsoft. Jesse Berst, editorial director of *ZDNet's* online "Anchordesk" and a longtime Microsoft follower, said if Microsoft is accused of an antitrust violation, MSNBC will report it. But it does not do original reporting on such issues or alert readers to bugs in Microsoft software.[96] Many computer users will recognize from the name that MSNBC has ties to Microsoft. Often that is not the case. Software and hardware companies have invested heavily in Web sites. "It is very difficult for online visitors to know whether the news they're reading is being written and distributed by sources that a have a stake in the events," Matt Welch wrote in *Online Journalism Review.*[97]

Not all journalists fear the rise of conglomerates. Media analyst and former CBS newsman Tom Wolzien stated that they might be good for journalism. "Who else can afford the risks or the cost of catastrophic libel insurance?" he asked. "Alone, television news organizations are not big enough to withstand the legal threats of huge, entrenched industries like tobacco or oil. Even a company the size of pre-Westinghouse CBS, with a stock market value of some $5 billion, could have been bankrupted by a jury award of the amount sought in some recent cases."[98]

Others believe it would be impossible for a conglomerate to kill a major story. They say there are too many sources of information, ranging from competing news organizations to the Internet. Journalists themselves will police efforts by corporate managers to subvert the news. They point out that journalists reported CBS's decision to kill the *60 Minutes* piece about cigarettes and that *The Wall Street Journal* broke the story when CBS backed off.

The Power of Advertisers

When advertisers buy an advertisement, do they also buy a say in the nature of the news? In an ideal world the answer to the question would be easy. If journalists are to live up to their ethical obligation of truth-telling, then the search for truth should not be influenced by advertisers. News media owners would be aware of this ethical imperative and would refuse to bend to advertisers.

Some have even argued that it is against advertisers' own best interests to use their ad dollars to muscle the media. Businesses buy advertisements so they can increase their sales and make more money. If they get upset about a story and cancel their advertisements, they hurt themselves by losing business. Since they need to advertise and since there's usually only one paper in town, their threats of withholding advertising are hollow.[99]

But that's not the way it has worked out.[100] The news media have become so dependent on advertising dollars that today as much as 80 percent of a newspaper's revenue,[101] and nearly all of a TV station's, come from advertisers. Paying this much of the tab, advertisers often have a lot of clout, and some are willing to use it. If a news organization carries a story they don't like, they threaten to move their advertising accounts either to other TV stations and newspapers that haven't offended them or to media that carry no news and therefore cannot offend them—media like direct mail, all-music radio or free "shopper" publications.

Many media owners take advertiser boycotts seriously. Editors and TV news directors say this kind of pressure is increasing; a few even consider it their top ethical concern.[102] All too often, advertisers and other influential members of the business community demand and receive special treatment. Sometimes this special treatment is indirect. Reporters may be expected to select sources from businesses that advertise with the paper and avoid sources from businesses that don't. For instance, the editor of a Pennsylvania newspaper complained when a travel story named three travel agents, none of whom advertised with the paper. If a story needs to be illustrated with local examples, the editor contended, "our policy is to use the ones who advertise. I don't think that's compromising anything. . . . If you're going to pick only a few people to talk to, pick the ones who spend money with us."[103] A small-city editor in Indiana directed a reporter who was preparing a story about merchants' Christmas preparations to exclude references to stores that did not advertise with the paper. A similar policy is in effect at the *Chicago Sun-Times*. On what he calls "discretionary" stories (which department store Santa to picture in the paper, for example), Larry Green, the paper's executive editor, said the paper uses advertisers rather than nonadvertisers.

Of more concern are those cases in which advertisers exert direct pressure on the news. Sometimes they demand that their press releases be used verbatim or that only favorable stories about their products and services be run. On occasion, editors and commentators are pushed to write editorials in support of political positions that advertisers favor.

Some Battle Ad Pressure

Some newspapers have battled publicly with advertisers who wanted to control the news content. When *The Salina (Kan.) Journal* endorsed a city sales tax, the city's car dealers who opposed the measure pulled their ads from the paper. Instead of bending to the boycotters' demands, the paper reported the dealers' actions and published a series of editorials criticizing them. "I think we should let the public know what organizations are trying to impose their will on us, trying to drive us out of business because we don't agree with their point of view," the editor of the paper said.[104]

Many other newspapers have also fought costly advertiser boycotts. *The Washington Post* once ran a story about a Harvard University study predicting a decline in the prices of houses in the Washington area. To provide balance, the reporter included comments from experts who disagreed with the prediction. But the story still did not sit well with the real estate community. Major builders withdrew an estimated $750,000 worth of advertising from the paper.[105]

When *The Seattle Times* and *Seattle Post-Intelligencer* ran stories about labor problems at Nordstrom, a large department store chain, James Nordstrom, co-chairman of the company, called the coverage "the worst in the nation." The chain stopped advertising in the papers and started using other media.[106] But the papers did not soften their coverage. "You can't sell your soul in little bits and pieces and expect readers will understand," the executive editor of the *Times* said. "A lot of newspapers don't understand that."[107]

Editors at *The Virginian-Pilot* and *The Ledger-Star,* sister newspapers in Norfolk, Va., and the *St. Louis Post-Dispatch* showed their independence from their advertising departments. When the advertising department rejected an ad for a winter festival sponsored by a gay and lesbian group, the Norfolk papers ran news stories about the festival and about the rejected ad. Editors at the *Post-Dispatch* took a similar stand. When their advertising department refused an anti-abortion group's ad that featured a graphic photo of a mutilated doll, the newspaper ran a story about the controversy and included the photo. The paper's ombudsman wrote a column explaining to readers the seeming inconsistency of a paper first rejecting an advertisement and then printing it for free as news. "That apparent anomaly," he said, "was the best demonstration of the separateness of a paper's news department and its business offices I've ever seen."[108]

But Advertisers Often Get Their Way

Examples of editors and TV news directors bravely battling advertisers may become less frequent as management scrambles to meet the profit expectations of their corporate owners. Reports in *CJR, AJR,* various regional journalism reviews and *The Wall Street Journal* have exposed apparent special treatment being given to advertisers and other influential groups. Auto dealers, real estate interests and department stores are frequently cited as recipients of favored status. These groups are among the heaviest advertisers in newspapers.

The Oregonian in Portland destroyed tens of thousands of copies of its own Sunday paper after advertising people pointed out a story that was sure to upset real estate firms that buy lots of advertising. The story suggested that homeowners could save money if they sold their homes without the help of real estate agents and pocketed the commissions that agents charge. The paper's managing editor explained that the timing of the story "could not have been worse in view of the assurances we had made" to real estate groups at a meeting shortly before the incident.[109]

The Oregonian is not alone in appeasing real estate people. Wendy Swallow Williams, a journalism professor at American University in Washington, found that 44 percent of the real estate editors she surveyed said publishers or senior editors would not allow them to present balanced coverage in their sections. "More than 80 percent said advertisers had threatened to pull their advertising because of negative coverage; a third said they knew of advertisers who had done so," she wrote. The attack on their journalistic ethics was painful for many of them. "Several editors said they had been ordered by senior editors or publishers to delay or kill a story that might offend advertisers. For each, the experience was devastating," she wrote.[110] Many editors filled their questionnaires with long diatribes attacking publishers and advertisers.

Hard-hitting journalism is also missing in the travel sections at many papers. Managers at the Contra Costa, Calif., *Times* stopped the presses when they saw a story in its Sunday travel section about the plight of passengers on a Caribbean cruise ship who were caught in a hurricane. They replaced that story with one less likely to offend the travel industry, which buys most of the advertising in that section.[111]

Automotive dealers also twist journalists' arms. In a column, a sportswriter for the Carbondale *Southern Illinoisan* compared the ineffective St. Louis Cardinal pitching staff to a bunch of used-car lemons polished up for quick sale by a shady dealer. After some dealers complained, the paper printed an apology and suspended the sportswriter and his editor. The publisher said it was an "obsolete stereotype" of used-car dealers.112

The *San Jose Mercury News* was hit by a boycott after it ran a story headlined "A Car Buyer's Guide to Sanity." Among other things, the story claimed buyers should rely on factory invoices for the cost of the car rather than take the dealer's word. The publisher of the paper apologized to car dealers, but they continued the boycott, which cost the paper more than $1 million. In an effort to make peace, the paper began printing a house ad telling readers why they were better off shopping with local authorized dealers.113

Another way to satisfy advertisers is to create special, noncritical sections. After a story critical of tactics used to sell cars, *The Birmingham (Ala.) News* lost between $300,000 and $500,000 a year in car ads. So the paper introduced a new automotive section that it promised would be advertiser-friendly.114 Other newspapers have done that with real estate sections. They allow advertisers to write news-like stories that are then printed as if they are news. Headlines gush "Sound Judgment the Basis for Buying at Boca Quay." This blending of ads and editorial copy is often called "advertorials." A growing trend is to have journalists use some of their time helping to prepare these sections.

How Often Do Editors Cave In?

The frequency of advertiser attempts to influence the press alarms many journalists. Philip Meyer, a former reporter and Knight-Ridder executive who conducted a survey of journalists' ethics for the ASNE, found that "advertising pressure is a concern at least some of the time on papers read by 79 percent of the American public. . . . And for 9 percent, it happens every week. That's a lot of advertiser pressure."115

Other research paints an even bleaker picture. A survey by professors at Marquette University found that more than 90 percent of the newspapers had been pressured by advertisers to change or kill a story and that about a third of the editors admitted that they had caved in and complied with advertisers' wishes.116 The ethics committee of the ASNE reported that its study found that in the early 1990s, about 90 percent of nation's largest 100 newspapers had advertisers cancel ads because they were upset by news stories. Only about 10 percent of the time did the newspapers inform readers of what was going on.117

These figures, as awesome as they are, may underestimate the influence of advertisers. Stephen Rynkiewicz, a copy editor at the

Chicago Sun-Times, has pointed out that editors rarely kill stories outright, "but any practical reporter or editor uses extra caution when they see a conflict coming. In that respect, business has bought influence in the news media as surely as it has with PAC money in Congress."118

The situation may be even worse for broadcast news. When TV news directors were asked in a survey what their major ethical concerns were, many cited the growing pressures to give special treatment to advertisers.119 Writing in a publication of the Investigative Reporters and Editors organization, consumer reporter Herb Weisbaum of KIRO-TV in Seattle wrote: "We don't even bother with most auto-related stories anymore. These days, even a simple consumer education story on how to buy a new car can draw the wrath of local car dealers. Trying to share such basic advice with your viewers can result in the loss of many thousands of dollars."120

Advertising Pressure Online

When allegations of an affair between President Clinton and Monica Lewinsky first became news, thousands of people turned to online sites for information. MSNBC's Web site had 830,000 visitors one day, double its normal load. CNN Interactive had 12.3 million page viewerships, its second-busiest day. *The New York Times* site had a 40 percent jump to 2.5 million visits a day during the week after the Lewinsky story broke.121

Yet for all their popularity, Web sites are not making much money. Nearly all of them depend on advertising for revenue, but in 1998 the advertising revenue of the entire World Wide Web was less than that of *Sports Illustrated* and *TV Guide.*122 Publishers were getting restless for a payback on their investments.

At many online news outlets, the wall between advertisers and journalists is being severely tested. "Perhaps the biggest question looming for a new media publication trying to meet costs is whether, even while preserving its editorial independence, it winds up losing its editorial soul," wrote Terry Eastland, an editor at *Forbes Digital Tool.*123 Fred Mann, the general manager of *Philadelphia Online,* the Web version of the *Inquirer* and *Daily News,* worries about crossing the line between advertising and editorial. "Many of our sites, mine included, have what we blithely call 'sponsored' content. Toyota sponsoring auto reviews." Other online papers have sports pages tied to the publicity departments of local teams. Most newspapers would balk at such an arrangement for the print version of their papers.

Front-page advertisements are rarely seen in American newspapers. Yet online versions almost always feature advertising banners. For a while in 1997, the *USA Today* logo itself became an ad on the opening page of its Web site. The words "USA Today" morphed into an Oldsmobile. Lorraine Cichowski, vice president for *USA Today*'s information network, called this an example of "out-of-the-box thinking. . . . Advertisers are trying a lot of innovative things on the Web, and where we can accommodate them we do."[124]

The use of news staff to prepare material for advertisers is becoming common at Web sites, even at publications that would never allow the practice in their regular newsrooms. Chris McKenna, a producer for *Time Online*, told *CJR*, "It's as if they're saying, 'Hey, we can compromise a bit, it's not our flagship product.'"[125]

Furthermore, to fund their online editions, many newspapers have worked out deals with other businesses. Mann described the process this way:

> Conventional wisdom (and in this case pretty undeniable wisdom) says that those companies that partner wisely will ultimately win the game online. OK. So you go out and form various types of business alliances with other companies.
>
> You sign a deal with AT&T because they can give you the Internet access you need to offer to your potential audience.
>
> You partner with your major local bank so that you can offer their online banking services on your site and draw a bigger audience and therefore sell more ads.
>
> You ally with a major health care provider because you want their doctor database online. You throw in with one of your local major league sports franchises to cosponsor an interactive game which drives your hit totals and gives the ball club lots of easy promotional mileage. You even do business with Microsoft because, while they may ultimately devour you, you need their technical support and, Jeez, they'll throw money at anything.
>
> Now that all that is in the works . . . post some credible business coverage online. Maintain your high standards for impartiality. Make sure your readers remember your impeccable credibility when they read that story about the high tech war-to-the-death between Netscape and Microsoft which appears right next to your advertising button which says "Powered by Microsoft" on the screen.

Mann agrees with those who say some rules may be different for online journalists. "We think we've put on enough safeguards to protect the editorial integrity of our information," Mann said. "But where we draw the line is not necessarily where [print journalists] would. We may all subscribe to the same traditional journalistic values, but how you implement them in a world of clicks and links and interlocking databases is not as clear as it used to be."[126]

Some online editors disagree. *Forbes'* Eastland contends that avoiding the appearance of advertising influence is "a necessity since so many judgments are made on the basis of appearances." He thinks Web designers should clearly separate links to advertisers from links to news sites and opposes placing commercial links in news stories themselves. Eastland is also concerned about Web editors doing special projects for advertisers. These special sections are sources of income, he admits. However, he said, "If a site frequently devotes editorial resources to such projects, even producing authentic journalism, it may wind up doing less and less of what it started out to do—indeed what impelled its editors to go online in the first place."

For some online editors, protecting the credibility of online journalism is crucial. "If there's even a hint of ethical compromise, we don't have a business," said Jai Singh, editor of *News.com,* a Web site that covers new technologies. "We all bring our journalism heritage into this."[127]

Improving the Profession

The alternatives for journalists who find that the demands of management clash with their consciences are not very inviting. Traditionally, ethical journalists have quit working for unsavory employers and found jobs at other stations or newspapers. That option has been made less achievable because of the shortage of jobs in journalism. Some journalists have decided to leave the profession altogether rather than lower their ethical standards.

A code of ethics for newspaper publishers and broadcast station owners would be one small step in improving the quality of American journalism. But there has been little discussion of extending codes of ethics to publishers, and it is difficult to imagine that the worst offenders, whose publications need codes the most, would agree to one. It is ironic that many of the same owners whose newsrooms have strict codes of ethics for journalists are not covered by codes of ethics themselves. These owners are willing to tell small-town reporters who barely make living wages that they cannot accept free admission to an amusement park for fear that they will compromise the integrity of the news. Yet the owners are not bound by any industry codes of ethics that deal with understaffing newsrooms, reducing the news hole or yielding to advertiser pressure.

Both former CBS newsman Jon Katz and *CJR*'s Karen Rothmyer urge journalists to try to make media managers understand the need for them to commit financial resources to strong news coverage.

Rothmyer believes that reporters and editors are going to have to take a more active role in the management of their papers. She wrote:

> For journalists, the challenge will be to learn to live with the financial realities while, at the same time, fighting against the corporate values that so often accompany them. That will require two forms of activity not now common in American newsrooms: serious financial analysis, by news employees, of their organizations; and collective action—not individual gestures or expressions of concern—aimed at giving journalists a voice as one of the stakeholders in media corporations.[128]

Katz urged broadcast journalists to take an even more aggressive approach because he believes that pressure from outside the broadcast industry is the only way to get station owners to invest in better newscasts. Katz suggested that TV news directors have lunch with local newspaper editors and encourage them to print stories about the "perilous position of local news" and to write editorials that "lean on the television industry to provide air time that's protected . . . from some of the profit pressure."[129]

Katz said that it may take the fear of renewed government regulation to improve local stations' commitment to news. Speaking to station managers, he said:

> Remember that this deregulatory era can't last forever. Sooner or later some congressman or -woman is going to notice that you're making obscene profits, that you're broadcasting little public affairs programming, that your children's programs exist only to sell sugared cereals, and that you've grown contemptuous of the notion of public airwaves as a public trust. When it hits the fan, you'll have little in the way of public support. Then you'll be forced to get serious. . . . Remember that in other fields executives have learned to view market research as a guide, not a bible.[130]

The answer to the problems of business interference in the newsroom is going to have to come from media owners themselves. Owners have made a lot of money from TV stations and newspapers. One stock analyst expects newspaper profit ratios to continue to be nearly twice that of other American industry in years to come.[131]

The problem is that these profit ratios may be lower than those media owners grew accustomed to during the high-flying 1980s. Too many owners want to maintain their high profit ratios by slashing at the heart of the news operation and undermining its commitment to telling the truth. Until these publishers and station owners learn to accept new realistic profit standards, too many journalists will not be allowed to practice their profession in keeping with its highest ethical principles.

13

Journalists
and Their
Communities

More than 300,000 people crowded the streets of Washington, D.C., carrying pro-choice banners and singing protest songs. They were hoping to send a message to the U.S. Supreme Court that they disagreed with its ruling in *Webster v. Reproductive Health Services,* which many believed was a signal that the court was going to overturn its decision in *Roe v. Wade* legalizing abortion.

A protest of this size was a major media event. Hundreds of journalists were on the scene. Among them was Linda Greenhouse, a *New York Times* reporter who covers the Supreme Court. But she wasn't there to report on the demonstration. She was there with the marchers who were protesting the decision. And she wasn't the only reporter who participated in the march. Dozens of journalists from papers all over the country were also among the protesters.

When these journalists returned to their newsrooms, many received a jolt. They got messages from their editors telling them that they had violated their newspapers' codes of ethics. The codes specified that they were not allowed to participate in activities that may create or appear to create conflicts of interest.

Many of these journalists and some of their editors said they did not know that participating in the march would be considered unethical. When Greenhouse told the Washington bureau chief for the *Times* about her participation, his first reactions were that she had done nothing wrong. "People's private expressions are their own business," he told her. Then he checked the *Times'* guidelines on ethics and found a clause that seemed to ban such activities:

> The integrity of *The Times* requires that its staff members avoid employment or any other undertakings, obligations, relationships or investments that create or appear to create a conflict of interest with their professional work for *The Times* or otherwise compromises *The Times*' independence and reputation.

But he still wasn't sure the rule would apply to Greenhouse's participation in the march. So he checked with *Times* editors in New York and learned that Max Frankel, then executive editor, was committed to the policy. He was told, "Max's view is that, as an example, you cannot cover the White House and wear a campaign button."[1]

Greenhouse and other *Times*' staffers were not punished by their paper for their participation in the march. She stayed on the Supreme Court beat because, her bureau chief said, "We have full faith and confidence in her professionalism. It's part of our profession that we try to discipline opinions, not that we're opinion-free."

But she was criticized by other journalists. "Most of my colleagues thought I was a jerk to be there," Greenhouse said, "and they let me know that, either politely or impolitely."[2] Some thought the *Times* let her off too easily. Eileen McNamara, who covered the abortion issue for *The Boston Globe* at the time of the march, said that Greenhouse had made "a terrible mistake" in marching and that the *Times* had "made a bad mistake in allowing her to continue to cover the issue." Greenhouse said she would follow the newspaper's policy and not participate in any more pro-choice rallies. "I don't intend to make a martyr of myself. I wouldn't want to do anything to undermine the credibility and objectivity of the profession," she told *Time* magazine.[3] She remained on the Supreme Court beat and won a Pulitzer Prize in 1998.

The journalists who joined the protest have encountered one of the thornier concerns facing journalists. Many want to be involved in their communities, yet they are aware that these involvements can lead to conflicts of interest—or the appearance of conflicts of interest. Conflicts of interest are part of our everyday lives. But when such conflicts occur for journalists, the public is apt to wonder whether these journalists have given up their independence and ability to report truthfully. Such doubts are taken seriously by those in a profession in which being believed is everything.

Journalists and Free Speech

When Greenhouse's editor heard of her participation in the march, his first response was that she had done nothing wrong since she was expressing her opinions on her own time. Bosses in most businesses would probably say the same thing: "At work, you live by our rules; after work you are free to do pretty much what you want." But often that's not the way it works in journalism.

On the job, reporters are sometimes encouraged to express their opinions in op-ed columns and news analysis pieces and to appear on TV and radio talk programs. Some small-town papers even pay bonuses to reporters who write editorials. But off the job, journalists are supposed to keep their opinions to themselves. Most newspapers and TV stations have policies limiting what reporters and editors can say and do when they are not at work.

Editors at many papers, including the *Chicago Tribune,* issued reminders of their conflict-of-interest rules when they learned that some of their staff members had participated in the abortion rights march. Some papers had newsroom meetings to discuss the matter. A few newspapers, like *The Washington Post,* went a step further. Editors prohibited all staffers who participated in the march from reporting or editing any stories about the abortion question. Leonard Downie Jr., who was managing editor at the *Post* during the pro-choice march, told *Time* that some of his staff members "found it kind of shocking that they are called on not to exercise some of their personal rights so that the paper can vigorously defend its own First Amendment rights."[4]

To head off potential problems, many newspapers and TV news departments reminded their staffs of their policies before the march on Washington by gays and lesbians in 1993. ABC News, the Associated Press and the *Post* were among the news organizations that specifically banned their journalists from participating in that demonstration. Other news organizations limited participation to staff members who did not cover issues involving gays.[5]

The Cox chain, which includes *The Atlanta Journal-Constitution* and several TV stations, took a different approach when a member of its Washington bureau wanted to participate in the Million Man March organized by Louis Farrakhan, leader of the Nation of Islam and considered by many to be racist and anti-Semitic. He told his editors that he wanted to participate "not because I believe in the messengers, but because I believe in the message" of the march, which was atonement and responsibility. His editor agreed to let him march as long as he was completely "passive," meaning he did not speak, carry placards or show any support or disapproval of the activities. Before the march, he wrote a column explaining his participation.

Marches are not the only ways that journalists have run afoul of conflict-of-interest codes. Reporters at many papers have been cautioned not to wear campaign buttons or put political bumper stickers on their cars. A pro-choice reporter at a newspaper in South Florida was fired after she mailed miniature coat hangers, symbols of the procedures used when abortions were illegal, to every member of the Florida Legislature. A reporter at *The Press Democrat* in Santa Rosa, Calif., was taken off coverage of the timber industry after a weekly paper quoted him as praising organizers of an anti-logging protest.[6] And some papers have asked reporters not to join groups like the National Organization for Women because these organizations become entangled in political issues.

A few journalists want to play an even more pivotal role in their communities. They want to hold political office. A reporter for the *Knoxville News-Sentinel* believed that although her local schools had a good reputation, they had some serious problems. So she decided to run for a seat on the Alcoa, Tenn., school board. "I thought that because I am a journalist that I could make a positive contribution," she said. "I've covered city council, county commissioners and those kinds of public governing bodies, and I know how to ask questions and get information."

But the paper's policy prohibited "participation of an employee in any political activity that could raise questions as to the newspaper's objectivity." Her editor gave her a choice: Keep the $25-a-month school board job or keep her job at the newspaper—but not both. She chose to fight, arguing that allowing her to serve on the school board would create no problems for the paper. Alcoa is 15 miles from Knoxville, she explained, and the paper hired a stringer (a part-time reporter) to cover the school board. She conceded that reporters should not run for mayor or city council while on the payroll of the local newspaper, but she thought a nonpartisan school board was a different kind of body.[7]

But people both in and out of journalism might argue that even nonpartisan school boards are just as political as city councils because they collect and spend big tax dollars. Others wonder if news coverage of the school board might not be compromised, especially at a smaller newspaper like the *News-Sentinel*. How would the reporter assigned to cover the meetings treat a colleague if she did or said something during a meeting that made her seem shallow or foolish? Might her editors be concerned that a story that reflected poorly on the reporter would cause her problems on her own beat?

The Knoxville paper's reactions to the reporter's candidacy illustrate the general newsroom taboo against reporters' getting involved in politics. Reporters from news organizations ranging from *The Miami Herald,* to the Duluth, Minn., newspapers, to WESH-TV in

Orlando, Fla., have quit or been fired when they decided to become political candidates. Many newspaper codes, like the *Standard-Examiner's* in Ogden, Utah, specifically ban newsroom employees from running for or holding any elective office.[8]

However, some reporters have covered themselves while they served on governmental bodies. In the 1980s, Dan Meckes covered a city council for *The Daily Herald* in Tyrone, Pa., while he served on it. A second member of that city council was a reporter for another paper; however, her paper assigned someone else to cover the meetings.[9] Two journalists for the Washington, Pa., *Observer-Reporter* covered themselves: One was a member of the city council and the other was on the county planning commission. Both resigned their political positions when another paper pointed out the obvious conflicts of interest.[10]

Some editors have used their dual roles as journalists and city council members to give themselves the final word. Jack Benson, the editor and publisher of the *Proctor (Minn.) Journal*, was criticized by the Minnesota News Council after he wrote stories about the Proctor City Council on which he served. Benson quoted himself as saying things he never said at the meetings, according to the news council, and used his stories to suggest that other members of the City Council were racists or bigots.[11]

Why Limit Journalists' Rights?

Many journalists believe that newspeople should not take part in public issues. They argue that as people participate in marches and organizations that promote causes, they become more deeply involved in these issues. These strong involvements may lead to bias unintentionally slipping into their reporting. The concern is not that reporters might deliberately slant their stories. Editors are supposed to keep that from happening. The fear is that while gathering information, they might treat people who agree with them more favorably and unconsciously rely on these sources more heavily.

Many people, both in the newsroom and among the public, have wondered whether this kind of unintentional bias may have affected media coverage of the abortion debate. "If you are a woman reporter under the age of about 50 . . . you are writing about something that could happen to you," said Cynthia Gorney, who covers abortion for *The Washington Post*. She told *Los Angeles Times* media writer David Shaw, "You're going to have a view on it. . . . There's no way you can set that aside. The issue is whether you can, while holding that view, listen seriously to people of all stripes on this issue . . . and really do what reporters are supposed to do . . . shed light and make clear why people hold the positions that they do."[12]

A few journalists have admitted that on the question of abortion, they cannot set aside their beliefs. Reporters at newspapers ranging from the *Vero Beach (Fla.) Press-Journal* to the *Los Angeles Times* have asked to be taken off coverage of abortion issues because they doubted they could be fair. The *Times* reporter did not want to cover planned blockades of clinics by Operation Rescue. "There were moments, probably in the wake of the demonstrations, when I was angry enough that I could not have written dispassionately about the matter," she told Shaw.

Many other reporters who cover abortion believe they can separate their personal feelings from their reporting. However, there are questions about how successful they have been at doing this. Some have charged that many reporters unconsciously ask tougher questions of anti-abortion leaders and seem less willing to take their opinions seriously. Shaw spent 18 months studying the media's coverage of the abortion issue and then wrote a four-part series in which he concluded:

> [W]hile responsible journalists do try hard to be fair, the culture in most big-city newsrooms automatically embraces the abortion rights side of the argument, and this results—however unwittingly—in scores of examples, large and small, that can only be characterized as unfair to the opponents of abortion, either in content, tone, choice or language or prominence of play.

Shaw cited a study of *The New York Times, The Washington Post,* and the evening news on ABC, NBC, and CBS that found that women reporters quoted twice as many supporters of abortion rights as they quoted opponents of abortion. Among women newspaper reporters, the tilt was 3–1. During the same time period, men reporters were evenly split on the use of supporters and opponents of abortion rights. News executives and reporters at these news organizations told Shaw that they thought their coverage was fair.

Abortion, of course, is not the only issue that may prompt concerns about unconscious bias in coverage. Objections have been raised about Jewish reporters who cover the Middle East and African-American reporters assigned to the civil rights beat.[13] Others have wondered if gay and lesbian journalists can cover gay rights issues fairly and write dispassionately about political issues involving AIDS or if reporters who have strong feelings about nature conservation should be on the environmental beat.[14]

Downie of *The Washington Post* is so concerned that journalists may allow their personal opinions to unconsciously slant their coverage of political issues that he would prefer reporters not to vote. Going through the process of judging a candidate's fitness for office may subtly influence what reporters write, in Downie's view. That's why he has refrained from voting in any election in which he played a role in the paper's coverage.[15] The *Post,* along with papers like *The Philadelphia Inquirer,* does not allow its staff to take part in any activity that might compromise the paper's credibility regardless of whether they are covering the issue.

Public Perceptions

Many reporters who marched in the Washington abortion rights rally were not only embarrassed by the criticism from their editors, but they were further chagrined when they learned that pro-life groups were using their participation in the march "to prove" their argument that the media were biased against them.

The possibility that people will presume bias is another reason many news organizations require their journalists to keep their opinions to themselves. Too many people are willing to discount the message if they believe the messenger has an ax to grind. Steven Brill, the founder of Court TV and *Content* magazine, discovered that lesson when he wrote an article critical of Kenneth Starr, the special prosecutor looking into a variety of accusations against President Clinton. Critics pointed out that Brill had donated money to the Clinton campaign.

Former *Washington Post* ombudsman Geneva Overholser also worries about the effects of journalists spouting their opinions in print or on TV talk shows. She notes that most newspapers won't allow staff members to moonlight or even head the local United Way because their objectivity might be questioned. Yet many of these same newspapers "are fine with journalists going on television and pronouncing upon the people and events they cover—complete with nameplates to make sure everyone knows whom they work for." Overholser is baffled by how these journalists can "tell viewers how abysmal the House majority leader's performance was, how pathetic the vice president's trip to China, where the latest scandal ranks on a scale of one to 10—and then turn around and report on the hapless officials involved."[16]

Kerry Sipe, the ombudsman at *The Virginian-Pilot* in Norfolk, Va., criticized his papers for allowing reporters to write opinion columns in which they made caustic comments about the people they cover. In one column, the reporter who covered local schools wrote that discipline in the schools was so bad that it was dangerous to enter a classroom. He further charged that administrators didn't care about these unsafe conditions. In another column, the city hall reporter told readers that there was no good reason to vote against a controversial $17.6 million bond issue a city utility was considering. Sipe wondered whether school officials would trust the reporter to give them a fair shake in future news stories after the reporter had accused them of not caring about safety in the schools. Sipe also asked whether citizens opposed to the bond issue would feel good about being interviewed by a reporter who has already gone on record as having dismissed their objections to it as unfounded.[17]

Too Many Restrictions?

Many journalists think the restrictions now in place at many newspapers intrude far too much into their private lives. They contend that they can express their opinions publicly and still do their jobs. Once the public sees that their stories are fair, there will be no loss of credibility.

A. Kent MacDougall, now a journalism professor at the University of California, argued that he did nothing wrong when he participated in an anti-Vietnam war protest while he was a reporter at *The Wall Street Journal*. In an op-ed piece for the *Journal,* he wrote, "A well-trained reporter with pride in his craft won't allow his beliefs to distort his stories, any more than a Republican surgeon will botch an appendectomy on a Democrat."[18] Helen Thomas, United Press International's veteran White House reporter, told talk show host Phil Donahue that she had a 40-year history of expressing her views and still reporting the news fairly.[19]

Many journalists would agree. They contend that placing limits on journalists' free speech is only a cosmetic effort to mask the fact that journalists have opinions. They argue that reporters' stories will be the same whether they keep quiet about their opinions or whether they express them openly. "There's a certain hypocrisy in trying to have the public think that just because a reporter doesn't march, he or she is somehow more objective than somebody who does march," *New York Newsday* columnist Gabriel Rotello told *American Journalism Review.*[20]

Other journalists argue that some issues are too important for them just to bury their heads in the sand. A *Chicago Tribune* reporter told *Time* magazine, "To me, the struggle for abortion rights is as important to women as the struggle against slavery. This isn't about whether they're going to build some bridge downtown. This is about my body."[21]

And a few contend that off-duty, journalists should have the same rights as other Americans. Sandy Nelson of the *Tacoma (Wash.) Morning News Tribune* argued that newspapers treat journalists "like serfs." She said, "We have become the company's property 24 hours a day." When Nelson openly campaigned in support of the city's ban on discrimination because of sexual orientation, her editors moved her from a reporting position to the copy desk. Nelson sued to get her reporting job back. She cited a state law prohibiting employers from discriminating against employees because of their political activities. However, the state Supreme Court ruled against her. The court decided newspapers were an exception because they needed to prohibit political activism by reporters to protect their credibility. The U.S. Supreme Court let the ruling stand.[22]

Many editors take a less extreme position. *Time* magazine, for example, does not impose a ban on staff members' engaging in political activity as long as it is unrelated to their regular beats. NBC News, the *Los Angeles Times* and *The New York Times* take essentially the same position.

Many editors understand the rationale for letting reporters express opinions about topics they do not cover. But, they say, such a policy would be hard to implement. Defending AP's ban on reporters participating in the gay and lesbian march in Washington, William Ahearn, executive editor of AP, said that its reporters cover all kinds of stories. It isn't possible for them to know in advance whether they may be called upon to report stories that may involve issues like abortion or homosexuality.

Some believe a blanket statement in a code of ethics banning any participation in public issues too sharply limits journalists' rights. But they also would acknowledge that when journalists feel very strongly about issues, they should not play a role in covering them. These writers, such as Deni Elliott of the University of Montana, believe all reporters have at least one issue they feel so strongly about that they should not be allowed to write about it.[23]

When Spouses, Family, Friends Cause Conflicts

When Charles W. Bailey was editor of the *Minneapolis Tribune*, his paper reported that his wife had made a large contribution to the campaign of a U.S. senatorial candidate. This prompted Bailey to get out a memo to his staff that read:

> The contribution may be a matter of some embarrassment to me. I hope it will not be a source of embarrassment for the *Tribune*. It didn't

seem to me that I had any business trying to tell my wife what she could do with her money as long as what she proposed to do was legal and would be a matter of public record.[24]

Most news executives agree they have no legal right to influence the activities of spouses. So when a conflict of interest does arise because of a spouse, all the news organization can do is to make sure the journalist is not involved in the coverage of the spouse. But many news organizations caution employees about the activities of their families. *The Washington Post* not only warns its staff members to "avoid active involvement in any partisan causes" but includes a statement about their families: "Relatives cannot fairly be made subject to *Post* rules, but it should be recognized that their employment or their involvement in causes can at least appear to compromise our integrity."[25]

In Seattle, Elaine Bowers, the new bride of *Seattle Times* managing editor Michael R. Fancher, quit her job as press secretary to the mayor after only a day. Her job qualifications were not in doubt. She had been a reporter for *The Star* in Kansas City and the *Houston Chronicle* and had worked as press secretary to Missouri Gov. Kit Bond for two years. But if she stayed on in her new job in the mayor's office, her husband was going to lose his. *Seattle Times* management informed him that his wife's new job put him in violation of the paper's ethics code. It states that staffers are not to make news judgments about individuals they are related to by blood or marriage. If she took the job, he would be transferred out of the newsroom. Bowers ended up taking a public relations job with the Seattle Public Health Hospital. Fancher was allowed to continue as managing editor but had to remove himself from any news involving the hospital. Later he was promoted to executive editor.[26]

The children of journalists can also raise conflict-of-interest problems. Bill Endicott resigned as Sacramento bureau chief for the *Los Angeles Times* after his editors told him that he would be transferred unless his 23-year-old daughter quit her entry-level secretarial job with Willie Brown, speaker of the California Assembly. Endicott, who was hired almost immediately by *The Sacramento Bee* to be its chief correspondent at the capital, said he could see no moral or legal basis for the request that he ask his daughter to quit her job. "My daughter is an independent adult," he added. "I can't tell her where to work."[27]

Other news organizations have taken less strident stands. CBS allowed Rita Braver to cover the Clinton White House even though her husband, Robert Barnett, was an old friend of the Clintons and worked for a while as a lawyer on the president's Whitewater defense team. According to Howard Kurtz of *The Washington Post,* Clinton thought Braver was unduly harsh on him just to prove her independence. He even joked to her, "You should get a divorce so you can go a little easier on me."[28] CNN reporter Christiane Amanpour married Jamie Rubin, a spokesman in the U.S. State Department, with the blessings of both CNN and CBS, where Amanpour worked as a *60 Minutes* correspondent.[29]

Many newspapers at one time had nepotism policies that prevented spouses from working in the same newsroom. Journalists sometimes postponed their marriages and simply lived together to get around such rules. It is common today to find husbands and wives both doing journalism, sometimes for the same employer but often for different news organizations. Sometimes they're on the same beat, as was the case with Charles Bierbauer and his wife, Susanne Schafer. Both covered the White House, she for AP and he for CNN.

Albert Hunt, chief of the Washington bureau of *The Wall Street Journal,* said that neither he nor his wife, Judy Woodruff, then chief correspondent for the *MacNeil/Lehrer NewsHour,* found that their marriage caused any problems in their professional lives. He contended that "good reporters can compete against their spouses during the day and sleep with them at night."[30]

Cokie Roberts of ABC News and National Public Radio believes her marriage benefits because both are journalists. She thinks they better understand the demands of the job and have more in common. Her husband, Steve, has been reporter for *U.S. News & World Report* and a columnist for the *New York Daily News.* When *New York Times* reporter Allison Mitchell was assigned to cover the Clinton White House, she received some insights about the job from her husband, Francis X. Clines, a *Times* reporter who had previously covered the White House.

A more common problem for journalists is with friendships. Donald Smith, editor of the *Monticello (Minn.) Times,* recalled an incident in which a friend's son was caught stealing goods from parked cars. Shortly before deadline, the friend called him. "The grieving parent knows me well. I could feel her pain. Publication of the young man's name in our newspaper would make the situation worse, she hinted, raising even the possibility of suicide due to publication and pending court action." She asked if her son's name could be removed from the sheriff's report. Smith told the woman that since his paper prints every arrest, in fairness, he would have to run her son's name.[31]

Other editors in small cities have also felt peer pressure. In Port Angeles, Wash., a local doctor was suspected, but not charged, in the smothering death of a newborn baby. When the *Peninsula Daily*

News printed the doctor's name, some of the doctor's friends tried to block editor John Brewer's nomination to the local Rotary Club.[32]

Civic Journalism

As we have seen, for the past three decades, most journalists have refused to take active roles in their communities. This has not always been the case. In the past, many newspaper publishers played powerful roles in their communities. They used their newspapers to determine which projects and causes would be publicized and which would not. Often, this control of information gave them a bigger say in local affairs than many elected officials. Also, since publishers could write strong endorsements and shape the coverage of political campaigns, they could help or hurt a candidate's chances of winning. Many publishers used this leverage. Katherine Fanning, former editor of the *Christian Science Monitor,* recalls that Col. Robert McCormick of the *Chicago Tribune* and Robert Atwood of the Anchorage, Alaska, newspapers "pretty much called the shots" in their communities. "There was only one viewpoint," she said.

Fanning said that kind of overbearing community activism is one reason so many journalists adopted "the objective, hands-off, concerned-about-conflict-of-interest style." They began to stay on the sidelines. They saw their jobs as being watchdogs, pointing out the shortcomings of society in hopes that others would do something about them. It was not their job to work directly to improve society.

At some news organizations, this orientation is changing. Journalists are easing their stands on potential conflicts of interest and are becoming more involved in their communities. But they are not becoming community leaders in the heavy-handed, almost dictatorial style of the McCormicks and Atwoods. "We are turning to a more bottom-up, grassroots, diverse kind of approach to community leadership for the newspaper," Fanning said, "one that involves the community and involves diverse voices within the community; one where the newspaper can help to spark a kind of involvement."

The Beginnings of a Movement

Although many editors and writers have contributed to the civic journalism movement, two editors, Davis "Buzz" Merritt in Wichita, Kan., and Jack Swift in Columbus, Ga., led campaigns that stirred journalists across the country to reconsider the role of the news media in society.

Merritt, editor of *The Wichita Eagle,* looked at his paper's coverage of the 1988 elections and did not like what he saw. The campaign had been dirty. One candidate would charge an opponent with some wrongdoing, and the opponent would respond with a countercharge. The papers and TV news were filled with racehorse coverage, reporting who was ahead in the polls this week but reporting little about the issues. When the campaigns were over, only about half the registered voters decided to go to the polls. Merritt thought something was clearly wrong. He suspected that voters were disenchanted with the candidates—and with the news coverage. He thought journalists could do better.

During the next election two years later, the paper conducted surveys and focus-group interviews to determine what issues were important to voters. Each Sunday before the election, the paper and its partner in the project, KAKE-TV, carried in-depth stories about these issues. Reporters at the newspaper and TV station had to change their reporting styles. "It took us a while to re-educate ourselves about the issues," managing editor Steve Smith wrote. "We had become transcribers to political campaigns—getting A's statement and B's response and so forth. We had to train ourselves to be a little nasty" in forcing candidates to answer specific questions about real issues.

Merritt was so satisfied with the election project that he decided to try reporting other issues using the same techniques. The *Eagle* hired researchers to interview Kansans about what they thought were the area's problems and how these problems could be answered. The paper then invited readers to offer their ideas about problems and solutions. When the stories appeared in the paper, "there were hundreds of voices . . . and not a single expert or politician," Merritt told *AJR.* The stories suggested ways people could get involved in fixing community problems, and many people responded. For example, after the paper ran stories on education, the number of school volunteers jumped by a third. The effort had another benefit that pleased Merritt. A survey showed that the paper's reader satisfaction was up more than 12 percent.

While Merritt was experimenting in Wichita, editor Jack Swift and his *Columbus (Ga.) Ledger-Enquirer* were also investigating a difficult social problem: racism. In a series of stories, the paper reported that the school system was largely segregated; the city's social life was segregated; nearly 40 percent of the residents were functionally illiterate; and the community had other serious troubles. After talking to experts, government leaders and citizens, the paper presented an agenda of how things could be improved. Although the stories were well reported, they had no impact, according to *AJR.*

Neither government leaders nor the public showed any interest in what the *Ledger-Enquirer* proposed.

Swift faced a difficult choice. His paper could either abandon the proposals or take a leadership role in bringing about change. Swift decided to take action. The *Ledger-Enquirer* began by sponsoring town meetings to rally support for more spending on schools and other community projects. The paper also threw barbeques, where many townsfolk had their first social encounter with people of other races.

Although reporters and editors at the *Ledger-Enquirer* agreed with Swift's cause, many objected to the paper's activism, which they thought had turned them into reformers rather than reporters. Staff morale was low, and employees complained about Swift to management, according to *AJR*. But four years after the project, Billy Winn, the chief reporter on the project, remained convinced Swift was right. "I maintain that anyone who cared about the community would have had a difficult time deciding to do otherwise. . . . If you didn't do something, people were actually going to suffer. It was that clear-cut."[33]

The actions of Merritt and Swift are considered by many to be the start of the civil or public journalism movement. Swift committed suicide while the campaign was under way. However, Merritt and New York University Professor Jay Rosen have become the movement's strongest advocates. Civic journalism has no official definition. The common theme, however, is an effort to involve the news media more directly in their communities. While not always agreeing on the cure, its supporters believe they know what's afflicting conventional journalism. Eric Black of the Minneapolis *Star Tribune* summed up three basic symptoms:

- Overreliance on experts. Most journalists base their stories on information from politicians, experts and celebrities, but not from the public. Some believe this encourages the public to be passive, to assume that the problems are out of their hands.
- The cynicism of journalists. Many argue that one reason the public has begun to distrust public institutions, including the media, is that journalists portray public institutions, including the news media, as not being trustworthy.
- The obsession with detachment. Traditional journalists believe that if they get involved in their communities, they will lose their objectivity. They want to remain outsiders observing and reporting on the actions of people in the communities. However, civic journalists believe this gives the impression that

journalists don't really care whether society thrives or falls apart. Former PBS anchorman Robert MacNeil warned journalists against acting like "amused bystanders watching the idiots screw it up."

Black wrote that civic journalists hope their movement will:

• Invite ordinary citizens back into public life by making their concerns the starting point of debate.
• Overcome journalistic cynicism and acknowledge the possibility that citizens working together might solve some of society's problems.
• Modify the rules of detachment by accepting that journalists have an interest in and responsibility for raising the level of public discourse and helping society find solutions to its problems.[34]

Hundreds of public journalism projects have been conducted by newspapers and TV stations in the last five years in large cities like Seattle and smaller communities like Madison, Wis., and Tallahassee, Fla. Many have been keyed to election coverage, but others have looked at social issues like crime and racism.

Public Journalism Works in Charlotte

Two police officers in Charlotte, N.C., began to chase a suspect and radioed for help. But by the time the backup team arrived, the officers were dead—both shot in the head. Their deaths sent shudders down many spines in Charlotte, a booming city with gleaming bank towers, thriving businesses and a growing crime problem.

The deaths of the officers made crime news an even bigger story for Charlotte's news media. But *The Charlotte Observer* didn't want to do traditional coverage. Rick Thames, the paper's city editor, explained, "It was clear to us and to readers that the city had a real problem. It was important to figure out some way to deal with it that would be constructive." The paper's editor, Jennie Buckner, agreed. She wanted crime covered "in a way that wouldn't just feed fear." She decided the *Observer* would begin a long-term project patterned after the "civic" or "public" journalism movement. Charlotte TV station WSOC joined in. Together they used polls, forums and in-depth reporting in hopes of bringing attention and solutions to community problems. The paper held town meetings in high-crime areas and listened to residents' concerns. Some reporters and editors even moved into high-crime areas so they could better understand the communities.

Both newspaper and TV reports profiled residents of the neighborhoods. What they found surprised the veteran city editor. "These people were living with violent crime to an extent the rest of us don't understand," he said. Reporters didn't stop with stories about these people's plight. They also looked for answers to the crime problem. They prepared stories about neighborhoods that were trying to solve their crime problem, and they found laws that could be used to close crack houses. They asked residents to make "wish lists" of what the city could do to help their communities and then did stories about how Charlotte's residents could help. In the 18 months following the shooting of the police officers, the *Observer* and WSOC

- Held a half-dozen town meetings in crime-riddled neighborhoods, where hundreds of residents accepted invitations to air their concerns.
- Inspired more than 700 groups or individuals to volunteer to meet various neighborhood needs.
- Triggered the city to raze dilapidated buildings, open long-promised parks and recreation facilities, and clear overgrown lots that were havens for illegal activity.
- Prompted 18 local law firms to file public nuisance suits, without charge, to close neighborhood crack houses.
- Captured the attention of their peers. The *Observer* was named a Pulitzer Prize finalist in the public service competition, and WSOC-TV won a prestigious Headliner Award.[35]

Perhaps the biggest reward to some of the journalists was the personal satisfaction they experienced. "I've been reporting 12 years— 10 in this market," said WSOC crime reporter Mark Becker. "This has given me an opportunity to do more in-depth work, looking in a constructive way toward solutions."

Concerns About Civic Journalism

While the results of projects like the one undertaken by *The Charlotte Observer* and WSOC are impressive, many people question whether conducting these activities is the proper role for journalists. They are ill at ease with the notion of journalists playing such a direct role in shaping the news. In particular, they worry about what happened to news coverage during another civic journalism project in North Carolina.

Sixteen of the state's newspapers, TV and radio stations cooperated in one of the largest experiments in civic journalism. Jointly, they began planning their coverage of the November 1996 U.S. Senate elections in January. Instead of individually chasing speeches by the candidates, the news organizations decided to poll voters to find out which issues they thought were important. Reporters then worked together to produce a 12-part series that concentrated on these issues. The series was a cooperative effort. Reporters who normally compete with one another shared bylines on the stories. Newspapers promoted segments about the topics when they appeared on local TV and radio stations, and the broadcast media urged viewers to read the stories in their local papers. After the election, surveys found that about a quarter of North Carolina voters read the series and used the information in deciding which candidates they supported.[36]

Journalists involved in the project were proud of their coverage. There were fewer racehorse stories and fewer charge-countercharge exchanges. The candidates' positions on the issues were emphasized. The project seemed to satisfy the hopes of many advocates of civic journalism like Edward Fouhy, director of the Pew Foundation, which helps fund civic journalism projects. "Civic journalists . . . aggressively ferret out issues of interest to citizens who are not members of the elite," he wrote. "That means things like the education of their children, the security of their families, and the economic future they face. That means covering an agenda that is set more by citizens, by the people, and less by those who would manipulate them. That means thinking about the news not only from the standpoint of conventional journalistic practice but taking it a step further and thinking about a subject from the standpoint of the public and public interest."[37]

However, some argue that this characteristic of civic journalism encouraged the news media to set the agenda for the North Carolina campaigns. Neither candidate was pleased by the coverage. Republican Jesse Helms called it a "fraud." Democrat Harvey Gantt's campaign manager was even more blunt. He called it "a bunch of crap, just nonsense, just bullshit, absolute bullshit."

The Gantt campaign was particularly upset over the media's use of polls to decide which issues to cover. Gantt's campaign manager complained that the issues were ignored if they did not fall into the categories picked by readers months before the election. For example, *The Washington Post* in a front-page story reported that the Jesse Helms Center, a foundation created to honor the senator, had been given $225,000 by the government of Taiwan, $100,000 by the government of Kuwait and hundreds of thousands by the tobacco industry. Helms is chairman of the Senate Foreign Relations Committee. Yet North Carolina's major papers, which were part of the joint campaign coverage, did not write any follow-up stories of their own about the contributions.

Gantt thought this was an important issue, but "you can't get them covered because they're not on the list of things voters supposedly care about," he said. To Gantt, the joint coverage gave an inaccurate picture of the race. "There are serious disagreements [between the candidates] here, but all the disagreements are sanitized, everything is put through the washing machine, and it all gets blurred together." He complained that the coverage was prepackaged and became "a crushing bore."[38]

Many journalists were also troubled by the experiment. Michael Gartner, publisher of the Ames, Iowa, *Daily Tribune* and former president of NBC News, thinks each news organization ought to do its own reporting of local races. "If five competing newspapers had gone after the stories, their reporters would have written the story in five different ways, held five sets of interviews, found five sets of facts," he stated. "At least one of the five might have uncovered something startling, something contradictory, something new."[39] He believes media coalitions, which are characteristic of many public journalism projects, "homogenize the news and reduce the number of voices gathering it." He also has concerns about the news judgments being left to "pollsters or, worse, to readers or viewers in focus groups who have no particular knowledge of a state, of politics or of politicians."

Robert Franklin, a veteran reporter at the Minneapolis *Star Tribune,* also worries about the use of polls: "Of course we should seek out the concerns of readers and citizens, whether by scientific sampling or old-fashioned reporting. But to let focus groups define a campaign would be as silly as letting politicians do it."[40]

That also concerns Anthony Marro, the editor of *Newsday.* His paper did an extensive series illustrating the devastating, but largely ignored, effects of segregated housing. He wonders how many readers would have named racism in the real estate industry as one of Long Island's major problems.

Other critics contend that civic journalism projects can become little more than marketing tools. *Washington Post* executive editor Leonard Downie Jr. said, "Too much of what's called public journalism appears to be what our promotion department does, only with a different name and a fancy evangelistic fervor." Journalists spend their time working on projects to improve the media organizations' relationships in the community instead of tracking down important stories.

Some are also concerned that civic journalism may lead to softer coverage of news events. One reporter covered a newspaper-sponsored town meeting that turned into a free-for-all. The reporter described the meeting as "verbal sparring, tit-for-tat argument." But an editor changed the story to read that the meeting "began with both groups still feeling pain and casting blame, but the ensuing discussion helped find some common ground for a new foundation of understanding."

Perhaps the major philosophic objection to public journalism is whether it is the proper role for journalists. Bill Babcock, director of the Silha Center for the Study of Media Ethics at the University of Minnesota, contends that journalists should stand by their traditional commitment not to get involved in the stories they cover. "I get worried when journalists put themselves in the role of advocates for anything, even something as harmless-sounding as civic connectedness," he said. "Journalism's job is to give the public a full array of information which they may choose to use or not use to become more connected."

Jane Eisner, editorial page editor of *The Philadelphia Inquirer,* agrees. She wrote, "Our central mission is to report the news, to set priorities, to analyze but not to shape or direct events or outcomes."[41] Their concerns are that when journalists lose the role of objective bystanders, they become like every other player in society. They lose their standing as independent watchdogs.

A more fundamental question is whether public journalism projects are successful in getting the public involved. During the 1996 Senate election, *The Bergen (N.J.) Record* printed 54 full pages of stories about the issues, the candidates' positions and voters' concerns. These pages included none of the horse-race or insider coverage. After the election, the paper surveyed its readers and found

- Fewer than one in five remembered seeing the "Campaign Center" pages.
- *Record* readers were no better informed about the issues and no more interested in the campaign than readers of other newspapers.
- Readers did not change their opinion of the paper's political coverage.

Glenn Ritt, the paper's vice president, concluded that a newspaper's role in getting voters involved is limited if people are turned off by the politicians and bored by the issues. "We are only part of the equation, and maybe not the most important part," he wrote.[42]

It's too early to know whether public journalists will reshape the profession. However, Carl Sessions Stepp, senior editor of *AJR,* offers that the movement may have come at the right time. News organizations have begun to think of readers and viewers as customers. The directive in many newsrooms is to give them a product they would like. The civic journalism movement may change that attitude. Civic journalists urge media management to consider readers and viewers as citizens. The job of the media, they contend, is to involve these citizens in public life by reporting on matters of importance. If that's the shift in news orientation that comes from the civic journalism movement, many journalists will welcome it.[43]

14

Freebies and Financial Concerns

The computer columnist for a major Southern newspaper was explaining new, faster ways to connect to the Internet. "At home, I've been using Global Village's new TelePort modem, which retails for $99 at most computer retail outlets," he wrote. "It was fairly easy to install, and I've been connecting to both America Online and a local Internet service provider at around 45 kbps. It is noticeably better than the performance I get with the 28.8 modem in my laptop computer." The TelePort modem was the only product mentioned by brand name.

The same week, 50 miles away, the computer columnist at another newspaper was also extolling the virtues of the TelePort modem. "Unlike my Accura, which is an internal model, the TelePort is external. That makes installation a snap. Simply plug it into an open COM port with the supplied connection cable, plug in the modem's power pack and flip the power switch." Not only is it easy to use, he wrote, but the TelePort's "sleek beige case, just 3 inches wide and 5.5 inches deep, fits easily on the desktop or computer." The column featured a picture of the TelePort's box and gave the Internet address of the manufacturer.

Readers considering buying faster modems may have believed they had just received some good advice. After all, computer columnists are paid to sort through all the technical gibberish and offer informed opinions. If they choose to use the TelePort modem, it must be a quality product. However, a less technological reason may have influenced the columnists' choice. The manufacturer, Global Village, had sent modems to dozens of computer writers.

Many papers, including the ones these writers worked for, have strongly worded bans preventing staffers from accepting free trips, free dinners, free visits to theme parks or any other valuable gifts. Yet applying these rules is not always easy—even at ethical stalwarts like *The New York Times.*

In 1996 the New York Yankees ripped through the regular season like the Bronx Bombers of legend and rekindled the fervor of Yankee fans. When all the tickets were sold for the first home game of the American League playoffs, police had to be called in to break up lines of angry fans at the ticket office. As the Yankees marched through the playoffs and prepared to meet the Atlanta Braves in the World Series, hysteria set in. *Editor & Publisher* magazine described the frenzy like this:

> It turned into a nightmare when World Series tickets went on sale as scalpers bused in homeless men from Jersey City to wait in line for them.
>
> The scalpers—peddling $25 bleacher seats for $500 and $70 box seats for $2,000—also worked the Major Deegan Expressway near the stadium, the coffee shops, the subways, the parking lots and the side streets.
>
> And there were the near-perfect counterfeit tickets going for black-market rates, with newspapers publishing poignant pictures of victims who bought them, and listing the names of the people charged with selling them.
>
> The television cameras focused on fans lying on the cold concrete sidewalks for up to 48 hours, while newspapers published stories about people using the pavement as a toilet while they waited to buy tickets.
>
> The Yankees had captured the core of the Big Apple, from Wall Street to Westchester, and everyone wanted to be in the South Bronx for an emotional baseball revival meeting.
>
> The news pages were filled with those stories, and local broadcasters aired sad sound bites of ticket-starved fans who were turned away.[1]

But some Yankee fans were not standing in long lines or crying in their beer because they couldn't get tickets. For these fans, tickets were only a phone call away. They were some of New York's top journalists. Depending on their pedigree, these journalists had been offered free tickets or the opportunity to buy tickets to the sold-out games. Some *New York Post* staffers accepted the free tickets, and three sat in Yankee owner George Steinbrenner's luxury box. Reporters and editors from other New York media, including *The New York Times, Daily News* and Associated Press, bought the tickets reserved for journalists. As *E&P* pointed out, "Those who acquired tickets went to the games as spectators—not as working journalists—a sore point to the thousands of fans who couldn't get them."

The journalists who accepted the tickets defended their actions. "I don't understand the conflict," Joseph Lelyveld, *New York Times* executive editor, told *E&P*. "I do not see it as a good, ethical issue of the day. We paid for our tickets." But many other journalists reacted differently. Long Island's *Newsday* refused to allow its staff to buy the special tickets, and William Marimow, managing editor of the Baltimore *Sun,* said, "To be honest, paying for a scarce ticket is a close call. But if something makes me hesitate or pause, I don't do it."

Goodbye, Free Lunch

The freebie problem is a comparatively new one in American journalism. Although would-be seducers of the press have existed for years, they were hardly mentioned in early literature on journalism ethics. Press leaders did not perceive their efforts as a serious threat to journalistic integrity, perhaps because freebies were not all that common.

That changed with the growth of the public relations movement, which developed during the 1920s. Government, business and other segments of society were advised to curry favor with the press. That often translated into gifts and free tickets, travel and meals.

Journalists in those days did not see free tickets to the theater, circus or baseball games as a problem. These perks went with the job; they made up for the notoriously low salaries. Many reporters assumed their news sources would pick up the tab for their drinks or meals. There was "a tradition in journalism of take what you could get," Richard B. Tuttle said when he was publisher and editor of the Elmira, N.Y., *Star-Gazette.*[2] Want to take the kids to an amusement park? Call the public relations office and tell them when you're coming. Can't afford a nice vacation? Promise travel agents and tour operators a flattering story in the Sunday travel section and go wherever you like.

Occasionally the voracity of some journalists shocked even the public relations practitioners who arranged the freebies. A Disney World executive recalled a reporter from a Midwestern paper who rejected the free room arranged for him in one of Disney's nicest hotels. The reporter demanded a suite. She complied and, as a peace offering, suggested that the reporter and his wife have a complimentary dinner in the hotel's restaurant. The executive said, "They ordered from the right-hand side of the menu," picking only the most expensive items.

Christmas used to be a festival of freebies. In the mid-1900s, newsrooms often looked like the gift-wrap sections of department stores as loot would roll in. Some, like baskets of apples from a well-known senator, would be for everybody; other gifts would be for specific writers or editors. Many older journalists can tell stories of newsrooms awash with fifths of whiskey and of journalists cheerfully trying to abide by early ethics rules that allowed them to keep as much as they could drink in one sitting.

Some newspapers placed their reporters in awkward positions. The newspapers were too cheap to pick up the travel expenses of reporters. So sports reporters had to depend on the team's publicity staff to arrange travel to the games. Even political reporters were expected to accept free travel and hotel rooms from the candidates they were covering. Today, the media pay the expenses of the reporters. Curt Matthews, a former Baltimore *Sun* reporter who sometimes traveled with the White House press corps, said he was always "kind of shocked" when the president and the reporters landed somewhere and he heard people standing at the fence grumbling, "It's outrageous that those reporters get to travel around with the president on my tax dollars."[3] Sending reporters, technicians and equipment to cover the Gulf War with Iraq cost the media millions of dollars in 1991.

If you were to graph the history of freebies in America, there would be a line rising slowly through the 1930s and 1940s, reaching its highest point in the late 1950s and early 1960s, and then dropping slowly through the 1970s and 1980s and into the 1990s. The decline was prompted by the increase in professionalism among journalists and the adoption of codes of ethics.

Today, most American newspaper reporters insist on paying for their own meals and drinks, and most news organizations reimburse them when they pick up the check for their sources. Gifts that are sent to reporters are given away: Food often goes to homeless shelters and flowers to hospitals. When reviewers have finished their reviews, the books and CDs are donated to libraries or schools.

However, the rules against freebies are not in force at some American news operations, especially business and trade publications. For example, writers for magazines aimed at people in the travel industry routinely accept free trips. They defend the free trips, saying their stories provide only the nuts-and-bolts information about tourists spots that others in the travel industry need. Less justifiable is the acceptance of freebies by small newspapers and magazines and some broadcast stations. Often these organizations still see freebies as a justification for paying low salaries.

However, even in the most unregulated American newsrooms, the freebies the journalists receive are small potatoes compared with what their counterparts accept in other countries. German reporters often are given personal computers and large discounts on automobiles. Some even receive tax breaks from local governments.[4] Many Mexican journalists are on government or political party payrolls. Before the Gulf War of 1991, it was widely reported that Kuwait routinely offered reporters Mercedes automobiles and that many British and European journalists accepted them without hesitation.

What's Wrong with Freebies?

Nearly every media code of ethics bans freebies for these reasons:

- **The motives of the givers.** Even the most naive reporters soon figure out that public relations practitioners, politicians and other newsmakers do not buy dinners or pay travel expenses because they think reporters are such nice people. They want to influence coverage. The modem company discussed at the beginning of this chapter expected journalists to mention its products. A favorable comment by a computer writer is both cheaper and more believable than advertisements.

    Occasionally, as in the case of the New York Yankees, the motives of the givers are harder to discern. The Yankees were selling out every game. They didn't need to give journalists ticket deals to get publicity. Yet many of the journalists who accepted the ticket deal recognized why the Yankees were being so generous. Owner George Steinbrenner was preparing to ask taxpayers to finance a new ballpark for his Yankees. It was a tough sell because the city had not yet paid off the $125 million tag for refurbishing the existing Yankee Stadium. He wanted the journalists who would be writing and editing stories about the controversy to have firsthand experience with New Yorkers' passion for his Yankees.

- **Perceptions of the public.** Imagine that a mayor accepts a vacation paid for by a local company. Shortly after she returns, she proposes a law that would benefit that company. Regardless of how sincerely she believes in the new law, many voters are going to doubt her intentions. They are going to believe that the company bought her support. And therein lies a second reason many news organizations do not allow journalists to accept freebies. Even if journalists were not influenced by the freebies, the public may suspect that they were. Those suspicions are not healthy for a profession like journalism that depends on being believed.

That's why Phil Mushnick, a columnist for *The New York Post,* criticized journalists who accepted the Yankee ticket offer. He wrote in *The Village Voice*: "When you're talking about tickets that people are jumping off buildings to get and top media guys and captains of industry are getting tickets, clearly there is a quid-pro-quo quality to it that can't be ignored." Other journalists also expressed this worry.

Steve Geimann, president of the Society of Professional Journalists at the time, said, "Our code says that journalists should be free of obligation to any interest other than the public's right to know. When a news executive or a reporter is sitting in the box of someone he covers, it raises questions about his objectivity."

- **A privileged class?** Journalists used to accept all kinds of special privileges. Katharine Graham, publisher of *The Washington Post,* wrote in her autobiography, *Personal History:*

> Shortly after Russ Wiggins became managing editor of *The Post* in 1947, he summoned his police reporter. Wiggins asked if he was having parking tickets fixed. "Yes, sir," said the reporter, for people throughout the building. "I just take them to the station and give them to the chief."

Few, if any, news organizations today would allow their staffs to fix parking tickets. First, they wouldn't like the idea of reporters being indebted to the police chief. Second, they know that getting such special treatment would be resented by the public, many of whom already distrust the media and believe journalists think they are above other citizens.

The lack of fairness in the Yankee ticket deal caused Bruce Webber, a *New York Times* reporter, to change his mind about Steinbrenner's offer. Webber had accepted the Yankee offer that allowed him to buy tickets to a sold-out American League playoff game. Then his editor assigned him to cover the extreme efforts made by some fans to get World Series tickets. His story's headline read, "Fans Dig Deep and Give It All They've Got for Series Ticket." After writing the story, Webber decided not to buy any of the reserved-for-journalists Series tickets. "It seemed unseemly to me," he explained.

- **The appearance of hypocrisy.** Although it is rarely stated in codes of ethics, many journalists avoid freebies and other financial relationships with people in power because of a fear of looking like hypocrites. For years, reporters have prided themselves in exposing politicians on the take. After all, it's news if the head of a congressional banking committee accepts gifts from bankers. Many journalists believe the media's moral stance on such matters is undermined if their colleagues are accepting gifts.

  The Yankee case involved just such hypocrisy. The Yankees had made the same ticket offers to New York politicians. When a group of politicians bought some of the tickets, editorials in the New York media "flared with indignation," according to *E&P*. The papers wanted to know why City Council members were getting to buy tickets while ordinary New Yorkers were left out in the cold. The irony is that many editors and reporters at those "indignant" publications were sitting alongside the politicians in Yankee Stadium and enjoying the same deal.

- **The possibility of influence.** Many journalists are convinced that freebies will not influence them. "Believe me," said Marc Kalech, the *New York Post* managing editor who accepted free Series tickets. "I won't be swayed by free tickets. I still expect to get calls from Steinbrenner complaining about our coverage."

  Yet opponents of freebies would argue that reporters who accept gifts are opening themselves to the possibility of having newsmakers shape their stories in more subtle ways. They see a parallel in politics. Major corporations often give legislators free trips. While on these trips, company officials present their case in a relaxed, social environment. The free trip has bought the company excellent access to the politician, access that most citizens could never have. The Yankees may have achieved the same goal. They were also able to present their product in its most favorable light—from a seat in the owner's private box during the excitement of the World Series.

  For those journalists who accepted the free modems, the influence is more direct and obvious. Dozens of companies make modems. But the only modem mentioned in the reporters' columns was the one that had been given to them. The advantages they cited for the modem were hardly unique to that brand. Any 56.6 modem is likely to be faster than a 28.8 model, and regardless of the manufacturer, external models are almost always easier to install than the internal variety.

- **Direct pressure from gift givers.** Some public relations people pressure reporters to write favorable stories, especially if they have accepted freebies. Sometimes the pressure is implied. Travel writers will not be told to write good things about a resort. But the publicists who arranged the free trip may ask to see tear sheets of the stories the writers produce. Travel writers understand that if their stories do not satisfy the people arranging the free trips, they won't be invited again.

  A few organizations are more up front about what they expect when they give the media a freebie. Disneyland provides transportation for radio and TV shows to do live remotes from the park in California. John McClintock, supervisor of publicity, said Disney expects a puff piece. "That will be a deal," he said. "No one is expecting objective reporting from that. That is a promotional relationship."[5]

  Movie critics can also feel pressure. Unlike theater critics who buy opening-night tickets, movie critics often attend special screenings so they can write their reviews before the movie opens to the public. These special screenings have become a weapon some studios use to get favorable reviews. If critics have panned previous movies by the studio, they may be banned from the special screening, meaning their reviews will appear after the movie opens. Even well-known critics Roger Ebert and Gene Siskel were excluded from a 20th Century Fox screening after they gave two thumbs down to another Fox release. Syndicated and free-lance reviewers are most susceptible to this pressure. If they can't get their reviews to newspapers on time, the papers may begin to buy reviews from someone who can.[6]

  Some publicists play even harder ball. Sony made it very clear to Jeremy Horwitz that it was not happy with an article he wrote for *Intelligent Gamer* about a Sony video game called Crash Bandicoot. "I personally was yelled at over the phone by [a Sony public relations person] who made it clear to us we would not be receiving copies of Crash, and potentially other Sony products," he told *Columbia Journalism Review*. Similarly, Sony officials also did not hesitate to call the office of Andy Pargh, who is a free-lance writer and the Gadget Guru on NBC's *Today*. Sony had provided Pargh with one of its digital cameras. But when Pargh reviewed digital cameras for *USA Today*, the review made no mention of Sony. Sony wanted to know why. Pargh's assistants explained that the newspaper had edited out the reference for space without telling them.[7]

Different Rules for Different Towns?

Some journalists in smaller cities believe the rules ought to be different for them. James Lowman, who spent four years as a one-person news bureau in two small communities for the Elmira, N.Y., *Star-Gazette,* said he believes it is permissible to accept "lunches, Cokes, beers and so on from sources" in rural settings, where "a different set of ethics" is at work. "You have to remember that the person offering the treat has a set of ethics, too," Lowman said. "The moment you turn him down, you are questioning his own ethics. It hurts people for the reporter to turn the treat down. People are grossly offended by that in a small community."

George Osgood Jr., who covered another small town for the Elmira paper, noted that people in small communities "know and trust each other, for the most part, and neighborliness gets more than just lip service." He claimed that turning down the gift of homemade bread by a public official's family may make it seem the reporter is "too 'big-headed' to accept simple friendship and too set in his city ways to understand rural hospitality."[8]

Lowman and Osgood argue that what might be seen as a freebie in an urban journalism setting is often a friendly gesture in a small town. Some journalists in big cities believe they too should be treated differently. One reporter who left a small-city newspaper for the *Chicago Tribune* was surprised when her editor suggested that she accept freebies. The editor contended that it was all right in Chicago because it is such a sophisticated city. The *Tribune*'s written code of ethics does not make this distinction.

Financial Entanglements

Philadelphia once was home to the Pen and Pencil Club, a drinking and social organization popular with local journalists. One of the club's irreverent acts was the creation of the Harry J. Karafin Award to memorialize the city's worst journalist. Karafin was a reporter who was fired by *The Philadelphia Inquirer* in 1967 after *Philadelphia Magazine* exposed how he used sources and his access to the news columns of the *Inquirer* to build up his public-relations sideline. Karafin would prey on shady businesses under investigation by some legal agency or other and get them to buy his services. Then he would turn the publicity faucets on or off in the *Inquirer* to suit his clients. He died while serving time in prison for blackmail after his exploits were exposed by a local magazine, not by the *Inquirer,* then owned by Walter Annenberg.[9]

If the Karafin award had existed in the 1980s, R. Foster Winans, a *Wall Street Journal* reporter, would have no doubt won it. At his trial on charges of securities fraud, Winans admitted that he had leaked information to a couple of hungry stockbrokers about what was to be published in the *Journal*'s "Heard on the Street" column, which Winans wrote. The stockbrokers then bought or sold the stocks they thought would be affected by what the columns stated. These transactions earned them a profit of about $700,000, of which Winans and his accomplice, David Carpenter, received only $30,000.

The *Journal,* which has for years had one of the strongest conflict-of-interest policies in the news business, fired Winans when it first heard he was under investigation. The paper printed an editorial that explained that leaking market-sensitive information was specifically prohibited by its policies. The credibility of the newspaper "could not be long sustained if readers come to believe that our articles are tainted by some hidden agenda other than informing the public," the editorial stated.[10]

One effect of the Winans episode is that many newspapers began to adopt very tough standards, especially for business writers. Most newspapers require business writers to check with editors before they buy stocks to reduce the chance of a conflict of interest, and some news outlets, like CNBC, prohibit business journalists from buying and trading stocks. The *St. Petersburg Times* fired a business writer who covered banking when it was discovered that he was short-selling bank stocks. (Short-selling is a financial move in which the investor is betting the price of the stock will go down.) Then, two days later, the editor who fired the business writer was himself fired when he acknowledged that some of the money in his retirement account was invested in a mutual fund that had bought stock in a bank-holding company.

Many in journalism circles were surprised at the severity of punishment. There was no indication that the reporter who covered Florida banking was planning to write anything that might affect the price of his stock in a West Coast bank. And the editor's mutual fund bought and sold stocks without advance notice to its shareholders. Karen Rothmyer, then a business journalism professor at Columbia University, said the firing of the editor "begins to get into the realm of the absurd."[11]

However, many thought the *Palm Beach (Fla.) Post* was too lax when it suspended for a week a business reporter who lobbied his colleagues to write praiseworthy stories about a gun-lock company. The reporter had invested in the company and maintained a Web page that compared the company's CEO to Jonas Salk, the inventor of the polio vaccine.[12]

Outside Jobs

Moonlighting, or holding down a second full- or part-time job, has become common in modern society. Other than possible damage to health, moonlighting seems to present few problems to most of its participants. But if you are a reporter, you need to be careful when selecting that second job. Writing a book is probably acceptable and, depending on the topic, may even be encouraged by your editors. It might make you some money and bring credit to you and your news organization. Before you write an article for a national magazine, you'd better get permission from your editor. But watch out if you want to write a promotional booklet for a local land developer. It could get you fired. Many news organizations have taken a dim view of outside jobs and activities that might cause the public to smell a conflict of interest.

Typical of their policies is the one at *The Boston Globe*. The *Globe* refused permission to a photographer who wanted to be the backup to the Boston Red Sox baseball team's official photographer. His role would have been to shoot pictures for the Red Sox yearbook, score cards and promotional materials. *Globe* editors also asked for the resignation of a political columnist when the paper learned that he was working part-time for two companies—doing public relations for a food brokerage firm and working as a news writer for a TV station.[13]

Similarly, an investigative reporter and the Hackensack, N.J., *Record* parted company after the newspaper learned that he was combining his reporting job with his outside job. He used his newspaper's resources to track down motor vehicle records and the like for clients of his private-eye company, Dig Dirt Investigations.[14]

TV journalists also have run into problems with conflicts of interest. When Bill Williams was news anchor for WBIR-TV in Knoxville, he received talent fees and expenses for work he did on a documentary for the Tennessee Valley Authority. He then used pieces of the documentary in a series on water quality that he did for his station. Neither Williams nor his news director saw anything wrong with Williams working for the TVA. However, a member of the SPJ ethics committee said he was appalled by the "obvious conflict of interest" in Williams' accepting money from a news source.[15]

Jim Warren, the Washington bureau chief of the *Chicago Tribune*, castigated journalists who accepted fees to speak to organizations they were covering. Warren reported that both ABC's Cokie Roberts and CBS's Lesley Stahl collected $20,000 from health insurance groups. At the time, the Clinton administration was pushing for a national health care plan, which most of the insurance industry opposed. "On this money stuff, I don't think there is much gray area," Warren said. "You don't enter into business relationships with anybody you might cover or whose issue you might cover. I mean, you just don't do it. I had a Cokie item a few months ago—she and her husband [also a reporter] took $45,000 from a bank in Chicago. That's indefensible; it's outrageous."[16] After Warren wrote a series of columns detailing the speaking fees paid to top journalists, many news organizations banned the practice.

Traditionally, most newspaper and newsmagazine journalists avoid anything to do with their own organizations' advertising departments in deference to long-standing rules about keeping news and advertising separate. But today, it is becoming more common for journalists to produce special sections developed for advertisers. Reporters may be asked to write puff pieces for yearly "progress" sections that highlight local businesses, and advertising departments may enlist copy editors to prepare sections with stories and photographs provided by advertisers. Often the journalists ask that their bylines not be used on such stories.

It's harder for broadcast journalists to hide their identities. At some local radio and TV stations, making commercials, even testimonials, is sometimes part of the job of their news staffs. This may add to the income of newscasters and their stations, but it certainly detracts from their credibility as reporters and presenters of the news. Some TV newspeople get around this problem by having split personalities. During the 1980s, Glenn Rinker was recognizable throughout most of the nation as the happy shopper in TV ads for a furniture store chain. But not in Orlando, Fla., where he was the serious-minded news anchor for the CBS affiliate. Rinker had a clause written in his contract with the advertising agency that prohibited it from showing his ads in Central Florida.

Of course, a great many broadcast journalists will not do advertisements. Carol Marin, a former anchor at then top-rated WMAQ in Chicago, refused to mix news and advertising. She was suspended for three days when she refused to read the names of two supermarkets that were passing out fire-prevention pamphlets. "I would not read the names of those stores so people could pick up a pamphlet and, maybe, buy a loaf of bread while they're there," she said.[17] Marin later quit the station when it hired Jerry Springer, host of a tabloid TV talk show, as a commentator.

The news departments at ABC, CBS and NBC have long had rules against full-time journalists doing ads. CNN followed suit after news executives discovered that correspondent Jonathan Karl was to be featured in advertisements for Visa credit cards. Visa was asked to drop the ad campaign, which was already scheduled to appear in several magazines.[18]

CNN executives also have restrictions on news personnel appearing in the movies. The decision came after a dozen CNN correspondents and anchors appeared in the science fiction movie *Contact*. CNN refused to allow its logo or personnel to appear in the movie *Deep Impact*. But MSNBC jumped at the chance of having its logo—but no reporters—in the film. ABC, CBS and NBC already had rules limiting the kind of roles that news personnel could play in motion pictures or TV programs.

Some argue that these rules are excessive: Readers and viewers recognize fiction and understand when reporters are simply acting. Nevertheless, others believe that it undermines the journalistic ideal that the profession is a public trust. Appearing in a movie "is good for individual journalists and bad for the profession," said Robert Lichter, president of the Center for Media and Public Affairs. "It gradually is draining it of any sense of higher purpose, which journalists are quick to claim for themselves when they talk about their right to know." An ABC official agreed: "We don't feel it's wise to create a blurring of the lines."[19]

Contests and News Judgment

Contests can be good ideas. An organization promotes a contest for reporting or editorial writing and lines up some respected editors and journalism professors as judges. Often the winners' work is reprinted and can serve as a model for other journalists, thus improving the craft. Many contests—the Pulitzers, SPJ Awards of Merit, the Society of Newspaper Design awards, and many regional contests sponsored by journalism groups—have achieved that goal.

However, some contests do not serve any altruistic purpose. The sponsors of these contests are trying to get their message to appear free in as many newspapers as possible. They hope that by announcing a contest for the best story that promotes whatever they want promoted and by promising a big cash prize, they can lure journalists into writing stories favorable to their causes. For example, the National Association of Realtors offered a cash prize for "articles dealing with real estate development, property tax relief, etc."[20]

Other contests define themselves even more directly. South Carolina sponsored a contest "for articles promoting travel in South Carolina," and the Mexican National Tourist Council wanted articles "that promote travel to Mexico." But whether or not a contest is this blatant, it often isn't difficult to guess the kinds of articles that are likely to win. Paul Poorman, former editor of the *Akron (Ohio) Beacon Journal,* said he doubted that an exposé on the use of faulty concrete in interstate highway construction was likely to win a contest sponsored by the National Highway Contractors' Association and the Cement Institute.[21]

The Milwaukee Journal did not have awards in mind when it assigned reporter Don Bluhm to check out major Mexican resorts after the 1985 Mexico City earthquake. But two months after Bluhm's articles were published, a flyer came to his desk announcing a contest to reward "outstanding press reports abroad which aided in clarifying the image of Mexico" after the quake. Bluhm saw nothing in the newspaper's 10-year-old policy about contests to keep him from entering. So he did, and he won a $12,500 second prize. The size of the award concerned Bluhm and his editors: At that time Pulitzer Prize winners got $1,000. His editors discovered that the contest was sponsored by Mexico's department of tourism, two travel organizations and a chain of Mexican hotels. The editors concluded that accepting the prize "in a contest intended to promote tourism in Mexico gives the appearance of a conflict of interest that compromises the newspaper's credibility." Bluhm agreed with the editors and returned the money.[22]

Many large newspapers now have written rules that limit the kinds of contests staff members can enter. And SPJ has also adopted guidelines for determining which contests fall within the society's code of ethics. SPJ rejects contests that "state or imply favorable treatment of a cause or subject." Approved contests should have judging panels that are "dominated by respected journalists or journalism educators." Cash awards should be accepted only if contests are wholly sponsored by professional journalism organizations, journalism foundations or universities.[23]

Improving the Profession

Perhaps of all the ethical concerns raised in this book, the ban on freebies seems the least fair. At many news outlets, publishers and station managers aren't bound by the rule. And upper-echelon editors and news directors usually make enough money that a ban on freebies is rarely a hardship for them.

That leaves two groups who are most tempted by freebies. One is the veteran moocher. We all know these people. They are always on the take. They never pick up the check; they never buy a round. If they are covering an event that offers freebies, they try to take two. And while we may be amused by their cheapness, it's a trait we don't respect. And neither does the public. They paint a tawdry picture of the profession.

The other group to whom freebies have appeal consists of young journalists and journalists at news organizations with ridiculously low pay. A few tickets to an amusement park—let alone a free vacation—can become a big deal when your salary is at or below the poverty line. Media owners who place news professionals in this quandary are doing the profession a disservice.

Yet all journalists must recognize that freebies aren't gifts. They are efforts to influence news decisions. The SPJ Code of Ethics states it very clearly: "Journalists should refuse gifts, favors, fees, free travel and special treatment, and shun secondary employment, political involvement, public office and service in community organizations if they compromise journalistic integrity." Turning down freebies is a small price to pay to help the profession regain the respect it must have.

Chapter 1

1. The "King Hog" series was written by Melanie Sill, Pat Stith and Joby Warrick. It ran in *The News & Observer*, Feb. 19 to Feb. 28, 1995. It is on the Internet at www.pulitzer.org. For the aftermath, see Craig Whitlock, "N&O Hog Series Takes Top Pulitzer; Public Service Prize Rewards Stories on Pork Industry," *The News & Observer*, April 10, 1996, p. A1.

2. Wm. David Sloan, James G. Stovall and James D. Startt, eds., *The Media in America: A History*, Worthington, Ohio: Publishing Horizons, 1989, p. 104. It has an interesting section on Colonial editors, pp. 99–120.

3. Interview with Gene Goodwin, Feb. 10, 1986.

4. The first is reported by John W.C. Johnstone, Edward J. Slawski and William W. Bowman in *The News People: A Sociological Profile of American Journalists and Their Work*, Urbana: University of Illinois Press, 1976. David H. Weaver and G. Cleveland Wilhoit have replicated and expanded on their research three times. See their books *The American Journalist: A Portrait of U.S. News People and Their Work*,

Bloomington: Indiana University Press, first edition, 1986, and second edition, 1991, and *The American Journalist in the 1990s: U.S. News People at the End of an Era*, Mahwah, N.J.: Lawrence Erlbaum Associates, 1996.

5. Times Mirror survey in 1989 cited by Peter Brown, "Squires Is Right—We Are out of Touch with Voters and Their Concerns," *ASNE Bulletin*, November 1992, p. 8.

6. *The People & The Press*, Los Angeles: Times Mirror, 1986.

7. David Shaw, "Poll Delivers Bad News to the Media," *Los Angeles Times*, March 31, 1993, p. A16.

8. "How Are We Doing?" *Columbia Journalism Review*, January/February 1992, p. 15.

9. AP, "Wary of the Media's Messengers," *The Miami Herald*, Dec. 14, 1996.

10. George Garneau, "Press Freedom in Deep Trouble," *Editor & Publisher*, April 20, 1991, p. 11. Wyatt's report is titled "Free Expression and the American Public" and was commissioned by the American Society of Newspaper Editors.

11. David Shaw, "Media: High Ratings Are Tempered," *Los Angeles Times*,

Aug. 11, 1985. Also see William
Schneider and I.A. Lewis, "Views on
the News," *Public Opinion,*
August/September 1985, pp. 6–11,
58–59.

12. Statistics were presented during the
"Credibility Matters" section on
PBS's *NewsHour,* April 7, 1997. A
transcript of the program is on the
PBS Web site.

13. Gerald Stone and John Less,
"Portrayal of Journalists on Prime
Time Television," *Journalism
Quarterly,* Winter 1990, p. 707.

14. Bill Mahon's findings in his master's
thesis at Penn State University are
cited in Chip Rowe, "Hacks on
Film," *Washington Journalism
Review,* November 1992, p. 277. A
study of the newspaper industry's efforts in the 1930s and '40s to have
journalists shown in a more favorable light can be found in Stephen
Vaughn and Bruce Evensen,
"Democracy's Guardians:
Hollywood's Portrait of Reporters,
1930–1945," *Journalism Quarterly,*
Winter 1991, pp. 829–837.

15. Debra Gersh, "Stereotyping
Journalists," *Editor & Publisher,*
Oct. 5, 1991, p. 18. The movie,
which starred Kirk Douglas, was
originally titled *Ace in the Hole* but
was reissued as *The Big Carnival.*

16. Glenn Garelik, "Stop the Presses!
Movies Blast Media. Viewers
Cheer," *The New York Times,* Jan.
31, 1993, national edition, pp. H11
and H18.

17. Eleanor Randolph, "The Other Side
of the Pen: Reporters in the News,"
*Messages: The Washington Post
Media Companion,* Boston: Allyn
and Bacon, 1991, p. 351.

Chapter 2

1. Gary A. Hogge, M.D., "You Can
Fight City Hall: Even When It's a
Newspaper," *Medical Economics,*
July 21, 1980, pp. 69–72.

2. *Problems of Journalism: Proceedings
of the ASNE 1923,* Washington,
D.C.: ASNE, pp. 39–52, 118–125.

3. Karen Schneider and Marc Gunther,
"Those Newsroom Ethics Codes,"
Columbia Journalism Review,
July/August 1985, p. 55.

4. Douglas A. Anderson and Frederic
A. Leigh, "How Newspaper Editors
and Broadcast News Directors View
Media Ethics," *Newspaper Research
Journal,* Winter/Spring 1992, p. 115.

5. Philip Meyer, *Ethical Journalism,*
New York: Longman, 1987, p. 18.

6. Clifford Christians, "Enforcing
Media Codes," *Journal of Mass
Media Ethics,* Fall/Winter 1985–86,
pp. 14–21.

7. Frank Sutherland, "Headquarters
Stays in Chicago; Quill Editor
Named," *Quill,* June 1985, p. 42.

8. Jeremy Iggers, "Journalism Ethics:
Right Name. Wrong Game?"
Newsworthy, Spring 1995.

9. Laurie A. Zenner, "Code Violations:
Codes Run Afoul of First
Amendment," *Newsworthy,* Spring
1995.

10. Mark Zieman, "Everyone Needs to
Know the Rules of the Game,"
Newsworthy, Spring 1995.

11. Interview by Gene Goodwin, Oct. 7,
1981.

12. Interview by Goodwin, March 14,
1986.

13. Jean Chance and Connie Bouchard,
"The Gainesville Slayings: A Study
in Media Responsibility and
Unnamed Sources," a paper pre-
sented at the AEJMC Southeast
Colloquium, 1993.

14. David Pritchard and Madelyn
Morgan, "Impact of Ethics Codes
on Judgments by Journalists: A
Natural Experiment," *Journalism
Quarterly,* Winter 1989, pp.
934–941.

15. "News Council Closes, Gives Files
to Minnesota," *Quill,* May 1984,
p. 44.

16. William MacPherson, "Sole
Newspaper Watchdog in U.S. Finally
Gets Some Company," *The Ottawa
Citizen,* Sept. 18, 1992, p. A11.

17. In 1992, chapters of the SPJ in
Oregon and Washington formed the
Northwest News Council and
planned to rely on volunteers to
keep it afloat. Their initial budget
was $300, compared with the well-
established Ontario Press Council's
$185,000 budget, funded by mem-
ber newspapers. The council has encountered problems getting news

media to cooperate with its investigations and has not been very active.

18. Kristin Tillotson, "Watching the Watchdog," *Star Tribune,* Nov. 2, 1996, p. 12A.

19. Martin Schram, "Bring back National News Council," *The Montgomery Advertiser,* Jan. 9, 1997, p. 15A.

20. Mike Wallace, Remarks at the 19th Annual Frank E. Gannett Lecture at the Media Studies Center, New York, N.Y., Dec. 4, 1996.

21. Tillotson.

22. John Lansing, "National News Council Would Lead to More Timid Press," *Star Tribune,* Dec. 21, 1996, p. 21A.

23. Troy Clarkson, "News Councils: Pro and Con," *Presstime,* May 1998, p. 35.

24. "Ethics Police," *American Journalism Review,* June 1993, p. 9.

25. Lou Gelfand, "Newspaper Ombudsmen Can Help to Retain Readers," *Presstime,* April 1992, p. 35.

26. Kate McKenna, "The Loneliest Job in the Newsroom," *American Journalism Review,* March 1993, pp. 41–44.

27. Interview by Goodwin, Oct. 7, 1981.

28. Richard Salant, "Ombudsmen—Worth Saving?" *Nieman Reports,* Fall 1992, p. 75.

29. Gelfand.

30. Reese Cleghorn, "Keeping Reporters Honest," Baltimore *Sun,* July 23, 1998.

31. Jerry Ceppos, "Dear Reader," *San Jose Mercury News,* June 19, 1996, p. 1.

32. Susan Paterno, "I Can Explain," *American Journalism Review,* July/August 1998.

33. Interview by Goodwin, Nov. 2, 1981.

Chapter 3

1. Information about the WCCO broadcast came from Gary Gilson, "WCCO and Northwest: Investigation of One Brought Scrutiny to the Other," *Star Tribune,* Nov. 10, 1996; "Determination 112, In the Matter of the Complaint of Northwest Airlines Against WCCO-TV, Channel 4," Minnesota News Council, Oct. 18, 1996; Kristin Tillotson, "Sweeps News Tells a Lot About Priorities," *Star Tribune,* Dec. 7, 1996, p. 10E; Kristin Tillotson, "WCCO, Northwest Have Showdown Today," *Star Tribune,* Oct. 18, 1996, p. 1B; Kristin Tillotson, "News Council Sides with NWA in Dispute over WCCO Report," *Star Tribune,* Oct. 19, 1996, p. 1A; "Northwest Case a 'Wake up Call' for TV News, Says WCCO's Shelby," *Newsworthy,* Spring 1997; John Lansing, "National News Council Would Lead to More Timid Press," *Star Tribune,* Dec. 21, 1996, p. 21A; "Wallace: Some Investigative Journalism Is Caricature," *WCCO Channel 4000 News,* May 17, 1996; "Will Ruling Have a 'Chilling Effect?'" *WCCO Channel 4000 News,* Oct. 18, 1996; "I-Team Reports on Northwest Airlines," *WCCO Channel 4000 News,* April 29, 1996; "Clash of Minnesota Titans Gets *Sixty Minutes* of Fame," *WCCO Channel 4000 News,* Nov. 14, 1996; AP, "Newspaper: Northwest Airlines Safer Than Many Carriers," *WCCO Channel 4000 News,* April 29, 1996; "Northwest Employees Defend Airline," *WCCO Channel 4000 News,* April 29, 1996; "Don't Rock the Boat," *WCCO Channel 4000 News,* April 30, 1996; "Shelby's Concluding Remarks," *WCCO Channel 4000 News,* May 1, 1996; "Newspaper Ad Refutes Broadcast," *WCCO Channel 4000 News,* May 5, 1996; "The Oversights Uncovered by I-Team," WCCO Channel 4000 News, April 29, 1996; and "I-Team: The Fall-out from Both Sides," April 30, 1996.

2. Wm. David Sloan, James G. Stovall and James D. Startt, eds., *The Media in America: A History,* Worthington, Ohio: Publishing Horizons, 1989, p. 71.

3. Theodore Peterson, "The Social Responsibility Theory of the Press," in *Four Theories of the Press,* edited by Fred Siebert, Theodore Peterson

and Wilbur Schramm, Urbana: University of Illinois Press, 1956 (paperback edition, 1973), p. 88.

4. Interview by Gene Goodwin, Oct. 8, 1981.

5. David Halberstam, *The Powers That Be*. New York: Knopf, 1979, p. 194.

6. Halberstam, p. 446.

7. Daniel C. Hallin, "Whose Campaign Is It, Anyway?" *Columbia Journalism Review*, January/February 1991, p. 44. Details of the incident are taken from his article.

8. Leon Sigal, *Reporters and Officials*, Lexington: Lexington Books, 1973.

9. Quoted in James Fallows, *Breaking the News: How the Media Undermine American Democracy*, New York: Pantheon Books, 1996, p. 246.

10. Quoted by Frank Bruni, "The Partial-Truth Abortion Fight," *The New York Times*, March 9, 1997, p. E3.

11. The headlines appeared in the Feb. 13, 1998, editions of the papers.

12. *A Free and Responsible Press: Report of the Commission on Freedom of the Press*. Chicago: University of Chicago Press, 1947 (midway reprint, 1974), pp. 20–29. Also see Peterson, pp. 73–104.

13. John Vivian, *The Media of Mass Communication*, Boston: Allyn and Bacon, 1991, p. 338.

14. Peterson.

15. Chuck Taylor, "Where Fact Meets Friction," *The Seattle Times*, June 6, 1997. Suarez was speaking to the National Association of Hispanic Journalists meeting in Seattle.

16. See Lawrie Mifflin, "Crime Falls, but Not on TV," *The New York Times*, June 6, 1997, sec. 4, p. 4; and Mark Fitzgerald, "Local TV News Lacks Substance," *E&P Interactive*, May 24, 1997.

17. Remarks from "Journalists, Violence and the News," a workshop sponsored by the Minnesota News Council and Minnesota Public Radio, May 1996, reprinted in Rhonda Hillberry, "Journalists, Violence and the News," *Newsworthy*, Summer 1996.

18. Fitzgerald.

19. Information about KVUE came from Janet Evans-Ferkin, "KVUE-TV Experiments with Crime Coverage," *Communicator*, May 1996, p. 23–26; Michelle Kemkes, "'If It Bleeds, It Leads,' Isn't the Motto at KVUE-TV," *Newsworthy*, Summer 1996; and Hillberry.

20. Jeffrey Weiss, "Crime Coverage Arrested," *The Dallas Morning News*, Dec. 22, 1996, p. 1A.

21. Robert P. Laurence, "KNSD Hires News Executive," *The San Diego Union-Tribune*, July 15, 1998.

22. Nigel Wade, "Why One Paper Kept Shootings off Page 1," *Star Tribune*, May 28, 1998.

23. References to Shaw in this section are from David Shaw, "The Pride and Perils of Fast Reporting," *Los Angeles Times*, Aug. 5, 1998, "New Media Playing Field Opens Way to More Errors," *Los Angeles Times*, Aug. 6, 1998, and "Letting Rivals Influence News Decisions Can Be Tricky," *Los Angeles Times*, Aug. 6, 1998.

24. Information taken from "Determination 112"; Gilson; and AP.

25. David Shaw, "How Media Gives Stories Same 'Spin,'" *Los Angeles Times*, Aug. 25, 1989, p. A1.

26. Interview by Goodwin, April 8, 1981.

27. John C. Merrill, *Journalism Ethics: Philosophical Foundations for News Media*, New York: St. Martin's Press, 1997.

28. Judith Lichtenberg, "In Defense of Objectivity," in *Mass Media and Society*, edited by James Curran and Michael Guervitch, London: Edward Arnold, 1991, pp. 216–231.

29. From her remarks in the 13th annual Otis Chandler lecture at the University of Southern California School of Journalism, quoted in M.L. Stein, "Here We Go Again!" *Editor & Publisher*, Nov. 28, 1992, p. 11.

30. Andy Newman, "Is It Opinion, or Is It Expertise?" *American Journalism Review*, March 1993, pp. 12–13.

31. Carl Sessions Stepp, "Ten Ways to Keep Your Readers," *American Journalism Review*, April 1993, p. 23.

32. Jeffrey Katz, "Tilt?" *Washington Journalism Review,* February 1993, p. 26.

33. An interesting account of the news coverage of the early medical findings about cancer and tobacco can be found in Karen Miller, "Smoking up a Storm," *Journalism Monographs,* December 1992.

34. Information in this section was drawn from Christiane Amanpour, "Television's Role in Foreign Policy," *Quill,* April 1996, pp. 16–17; and Sherry Ricchiardi, "Over the Line?" *American Journalism Review,* September 1996, pp. 24–31.

Chapter 4

1. The original story was "Dean Probes Sexism Issue," *Calgary Herald,* Nov. 15, 1991, p. B1. The correction was printed the next day. The newspaper's ombudsman, Jim Stott, discussed the incident in "More Flexible Error Correction Policy Would Serve All," *Calgary Herald,* Dec. 8, 1991, p. A7.

2. Michael Singletary and Richard Lipsky, "Accuracy in Local TV News," *Journalism Quarterly,* Summer 1977, pp. 363–364.

3. George Kennedy, "Newspaper Accuracy: A New Approach," *Newspaper Research Journal,* Winter 1994, pp. 55–62.

4. "Darts and Laurels," *Columbia Journalism Review,* March/May 1993, p. 22.

5. Rolf Rykken, "New Tactics Mark the Push for Accuracy," *Presstime,* July 1991, pp. 6–8.

6. Alicia C. Shepard, "To Err Is Human, to Correct Divine," *American Journalism Review,* June 1998, pp. 50–57.

7. Nancy Davis, "Views from City Hall," *Presstime,* August 1998, p. 29.

8. Reprinted in "The Lower Case," *Columbia Journalism Review,* November/December 1990, p. 65.

9. Dennis Foley, "Speed Can Spell Trouble at Newspaper," *The Orange County (Calif.) Register,* July 12, 1998, p. B4.

10. "Errors in Print a Firing Offense?" *News Photographer,* April 1998, p. 4.

11. Richard P. Cunningham, "Gov. Lamm and the 'Duty to Die,'" *Editor & Publisher,* May 19, 1986, p. 7.

12. H.L. Mencken, *Promises: Sixth Series,* New York: Knopf, 1927, p. 15.

13. Deborah Potter, "Competence in the Newsroom," *Poynter Report,* Spring 1998, p. 5.

14. Geneva Overholser, "Reading into What You Read," *The Washington Post,* June 2, 1996.

15. "F.Y.I." *Washington Journalism Review,* January/February 1993, p. 13.

16. Cortland Anderson, remarks to APME Convention, Toronto, Oct. 21, 1981.

17. Craig Branson, "Covering Government in a Time of Change," *The American Editor,* June 1997.

18. Business Week, Nov. 11, 1996.

19. Sandra Mims Rowe's comments were taken from her remarks at the Asian American Journalists conference in Boston, Aug. 15, 1997, and from "Journalism Values in an Era of Change," a speech to the Poynter Institute Conference in New York, Feb. 14–16, 1996.

20. Interview by Gene Goodwin, Nov. 25, 1980.

21. Seymour Topping, "'Expert Journalism' Requires a Broad Education," *ASNE Bulletin,* November 1992, p. 2.

22. David Shaw, "New Media Playing Field Opens Way to More Errors," *Los Angeles Times,* Aug. 6, 1998.

23. Smith's and Sesno's comments were made on *The NewsHour with Jim Lehrer,* Jan. 29, 1998.

24. Information taken from reports on the CNN Web site, July 2, 1998.

25. Eleanor Randolph, "The Other Side of the Pen," *Messages: The Washington Post Media Companion,* Boston: Allyn and Bacon, 1991, p. 351.

26. Alicia C. Shepard, "Show and Print," *American Journalism Review,* March 1996, pp. 40–44.

27. Interview by author, Sept. 10, 1998.

28. Rykken, pp. 6–8.
29. Jay Matthews, "When in Doubt, Read It Back," *Washington Journalism Review,* September 1985, pp. 33–35.
30. Steve Weinberg, "So What's Wrong with Pre-Publication Review?" *Quill,* May 1990, p. 27.
31. David Armstrong, "Mercury News Lets Executives See Reporter's Draft," *San Francisco Examiner,* Sept. 3, 1998.
32. Interview by author.
33. Miriam Pepper, "To Identify or Not, a Tough Question for Papers," *The Star,* April 4, 1998.
34. "*Newsweek* Recalling Issue on Kids from Newsstands," *The Orlando Sentinel,* May 6, 1997, p. A24.
35. Lawrence K. Grossman, "To Err Is Human, to *Admit* It Divine," *Columbia Journalism Review,* March/April 1997, p. 16; and Dorothy Giobbe, "Better Late Than Never," *E&P Interactive,* June 1, 1996.
36. "Mercury News Editor Admits Weakness in Series," *San Francisco Chronicle,* May 12, 1997, p. A2.
37. Rykken, p. 6.
38. Howard Kurtz, "Why the Press Is Always Right," *Columbia Journalism Review,* May/June 1993, pp. 34–35.
39. Grossman, p. 16.
40. "TV News: Truth? Consequences?" *Newsworthy,* Summer 1993.
41. Michael Cremedas, "Corrections Policies in Local Television News: A Survey," *Journalism Quarterly,* Spring 1992, pp. 166–172.
42. Grossman, p. 16.
43. Ralph Holsinger, *Media Law,* New York: Random House, 1987, p. 119.
44. Stott.
45. Quoted in Richard Cunningham, "Speak Softly and Carry an Ombudsman," *Quill,* April 1992, p. 4.

Chapter 5
1. Tamala M. Edwards, "Not the Boys on the Bus," *Media Studies Forum,* Winter 1997.
2. Keith Woods, "Facing Race," *Presstime,* October 1996, p. 61.
3. Interview by author.

4. Roland Wolseley, *The Black Press, U.S.A.,* Ames: Iowa State University Press, 1990, pp. 68–69.
5. Brent Staples, "Citizen Sengstacke," *The New York Times Magazine,* Jan. 4, 1998, pp. 27–28.
6. Ed Morales, "Brown Out: Searching for the Missing Latinos in the Media," *The Village Voice,* July 30, 1996, p. 24.
7. Rick Marks, "A Community Connection," *Communicator,* August 1996, pp. 22–24. Spanish station ratings are also from this article.
8. Myriam Marquez, "In Any Language, the News Media Can Do Better for Hispanics," *The Orlando Sentinel,* Sept. 12, 1997, p. A14.
9. "Newsroom Diversity Numbers: Flat," *Presstime,* May 1997, p. 72.
10. Erika D. Peterman, "For Journalists of Color: Too Little, Too Late," *St. Petersburg Times,* July 15, 1997.
11. Michele Vernon-Chesley, "On Adding Color," *Presstime,* cover story supplement, July 1996, pp. 8–9.
12. "Pioneer Profile: Claudia Elisa Ortega," *Presstime,* cover story supplement, July 1996, p. 6.
13. "APME Newsroom Diversity Study," MORI Research, September 1996. Also see Jodi B. Cohen, "Race Colors Newsroom Views," *Editor & Publisher,* Nov. 2, 1996.
14. Mark Fitzgerald, "Black Columnists, 'White' Papers," *Editor & Publisher*, Sept. 7, 1996.
15. Vernon Stone, "Minorities and Women in Television News," printed on the Web site of the School of Journalism at the University of Missouri. Data concerning minorities and women in broadcast newsrooms are taken from this site.
16. Peterman.
17. Fitzgerald.
18. "Diversity Dilemmas," *Columbia Journalism Review,* October 1993, pp. 19–20.
19. Sherri Owens, "Image Problem," *Black Family Today,* December/January 1996, p. 39.
20. William McGowan, "The Other Side of the Rainbow," *Columbia Journalism Review,* November/December 1993, pp. 53–57.

21. David H. Weaver and G. Cleveland Wilhoit, *The American Journalist in the 1990s: U.S. News People at the End of an Era,* Mahwah, N.J.: Lawrence Erlbaum Associates, 1996.

22. "Power of the Press," *Working Woman,* October 1991, p. 81.

23. Quoted by Christi Harlan, *Quill,* July/August 1995, p. 40.

24. Mark Jurkowitz, "Editors of Invention," *The Boston Globe,* Aug. 26, 1998, p. D1.

25. Alicia C. Shepard, "A Bureau's 'Woman Problem,'" *American Journalism Review,* December 1997, p. 27.

26. See Mary Schmitt, "Women Sportswriters—Business as Usual," *Media Studies Journal,* Spring 1997; Jennifer Frey, "A Look Inside the Women's Locker Room," *The Washington Post,* July 27, 1977, p. D11; and Virginia Watson-Rouslin, "The Men's Room," *Quill,* January 1987, pp. 20–24.

27. Mark Fitzgerald, "Blacks Most Upset by News Coverage," *Editor & Publisher,* Aug. 6, 1994, p. 15.

28. Carolyn Terry, "Hispanic Links Publisher Gives Latinos a Voice," *Presstime,* April 1995, p. 25.

29. Fitzgerald, "Blacks Most Upset by News Coverage."

30. Charlie Huisking, "*Journalists:* Media Not Tuned in to Blacks," *Sarasota Herald-Tribune,* Oct. 26, 1996, p. 11A.

31. David Shaw, "Coloring the News," *A Los Angeles Times* report reprinted in *Quill,* May 1991, pp. 15–23.

32. Howard Kurtz, "TV Viewers Often Assume Suspects Are Black," *The Washington Post,* April 28, 1997, p. C1.

33. Peterman.

34. Lynn Feigenbaum, "When Photos Tell a Different Story from Reality," *The Virginian-Pilot,* May 4, 1997, p. J5.

35. Peter Downs, "Imbalanced Coverage of Victims Decried," *The St. Louis Journalism Review,* June 1995, p. 1.

36. Gilbert Bailon, "Immigration Issues Provoke Poor Reporting by the Press," *ASNE Bulletin,* March 1995, pp. 42–43.

37. Howard Kurtz, "Bosses' Words Irk Journalists," *The Washington Post,* May 21, 1998, p. C1.

38. Interview of Vernon-Chesley by Michelle Martinez, Fall 1997.

39. Alicia Shepard, "Blowing up the Wall," *American Journalism Review,* December 1997, p. 26.

40. Peterman.

41. Potter's remarks can be found on the Poynter Institute's Web page at www.poynter.org.

42. Carolyn Terry, "Look in to Reach out," *Presstime,* April 1993, pp. 49–51.

43. Shaw, p. 19.

Chapter 6

1. Glass' fabrications were widely reported, including Ann Reily Dodd, "How a Writer Fooled His Readers," *Columbia Journalism Review,* July/August 1998, pp. 14–15; and Howard Kurtz, "*New Republic* Fires Writer over 'Hoax,'" *The Washington Post,* May 11, 1998, p. D1; "At *New Republic,* the Agony of Deceit," *The Washington Post,* June 12, 1998, p. B1, and "*George*'s Sorry Statement of Affairs," *The Washington Post,* June 8, 1998, p. D1.

2. Mark Jurkowitz, "Boston Globe Columnist Resigns After Admitting Fabrications," *The Boston Globe,* June 19, 1998; AP, "Globe Details Scrutiny, Dismissal of Columnist," *Los Angeles Times,* June 21, 1998; and Patricia Smith, "A Note of Apology," *The Boston Globe,* June 19, 1998.

3. Interview by Gene Goodwin, Oct. 8, 1981.

4. Jessica Savitch, *Anchorwoman,* New York: G.P. Putnam's Sons, 1982, pp. 172–173.

5. Ellen Warren, "The Poetic Columnist Who Fell from Grace," *Chicago Tribune,* Aug. 12, 1998; and Lamar B. Graham, "An Unbelievably Good Story," *Boston Magazine,* August 1991.

6. Janet Cooke, "Jimmy's World," *The Washington Post,* Sept. 28, 1980.

7. *After Jimmy's World,* report by the National News Council, New York, 1981, pp. 16–22.
8. William Green, "The Confession," *The Washington Post,* April 19, 1981.
9. NBC's *Today,* Feb. 1 and 2, 1982; AP, "She Knew She'd Be Caught After Winning Pulitzer," *Leesburg (Fla.) Commercial,* Feb. 2, 1982.
10. Gail Sheehy, "Wide Open City/Part 1: The New Breed," *New York,* July 26, 1971, pp. 22–25, and "Wide Open City/Part II: Redpants and Sugarman," *New York,* Aug. 2, 1971, pp. 26–36.
11. For two views on Woodward's books, see Stephen Banker, "In Bob We Trust," *Washington Journalism Review,* June 1991, p. 33; and Bill Monroe, "Woodward Reporting Yields Inside Grit," *Washington Journalism Review,* July/August 1991, p. 6.
12. Interview by Goodwin, June 4, 1981.
13. Tal Sanit, "Stand and Deliver," *Columbia Journalism Review,* July/August 1992, pp. 15–16.
14. "Darts & Laurels," *Columbia Journalism Review,* March/April 1997, p. 21.
15. *Dateline NBC,* Feb. 9, 1993. A detailed account of NBC's story can be found in "TV's Credibility Crunch," *The Washington Post National Weekly Edition,* March 8–14, 1993, p. 6.
16. Jonathan Adler, "On the Ropes at NBC News," *Newsweek,* March 8, 1993.
17. Interview by Goodwin, Nov. 10, 1981.
18. "2 Plead Guilty to Buying Beer for Teens for TV Story," *The Orlando Sentinel,* Feb. 24, 1993, p. A6; and "TV News Pair Get Jail Time for Buying Beer for Teens," *The Orlando Sentinel,* March 24, 1993, p. A10.
19. UPI, "TV Reporter on Trial for Staging Dog Fights," July 23, 1991, and "Reporter Convicted in Pit Bull Trial," Aug. 7, 1991.
20. Quoted by John Leo, "Image-Based Truth as Reality: No Apology Necessary, or Is It?" *The Orlando Sentinel,* March 3, 1993, p. A19.
21. David Shaw, "Poll Delivers Bad News to the Media," *Los Angeles Times,* March 31, 1993, p. A16.
22. Interviews by Goodwin of Lovelady and *Inquirer* executive editor Eugene L. Roberts Jr., May 28, Sept. 15, and Sept. 16, 1981.
23. Leslie Miller, "Globe Columnist Asked to Resign," *The Boston Globe,* Aug. 5, 1998.
24. Roy Peter Clark, "The Unoriginal Sin: How Plagiarism Poisons the Press," *Washington Journalism Review,* March 1983, pp. 43–47.
25. Larry Tye, "Plagiarism Seen as Common but Little Discussed," *The Boston Globe,* July 16, 1991, metro section, p. 1.
26. Tye.
27. Alicia C. Shepard, "Does Radio News Rip Off Newspapers," *American Journalism Review,* September 1994, pp. 15–16.
28. Mark Fitzgerald, "*Sun-Times* Drops Columnist over Plagiarism," *Editor & Publisher,* June 27, 1990, p. 17.
29. James Cox, "A Plague of Plagiarism," *USA Today,* July 25, 1991, p. 1B.
30. Eleanor Randolph, "Plagiarism and News," in *Messages: The Washington Post Media Companion,* Boston: Allyn and Bacon, 1991, p. 344.
31. Steve Polilli, "More Plagiarism Incidents Plague Texas Daily," *Editor & Publisher,* Jan. 19, 1992, p. 11.
32. William Henry III, "Recycling the News," *Time,* July 29, 1991, p. 59.
33. Randolph, p. 345.
34. Kevin McManus, "The, Uh, Quotation Quandary," *Columbia Journalism Review,* May/June 1990, pp. 54–56.
35. Jacques Leslie, "The Pros and Cons of Cleaning up Quotes," *Washington Journalism Review,* May 1986, pp. 44–46.
36. Quoted by McManus, p. 54.
37. John Drury, "Should Reporter Quote What They Say, or What They Mean? *Solutions Today for Ethics Problems Tomorrow,* Chicago: SPJ, October 1989, pp. 11 and 21.

38. Ronald Turovsky, "Did He Really Say That?" *Columbia Journalism Review,* July/August 1980.

39. Ron Lovell, "Wrong Way Stretch: Scoops Vanish, Credibility Remains—As One Reporter Learned After Re-Creating Quotes," *Washington Journalism Review,* May 1986, pp. 44–46.

40. Details of the Malcolm case were widely reported. See "The Jeff and Janet Show," *Newsweek,* May 31, 1993, p. 59.

41. The Malcolm case was also reported in "Two Media Cases Remanded," *Presstime,* July 1991, p. 48; "The Malcolm Case," *Columbia Journalism Review,* May/June 1990, p. 56; "Ruling Slices into Libel Defenses," *Presstime,* June 1992, p. 52; and Lyle Denniston, "New Yorker Libel Case Threatens the Press," *Washington Journalism Review,* March 1991, p. 54.

42. AP, "Court Rejects Appeal in Libel Case Against Writer, Magazine," *The Fresno Bee,* June 6, 1996, p. B4.

43. David Shaw, "The Press and Sex: Why Editors Lean to Dots, Dashes, Euphemisms," *Los Angeles Times,* Aug. 19, 1991, p. A19.

44. Mitchell Stephens and Eliot Frankel, "All the Obscenity That's Fit to Print," *Washington Journalism Review,* April 1981, pp. 15–19.

45. AP, "There He Goes: Reagan's Mike Tattles on Him," *The Orlando Sentinel,* March 1, 1986.

46. Shaw, "The Press and Sex."

47. Chip Rowe, "'Maledicta' Favors the Whole F___ing Truth," *Washington Journalism Review,* January/February 1992, pp. 14–16.

48. Shaw, "The Press and Sex."

49. Shaw, "The Press and Sex."

50. Lou Gelfand, "Photo, Headline Gave Some Readers Offense," *Star Tribune,* Oct. 29, 1995.

51. Jacques Leslie, "Digital Photopros and Photo(shop) Realism," *Wired,* July 22, 1998.

52. Thomas Collins of *Newsday,* "News Photographers Under Fire," *The Orlando Sentinel,* Dec. 12, 1981.

53. Ray Moseley, "TV Filmmaker Accused of 2nd Fake," *Chicago Tribune,* June 10, 1998.

54. "Darts & Laurels," p. 22. Also see Robert King, "The Amazing Growing Sweater," on the Poynter Institute Web site, www.poynter.org. King was presentations editor at the time.

55. Kenny Irby, "Missing Woman Stirs Dialogue, Creates Policy at *Journal-Constitution,*" *Poynter Report,* Spring 1998, pp. 7–8.

56. James R. Gaines, "To Our Readers," *Time,* July 4, 1994.

57. Quoted in Don E. Tomlinson, "Legal and Ethical Ramifications of Computer-Assisted Photograph Manipulation," in *Protocol,* Washington: NPPA, 1991, p. 5.

58. "The Trouble with Harry," *Columbia Journalism Review,* January/February 1990, pp. 4–5.

59. David Zurawik and Christina Stoehr, "Money Changes Everything," *American Journalism Review,* April 1993, p. 30.

60. Nancy M. Davis, "Electronic Photo Manipulation: Many Are Doing It, and Editors, Photojournalists Urge Strict Guidelines to Protect Credibility," *Presstime,* February 1992, pp. 22–23.

61. Deni Elliott, "Deception and Imagery," in *Protocol,* Washington: NPPA, 1991, p. 3.

62. Lou Hodges, "The Moral Imperative for Photojournalists," in *Protocol,* Washington: National Press Photographs Association, 1991, pp. 7–8.

63. Shiela Reeves, "What's Wrong with This Picture? Daily Newspaper Photo Editors' Attitudes and Their Tolerance Toward Digital Manipulation," *Newspaper Research Journal,* Fall 1992/Winter 1993, pp. 131–155.

64. Patrick Boyle, "Standards for Photography's Cutting Edge," *Washington Journalism Review,* November 1992, p. 12.

65. "Time Manipulates Photograph," *The Washington Post,* June 22, 1994, p. 2.

Chapter 7

1. Caroline Lowe, "Heat on the Beat," *Newsworthy,* Winter 1994.

2. Jeremy Iggers, "Journalism Ethics:

Right Name. Wrong Game?"
Newsworthy, Spring 1995.

3. Interviews by author, March 21, 1997.

4. Interview by Gene Goodwin, Feb. 15, 1981.

5. Details of the Foreman story are taken from "Inquirer Conflict in Cianfrani Case," *The Philadelphia Inquirer,* Aug. 27, 1977, p. 1; "Reporter Linked to a Senator's Gifts," *The New York Times,* Aug. 28, 1977, p. 4; and Donald L. Barlett and James B. Steele, "The Full Story of Cianfrani and the Reporter," *The Philadelphia Inquirer,* Oct. 16, 1977.

6. Eleanor Randolph, "Conflict of Interest: A Growing Problem for Couples," *Esquire,* February 1978, pp. 55–59, 124–129.

7. David Barstow, "Two Newspapers, Two Sides to the Same Story," *The American Editor,* July/August 1996. His story originally appeared in the *St. Petersburg Times.* Most of the details about this reporter's handling of this case were taken from this article. Details about the crime and the legal proceedings were taken from reports in *The Orlando Sentinel.*

8. John Haile, "Witness Is a Liar, but There's Other Proof," *American Editor,* July/August 1996.

9. The case was widely reported. Details here were taken from Alex S. Jones, "Weighing the Thorny Issue of Anonymous Sources," *The New York Times,* March 3, 1992, p. A14; and Frank Green, "Adams Case Spurs Debate on Use of Unnamed Sources," *The San Diego Union-Tribune,* March 4, 1992, p. A2. Also see Cheryl Reid, "Anonymous Sources Bring down a Senator," *Washington Journalism Review,* April 1992, p. 10.

10. Green.

11. Gina Lubrano, "Anonymous Sources Test a Newspaper," *The San Diego Union-Tribune,* March 9, 1992, p. B7.

12. Quoted by Alex S. Jones, "Anonymity: A Tool Used and Abused," *The New York Times,* June 25, 1991, p. A20.

13. Interview by Goodwin, Oct. 5, 1981.

14. Interview by Goodwin, Oct. 16, 1981.

15. Interview by Goodwin, Oct. 6, 1981.

16. Jean C. Chance and Connie Bouchard, "The Gainesville Slayings: A Study in Media Responsibility and Unnamed Sources," a paper presented at the AEJMC Southeast Colloquium at the University of Alabama, March 25–27, 1993, p. 14.

17. See. F. Dennis Hale, "Unnamed News Sources: Their Impact on the Perceptions of Stories," *Newspaper Research Journal,* Winter 1983, pp. 49–56.

18. Results of four opinion polls are reported in David Weaver and LeAnne Davis, "Public Opinion on Investigative Reporting in the 1980s," *Journalism Quarterly,* Spring 1992, pp. 146–155.

19. Howard Kurtz, "Sez Who? How Sources and Reporters Play the Leak Game," *The Washington Post,* March 7, 1993, p. C5.

20. Jeff Testerman, "Media Firestorm," *St. Petersburg Times,* April 12, 1992, Perspective section, p. 10.

21. Kurtz.

22. Tom Fiedler, "Don't Let Gossip Take over the News," *The Miami Herald,* April 2, 1998.

23. Eleanor Randolph, "Journalists Face Troubling Questions About Leaks from Criminal Probes," *The Washington Post,* Aug. 12, 1989, p. A4.

24. For an example of this, see Andrew Rosenthal, "Inquiry Raises Questions on Anonymous Sources," *The New York Times,* June 27, 1998, p. A13, or Randolph, "Journalists Face Troubling Questions."

25. David Heckler, "Danger Ahead: Sex Abuse Cases," *Washington Journalism Review,* September 1991, p. 38.

26. References to Kurtz in this section are from his "Sez Who?" article.

27. David Rosenbaum, "The House, the Press and Bad Feelings," *The New York Times,* June 7, 1989, p. A25.

28. Doris Graber, *Mass Media and American Politics,* Washington: CQ Press, 1989, p. 254.
29. "Lesson on Flacking for Government," *The New York Times,* Aug. 30, 1984, p. B10.
30. Howard Kurtz, *Spin Cycle: Inside the Clinton Propaganda Machine,* New York: The Free Press, 1998.
31. Quoted by Kurtz, "Sez Who?"
32. Randolph, "Journalists Face Troubling Questions."
33. Frank Smyth, "'Official Sources,' 'Western Diplomats,' and Other Voices from the Mission," *Columbia Journalism Review,* January/February 1993, p. 35.
34. James McCartney, "Perhaps Every Reporter Should Take an Oath to Walk out on Officials Who Insist on Talking 'Off the Record,'" *ASNE Bulletin,* October 1984, pp. 14–15.
35. Jones, "Anonymity: A Tool Used and Abused."
36. Interview by Goodwin, Nov. 4, 1981.
37. Howard Kurtz, "The Stream of Anonymous Sources," *The Washington Post,* Aug. 8, 1998.
38. Larry Lough, "Our Readers Must Know Our Sources," Muncie (Ind.) *Star Press,* May 26, 1997.
39. William Blankenburg, "The Utility of Anonymous Attribution," *Newspaper Research Journal,* Winter/Spring 1992, pp. 10–23.
40. Quoted by Kurtz, "Sez Who?"
41. Chance and Bouchard.
42. Phil Record, "Who Said So?" Fort Worth *Star-Telegram,* June 29, 1997, p. 5.
43. Carl Bernstein and Bob Woodward, *All the President's Men,* New York: Simon and Schuster, 1974, p. 71.
44. Gary Ruderman, "Off-the-Record Comments Should Be Just That," *Solutions Today for Tomorrow's Ethical Problems,* Chicago: SPJ, October 1989, p. 8.
45. Allan Wolper, "Off the Record," *E&P Interactive,* July 26, 1997.
46. Ruderman, p. 8.
47. Kurtz, *Spin Cycle,* pp. 40–41.
48. Walter Isaacson, "The 'Senior Official,'" *Washington Journalism Review,* November 1992, pp. 30–34.
49. Kurtz, *Spin Cycle.*
50. Laurence Zuckerman, "Breaking a Confidence," *Time,* Aug. 3, 1987, p. 61; Eleanor Randolph, "Managing Confidential Sources," *Messages: The Washington Post Media Companion,* Boston: Allyn and Bacon, 1991, pp. 347–349.
51. Milton Coleman, "A Reporter's Story: 18 Words, Seven Weeks Later," *The Washington Post,* April 8, 1984.
52. Interview by Goodwin, Feb. 25, 1986.
53. See Bill Salisbury, "Burning the Source," *Washington Journalism Review,* September 1991, pp. 18–22, and "No Way to Treat a Tipster," *Columbia Journalism Review,* January/February 1986, pp. 10–11.
54. "Reporter Decides to Serve Jail Time," *St. Petersburg Times,* March 11, 1993, p. A1; and "Protecting a Principle," *St. Petersburg Times,* March 11, 1993, p. A18. Background to the case is in Bruce Sanford and Anne Noble, "Threats Escalate to Strip Confidential Sources from the Reporter's Tool Kit," *Quill,* April 1992, pp. 10–11.
55. "I'll Shield Sources, Reporter Vows," *Newsday,* Feb. 14, 1992, p. 17; and "NPR Reporter Won't Reveal Sources," *The Washington Post,* Feb. 25, 1992.
56. "Source Saves Reporter from Jail Term," *News Media & the Law,* Summer 1985, pp. 26–27.
57. Ralph Holsinger, *Media Law,* New York: Random House, 1987, pp. 270–271.
58. *Facts About Newspapers '93,* Reston, Va.: Newspaper Association of America, p. 27.
59. "Confidential Sources," *Freedom of Information Annual Report 1979,* APME, pp. 4–5.
60. Tamara Jones, "Reporters in Germany open Wallets for Stories," *Los Angeles Times,* March 26, 1991.
61. Michael Dobbs, "Psst! Kremlin News for Sale: Hard Cash Only," *The Washington Post,* Feb. 5, 1992, p. A21.
62. Anthony Lewis, "Hire and Salary," *The New York Times,* Jan. 26, 1978; John Herbers, "Former Aide

Interviews Nixon," April 9, 1984, p. C18; Tom Wolfe, *The Right Stuff,* New York: Farrar-Straus-Giroux, 1979, pp. 277–296, 352–379.

63. Interview by Goodwin, Nov. 2, 1981.

64. Ann Hodges, "Cult Interviews Worth Big Bucks to News Shows," *The Houston Chronicle,* April 24, 1993, p. 6.

65. Michael Hedges, "Media Mull the Ethics of Buying Tawdry Tales," *The Washington Times,* Jan. 29, 1992, p. A1.

66. April Lynch, "*Newsweek* Paid Hooker After Photo, Interview," *San Francisco Chronicle,* July 19, 1990, p. A6.

67. Kenneth Jost, "The Dawn of Big-Bucks Juror Journalism," *Legal Times,* July 20, 1987, p. 15.

68. Lyle Denniston, "Making Checkbook Journalism a Crime," *American Journalism Review,* April 1995, p. 58.

69. "Newspaper Suspends 2 for Ethics Violations," *Chicago Tribune,* Nov. 13, 1989, p. 3.

70. Renee Montage, *Morning Edition,* National Public Radio, June 1, 1993.

71. Charles Walston, "Tabloid TV Has Changed the Rules," *The Atlanta Journal-Constitution,* Nov. 17, 1991, p. G1.

72. Josef Adalian, "'Minutes' Man Hewitt Blasts NBC's 'Dateline,'" *New York Post,* Jan. 14, 1998.

73. Michael D. Shear, "Families Struggle with Private Matter—and Glare of Media Spotlight," *The Washington Post,* Aug. 16, 1998, p. B1.

74. Interview by author, Aug. 21, 1997.

75. Walston.

76. John Tierney, "Cash on Delivery," *The New York Times,* April 18, 1993, sec. 6, p. 64.

77. *Nightline,* ABC, April 8, 1993. On this program, Donahue said his show had not paid for interviews, but he said he would not rule out paying for them. About two weeks later, New York *Daily News* and National Public Radio reported his show had paid for appearances by two of the police officers in the Rodney King incident in Los Angeles.

78. Interview by Goodwin, Sept. 21, 1981.

79. ASNE poll cited in Julie Dodd and Leonard Tipton, "Shifting Views of High School Students About Journalism Careers," *Newspaper Research Journal,* Fall 1992/Winter 1993, pp. 111–119.

80. Weaver and LeAnne Davis.

Chapter 8

1. Information about the Hussey story came from Mark Brunswick, "Relatives Plead for Safe Return; Search for Missing Youth and Man Continues near Mora," *Star Tribune,* Nov. 18, 1993, p. 1B, and "Bodies of Man, Teen Found; Both Had Gunshot Wounds in the Head," *Star Tribune,* Nov. 20, 1993, p. 1A; Kurt Chandler, "Group for Troubled Teens Had Counseled Hussey," *Star Tribune,* Nov. 20, 1993, p. 8A, and "Youth Program Says It's in 'Hiding' over Hussey Furor," *Star Tribune,* Nov. 24, 1993, p. 1B; Doug Grow, "From Tragedy of Boy's Murder, Another Anger Rises," *Star Tribune,* Nov. 26, 1993, p. 3B; Lou Gelfand, "Readers Infuriated by Violation of Hussey's Privacy," *Star Tribune,* Nov. 28, 1993, p. 29A, and "Readers Question Details Used in Story of Teen's Disappearance," *Star Tribune,* Nov. 21, 1993, p. 35A; Jennifer Juarez Robles, "Teenagers Often Struggle in Secret; They Need to Know System Won't Betray Them, as It Did Hussey," *Star Tribune,* Dec. 3, 1993, p. 29A; "Right to Privacy—Right to Know: Whose Rights Prevail?" *Newsworthy,* Spring 1994; "An Adamant Dissent: The Hussey Family's View," *Newsworthy,* Spring 1994; and "Anguish, Too, in the Newsroom: The Scene on Deadline," *Newsworthy,* Spring 1994.

2. Greg Ring, "Are Exact Addresses Always Part of the News?" *ASNE Bulletin,* February 1985, p. 5.

3. Frank Thayer and Steve Pasternack, "Policies on Identification of People in Crime

Stories," *Newspaper Research Journal,* Spring 1994, pp. 56–64.

4. Pamela Terrell, "Full Name, Age and Address—or Not?" *Presstime,* December 1990, pp. 30–33.

5. Daniel Lynch, "AIDS: The Number 11 Killer," *Washington Journalism Review,* January/February 1992, pp. 19–21.

6. Thomas Collins, "When News Gets Explicit," *Newsday,* Aug. 13, 1990, sec. 2, p. 4.

7. "Mama Mia! Breast Pic Offends Readers," *Quill,* April 1992, p. 5.

8. Thomas Oliphant, "Invaded—by the Press," *The Boston Globe,* April 19, 1991, p. 19.

9. Toni Locy, "Handymen Did Job on Elderly D.C. Woman," *The Washington Post,* Aug. 10, 1997, p. A1.

10. Thayer and Pasternack.

11. Lou Gelfand, "Paper Shouldn't Name Suspect Until Charge Is Filed," *Star Tribune,* Nov. 24, 1996, p. 27A.

12. Sam Walker, "Media's Publishing of Sensitive Material Raises Ethical Questions," *Christian Science Monitor,* March 7, 1997. Also see Ed Bark, "Media Ponder Their Own Ethics," *The Seattle Times,* Aug. 24, 1996. Bark is a *Dallas Morning News* reporter.

13. David Noack, "Publishing Sex Offender Data," *E&P Interactive,* Aug. 8, 1997.

14. Si Liberman, "The Harlotry Project," *E&P Interactive,* April 12, 1997.

15. Rosalind C. Truitt, "Juvenile Justice," *Presstime,* July/August 1996, pp. 63–67; and Thayer and Pasternack.

16. LynNell Hancock, "Naming Kid Criminals," *Presstime,* July/August 1998, pp. 18–19.

17. Collins, "When News Gets Explicit."

18. Bruce DeSilva, "Views of Newspaper Gatekeepers on Rape and Rape Coverage," unpublished paper presented at AEJMC Convention, Corvallis, Ore., 1983.

19. D.D. Guttenplan, "Not Naming Names," *Newsday,* May 3, 1989, p. 2.

20. Dershowitz made similar observations about both the New Bedford and William Smith (discussed later in the chapter) trials. His comments are widely quoted, including Robin Benedict, *Virgin or Vamp: How the Press Covers Sex Crimes,* New York: Oxford University Press, 1992, p. 253; and Rita Ciolli, "Naming Rape Accusers: A Policy under Review," *Newsday,* May 5, 1991, p. 6.

21. Paul R. LaRocque, "Naming Rape Victims," *APME News,* Summer 1996.

22. Benedict, pp. 252–253.

23. Jane Schorer, "The Story Behind a Landmark Story of Rape," *Washington Journalism Review,* June 1991, pp. 20–26.

24. Ellie Dixon, "We List Abuse Victims' Names. Why Don't You?" *The American Editor,* December 1996.

25. Eleanor Randolph, "Naming Rape Victims," *Messages: The Washington Post Media Companion.* Boston: Allyn and Bacon, 1991, p. 361.

26. Ciolli, p. 6.

27. Benedict, p. 254.

28. Cited by Elizabeth Culotta, "Naming Alleged Rape Victims: Two Policies Within 30 Miles," *Washington Journalism Review,* July/August 1992, p. 14.

29. Ciolli.

30. Dick Haws, "Rape Victims: Papers Shouldn't Name Us," *American Journalism Review,* September 1966, pp. 12–13.

31. Tommy Thomason, Paul LaRocque and Maggie Thomas, "Editors Still Reluctant to Name Rape Victims," *Newspaper Research Journal,* Summer 1995, pp. 42–51.

32. Thomason, LaRocque and Thomas.

33. Thomason, LaRocque and Thomas.

34. Fred Friendly, "Gays, Privacy and a Free Press," *The Washington Post,* April 8, 1990, p. B7.

35. Pat Murphy, "Ford Hero's Mother Has Misgivings," *The Detroit News,* Sept. 26, 1975.

36. Charles B. Seib, "How the Papers

Covered the Cinema Follies Fire," *The Washington Post,* Oct. 30, 1977; and George Beveridge, "Identifying the Movie-Fire Victims," *Washington Star,* Oct. 31, 1977.

37. For a discussion of outing, see Randy Shilts, "Is 'Outing' Gays Ethical?" *The New York Times,* April 12, 1990, p. A23.

38. Deni Elliott, *St. Petersburg Times,* March 26, 1989.

39. Friendly.

40. William A. Henry III, "To 'Out' or Not to 'Out,'" *Time,* Aug. 19, 1991, p. 17.

41. Mitchell Hartman, "When to Say Someone Is Gay," *Quill,* November/December 1990, p. 7.

42. Art Nauman, "Gory Photo Offends Many," *The Sacramento Bee,* Jan. 14, 1996.

43. Interview by Gene Goodwin, Jan. 8, 1982.

44. "Graphic Excess," *Washington Journalism Review,* January 1986, pp. 10–11.

45. Richard Harwood, "Sometimes Compassion," *The Washington Post,* April 28, 1991, p. C5.

46. George Padgett, "Let Grief Be a Private Affair," *Quill,* February 1988, p. 13.

47. Richard Cunningham, "Child Photos: Drawing the Line," *Quill,* February 1988, pp. 8–9.

48. Quoted in Richard Cunningham, "Seeking a Time-out on Prurience," *Quill,* March 1992, p. 6.

49. John Long, "Reflections by NPPA's Ethics and Standards Committee Co-Chairs," *News Photographer,* April 1998, p. 47.

50. Michael D. Sherer, "Chapter 5: Ethics and Expectations," *Excellence in Television Photojournalism,* published on the Web site of the NPPA, 1995.

51. Ann Zimmerman, "By Any Other Name . . .," *Washington Journalism Review,* November/December 1979, pp. 43–45.

52. Interview by Goodwin, Oct. 15, 1981.

53. "Long Ears in Louisville," *Time,* Oct. 14, 1974.

54. Interview by Goodwin, Oct. 23, 1981.

55. Philip Meyer, *Ethical Journalism: A Guide for Students, Practitioners and Consumers,* Lanham Md.: University Press of America, 1987 p. 83.

56. Meyer, p. 203.

57. Frank Sutherland, "Jerry Thompson: Before and After the Klan Series," *Gannetteer,* April 1981, pp. 10–11.

58. Interviews by Goodwin of Larry Beaupre and Robert Giles, then editors at the *Times-Union,* Oct. 15, 1981.

59. "Digging out the News," *Washington Journalism Review,* September 1985, pp. 12–13.

60. Interview by Goodwin, Sept. 2, 1981.

61. Interview of William Deibler, managing editor of the *Pittsburgh Post-Gazette,* by Goodwin, Oct. 22, 1981.

62. Richard Turner and Peter Annin, "Leaving Messages, Sending Messages," *Newsweek,* July 13, 1998, p. 65; and John Fox, "Journalism on the Run," *CityBeat,* July 30–August 5, 1998.

63. "Privacy and the Need to Know," *Presstime,* October 1992, p. 24.

64. "Shattering the Illusion of Privacy," *Macworld,* July 1993, p. 128.

65. See "Privacy in the Internet Age," a 41-page special report in *PC World,* September 1998.

66. "Privacy and the Need to Know."

67. Sigman L. Splichal, "How Florida Newspapers Are Dealing with Access to Computerized Government Information," *Newspaper Research Journal,* Fall 1992/Winter 1993, pp. 73–83.

68. Larry J. Sabato, *Feeding Frenzy: How Attack Journalism Has Transformed American Politics,* New York: Free Press, 1991, p. 27.

69. John Seigenthaler, "The First Amendment: The First 200 Years," *Presstime,* February 1991, pp. 24–30.

70. Seigenthaler.

71. Michael Wines, "Supreme Leader, Pigeon in Chief," *The New York Times,* March 23, 1997, p. A4.

72. Seigenthaler, p. 29.
73. Wines.
74. Details taken from David Shaw, "Stumbling over Sex in the Press," *Los Angeles Times,* Aug. 18, 1991, p. A1; Seigenthaler; and Sabato.
75. Details of the 1884 campaigns are reported both by Sabato, pp. 25–51, and Seigenthaler, p. 30.
76. See Gloria Borger, "Private Lives, Public Figures," *U.S. News & World Report,* May 18, 1987, p. 20; and Sabato, pp. 25–52.
77. Sabato, p. 30.
78. That FDR had a mistress is widely reported. See Borger, Seigenthaler or Sabato.
79. Sabato, p. 30.
80. Sabato, p. 31.
81. Sabato, p. 40.
82. See Sabato or Borger.
83. Seigenthaler, p. 24.
84. David Shaw, "Trust in Media Is on Decline," *Los Angeles Times,* March 31, 1993, p. A1.
85. Sabato, p. 46.
86. Harry F. Waters, "Public or Private Lives?" *Newsweek,* Feb. 17, 1975, p. 83.
87. Interview with Goodwin, Oct. 7, 1981.
88. Waters.
89. Waters.
90. The Hart-Rice story is widely told. For instance, Borger has a good discussion.
91. Seymour Hersh, *The Dark Side of Camelot,* Boston: Little, Brown and Co., 1997, pp. 238–246.
92. Sabato, p. 36.
93. Hersh, p. 106.
94. Shaw, "Trust in Media Is on Decline."
95. Phil Donahue, "Infidelity Is a Valid Campaign Issue," *The New York Times,* Aug. 26, 1992, p. A21.
96. Quoted in "Why Must Our Candidates Be Choirboys?" *Newsday,* Jan. 29, 1992, p. 77. Reeves' book is *A Question of Character: A Life of John F. Kennedy,* published by Free Press.
97. Shaw, "Trust in Media is On Decline."
98. AP, "Most Americans Believe Clinton Lied," *USA Today,* Aug. 4, 1998, p. 1.

99. David S. Broder, "No One to Blame but Himself," *The Washington Post,* Aug. 2, 1998, p. C7.
100. See David Whitman, "Was It Good for Us?" *U.S. News & World Report,* May 19, 1997, p. 58; and Francis X. Clines, "America's Jaded Eye on Sex in Public Life," *The New York Times,* June 1, 1997, sec. 4, p. 5.
101. Douglas Stanglin, "The New Politics of Forgive and Forget," *U.S. News and World Report,* March 3, 1997, pp. 37–40.
102. Quoted by Clines.
103. "Privacy and the Need to Know."
104. John Broder, "The Lewinsky Legacy (If There Is One), *The New York Times,* Aug. 2, 1998, sec. 4, pp. 1 and 4.
105. Mona Charon, "Parents Are Fair Game, but Leave Chelsea Alone," *The Atlanta Journal-Constitution,* Nov. 17, 1992, A23.
106. Myriam Marquez, "Media Shouldn't Hound Chelsea," *The Sunday Gazette Mail,* Feb. 14, 1999. Marquez is a member of *The Orlando Sentinel*'s editorial board.
107. "Privacy and the Need to Know," p. 24.
108. Interview by Goodwin, Oct. 10, 1981.
109. Interview by Goodwin, Nov. 4, 1981.
110. Eric Schmitt, "Absence of Pity," *Quill,* July/August 1984, pp. 10–11.
111. John Sullivan, "Celebrity Pulls Advertising," *E&P Interactive,* July 19, 1997.
112. John Sullivan and John Consoli, "Devil or Angel?" *E&P Interactive,* May 31, 1997.
113. Jonathan Rowe, "When Private Sins Are Public News," *Christian Science Monitor,* April 10, 1989, p. 13. The quotes from Gee are from this article.
114. Interview by Goodwin, May 28, 1981.
115. "Mutual Respect Needed to Improve Relations Between Athletes, Media," *Athletes and the Media,* a Freedom Forum report, Jan. 29, 1994.

116. Minnesota News Council, Determination 73, 1988.
117. See Kenny Moore, "The Eternal Example," *Sports Illustrated,* Dec. 21, 1992, pp. 16–27.
118. Quoted in "Arthur Ashe AIDS Story Scrutinized by Editors, Columnists," *Quill,* June 1992, p. 17.
119. "Arthur Ashe AIDS Story."
120. Christine Spolar, "Privacy for Public Figures?" *Washington Journalism Review,* June 1992, pp. 20–22.
121. "Arthur Ashe AIDS Story."
122. "Arthur Ashe AIDS Story."
123. Victor Zonana, "Ashe Case Raises Fame vs. Privacy Case," *Los Angeles Times,* April 10, 1992.
124. Spolar, p. 22.
125. "Arthur Ashe AIDS Story."
126. Spolar, p. 21.
127. Marlene Cimons, "Ashe Calls for Sensitivity from the Media," *Los Angeles Times,* May, 27, 1992, p. C2.

Chapter 9
1. Details are from Cliff Brown, "The Public's Right to Know Can Kill You," unpublished paper; "The *American* Did Not Take Part in Hoax," *Hattiesburg (Miss.) American,* Dec. 11, 1984; Duane McAllister, "Publisher Goes on Donahue Show to Defend a Tough Ethics Decision," *Gannetteer,* March 1985, pp. 6–7; Janet Braswell, "Police Stage Hoax to Stop Contract 'Hit,'" *Hattiesburg (Miss.) American,* Dec. 10, 1984; Frank Sutherland, "A Man Threatens Murder in Hattiesburg—and Debate Rages on Using False Stories," *Gannetteer,* August 1986, pp..4–8.
2. Sissela Bok, *Secrets: On the Ethics of Concealment and Revelation,* New York: Vintage, 1984, p. 177.
3. Donald Asher, "The State of Secrecy," *Quill,* April 1998, pp. 17–23.
4. Rosalind C. Truitt, "Citizen Concerns Augment Government Officials' Increased Efforts to Curtail Press Privileges," *Presstime,* May 1996.
5. Truitt.

6. Howard Simons, "Government and National Security," excerpt from talk to ASNE Convention in *Editor & Publisher,* April 26, 1986, pp. 80–89.
7. Bok, p. 208.
8. Frank Aukofer and William Lawrence, *The Odd Couple: A Report on the Relationship Between the Media and the Military,* published by the Freedom Forum, 1995.
9. Malcolm W. Browne, "The Fighting Words of Homer Bigart: A War Correspondent Is Never a Cheerleader," *New York Times Book Review,* April 11, 1993, p. 13.
10. "Pentagon Activates Press Pool to Cover Libya Bombing," *Presstime,* May 1986, p. 69.
11. William Boot, "Wading Around in the Panama Pool," *Columbia Journalism Review,* March/April 1990, pp. 18–20.
12. Pete Yost, "U.S. Sharply Distorts War News, Study Says," *Chicago Tribune,* Jan. 19, 1992.
13. Stanley W. Cloud, "Covering the Next War," *The New York Times,* Aug. 4, 1992, p. A19.
14. Chris Hedges, "The Unilaterals," *Columbia Journalism Review,* May/June 1991, pp. 27–29.
15. Aukofer and Lawrence.
16. Interviews by author, September 1998.
17. David Shaw, "Onetime Allies: Press and LAPD," *Los Angeles Times,* May 24, 1992, p. A1.
18. "Police, TV Agree on Broadcast Restrictions," *News Photographer,* May 1998, pp. 18–19.
19. Steve Brill, "Pressgate," *Brill's Content,* August 1998, pp. 128–129.
20. Bill Boyarsky, "Motives Sought in Suicide of Oakland Publisher Knowland," *Los Angeles Times,* Feb. 25, 1974.
21. Joe Shoquist, "When Not to Print the News," 1974 report of APME Professional Standards Committee.
22. Thomas Collins, "When the Press Restrains Itself," *Newsday,* March 30, 1983.
23. Paula Moore, "Two Boys Are Kidnapped in El Paso—and the Media Weigh Withholding the

Story," Editorially speaking section of *Gannetteer,* August 1986, pp. 2–3.

24. Roger Roy, "He's Using Her as a Shield," *The Orlando Sentinel,* Dec. 13, 1997, pp. A1 and A18.

25. David Shaw, "How Media Gives Stories Same Spin," *Los Angeles Times,* Aug. 25, 1989, pp. 32–34, and "Opinion Leaders Dictate the Conventional Leaders," *Los Angeles Times,* Aug. 26, 1989, pp. 24–26.

26. Matt Drudge made the comment during a speech to the National Press Club, June 1998. Also see M.L. Stein, "Slipping Journalism Standards, Are Basic Rules Crumbling on Web?" *Editor & Publisher,* June 12, 1998.

27. "Press 'Unfair, Inaccurate and Pushy,'" Pew's "The People and the Press" poll, 1997. Pew's polls are available on the Pew Web site, www.people-press.org.

28. Peter A. Brown, "Squires Is Right— We Are out of Touch with Voters and Their Concerns," *APNE Bulletin,* November 1992, p. 8.

29. David H. Weaver and G. Cleveland Wilhoit, *The American Journalist: A Portrait of U.S. News People and Their Work,* second edition, Bloomington: Indiana University Press, 1991, p. 24.

30. William Schneider and I.A. Lewis, "Views on the News," *Public Opinion,* August/September 1985, pp. 6–11 and 58–59.

31. David Croteau, "A Report Examining the 'Liberal Media' Claim," June 1998, posted on the FAIR Web page.

32. Todd Gitlin, "Media Lemmings Run Amok!" *Washington Journalism Review,* April 1992, p. 31.

33. Endorsement numbers found in N. Thimmesch, "The Editorial Endorsement Game," *Public Opinion,* October/November 1984, pp. 10–13; George Garneau, "Clinton's the Choice," *Editor & Publisher,* Oct. 24, 1992, p. 9; "Endorsement Addendum," *Editor & Publisher,* Nov. 7, 1992; and Stacy Jones, "Fear of Favor, Local Flavor, Increasingly Drive Newspapers to Stay Neutral on

Presidential Candidates," *E&P Interactive,* Oct. 26, 1996.

34. Byron St. Dizier, "Editorial Page Editors and Endorsements: Chain-Owned vs. Independent Newspapers," *Newspaper Research Journal,* Spring 1987, pp. 63–68.

35. Jones.

36. See Lawrence Mullen, "Close-ups of the President," *Visual Communication Quarterly,* Spring 1998, pp. 4–6.

37. David Shaw, "Of Isms and Prisms," *Columbia Journalism Review,* January/February 1991, pp. 56–57.

38. Michael Robinson and Maura E. Clancey, "Network News, 15 Years After Agnew," *Channels,* January/February 1986, p. 34.

39. A good review of the research can be found in Mark D. Watts, David Domke, Dhavan V. Shah and David P. Fan, "Actual and Perceived Media Bias in Presidential Campaigns: Explaining Public Perceptions of a Liberal Press," a paper presented at the AEJMC national convention, August 1998.

40. David Domke, "News Media, Candidates and Issues, and Public Opinion in the 1996 Presidential Campaign," a paper presented to AEJMC National Convention, August 1997.

41. Robinson and Clancey, p. 34.

42. Doris Graber, "Kind Pictures and Harsh Words: How Television Presents the Candidates," in *Elections in America,* edited by Kay Schlozman, Boston: Allen & Unwin, 1987, pp. 115–141.

43. Watts, Domke, Shah and Fan.

44. John Robinson, "Just How Liberal Is the News? 1980 Revisited," *Public Opinion,* February/March 1983, pp. 55–60.

45. Robinson and Clancey, p. 38.

46. Sandra H. Dickson, Cynthia Hill, Cara Pilson and Suzanne Hanners, "A Cynical Press: Coverage of the 1996 Presidential Campaign," a paper presented to AEJMC National Convention, August 1997.

47. Quoted in David Shaw, "Press Turns the Mirror on Itself," *Los Angeles Times,* June 19, 1988, p. 1.

48. Shaw, "Of Isms and Prisms," p. 56.

49. William A. Henry III, "Are the Media Too Liberal?" *Time,* Oct. 19, 1992, p. 47.
50. ASNE poll cited in Schneider and Lewis, p. 11.
51. Raspberry's comments were reported in *Newsworthy,* Winter 1994.

Chapter 10
1. Ben H. Bagdikian, "No. 50061, Inside Maximum Security," *The Washington Post,* Jan. 31, 1972.
2. Letter to Gene Goodwin, Nov. 14, 1981.
3. David Shaw, "Deception-Honest Tool of Reporting?" *Los Angeles Times,* Sept. 20, 1979.
4. *60 Minutes,* Sept. 27, 1981.
5. William J. Coughlin, "Tell It to the Marines," *Washington Journalism Review,* July/August 1984, pp. 54–55.
6. Neil Henry, "The Black Dispatch," *The Washington Post,* Oct. 9–14, 1983.
7. Interview by Donna Shaub in "Undercover Reporting: Is It Always Ethical?" unpublished paper.
8. Interview by Goodwin, Feb. 19, 1986.
9. Russ W. Baker, "Damning Undercover Tactics as 'Fraud,'" *Columbia Journalism Review,* March/April 1997, p. 32.
10. Michael Salwen, "Getting the Story by Hook or Crook," *Quill,* January 1981, pp. 12–14.
11. Daniel Anderson and Peter Benjaminson, *Investigative Reporting,* Bloomington: Indiana University Press, 1976, p. 109.
12. Steven Stark, "Investigating Bob Greene," *Quill,* June 1993, p. 12.
13. Tony Case, "In Disguise," *Editor & Publisher,* November 14, 1992, p. 14; and Richard Harwood, "Knights of the Fourth Estate," *The Washington Post,* Dec. 5, 1992, p. A23.
14. Interview by Goodwin, Nov. 4, 1981.
15. David Halberstam in his essay in "Dangerous Liaisons," *Columbia Journalism Review,* July/August 1989, p. 31.
16. David Weaver and LeAnne Daniels, "Public Opinion on Investigative

Reporting in the 1980s," *Journalism Quarterly,* Spring 1992, p. 151.
17. Interview by author, March 17, 1997.
18. Letter to Goodwin, Nov. 14, 1981.
19. Linda Mainiero, ed., *American Women Writers from Colonial Times to the Present: A Critical Reference Guide,* New York: Frederick Ungar, 1979, pp. 381–383.
20. Silas Bent, *Newspaper Crusaders: A Neglected Story,* New York: Whittlesey House, 1939, p. 198.
21. Frank Luther Mott, *News Stories of 1934,* Iowa City: Clio Press, 1935, pp. 258–260, 264–271.
22. Doug Struck, "Inside Crownsville," Annapolis *Evening Capital,* Oct. 6–25, 1975.
23. Interview by Goodwin, Sept. 9, 1981.
24. "Undercover," research report of the Times Publishing Co., St. Petersburg, Fla., and the Department of Mass Communication, University of South Florida, Summer 1981.
25. Howard Kurtz, "Hidden Network Cameras: A Troubling Trend," *The Washington Post,* Nov. 30, 1992, p. A1.
26. Details are taken from Kurtz; "Another Missing Union Label at ABC," *The Washington Times,* April 27, 1993, p. F2; and Diane Kunde, "Food Lion Roars back at Critics in Ad Blitz," *The Dallas Morning News,* Nov. 5, 1992, p. D1.
27. Kenneth Clark, "Hidden Meanings: Increasing Use of Secret Cameras and Microphones Raises Ethical Questions About TV Journalists," *Chicago Tribune,* June 30, 1992.
28. Kurtz.
29. "Darts & Laurels," *Columbia Journalism Review,* March/April 1997, p. 22.
30. Clark.
31. Quoted by Colman McCarthy, "Getting the Truth Untruthfully," *The Washington Post,* Dec. 22, 1992, p. D21.
32. Shaw.
33. AP, "ABC Must Pay Food Lion $5.5 million," *The Orlando Sentinel,* Jan. 23, 1997, p. B1.
34. Kurtz.

35. Details are taken from Beth Nissen, "An Inside View," *The Wall Street Journal,* July 28, 1978; interview with Lawrence O'Donnell, *Journal* associate editor, by Goodwin, Feb. 22, 1982; and a letter to Goodwin from Ed Cony, then publisher of the *Journal,* June 10, 1984.
36. Leslie Linthicum, "When to Go Undercover? As Last Resort to Get Story," 1983–84 report of the SPJ-SDX Ethics Committee, p. 20; Leslie Linthicum, "Undercover Student" series, *Albuquerque Tribune,* March 7–14, 1983; and Deni Elliott, "End vs. Means: Comparing Two Cases of Deceptive Practices," a 1985 report of SPJ-SDX Ethics Committee, pp. 15–16.
37. Kurtz.
38. Interview by Goodwin, Sept. 8, 1981.
39. Clark.
40. "Undercover."
41. Pat Widder, "Playing with Fire: Blur of Fact and Fiction Costs NBC," *Chicago Tribune,* Feb. 11, 1993, p. 1.
42. Russ W. Baker, "Truth, Lies and Videotape," *Columbia Journalism Review,* July/August 1993, pp. 25–28.
43. Baker, "Truth, Lies and Videotape."
44. Details are taken from Paul Shannon, "For Rent or Not for Rent," *IRE Journal,* Fall 1985, pp. 21–22; and an interview by author of Heath Meriwether, Feb. 21, 1986.
45. Marcel Dufresne, "To Sting or Not to Sting?" *Columbia Journalism Review,* May/June 1991, pp. 49–51. Details of the *Newsday* project are from this article.
46. These criteria came from participants in an ethical decision-making seminar at the Poynter Institute for Media Studies, reported in Jay Black, Bob Steele and Ralph Barney, *Doing Ethics in Journalism,* Greencastle, Ind.: Sigma Delta Chi Foundation, SPJ, 1993, pp. 112–113.

Chapter 11
1. Ramon Coronado, "Broken Goblet, Broken Table: The Media Cover a Hostage Family," and "How Far Should the Media Go to Get a Story?" in Editorially Speaking section, *Gannetteer,* May 1981, pp. 2, 4.
2. Craig Kelford Family, "Compassion from Reporters," *Los Angeles Times,* April 29, 1997.
\ 3. *The People & The Press,* Los Angeles: Times Mirror, 1986.
4. Ginger Casey, "Playground Vultures," *Quill,* November/December 1992, p. 27. The *Quill* piece is an excerpt from an article she wrote for the *San Francisco Examiner.*
5. David Pritchard, "The Impact of Newspaper Ombudsmen on Journalists' Attitudes," *Journalism Quarterly,* Spring 1993, pp. 77–86.
6. Remarks made by her in the 13th annual Otis Chandler lecture at the University of Southern California School of Journalism, quoted in M.L. Stein, "Here We Go Again!" *Editor & Publisher,* Nov. 28, 1992, p. 11.
7. Editor's Note to "Dangerous Liaisons," *Columbia Journalism Review,* July/August 1989, pp. 21–35. This article is a collection of short essays. Quotes from writers and journalists in this section are taken from this collection.
8. Janet Malcolm, "Reflections: The Journalist and the Murderer," *The New Yorker,* March 13 and 20, 1989. The article also appeared in Malcolm's *The Journalist and the Murderer,* New York: Knopf, 1991.
9. Casey.
10. John Tierney, "Cash on Delivery," *The New York Times,* April 18, 1993, sec. 6, p. 64.
11. Frank Fisher, "Trucker, Firm Awarded $525,000 in Suit Against 'Dateline NBC,'" *The Washington Post,* July 9, 1998, p. A7. Fisher writes for the AP. Also John Leo, "Media Ethics Come Under Increasing Court Scrutiny," column distributed by Universal Syndicate, July 12, 1998.
12. Richard Cunningham, "When News Features Hurt the Innocent," *Quill,* March 1987, p. 7. Details of this incident are taken from this article.
13. "Dangerous Liaisons."

14. Cunningham.
15. Richard Cunningham, "A Byrd's-Eye View of Ethics Inside *The Washington Post*," *Quill*, November/December, 1992, p. 10.
16. Bob Greene, "By Any Other Name," *Esquire*, September 1981, pp. 23–24.
17. Interview by Gene Goodwin, Sept. 23, 1981.
18. Quoted in "Dangerous Liaisons."
19. Elise S. Burroughs and Barbara Z. Gyles, "When a Tragedy Wounds Your Town, Coverage Often Adds to the Pain," *Presstime*, October 1997.
20. Interviewed by author.
21. Burroughs and Gyles.
22. Richard P. Cunningham, "Aside from That, How Was the Play, Mrs. Lincoln?" *Quill*, April 1988, pp. 8–9. Details and quotes about this incident are taken from this article.
23. William Coté and Bonnie Bucqueroux, "Covering Crime Without Re-Victimizing the Victim," a paper presented to the National Newspaper Association's Annual Convention, Nashville, Tenn., Sept. 25, 1996.
24. Fawn Germer, "How Do You Feel?" *American Journalism Review*, June 1995, pp. 36–43.
25. Phil Record, "Victims of Violence Have Good Advice for Fourth Estate," Fort Worth *Star-Telegram*, June 25, 1995. Day's comments are from this article (as are Witherspoon's; see preceding section, Chapter 11).
26. Susan Paterno, "The Intervention Dilemma," *American Journalism Review*, March 1998, pp. 37–43. Details of the story were taken from this article.
27. Anna Shaw, "Natasha's Story: Judgment Call in Sarajevo," *Columbia Journalism Review*, September/October 1992, p. 22.
28. Charles B. Seib, "Could a Little Caring Have Prevented Hoax?" *Presstime*, June 1981, p. 35.
29. Thomas Bray, "What If the 'Jimmy' Story Had Been True?" *The Wall Street Journal*, April 17, 1981.
30. John Troan, "The Lesson in the Janet Cooke Case," *Pittsburgh Press*, May 3, 1981.

31. Interview by Goodwin, June 5, 1981.
32. Interview by Goodwin, March 27, 1982.
33. H.L. Stevenson, "Bill Murphy and the Bridge Jumper," *Editor & Publisher*, Nov. 12, 1977, p. 34.
34. Interview by Goodwin, March 27, 1982.
35. Gannett News Service, *News Watch*, June 2, 1991.
36. Interview by Goodwin, Feb. 24, 1986.
37. "Pictures of the Month," *News Photographer*, April 1998, p. 53.
38. Liz Nakahara, "In the Eye of the Story," *The Washington Post*, Nov. 6, 1983, K1, 6, and 7.
39. Heather Lourie, Tony Saavedra and Stephen Lynch, "Freeway Suicide Televised," *The Orange County (Calif.) Register*, May 1, 1998; Greg Braxton and Brian Lowry, "TV Stations Reconsider Live Coverage Policies," *Los Angeles Times*, May 4, 1998; Howard Rosenberg, "The Russian Roulette of Live News Coverage," *Los Angeles Times*, May 5, 1998; and D.M. Osborne, "Overwhelmed by Events," *Brill's Content*, August 1998, pp. 67–69.
40. Nathan Kvinge, "Death on Tape," *News Photographer*, April 1998, pp. 48–50.
41. Interview by Goodwin, July 27, 1983.
42. "The Double Fire," *The New York Times*, March 13, 1983.
43. "Ethics Led Photog to Miss News Shot," *Editor & Publisher*, Aug. 3, 1985, p. 44.

Chapter 12
1. David Rudenstine, *The Day the Presses Stopped: A History of the Pentagon Papers*. Berkeley: University of California Press, 1996, p. 134. Details of the decision process at the *Post* are taken from this book.
2. "Wallace: Some Investigative Journalism Is Caricature," *WCCO Channel 4000 News*, May 17, 1996. A transcript of an interview between Wallace and Don Shelby.
3. Among the sources for the discussion of CBS were Lawrence K. Grossman, "Lessons of the 60

Minutes Cave-In," *Columbia Journalism Review,* January/February 1996, p. 39–51; Tom Wolzien, "The Consequences of Media Empires in the United States," *Media Studies Journal,* Spring/Summer 1996; "With Friends like These," *Mother Jones,* March 1996; "Up in Smoke," *Frontline* documentary (lengthier versions of the interviews with Ben Bagdikian, James C. Goodale and Lawrence Grossman were carried on PBS's WWW site); and transcripts of *60 Minutes,* Feb. 4, 1996.

4. "Journalistic Ethics: Some Probings by a Media Keeper," *Nieman Reports,* Winter/Spring 1978, 9–10.

5. Robert P. Clark, "Greed is Dangerous," *ASNE Bulletin,* July/August 1990, p. 27.

6. Dale Nelson, "Riding out the Storm," *Quill,* April 1991, p. 15.

7. Quoted in Karen Rothmyer, "The Media and the Recession: How Bad Is It—and Who's Really Getting Hurt?," *Columbia Journalism Review,* September/October 1991, p. 27.

8. Steve Gelsi, "They're Not Dead Yet," *Forbes Digital Tool,* May 14, 1997.

9. Jon Katz, "Memo to Local News Directors, Re: Improving the Product," *Columbia Journalism Review,* May/June 1990, p. 45.

10. Christopher H. Sterling and Timothy R. Haight, *The Mass Media: Apsen Institute to Communication Industry Trends.* New York: Praeger, 1978, p. 83.

11. Interview by Gene Goodwin, June 4, 1981.

12. Clark, p. 24.

13. John L. Hulteng, *The Messenger's Motives: Ethical Problems of the News Media.* Englewood Cliffs: Prentice-Hall, 1976, pp. 214–220.

14. Richard Norton Smith, *The Colonel: The Life and Legend of Robert R. McCormick,* Boston: Houghton Mifflin, 1997.

15. Ben Bagdikian, *The Media Monopoly,* third edition, Boston: Beacon Press, 1990, pp. 226–227.

16. Quoted by Clark, p. 27.

17. Mark Fitzgerald, "A Year of Expansion," *E&P Interactive,* Jan. 4, 1997; Mary Anderson, "Ranks of Independent Newspapers Continue to Fade," *Presstime,* August 1987, p. 22; and Loren Ghiglione, "The Price of Independence," *Presstime,* August 1996, p. 40.

18. David B. Martens, "A Newspaper Exec Looks at the Pain of Estate Taxes," *Presstime,* March 1997.

19. Anderson, pp. 16–23; and Ghiglione, p. 42.

20. Alex Ben Block, "Communications Media," *Forbes,* Jan. 12, 1987, p. 99.

21. Block, p. 99.

22. William Glaberson, "Times Co. Acquiring Boston Globe for $1.1 Billion," *The New York Times,* June 11, 1993, p. 1.

23. Elizabeth Gleick, "Read All About It," *Time,* Oct. 21, 1996, p. 66.

24. See Bagdikian, *The Media Monopoly,* p. 5.

25. For a review of some research in this area, see F. Dennis Hale, "The Influence of Chain Ownership on News Service Subscribing," *Newspaper Research Journal,* Fall 1991, pp. 34–46.

26. Interviews by Goodwin, May 28 and Sept. 18, 1981.

27. Stephan Barr, "Personal Best," *News Inc.,* November 1992, p. 25.

28. Barr, p. 26.

29. Neil Hickey, "Money Lust: How Pressure for Profit Is Perverting Journalism," *Columbia Journalism Review,* July/August 1998.

30. Tim Jones, "In Miami, the Owner Wants Bigger Profits, and a Paper Feels the Pressure," *Chicago Tribune,* Aug. 16, 1998.

31. Interview by Goodwin, Oct. 15, 1981.

32. Gannett owned 92 daily newspapers in 1997, according to '97 *Facts About Newspapers,* Reston, Va.: NAA, 1997, p. 22. The number of papers owned and circulation figures for Gannett, Thomson and Knight-Ridder come from this booklet.

33. Kay Lazar, "Provincial Profits," *News Inc.,* March 1990, p. 25.

34. Ann Lallande, "Alive and Kicking," *Presstime,* January 1997, pp. 31–37.
35. Interview by Goodwin, Oct. 21, 1981.
36. Quoted in Lazar, p. 23.
37. "A Harsh Farewell," *American Journalism Review,* June 1997, p. 45.
38. Sara Brown, "The Big Get Bigger," *Broadcasting & Cable,* April 6, 1998.
39. David Zurawik and Christina Stoehr, "Money Changes Everything," *American Journalism Review,* April 1993, p. 29; and Neil Hickey, "So Big: The Telecommunications Act at Year One," *Columbia Journalism Review,* January/February 1997, p. 24.
40. Tim Jones, "News Flash: It's Economics," *Chicago Tribune,* May 4, 1997; and Zurawik and Stoehr, p. 29.
41. Hickey, "Money Lust."
42. Bob Papper, Andrew Sharma and Michael Gerhard, "News Departments: Producing Profits," *Communicator,* April 1996, pp. 18–22.
43. Harry A. Jessell and Elizabeth A. Rathbun, "David Smith: Striking It Rich with Sinclair," *Broadcasting & Cable,* Aug. 19, 1996.
44. Bob Papper, Michael Gerhard and Andrew Sharma, "More News, More Jobs," *Communicator,* June 1996, pp. 20–26.
45. James Squires, *Read All About It,* New York: Times Books, 1993, p. 217.
46. Rebecca Ross Albers, "Extra! Extra?" *Presstime,* June 1994, p. 54.
47. Hickey, "Money Lust."
48. Roger Parloff, "How the Times Nailed a Health Care Giant," *Brill's Content,* August 1988, p. 106.
49. Donald E. Lippincott, "Investigative Reporting: Tighter Newsroom Budgets Are Forcing Editors to Be More Selective in Initiating Long-Term Projects," *Presstime,* February 1991, p. 15.
50. Papper, Gerhard and Sharma.
51. Comments made during a panel discussion on ethics at the Central Florida Press Club, April 10, 1997.
52. Dow C. Smith, "Slowing the Revolving Door," *Communicator,* December 1996, p. 22.
53. Saul Halpert, "Doing More with Less," April 1995, p. 37.
54. Lawrie Mifflin, "Crime Falls, but Not on TV," *The New York Times,* June 6, 1997, sec. 4, p. 4.
55. Robert Rutherford Smith, "Mystical Elements in Television News," *Journal of Communication,* Fall 1979, pp. 75–82.
56. Randall Rothenberg, "Playing the B-Roll Bop," *Quill,* September 1990, pp. 27–31.
57. Bob Sonenclar, "The VNR Top Ten: How Much Video PR Gets on the Evening News," *Columbia Journalism Review,* March/April 1991, p. 14.
58. Rothenberg, p. 29.
59. Guild wages were posted on the home page of the Dayton, Ohio, Guild local.
60. Kris Kodrich, "Show Us the Money: Studies Find That Journalists Still Don't Earn Much," an SPJ publication, 1998.
61. Vernon Stone, *Paychecks and Market Baskets: Broadcast News Salaries and Inflation in the 1990s,* 1997. Stone's research is posted on the University of Missouri School of Journalism's Web site.
62. Heidi Evans, "Working for Peanuts," *Quill,* April 1991, pp. 11–13.
63. Steve Nash, "With an Efficiency, Used Car, Peanut Butter and Byline, What More Could One Want," *Presstime,* April 1985.
64. Smith, "Slowing the Revolving Door," p. 22.
65. Statistics cited in Mary Alice Bagby, "Transforming Newspapers for Readers," *Presstime,* April 1991, p. 20.
66. John P. Robinson, "Thanks for Reading This," *American Demographics,* May 1990, p. 6.
67. "Times Mirror Studies Find Lagging Interest in News," *Presstime,* August 1990, p. 40.
68. Robinson, p. 6.
69. David Shaw, "Trust in Media Is on Decline," *Los Angeles Times,* March 31, 1993, p. A1.

70. Nelson, p. 15.
71. Information about the changes at the *Times* is from David Holmstrom, "Journalists Give Business Priorities a Wary Welcome," *Christian Science Monitor*, May 28, 1998; Mark Willes, "On L.A. Times Changes: Willes in His Own Words," *Editor & Publisher Interactive: The Media Info Source*, Nov. 29, 1997; Alicia C. Shepard, "Blowing up the Wall," *American Journalism Review*, December 1997; Hickey, "Money Lust"; David Shaw, "An Uneasy Alliance of News and Ads," *Los Angeles Times*, March 29, 1998; Charles Rappleye, "Cracking the Church-State Wall," *Columbia Journalism Review*, January/February 1998, pp. 20–23; Doug Underwood, "It's Not Just in L.A.," *Columbia Journalism Review*, January/February 1998, pp. 24–26; and William F. Woo, "Why Willes Is Wrong," *Columbia Journalism Review*, January/February 1998, p. 27.
72. John Lansing, "The Pressure for Ratings Is Hard to Underestimate," remarks prepared for the "Journalism Values in an Era of Change" seminar, Poynter Institute for Media Studies, Feb. 14–16, 1996.
73. Ben Bagdikian, "Fast-Food News: A Week's Diet," *Columbia Journalism Review*, March/April 1982, pp. 32–33.
74. Carl Sessions Stepp, "When Readers Design the News," *Washington Journalism Review*, April 1991, p. 24.
75. "Darts and Laurels," *Columbia Journalism Review*, July/August 1992, p. 22.
76. Stepp, p. 24.
77. Lippincott, "Investigative Reporting," p. 16. Editors from *The News* made similar comments when speaking to the Central Florida chapter of the SPJ's spring 1991 meeting.
78. David H. Weaver and G. Cleveland Wilhoit, *The American Journalist in the 1990s: U.S. News People at the End of an Era*, Mahwah, N.J.:

Lawrence Erlbaum Associates, 1996. Also see their book *The American Journalist: A Portrait of U.S. News People and Their Work*, second edition, Bloomington: Indiana University Press, 1991, p. 114.
79. Shaw, "An Uneasy Alliance."
80. John Morton, "Newspapers Are Losing Their Grip," *Washington Journalism Review*, May 1987, p. 52.
81. Stephen Lacy and Frederick Fico, "The Link Between Newspaper Content Quality & Circulation," *Newspaper Research Journal*, Spring 1991, pp. 46–57.
82. Robert Lenzner and Carrie Shook, "Texas Darwinist," *Forbes*, Jan. 26, 1998.
83. Bailey Thomson, "Mobile's Transformation Succeeds in Tiner's Hands," *American Editor*, May 1998.
84 James McCartney, "USA Today Grows Up," *Columbia Journalism Review*, September 1997, pp. 18–25.
85. "Occasional Readers Might Read More If Newspapers Targeted Their Needs, Study Says," *Presstime*, April 1991, p. 58.
86. Bagby, pp. 20–22.
87. Jon Katz, "Memo to Local News Directors, Re: Improving the Product, *Columbia Journalism Review*, September/October 1991, p. 42.
88. Ed Bishop, "Giant Conglomerates Devour News Media—Limit Scope of American Journalism," *St. Louis Journalism Review*, June 1996, p. 1.
89. Bagdikian, *The Media Monopoly*, p. xxii.
90. Marc Gunther, "All in the Family," *American Journalism Review*, October 1995, p. 38.
91. Lawrence Grossman, "Regulate the Medium, Liberate the Message," *Columbia Journalism Review*, November/December 1991, pp. 72–73.
92. "Darts and Laurels," *Columbia Journalism Review*, January/February 1990, p. 24.
93. Gunther, p. 40.

94. Gunther, p. 36.
95. Alexandra Marks, "New Media Alliances Test Press Objectivity," *Christian Science Monitor,* July 2, 1996, p. 1.
96. Steve Gelsi, "MSNBC's Declaration of Independence from Microsoft," *Digital Tool,* Sept. 24, 1997.
97. Matt Welch, "Who Owns Internet News?" *Online Journalism Review,* June 23, 1998.
98. Wolzien.
99. See John L. Hulteng and Roy Paul Nelson, *The Fourth Estate: An Informal Appraisal of the News and Opinion Media,* second edition, New York: Harper & Row, 1983, p. 104.
100. For a clear discussion of this issue, see Ronald K.L. Collins, *Dictating Content: How Advertising Pressure Can Corrupt a Free Press,* Washington: Center for the Study of Commercialism, 1992.
101. "Some Industry Averages," *Presstime,* January 1993, p. 15.
102. Douglas Anderson and Frederic A. Leigh, "How Newspaper Editors and Broadcast News Directors View Media Ethics," *Newspaper Research Journal,* Winter/Spring 1992, pp. 118–119.
103. Interview of James A. Dunlap of Sharon, Pa., *Herald* by Goodwin, Oct. 28, 1981.
104. Quoted in Charles Brewer, "Automobile Dealer Boycotts: How Widespread?" unpublished student paper at Penn State University in possession of author.
105. Elizabeth Lesly, "Realtors and Builders Demand Happy News and Often Get It," *Washington Journalism Review,* November 1991, p. 21.
106. Doug Underwood, "Retail Stores and Big-City Papers," *Columbia Journalism Review,* September/October 1990, pp. 33–35.
107. G. Pascal Zachary, "Many Journalists See a Growing Reluctance to Criticize Advertisers," *The Wall Street Journal,* Feb. 6, 1992, p. A9.
108. "Darts and Laurels," *Columbia Journalism Review,* May/June 1993, p. 23.

109. Zachary.
110. Wendy Swallow Williams, "Two New Surveys Show the Industry's Reach," *Washington Journalism Review,* November 1991, p. 24. Also see Wendy Swallow Williams. "For Sale! Real Estate Advertising & Editorial Decisions About Real Estate News," *Newspaper Research Journal,* Winter/Spring 1992, pp. 160–168.
111. "Darts & Laurels," *Columbia Journalism Review,* January/February 1996, p. 19.
112. "Darts and Laurels," *Columbia Journalism Review,* July/August, 1990, p. 14.
113. Alicia C. Shepard, "Those Sensitive Auto Dealers Strike Again, and Another Newspaper Caves," *American Journalism Review,* September 1994, p. 14.
114. Steve Singer, "When Auto Dealers Muscle the Newsroom," *Washington Journalism Review,* September 1991, pp. 25–28.
115. Philip Meyer, *Ethical Journalism: A Guide for Students, Practioners and Consumers,* New York: Longman, 1987, p. 39.
116. Ann Marie Kerwin, "Advertiser Pressure on Newspapers Is Common: Survey," *Editor & Publisher,* Jan. 16, 1993, pp. 28–29, 39.
117. ASNE Ethics Committee Report cited by Gil Cranberg, "Newspapers Face More Advertising Pressure Than They Report," *Editor & Publisher,* May 15, 1993, p. 52.
118. Stephen Rynkiewicz, "Can Editorial and Advertising Departments Exist in Piece?" *Solutions Today for Ethics Problems Tomorrow: A Special Report by the Ethics Committee of the Society of Professional Journalists,* 1989, p. 18.
119. Anderson and Leigh, p. 118.
120. Quoted by Lesly, p. 28.
121. Martha L. Stone, "News Rush on the Net," *ZDNet,* Jan. 30, 1998.
122. "Ticker," *Brill's Content,* August 1998, p. 152.
123. Terry Eastland, "Ad-ding up on-line," *Forbes Digital Tool,* Sept. 10, 1997.

124. Howard Kurtz,"Tattoo Catches Reporters Napping," *The Washington Post,* July 28, 1997.
125. Andie Tucher, "Why Web Warriors Might Worry," *Columbia Journalism Review,* July/August 1997, p. 35.
126. Mann's remarks are taken from Fred Mann, "Moving Beyond 'Code First, Ask Questions Later,'" *The American Editor,* November 1996, pp. 4–5; and Fred Mann, "Do Journalism Ethics & Values Apply to New Media?" A speech to the Journalism Values & Ethics in New Media conference at the Poynter Institute, St. Petersburg, Feb. 22, 1997.
127. Paul Sagan, "News.com: One Site's Struggle to Stand out on the Web," *Columbia Journalism Review,* July/August 1997, p. 37.
128. Rothmyer, pp. 23–28.
129. Katz 1990, p. 43.
130. Katz 1990, p. 49.
131. John Morton, "Shed No Tears for the Newspaper Industry," *Washington Journalism Review,* October 1992, p. 64.

Chapter 13
1. Eleanor Randolph, "The Media and the March," *Messages: The Washington Post Media Companion,* Boston: Allyn and Bacon, 1991, pp. 341 and 342.
2. David Shaw in "Can Women Reporters Write Objectively on Abortion Issues?" *Press Woman,* April 1991, p. 14.
3. Laurence Zuckerman, "To March or Not to March," *Time,* Aug. 14, 1989, p. 45.
4. Zuckerman.
5. Elizabeth Kolbert, "Covering Gay Rights: Can Journalists Be Marchers?" *The New York Times,* April 24, 1993, sec. 1, p. 10.
6. "May Reporters Speak out on Topics They Cover?" *Quill,* March 1991, p. 37.
7. Interview by Gene Goodwin, March 19, 1986.
8. The paper's code is excerpted in Kim Mills, "Taking It to the Streets," *American Journalism Review,* July/August 1993, pp. 22–26.

9. "Councilman's Dual Hats Are Front-Page News in Tyrone," Johnstown, Pa., *Tribune-Democrat,* July 1, 1985.
10. "An Editorial Leads to Two Newsmen's Resignations from Public Office," *Quill,* May 1980, p. 6.
11. Minnesota News Council, Determination 45.
12. Shaw. Subsequent references to Shaw in this section are to this article.
13. Shaw, p. 13.
14. "No Cheering in the Press Box," *Newsweek,* July 19, 1993.
15. His remarks were made to the AEJMC conference in Washington, August 1989.
16. Geneva Overholser, "Just Say No to the PTA," *The Washington Post,* April 27, 1997, p. C6.
17. The incidents at the Norfolk papers were reported by Richard Cunningham, "Reporters Op/ed Pieces Muddy the Fairness Line," *Quill,* June 1991, pp. 6–7.
18. Zuckerman.
19. "Journalists Vote on War: 4 Yes, 2 No," *Washington Journalism Review,* March 1991, p. 14.
20. Mills.
21. Zuckerman.
22. "No Cheering in the Press Box"; "Court Lets Newspaper Curb Reporter's Activism," *The Orlando Sentinel,* Feb. 21, 1997, p. A18; and "Court: Papers Can Bar Reporter Activism," *The Orlando Sentinel,* Oct. 7, 1997, p. A7.
23. Cited in "To March or Not to March."
24. Charles W. Bailey, *Conflicts of Interest: A Matter of Journalistic Ethics,* New York: National News Council, 1984, p. 10.
25. *The Washington Post*'s code on conflicts of interest is excerpted in Mills.
26. "Can Marriage and Ethics Mix?" 1983–84 report of SPJ-SDX Ethics Committee.
27. "Appearances Are Deceiving, or So Some Editors Think," *Feed/back,* Summer 1985, p. 1.
28. Howard Kurtz, *Spin Cycle,* New York: Basic Books, 1998, p. 44.

29. William Drozdiak, "The Ultimate Joint Statement," *The Washington Post,* Aug. 10, 1998.
30. Susan Page, "'Till Death Do Us Part," *Washington Journalism Review,* March 1985, pp. 45–48.
31. Donald Q. Smith, "Community Role Requires Being Part . . . and Apart," *Newsworthy,* Fall 1995.
32. Susan Paterno, "I Can Explain," *American Journalism Review,* July/August 1998.
33. Information and quotations about the *Columbus (Ga.) Ledger-Enquirer's* campaign were taken from Alicia C. Shepard, "The Death of a Pioneer," *American Journalism Review,* September 1994, p. 35.
34. Eric Black, "Journalism and the Public," *Star Tribune,* April 8, 1996, p. A1.
35. The Charlotte case is widely discussed. Most of the material here was drawn from "Journalists, Violence and the News," *Newsworthy,* Summer 1996; and *Civic Journalism: Six Case Studies. A Joint Report by the Pew Center for Civic Journalism and the Poynter Institute for Media Studies,* Tides Foundation, 1995. Reprinted on the CPN home page.
36. Tinker Ready, "Media's Election Project Draws Mixed Reaction," Raleigh *News & Observer,* Dec. 9, 1996; and Jennie Buckner, "Public Journalism—Giving Voters a Voice, *Media Studies Forum,* Winter 1997. Buckner is editor of *The Charlotte Observer.*
37. Edward M. Fouhy, "Civic Journalism: Rebuilding the Foundations of Democracy," *Civic Partners,* Spring 1996.
38. Curtis Wilkie, "'Public Journalism' Plays out in N.C.," *The Boston Globe,* Oct. 30, 1996, p. A1.
39. Ready; and Michael Gartner, "Public Journalism—Seeing Through the Gimmicks," *Media Studies Forum,* Winter 1997. Gartner's comments in this section are from this article.
40. Black.
41. Mike Hoyt, "Are You Now, or Will You Ever Be, a Civic Journalist?" *Columbia Journalism Review,* September/October 1995, pp. 27–33. Marro's and Downie's comments also come from this article.
42. Howard Kurtz, "A Controversial Twist on Undercover 'Reporting,'" *The Washington Post,* June 9, 1997, p. D1.
43. Carl Sessions Stepp, "Public Journalism: Balancing the Scales," *American Journalism Review,* May 1996, pp. 38–40.

Chapter 14
1. Allan Wolper, "Editors Enjoy Ticket Windfall," *E&P Interactive,* Oct. 26, 1996. Most of the subsequent information about the Yankee ticket offers is taken from this article.
2. Interview by Gene Goodwin, Oct. 14, 1981.
3. Interview by Goodwin, June 3, 1981.
4. Tamara Jones, "Reporters in Germany Open Wallets for Stories," *Los Angeles Times,* March 26, 1991.
5. Eric Hubler, "Freebies on the Tube," *Quill,* March 1991, p. 27.
6. Glenn Lovell, "Movies and Manipulation: How Studios Punish Critics," *Columbia Journalism Review,* January/February, 1997, p. 12.
7. Trudy Lieberman, "Gimme!" and "Perceived Neutrality," *Columbia Journalism Review,* January/February 1998, pp. 45–49.
8. George E. Osgood Jr., "Ethics and the One-Reporter, Rural Bureau" (Master's paper, Pennsylvania State University, July 1981), pp. 22–23.
9. "The Reporter," *Philadelphia Magazine,* April 1967, pp. 42–45, 92.
10. "Dirty Linen," *Wall Street Journal,* April 2, 1984, p. 32.
11. Howard Kurtz, "Firings Cause Stir in St. Petersburg," *The Washington Post,* Oct. 13, 1990, p. D1.
12. "Newspaper Purgatory," *American Journalism Review,* January/February 1997, p. 8.
13. "Columnist Resigns After Paper Learns of His Outside PR Work," *Editor & Publisher,* Nov. 9, 1985, p. 12.

14. "Darts & Laurels," *Columbia Journalism Review,* January/February 1997, p. 22.
15. Randell Beck, "TV Reporter Covers TVA—and Free-Lances for It," 1985–86 report of SPJ-SDX Ethics Committee, p. 22.
16. Iris Krasnow, "Mr. Warren's Profession," *Chicago,* May 1995; and Joan Konner, "A Rogue from the Heartland," *Columbia Journalism Review,* September/October 1995.
17. Bill Carter, "Chicago TV Anchor Quits After Station Hires Talk-Show Host for Commentary," *The New York Times,* May 4, 1997, p. A16.
18. "Visa Asked to Drop CNN reporter," *The Orlando Sentinel,* June 14, 1997, p. C1.; and Thomas Collins, ". . . Newspeople Shouldn't Sell More Than the News," *The Orlando Sentinel,* May 30, 1989, p. A7. Collins is the media writer for *Newsday.*

19. The CNN-*Contact* dispute is discussed in Skip Thurman, "Marquee Journalists Star in Ethics Debate," *Christian Science Monitor,* July 25, 1997, p. 3; Richard Wilner, "MSNBC: Fact or (Science) Fiction?" *New York Post,* May 8, 1998; Fred Davis, "When Reporters Blur the Line Between Fact and Fiction," *The Seattle Times,* July 25, 1997; and "New CNN Movie Policy Will Benefit Media Credibility," SPJ news release, July 18, 1997.
20. "National and International Journalism Competitions," *Editor & Publisher,* Dec. 28, 1985, p. 10.
21. Interview by Goodwin, April 8, 1981.
22. Richard P. Cunningham, "Of Mice and Mysids," *Quill,* June 1986, p. 10.
23. "Contests: Which Programs Qualify Under Codes of Ethics?" 1984–85 report of SPJ Ethics Committee.

Bagdikian, Ben. *The Media Monopoly.* Fourth edition. Boston: Beacon Press, 1992.

Bailey, Charles W. *Conflicts of Interest: A Matter of Journalistic Ethics.* New York: National News Council, 1984.

Bayley, Edwin R. *Joe McCarthy and the Press.* Madison: University of Wisconsin Press, 1981.

Benedict, Robin. *Virgin or Vamp: How the Press Covers Sex Crimes.* New York: Oxford University Press, 1992.

Bernstein, Carl, and Bob Woodward. *All the President's Men.* New York: Simon and Schuster, 1974.

Black, Jay, Bob Steele and Ralph Barney. *Doing Ethics in Journalism.* Greencastle, Ind.: Sigma Delta Chi Foundation, Society of Professional Journalists, 1993.

Bok, Sissela. *Lying: Moral Choice in Public and Private Life.* New York: Vintage, Random House, 1984.

Christians, Clifford G., Kim B. Rotzoll and Mark Fackler. *Media Ethics: Cases and Moral Reasoning.* Third edition. New York: Longman, 1991.

Commission on Freedom of the Press. *A Free and Responsible Press.* Chicago: University of Chicago Press, 1947.

Crawford, Nelson A. *The Ethics of Journalism.* New York: Knopf, 1924.

Fallows, James. *Breaking the News: How the Media Undermine American Democracy.* New York: Pantheon Books, 1996.

Goldstein, Tom. *The News at Any Cost: How Journalists Compromise Their Ethics to Shape the News.* New York: Simon and Schuster, 1985.

Halberstam, David. *The Powers That Be.* New York: Knopf, 1979.

Hohenberg, John. *The News Media: A Journalist Looks at His Profession.* New York: Holt, Rinehart and Winston, 1968.

___. *The Professional Journalist.* New York: Holt, Rinehart and Winston, 1983.

Isaacs, Norman E. *Untended Gates: The Mismanaged Press.* New York: Columbia University Press, 1986.

Johnstone, John W.C., Edward J. Slawski and William W. Bowman. *The News People: A Sociological Portrait of American Journalists and Their Work.* Urbana: University of Illinois Press, 1976.

Knightly, Phillip. *The First Casualty: From the Crimea to Vietnam, the War Correspondent as Hero, Propagandist and Myth Maker.* New York: Harvest, Harcourt Brace Jovanovich, 1975.

Kurtz, Howard. *Media Circus.* New York: Times Books, 1993.

___. *Spin Cycle: Inside the Clinton Propaganda Machine,* New York: The Free Press, 1998.

Lambeth, Edmund B. *Committed Journalism: An Ethic for the Profession.* Second edition. Bloomington: Indiana University Press, 1991.

Malcolm, Janet. *The Journalist and the Murderer.* New York: Knopf, 1991.

Merrill, John C. *Existential Journalism.* New York: Hastings House, 1977.

___. *The Dialectic in Journalism.* Baton Rouge: Louisiana State University Press, 1989.

___. *Journalism Ethics: Philosophical Foundations for News Media.* New York: St. Martin's Press, 1997.

Merrill, John C., and S. Jack Odell. *Philosophy and Journalism.* New York: Longman, 1983.

Meyer, Philip. *Editors, Publishers and Newspaper Ethics. A Report to the American Society of Newspaper Editors.* Washington, D.C.: American Society of Newspaper Editors, 1983.

___. *Ethical Journalism: A Guide for Students, Practitioners and Consumers.* Lanham, Md.: University Press of America, 1987.

Rudenstine, David. *The Day the Presses Stopped: A History of the Pentagon Papers.* Berkeley: University of California Press, 1996.

Sabato, Larry J. *Feeding Frenzy: How Attack Journalism Has Transformed American Politics.* New York: Free Press, 1991.

Schudson, Michael. *Discovering the News. A Social History of American Newspapers.* New York: Basic Books, 1978.

Siebert, Fred S., Theodore Peterson and Wilbur Schramm, eds. *Four Theories of the Press.* Urbana: University of Illinois Press, 1956 (paperback edition, 1973).

Sloan, Wm. David, James G. Stovall and James D. Startt, eds. *The Media in America.* Worthington, Ohio: Publishing Horizons, 1989.

Squires, James. *Read All About It.* New York: Times Books, 1993.

Swain, Bruce M. *Reporters' Ethics.* Ames: Iowa State University Press, 1978.

Thayer, Lee, ed. *Ethics, Morality and the Media.* New York: Hastings House, 1980.

Weaver, David H., and G. Cleveland Wilhoit. *The American Journalist: A Portrait of U.S. News People and Their Work,* Bloomington: Indiana University Press, first edition, 1986, and second edition, 1991.

___. *The American Journalist in the 1990s: U.S. News People at the End of an Era,* Mahwah, N.J.: Lawrence Erlbaum Associates, 1996.

Wicker, Tom. *On Press: A Top Reporter's Life in and Reflections on American Journalism.* New York: Viking, 1978.